The Desert Air Force in World War II

This book is dedicated to all those who lost their lives in the Desert War.

Tomb-stone of "Hoppy" — the prop. of his aircraft

The day before his death he jokingly said that when he dies he wants "all the kings horses and all the kings men could not put "Hoppy" together again" put on his 'stone. — Its on.

PILOT
2 SQUADRON
S·A·A·F
Lt A·E·HOPKINS
Nº 17838

☆·24· 11·1916·
†·31 ·3·1942

C. of E.

"ALL THE KINGS HORSES AND ALL THE KINGS MEN
COULD NOT PUT "HOPPY" TOGETHER AGAIN".

Grave marker for Lieutenant Hopkins, killed in action 31 March 1942; his diary entry was used to add the words at the bottom of the grave marker. (George Hilary, SAAF).

The Desert Air Force in World War II

Air Power in the Western Desert 1940–1942

Ken Delve

Pen & Sword
AVIATION

First published in Great Britain in 2017 by
Pen & Sword Military
an imprint of
Pen & Sword Books Ltd
47 Church Street
Barnsley
South Yorkshire
S70 2AS

ISBN 978 1 84415 817 1

A CIP catalogue record for this book is available from the British Library

Typeset in Ehrhardt by
Mac Style Ltd, Bridlington, East Yorkshire
Printed and bound in the UK by CPI Group (UK) Ltd,
Croydon, CRO 4YY

Pen & Sword Books Ltd incorporates the imprints of Pen & Sword Archaeology, Atlas, Aviation, Battleground, Discovery, Family History, History, Maritime, Military, Naval, Politics, Railways, Select, Transport, True Crime, and Fiction, Frontline Books, Leo Cooper, Praetorian Press, Seaforth Publishing and Wharncliffe.

For a complete list of Pen & Sword titles please contact
PEN & SWORD BOOKS LIMITED
47 Church Street, Barnsley, South Yorkshire, S70 2AS, England
E-mail: enquiries@pen-and-sword.co.uk
Website: www.pen-and-sword.co.uk

Contents

Acknowledgements

I have used a variety of sources in this book, both primary (official documents and personal accounts) and secondary (some of the very fine books published by historians, units or individuals, and, increasingly, internet references, especially from squadron associations). Two of the main primary sources that you will see mentioned frequently are the ORBs (Operational Record Books) of the squadrons; these are sometimes a mine of information and sometimes a struggle, where they say very little or allude to something really important – and then say nothing about it! There is also frequent reference to the AMB (Air Ministry Bulletin); the ones I have referenced here are those that detail the medals (gallantry awards) – the same data that would subsequently be published in the *London Gazette*.

The Air Historical Branch (AHB) has remained a source of great help and support, and visits to the Branch are always productive, so my thanks, as always, to the team there. I have made use of several published works as reference, both printed primary sources or memoires, as well as a range of books from historians and enthusiasts, especially the first-hand accounts of 'those who were there'. I have been fortunate over the years to meet a great many veterans, and I now wish I had made far more comprehensive recordings of their memories and impressions – the notes I have seem all too thin.

Photographs are invariably a challenge for authors, with access to 'official collections' increasingly difficult or expensive. The Desert War is easier than some theatres in that there seemed to be more access to film and less restriction on taking photos – or more people (especially the South Africans) inclined to ignore or work around the restrictions. All those photographs that have SAAF in the caption credit are via the superb website run by Tinus Le Roux. They are credited by name to the family collection; for example, (Peter Metelerkamp SAAF) relates to albums provided by Peter's family to Tinus for the website. In more than forty years of aviation research I have never seen such a superb collection of material gathered in one place that is easy and free to view. The number of photos in this book that are credited to these albums is very high. This is for a number of reasons: firstly, the contribution of the SAAF units to the Desert War was very high; secondly, SAAF personnel seem to have taken more photos (this is also true in other theatres and of other nationals, such as those from the RAAF, where cameras/film were more readily available and a freer attitude to security was applied), and finally, and critically for a researcher, the availability of material – much RAF material is difficult to find or, if in official collections, is hard to access or too costly to use.

The site created by Tinus as a tribute to SAAF operations contains more than photographs, and it continues to grow as more material is provided by families. http://biltongbru.wix.com/ww2-saaf-heritage#!photo-albums/c8r3

My sincere thanks to Tinus for his help with providing images for this book (and the subsequent planned books).

Aviation History Research Centre

I have aspired for some years to create a similar Aviation Research History Centre and this is close to being realised. If you would like more information then please email me at kendelve222@gmail.com

Ken Delve
Swaffham, 2017

Chapter 1

Introduction

In the vast area covered by the 'Middle East' theatre – stretching from the western Mediterranean to the centre of Africa, air power played a crucial role in almost every campaign. Campaigns within the Middle East/Mediterranean theatre went well for the British while they were engaged against the Italians, although these forces were invariably larger and better equipped; however, the arrival of combat-experienced German forces in 1941 was a turning point that almost brought disaster. A point that must be made is the degree of contribution made by the South African Air Force (SAAF) in most of the campaigns in this theatre; in the later stages of the war in the Middle East and into Italy numerous SAAF squadrons operated within the Allied air forces, often as integral parts of RAF wings (or vice versa). The main battle ground was a narrow strip adjacent to the coast and which stretched for more than 1,000 miles; the distance from Alexandria (in the east in Egypt) to Tripoli (in the west and 100 miles or so from the border with Tunisia) was roughly the same as from Berlin to Moscow. The name Western Desert refers to this strip and it was in this area that the conflict covered in this book raged in a series, for the Allies, of retreat–advance–retreat–advance to victory.

The Middle East had long been a strategic area for the British, as a route, courtesy of the Suez Canal, to India and the Far East empire, but also with the increased importance of oil resources. Indeed, in the 1920s the majority of RAF squadrons were based outside the UK. Middle East Area had control of three groups on a regional basis – Egypt, Palestine and Iraq. Each group was small and covered the full range of RAF 'colonial' tasks, primarily reconnaissance and support of the local ground forces. However, this changed somewhat following the 1921 Cairo Conference when it was decided that the RAF should be given full control of military operations in Mesopotamia – the introduction of the so-called 'Air Control Policy'. Expansion of the RAF organization overseas brought two new groups under the control of ME Area in the early 1920s: Indian Group and Mediterranean Group. Once again these groups were quite small but the foundations of a chain of command suited for further expansion had been laid. RAF Middle East was formed on 1 April 1922 by renaming Middle East Area. The command had control of Egyptian Group and Aden Flight, plus, for supply and equipment purposes only, RAF Palestine and RAF Transjordan.

By the 1930s the growth of German military power led to a focus on UK-based air power, especially around the strategic bomber, and the Middle East (and Far East) became somewhat of a backwater for both numbers and equipment. It was very much a biplane RAF in the region in the mid-1930s, and while the UK units started to equip with modern types, the Middle East soldiered on with, for example, the Gloster Gladiator as its main fighter.

Mussolini's Italy had started to drive towards its new Roman Empire by increasing strength in the Italian provinces of North Africa, and also seeking an African Empire, the first major campaign being against Abyssinia (Ethiopia) from October 1935 to May 1936. The campaign was essentially one-sided as the Italians had technological superiority, in which the Regia Aeronautica played a significant part. For our story, it is the growth of fascist power and influence, and the use of air power, that is significant. For the British strategists, having the Italians in control of Ethiopia posed a potential threat to British interests in Africa (such as Kenya) but also the Sudan and Egypt. But for now, Italy and Britain were at peace. June 1940 brought the Italian declaration of war against Britain and campaigns in East Africa and Western Desert – the focus of our first few chapters.

The thirty-month period covered by this book, from the first Italian offensive of June 1940 to Montgomery's El Alamein offensive of autumn 1942 saw a transformation of Allied air power in terms of size and capability. From a campaign that involved biplane fighters on both sides (Fiat CR.42 and Gladiator) and limited and generally ineffective bombing capability, to hundreds of fighters and fighter-bombers of the Desert Air Force, along with tactical and strategic bombers. It was a war of airfields – those who had them could support the ground operations and also, if they were in the right places, could dominate the sea lanes over which critical supplies had to flow.

'The continuous and very heavy attacks of the R.A.F.,' said Rommel, 'absolutely pinned my troops to the ground and made impossible any safe deployment or advance according to schedule.' And General Bayerlein, Chief of Staff of the Afrika Korps, afterwards declared: 'Your air superiority was most important, perhaps decisive.... We had very heavy losses, more than from any other cause.'

There are two other aspects of this campaign/theatre that stand out … the desert itself both as a theatre of war and a place to 'live' and fight, and the many stories of aircrew who 'walked out' (the Late Arrivals Club).

The Desert …

George Beckett comments: 'The desert wind, the "Khamsin", made life even worse as the sand got into everything, food, drink and clothing. There were also clouds of vicious flies that descended on any exposed food, making an already unpalatable diet even worse. Newcomers to the desert took quite a while to get used to conditions. Also, it was prudent to check beds and clothes for scorpions and other desert nasties.'

'Duke' Ellington, 57th FG: 'The desert is a unique environment. In many ways, if one has to go to war, it is the ideal area. You do little damage to anything but the enemy. Usually the weather is ideal, but it can also be a virtual hell when you are trying to survive a dust storm. These can go on for days. Visibility is nil. You can get lost just navigating from one tent to another. The fine sand permeates every part of your living, eating and equipment. One of the virtues of the old P-40 was its superior insensitivity to blowing sand. But it was not immune. The crews had to spend a lot of time after one of these storms cleaning sand out of every corner and niche of the plane.'

Losses … and 'Walking Out' (the Boomerang Club or Late Arrivals Club)

'After only a few hours walking in flying boots over the terribly rough ground in this region we were all worried with blisters. About two o'clock we almost bumped into an enemy tank and in trying to get round it came across some more. Whichever way we turned we saw tanks; we must have walked into the middle of an enemy laager in the darkness so decided the only thing to do was to try to work our way through them. In single file we crept past tank after tank and although we could hear the crews coughing and talking we were not seen and when we finally realized that we had passed through safely we were six considerably shaken men … .' (148 Squadron, Sergeant Spence).

No.14 Squadron's Operational Record Book (ORB) recorded: 'The astounding safe arrival of Fg Off Mackenzie's crew after five days in the desert without food or water needs recounting. Fg Off Mackenzie's aircraft, after having successfully attacked Maleme aerodrome, did not find the coast, and force-landed some 70 miles South of Daba in the desert. All three of the aircraft crew jumped and landed quite safely. They had pre-arranged to meet at the aircraft, but Sergeant Fearn and Sergeant McConnell landed so far away from the aircraft they decided to head North. They were found four days later amongst some swamps, living on desert snails, berries, and what water they could find by digging. They had covered about 30 miles of desert to this area in three days without food and water. Fg Off Mackenzie, although not at his aircraft, which was found two days after it crashed, laid out strips by the aircraft but has never been found since. This search was given up after an 8-day hunt, the previous three days having been spent on motor bicycles scouring the area, but no trace was found.'

The aircraft, a Blenheim, had failed to return from an attack on troop concentrations in Crete. A second Blenheim (V5593) was lost on the same sortie, the crew became lost and Flying Officer J. Le Cavalier ordered Sergeant Page and Sergeant Bury to bail out, which they did. Sergeant Page survived and walked back to Mersa Matruh.

'This line of knocks reduced the squadron to four crews and 3 serviceable aircraft. However, reinforcements are arriving, but will need a little careful training before they go on their "blooding" flights.'

No matter how much research and writing I do around RAF air operations, I never cease to be amazed by the way in which squadrons, or rather the people on them, were able to cope with such high loss rates.

This short account is not a detailed history but rather it is an impression; to that end I have not attempted to provide details on every action and every unit; some squadrons get barely a mention … but the accounts for one Hurricane or Tomahawk squadron, or one Blenheim or Wellington squadron stand for all such units. As always with such air action books, the focus is invariably on the aircrew – but without the long-suffering ground crew no aircraft flew, without fuel, bullets and bombs, no ops could be flown. The ability of the RAF to recover and repair its aircraft, thanks to the work of the Repair and Salvage (RSU), likewise deserves recognition and praise, but gets scant mention in the few pages available.

My respect and admiration is unbounding for all those who were part of the RAF, RAAF (Royal Australian Air Force) and SAAF units in the campaigns; I have been fortunate enough over the years to meet many of them and to hear their tales; sadly, I never met enough of them and was never able to document even a fraction of the fascinating lives of these now rapidly vanishing group of men (not too many women in the desert).

Chapter 2

Beating the Italians in the Desert

During the 1920s British air strength in the Middle East was limited, and in most cases oriented around the Air Control Policy, which had been adopted at the 1921 Cairo Conference as a cost-effective way of controlling native disturbances without the expense and risk of using ground forces. The same policy was applied across the Middle East and, slightly later, in the tribal districts of the North-West Frontier Province (NWFP) of India, where the 1931 Frontier Defence Enquiry gave the RAF a leading role. This was the era of biplane bombers such as the Westland Wapiti and Hawker Hart, and in the absence of an air threat, or even an effective ground-to-air threat, it worked well. However, by the early 1930s the situation for the British in the Middle East was changing, with the aggressive Italian search for an empire. The 1935 Italo–Abyssinian Crisis clearly demonstrated Italian ambitions, and the use of air power.

'The threat of an apparently powerful Italian Air Force was sufficient to force a withdrawal of British naval units from Malta to Alexandria, and even there they were vulnerable to Italian bombers operating from airfields outside the range of available RAF aircraft based in the Suez Canal zone. This crisis passed but valuable experience was gained by a force of nine squadrons under Ashton McCloughry which moved forward into the desert with an advanced headquarters at Mersa Matruh.' (*RNZAF in the Desert War* official document)

'Operations,' wrote Mitchell, the air officer commanding-in-chief in the official RAAF History, 'would undoubtedly have been seriously affected by the dust … This had a bad effect on engines, aeroplanes, guns and bomb gear … Mechanical transport suffered to an even higher degree than aircraft engines, but the effect on personnel was as serious as that on material … The factor of dust today may be as important as that of mud in former wars.

'The technical and tactical difficulties inherent in this situation were patiently studied during the succeeding years when war seemed ever more probable as with each crisis in international affairs Italy aligned herself more positively with Germany. Major RAF preparations were impeded, however, by the desire of His Majesty's Government to do nothing which might impair the existing relations with that country (Italy).'

With the rise of Hitler, Germany became the main focus of British attention and military planning, and the Middle East became a backwater – although not totally so, as an infrastructure plan was put into place under the 1936 Anglo-Egyptian Treaty that included the construction of twelve new airfields.

Backwater of the Empire?

On 25 May 1939 the newly reformed 112 Squadron arrived at Alexandria aboard HMS *Argus*; under the command of Squadron Leader D.M. Somerville the Squadron's Gloster Gladiator IIs were tasked with the air defence of Cairo and the Delta. Part of 252 Wing, along with 80 Squadron, the new arrivals were destined to be one of the longest-serving and most successful RAF units in the Desert Air Force; indeed, a history of 112 Squadron is a mini-history of the Desert Air Force! In common with the rest of the RAF, the units in the Middle East went on standby on 3 September when war was declared, not that there was any specific indication of a threat to Egypt. The initial excitement lasted less than a week and it was back to peacetime training. A milestone occurred on 25 September when Flight Lieutenant Fry air-tested the first Hurricane to arrive in the command, although this did not signify all-round re-equipment.

In November 1939, RAF Middle East was primarily based in Egypt and had twelve squadrons, with only one modern – but soon to be shown as flawed – type, the Blenheim, in its inventory. HQ was in Cairo and the squadrons were based at:

Location	Squadron	Type
Heliopolis	113	Blenheim
	216	Bombay
Ismailia	30, 55	Blenheim
	14	Wellesley
Helwan	112	Gladiator
	70	Valentia
Fuka	45	Blenheim
Daba	211	Blenheim
Qasaba	14 (Flight)	Wellesley
	208	Lysander
Mersa Matruh	33	Gladiator
Amriya	80	Gladiator

80 Squadron Gladiators at Ismailia; the squadron arrived in the Middle East in May 1938.

The Gladiator had a long combat history in this theatre – through to 1941 – when in Europe the era of biplane fighters had essentially been ended by the start of the war.

Blenheims of 45 Squadron as part of a show of air power for King Farouk in Egypt.

Helwan was one of the pre-war stations and was provided with good facilities for two squadrons.

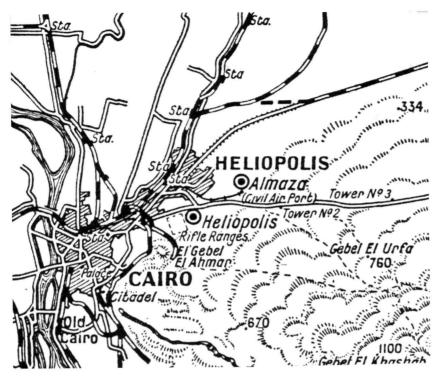

Heliopolis was another of the pre-war airfields, on the outskirts of Cairo. As can be seen from this 1937 plan, there were two aerodromes divided by the Suez Road. The overall dimension of this grass area was limited, but the airfield underwent significant expansion.

M.S.A.M.Nº 1133.

In addition, it controlled squadrons in the Sudan (47 and 223 Squadrons, both Wellesley) and Palestine (6 Squadron, Lysander). The first half of 1940 saw a gradual build-up of air strength, albeit the majority with outdated types! During the major Delta Defence Exercise of 7–17 May 1940 the Gladiators were hard-pressed to intercept the 'enemy' Blenheims, as the latter had a significant speed advantage. The German assault into France in early May brought the realization that the Phoney War was over, and it seemed likely that it would soon reach the Middle East, as Italy, a German ally, would seek to expand its existing Africa empire. On 22 May a show of strength overflight of Cairo was made by formations from 30, 33, 45, 80, 113, 208, 211 and 216 Squadrons; it is rumoured that one Egyptian observer commented, 'There are more than three – it must be the Italians.'

Sir Arthur Longmore took over command of Middle East Forces from Sir William Mitchell in May 1940 and issued a directive that defined the primary role of his air forces as 'the defence of Egypt, the Suez Canal and the communications route through the Red Sea. All Royal Air Force units stationed or operating in Egypt, the Sudan, Palestine and Transjordan, East Africa, Aden and Somaliland, Iraq and adjacent territories, Cyprus, Turkey, the Balkans, the Mediterranean Sea, the Red Sea and the Persian Gulf came under his control. This magnificent geographical responsibility was backed, however, by pitifully small means. Discounting the small Egyptian Air Force, whose degree of co-operation was unpredictable except that they might be expected to help with the fighter defence of Cairo, Longmore disposed in Egypt and Palestine only 40 Gladiators, 70 Blenheims, 24 Bombay and Valentia transports, 24 Lysanders and 10 Sunderlands. Farther afield in Kenya, the Sudan and Aden there were 85 Wellesleys and Blenheims and a few more Gladiators. In Kenya there were also three squadrons of the South African Air Force, one of Gladiators, one of Battles and one of Ju-86 aircraft.' (RAAF history). Note: It was indeed a massive and diverse geographical region, impossible for a single command organization or command. This theatre of war underwent frequent, and at times confusing, changes of command structure, especially as the scale and complexity of air forces increased.

Of the areas above, Sudan and East Africa are covered here briefly but with the exception of limited coverage of Syria and Iraq, and the Greek islands, the others are outside the scope of this book. On 1 June, 112 Squadron sent 'B Flight' to join 254 Wing of the Advanced Striking Force at Port Sudan, which became 203 Group, under the command of Air Commodore L.H. Slatter. The group included the Gladiators of 112 and 223 squadrons and Wellesleys of 14 and 47 squadrons; a total of fifty antiquated aircraft that could face an Italian air strength of around 150 aircraft.

'Longmore felt confident that what his forces lacked in quantity would, in any real prolonged test of strength, be compensated for by the offensive spirit and more solid experience and training of his air and ground crews. Accordingly, the outline plan for the defence of Egypt (revised on 7 June) showed no sign of pessimism. No.202 (Bomber) Group at Maaten Bagush was to control four bomber, one fighter, and one army-co-operation squadron for offensive action in the forward area, either independently or in concert with naval or ground forces. No.252 (Fighter) Wing at Alexandria was to control all other fighters with the general role of destroying enemy aircraft attacking any objective in lower Egypt, with particular reference to the protection of Cairo, the Suez Canal and the fleet base at Alexandria. Headquarters R.A.F. Middle East at Cairo was to keep under its own direct operational control the flying-boats of No.201 (Naval Co-operation) Group, the bomber-transport squadrons and reserve units.' (RAAF History)

During early June the rest of 112 Squadron, along with other RAF units, was redeploying in preparation for potential operations against the Italians in North Africa. At the same time the first South African pilots joined the squadron; they did not stay long, and neither did the small number

Although a monoplane, the open-cockpit Wellesley was out of date by the outbreak of war; 45 Squadron, shown here, re-equipped with Blenheims in June 1939, but 14 Squadron retained the type to December 1940.

Gladiator of 112 Squadron. (*Angus Farrell SAAF*)

of SAAF airman who were attached, but the significance was that this was the start of what was to be a major Dominion, and especially South African, contribution to the Desert War. As an example of unit confusion, although 112 Squadron was still part of 252 Wing, it co-operated with 202 Group, the operational group in Egypt, and assigned to offensive operations.

Longmore visited 80 Squadron during his tour of deployed squadrons, as the squadron ORB reported: 'He arrived [at Amriya] by air from Heliopolis. He was met by the OC, Squadron Leader R.C. Jones and shown around the camp. The AOC visited the three flights in their dispersed positions around the aerodrome, inspected the control room, and the defence scheme. He left by road to visit 256 Wing.'

It would be interesting to know Longmore's thoughts on his squadrons, especially their equipment and readiness. The ORB continued: 'During this stage of intense and increasing activity between the Italian and Allied Governments, the Squadron was held at short notice for patrols. The Operations Room was manned day and night and a duty flight was kept standing by for interceptions. Many convoys passing through the camp, all showing a state of complete readiness, should anything break out between the Governments. The camp was blacked out each night.'

Another aspect that was to be a feature of the campaigns in the North Africa theatre was the use of advanced airfields. 'The use of enemy captured and consequently forward landing grounds has been utilized for rearming and refueling, thus stepping up the total bomb load possible to drop by about 50 per cent' (33 Sqn ORB). The weight of bombs on target and the shorter time from airfield to target were key elements in Air Support.

On 30 May all leave was cancelled as 33 Squadron was put on standby in the expectation of the outbreak of war with Italy. The following day the squadron was brought to four-hour notice and the Gladiators were fully armed and ready. It was another ten days before Italy declared war. This was recorded on 10 June by 80 Squadron as: 'In the evening information was received that the

Oops – a not infrequent sight, a Gladiator on its nose; this is an 80 Squadron machine at Helwan in 1939.

The Lysander was primarily used for Army co-operation duties. (*Bomb Finney, SAAF*)

Italian Government had decided to open hostilities with France and Great Britain. The Squadron was instantly brought to readiness and arrangements made for full defence schemes and stand by arrangements to come into force. Guards were doubled, men armed and a complete feeling of readiness and calmness prevailed amongst all ranks.'

And the following day: 'At commencement of hostilities the Squadron was equipped with 22 Gladiators, for immediate use, and one Hurricane. All Flights were brought to readiness at 0330 hours and all airmen and officers were armed. Armed tenders were ready to patrol the boundaries of the camp, if necessary and barriers were placed in the road, to stop traffic for inspection.'

The first war patrol was flown at 0430; three Gladiators (Flight Lieutenant Jones, Flight Sergeant Morris and Flight Sergeant Vaughan) flying a dawn patrol at 16,000ft, fifteen miles west of Alexandria. Three more patrols were flown during the day, the main Allied concern being a bomber attack on Alexandria.

The AOC, Air Marshal Longmore, had decided on an offensive strategy with his very limited bomber force, which comprised a small number of Blenheim squadrons. Blenheims of 45 Squadron (eight aircraft from Fuka Main) and 113 Squadron (nine aircraft from Maaten Bagush) attacked El Adem airfield; two 45 Squadron aircraft were shot down by flak with the loss of all crew, and one 113 Squadron aircraft was brought down by three Italian fighters, with all crew escaping the aircraft and walking through the desert for eight hours before being taken prisoner near Tobruk. The attack itself had met with some success and in the first few weeks of the war the RAF bombers managed to create enough damage (for no further losses) to give concern in the Regia Aeronautica as to the strength of the Allied air forces and the ability of the RAF to maintain operations!

The Blenheims of 113 Squadron had moved from Heliopolis to Maaten Bagush on 10 June. Squadron Leader Mike Shekleton recalled they arrived in the late afternoon, 'to find our convoys have got in and tents are up for us. Darkness falls. A staff car is seen racing madly along (the road?) from 202 Group Headquarters. We are shouted into the Mess Tent. Barney says: "Italy has come in. Standby and I'll let you know the bomb load later." We expect to take off there and then but hang about until 11pm. and are then sent to bed!

The following day: 'Turned out at dawn. We're to raid Menistir or if there's nothing there then El Adem. From 4am. till 6.45pm. we hang around our aircraft. At last we're off. Menistir is 150 miles. We fly out to sea. I'm with Bob Bateson. Barney (Squadron Leader Keily) is leading with John up. On ETA we turn in and sweep over the coast. There is Menistir but there's nothing much there except for a couple of Savoias. Barney turns west and we follow. We're down to 1000ft. calmly flying along a main road. In a great wadi are hundreds of transports. We steam past a convoy. Sixty-five miles of this and here's El Adem. Bob yells: "Lord, look at 'em!" I clean forget to be scared. John drops a stick on the hangars. We follow. A crowd of men on the tarmac (apron) is staring up at us stupidly. They turn and run as I ping off. I have no feelings at all.

'John's bombs burst beside the hangars, mine go through the roofs. On the tarmac are about 30 a/c. I'm sure I miss them and my second stick goes on the field. There's a ghastly racket under our aircraft. We circle and return. I loose my third stick. Everything is covered in smoke. Can't see if I do any good. 'B' Flight's incendiaries are burning everywhere. Thompson yells "Fighters!" but I've still got bombs. Round we go again and I drop my stick on some buildings. Things are hitting our machine. Bursts of ack-ack smoke are filling the sky. We dive with Bob using the front-gun. It's a circus. We are down to ten or fifteen feet. O-omph! There's a stink of petrol. It's our starboard tank. We're off now streaking toward the sea with fighters on our tail. And there's 'Basher' (Beauclair) burning in front of us. Barney's shouting. "Join up! Join up!" 'Basher's' going down. Two fighters are attached to us. We hear their guns but we are too fast for them. (Later identified as CR32s). We're away. 'Basher' has belly-landed.'

45 Squadron, Fuka 1940; Flying Officer Sooty Wright. The squadron had moved to Fuka in August 1939, which remained its base for about a year. (*45 Squadron*)

Blenheims of 113 Squadron at Heliopolis. The squadron had exchanged Hinds for Blenheims at this airfield in June 1939.

These were the first RAF bomber losses in the Desert War:

1. 45 Squadron: Blenheim L8476; hit by flak over target, caught fire and crashed into sea east of Tobruk, all killed (Sergeant P. Bower, Sergeant S.G. Fox, Aircraftman 1st class J.W. Allison), commemorated on Alamein memorial.
2. 45 Squadron: Blenheim L8519; hit by flak, force-landed at Sidi Barrani (LG02) but aircraft burst into flames and all killed (Sergeant M.C. Thurlow, Sergeant B.A. Feldman, Aircraftman 1st class H. Robinson).
3. 113 Squadron: Blenheim L4823; attacked by fighters and shot down in flames; all three suffered burns but walked for eight hours before being taken prisoner (Flight Lieutenant D.A. Beauclair, Warrant Officer H.J. Owen, Sergeant J. Dobson).

Sudan and East Africa

With the Italian entry into the war in June 1940 the previously quiet East African states were under immediate threat from superior Italian forces. The outnumbered British forces were forced to withdraw from British Somalia as the Italians advanced in August and captured Berbera. However, it was only a temporary move while the British were reorganized and reinforced.

The RAF presence was very small, although Wellesleys did undertake a number of bombing missions. The major effort was applied by the squadrons based at Sheikh Othman, Aden, and this became a critical factor in denying the Italian forces access to other British states in the area and in keeping control of the all-important Red Sea communications route. The Aden base had received new squadrons in June with the arrival of the Blenheim-equipped units, 11 and No 39 Squadrons, of 2 (Indian) Wing. These aircraft were heavily involved in the recce of ports and airfields as well as bombing missions on a wide range of Italian targets in Abyssinia and Somaliland, the airfield at Diredawa being a particular favourite. Losses mounted in the face of opposition from CR.42 fighters but overall the squadrons gave a good account of themselves by keeping up the pressure on the Italians. The build-up of forces in Sudan and Kenya was

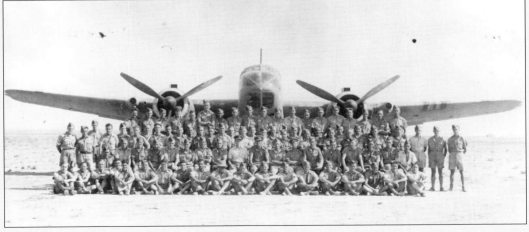

39 Squadron crews pose with a Blenheim, having moved from India to the Middle East as part of the reinforcement policy of early 1940.

Blenheim of 39 Squadron over Sheikh Othman, Aden, in summer 1940.

prompted by Churchill's insistence that the lost territory be regained as soon as possible. After a swift campaign the area was regained, along with Abyssinia – Addis Ababa being captured on 6 April 1941.

Fighting began with an Italian bombing raid on the Southern Rhodesian Forces base at Wajir in Kenya on 13 June 1940. The initial attack was made by three Caproni bombers, which attacked the landing ground and fort, the base of 237 Squadron.

'On the outbreak of war with Italy the Squadron duties were most varied, from bombing to low-level reconnaissance. Hostile forces could enter Kenya at any point on an eight hundred-mile frontage. It was of vital importance for the army to know where the enemy was massing his troops and transport, how far into British territory his patrols were moving, what artillery and armour he was about to use, and where his supply lines were.' (237 Squadron history)

At this time the Italians had 200,000 troops in Eritrea and Abyssinia as against 9,000 British and allied troops in the Sudan and 9,000 in Kenya. They also had around 200 aircraft, although very few modern types. In July they occupied Kassala (12 miles inside the Sudan) and in August they moved into British Somaliland, the defenders of which were eventually evacuated from Berbera. Meanwhile, British forces had been built up to 75,000 men in Kenya and 28,000 in the Sudan and Churchill ordered attacks to be launched from Kenya at the earliest opportunity.

No.14 Squadron with Vickers Wellesley 'bombers' moved to Port Sudan in May 1940. The arrival of Gladiator fighters in June 1940 gave the squadron in effect a dual role, although it remained primarily a bomber unit, with, at last, a more modern type, the Blenheim, arriving in September 1940. Wellesleys were also operated by 47 Squadron from June 1939 (and right up to March 1943!). On 11 June they were tasked to attack Asmara, and Wellesley K7730 became the first bomber casualty of the campaign. The two crew, Pilot Officer B. Fuge and Flight Sergeant S. Elsy, became PoWs when the aircraft force-landed.

At Port Sudan the officers of 112 Squadron were billeted in the Red Sea Hotel; squadron personnel were not impressed with Port Sudan: 'The town festered in a humid shade temperature of 110 degrees and sometimes more. In the cockpits of the aircraft patrolling down the Red Sea the temperature was sometimes 130 degrees. Many in the town were suffering from prickly heat, the rash which blotches your face and arms with red scabs. The water in the pool at the front of the Red Sea Hotel was so warm that it was a sight relief in the evening to emerge from it into slightly less warm air. In the hotel it was wise to fill your bath in the evening so that by morning the standing water would have dropped a degree or two below the temperature of the flat, hot fluid that steamed out of the tap.' (112 Squadron history).

The first operational sortie of the war for 39 Squadron took place on 12 June, when seven aircraft attacked the airfield at Diredawa in Abyssinia. Sergeant Sid Sills remembers the occasion clearly: 'My aircraft, Blenheim 1, L8384, piloted by P/O White and A/C Wright as WOP/AG, had been detailed to carry out a low-level dive-bombing attack on the Diredawa petrol dump, so we took off in the second vic of aircraft, joined in open formation at 14,000ft and set a direct course to the target. This took us across the Gulf of Aden, crossing the Somaliland coast a mile or so South of Djibouti, and then across the wild territory of Abyssinia. It was not a long flight, only about 1 hr 50mins, so that we arrived over Diredawa at breakfast time – in the hope that the station would be unprepared and have no aircraft airborne.

'And so it was. There was no sign of life as the first vic dropped its bombs from 14,000ft, and as the smoke and dust rose from their strike our vic made its shallow dive, aiming at the clearly marked petrol dumps. On the pilot's 'now' we released the bombs in a short stick at about 2,000ft – the front gun could be heard chattering away. The aircraft began to lift because of its reduced weight, and as we flew low across the airfield, we could see people running hither and thither, confused. Turning through 180 degrees we flew back across the main buildings with front and rear guns firing until we passed the airfield boundary. Then we climbed to about 10,000ft to rejoin the formation for the return to Aden where we landed some 3 hrs 50mins after take-off.' (*The Winged Bomb*, history of 39 Squadron, Ken Delve, Midland Counties).

The Italian defences had improved and a raid on Diredawa a few days later met a hot reception from heavy but inaccurate flak. The formation made a dive-bomb attack from 10,000 to 6,000ft but results were not observed. As Diredawa was one of the main Italian airfields it received a great deal of attention from 39 and other squadrons. So far very little had been seen of Italian fighters but another Diredawa raid, on the 24th, was intercepted by Fiat CR.42 fighters that attacked the formation vigorously. Blenheim L4920 dropped out of the formation and was last seen heading east on one engine. The aircraft eventually crash-landed in Somalia; two of the crew were rescued by the Somali Field Force and returned to Sheikh Othman, but the third crewman was killed.

It was not until the 29th that the scoreboard for 112 Squadron started, when Pilot Officer Hamlyn in Gladiator L7619 shot down an SM.71 south of Port Sudan. 'He climbed and delivered a quarter attack, followed by a tail chase. The enemy aircraft sheered off to the right and dived from 6,000ft down to 4,500ft. After firing approximately 1,000 rounds the enemy aircraft exploded and fell in flames into the Red Sea. Pilot Officer Hamlyn was about 30 yards astern of the Savoia when it exploded and parts of it damaged his windscreen, airscrew and ring and bead sight. A large piece of piping also lodged itself in his engine." (112 Squadron history).

The same day, Pilot Officer Wickham shot down two Italian fighters over the Western Desert while attached to 33 Squadron at Maaten Gerawla, claims that 33 Squadron records but 112 Squadron believe belong to them! On the same day, five Blenheims of 11 Squadron arrived, and were attached to 39 Squadron for operations.

The Italians crossed the Sudan border in early July and the British forces had to react. The Italians seized the fortress at Kassala, but stopped their advance at Gallabat, deciding instead to fortify the Kassala area, which became one of the targets for air attack. Ground force reinforcements arrived in the shape of 5th Indian Division, and 237 Squadron and other units supported the ground operations.

At the end of August, intelligence reports were received that Arab dhows were massing in Assab harbour, and it was feared that they might be used to ferry a large armed force across the Red Sea to attack Aden. It was decided to use the squadrons in Aden to conduct a one-day intensive bombing campaign of Assab and its environs. Thus, from one hour after dawn to one hour after dusk on 1 September, twenty-four raids were flown by the Aden squadrons. As attacks were made from high level results were difficult to observe; however, reports were later received that a great many of the natives had left with their dhows rather than risk a repeat bombing.

Throughout September and October, the Aden squadrons continued day and night operations against Italian positions across the Red Sea, as well as anti-submarine and shipping patrols along the Red Sea. On 6 November the British took back Gallabat, an attack supported by the RAF. The Italians were determined to hold on to the parts of Sudan they had seized and at Gondar launched a counter-offensive, heavily supported by aircraft, which led to largest air battle of the war in this area, with the Italians claiming seven Gladiators for the loss of five CR.42s. The front lines stabilized whilst air actions continued; the RAF made a particularly successful set of attacks on ground troops between 6 and 10 December in the Kassala area. By late 1940/early 1941, the SAAF contribution comprised 1 and 2 squadrons in the fighter role, 11 and 12 squadrons in the bomber role, and 40 Squadron in the army co-operation role.

As the No.14 Squadron ORB states, January brought an increase in air activity, with C Flight flying a record 270 hours. Much of this was in support of the Army advance through Kassala, Biscia and Agordat, with the squadron strafing the retreating enemy columns, and also involved attacks on the IAF bases at Asmara and Gura. The squadron was frequently accompanied by the SAAF Hurricanes.

Early 1941 brought increased activity along the Sudan front. Air action included bombing of enemy transport, convoys, and landing grounds, with aircraft ranging over Eritrea to attack

2 Squadron SAAF Gladiator at Wajir, with lookout up the tree.
(*45 Squadron*)

targets at Tessenei, Barentu, and Umm Hagar. It was on one such attack on 4 January that Sergeant A.K. Murrell won the DFM when bombing a target near Metemma.

January also saw the arrival of the Hurricane-equipped 3 Squadron SAAF to support the advance into Italian Somaliland. It was joined by 1 Squadron SAAF, which had re-equipped with Hurricanes having previously operated the Hawker Fury in Kenya (since May 1940). On 19 January the advance into Eritrea opened, the 4th Indian Division having arrived from the Western Desert to add experience and numbers.

The SAAF also took part in the East African campaign; Gladiator of 2 Squadron SAAF. (*SAAF*)

Attack on Diredawa 15 March 1941. (*Bob Kershaw SAAF*)

SAAF Hurricanes hiding in the bush! (*Bob Kershaw SAAF*)

SAAF Ju 86 bombing up; this was the only campaign in which the German type, operated by the South Africans, took an offensive role. (*Allan Mossop SAAF*)

Agordat fell in early February, but this coincided with an incident when Flying Officer Mackenzie's Blenheim (2115) was attacked by Hurricanes and had to crash-land at Port Sudan. A few days later, 7 February, the squadron starting using the captured airfield at Barentu, and increased attacks on Italian installations such as the CITAO workshops and transport park at Asmara; the attack on 8 February saw the loss of T1818, shot down by ground fire with the loss of Pilot Officer Renniker and his three crew.

Mogadishu was captured on 25 February. The pace of operations increased in March and 14 Squadron flew 235 operational sorties, many in support of the Battle of Keren, with 'blitz tactics against Chesen and its fortifications and lines of supply' and daily 'Movement Control'.

'It was decided that the 'big push' by the Army against Keren would be launched on March 15, and air operations for the four days previous to this date were organized with this step in mind. At 0340 hours (on 15th) two formations each consisting of three Blenheims made sorties against targets in the Keren area. Due to the fact that other aircraft were operating over these targets, there was much haze and ground dust, and it was therefore difficult to assess all the damage caused by the bombs. However, it is certain that the morale effect of the shower of bombs and machine-gun fire will have been very considerable, and this, together with the direct hits and near misses scored, lent the required support to our advancing troops.' (ORB)

This also coincided with an Allied thrust from Kenya to drive the Italians back in Ethiopia and Somaliland. John ('Jack') Frost was in action in February: 'The Transvaal Scottish position near Dif was being bombed by a flight of three Caproni Ca 133s when he intercepted. As he attacked the rear bomber, two Fiat CR 42 fighters of the escort came down at him, but he managed to elude them and climbed to intercept the two leading bombers. The Fiats came in again, head on, but he got in a long burst at one of them just before he broke into a steep climb. The Fiat went straight down into the bush and burst into flames. Jack Frost returned to attack the Capronis, which broke formation, the pilot of the first bailing out, and leaving the second pilot to make a crash landing. The second was shattered by the Hurricane's eight Browning .303 machine guns, harmonized in a deadly cone, and the third crash-landed after two passes from Jack had probably damaged it.' (SAAF History)

He was awarded an immediate DFC, the citation for which stated: 'In February, 1941, whilst on a patrol covering a distance of 180 miles inside enemy territory, this officer attacked an enemy bomber on the ground, at Afmadu, and destroyed it. The next day, he intercepted a formation of three enemy bombers escorted by two fighters, which were attacking our ground forces. He immediately attacked the bombers, two of which lost height rapidly and crashed. Captain Frost was then himself engaged by the fighters. He destroyed one, drove the other off, and then shot down the remaining bomber. He displayed great courage, skill and determination against a superior number of enemy forces.' (AMB 3050).

A few weeks later, 15 March, he was shot down during an attack on Diredawa airfield. 'Two Fiat CR 32s and a 42 came up to defend but were all shot down, the six Hurricanes shooting up Italian aircraft on the ground. Three Savoias and three Fiat 32s and a 42 were set on fire while yet another Caproni and three more fighters were damaged. The Hurricanes returned to Diredawa, after refuelling and re-arming at the captured Italian airfield at Daghadur. During this attack, Jack Frost's aircraft was hit and glycol coolant streamed back in the usual white mist; this was always a nerve-racking time; one never knew when a blast of flame would come from the violently overheated engine. He landed at a satellite airfield a few miles from Diredawa, and jumped out of his Hurricane, intent on setting fire to it before the Italians could reach him. The guns in the surrounding hills started to fire on him and he was in a tight spot. Lieutenant R. H. C. (Bob) Kershaw had seen his Flight Commander go down, however, and circled the field to keep off any Italian ground forces that might have tried to capture Jack, and then landed and taxied his Hurricane towards his Flight Commander, shouting to him to jump in. With artillery fire crashing around them, Jack climbed in and flew the Hurricane, sitting on Bob's lap.' (SAAF history)

SAAF pilots gallantry awards for the campaign: Jack Frost DFC, Bob Kershaw DSO (first to a South African in the Second World War), S. v. B. Theron DFC. (*Allan Mossop SAAF*)

This resulted in his award of a DSO – the first such award to the SAAF in the Second World War.

Keren fell on 27 March, having been subject to 591 air sorties over a five-day period; the Italians made a rapid retreat to Asmara and the expectation of the Allies was that the whole of Eritrea would be 'cleared up within the month of April', The expectation proved true, and air assets were being redeployed by early April; 14 Squadron flew its last sorties in the first week of April, in conjunction with 223 Squadron and Fleet Air Arm (FAA) units. The Blenheims moved to Heliopolis on 12 April to be refitted, get new crews and be reorganized as fully mobile with two flights – ready to join the Desert War.

Meanwhile, the Allies were also retaking Somaliland, Hargeisa being captured on 20 March, and Mogadishu a few days earlier. Diredawa fell on 29 March, a location that had been a frequent target for the bombers. Finally, Addis Ababa was captured on 6 April 1941. The last Italian formations surrendered on 18 May 1941 and the East Africa campaign was over, albeit some hold-outs remained until October.

At Amriya, 80 Squadron was delighted to see the arrival of three Hurricanes, which had flown in from Mersa Matruh following their long-range transit from the UK, supported by a Hudson that carried guns and ammunition. The Hurricanes were handed to 'A' Flight. By the 28th it had seven aircraft, and a Hurricane Flight was formed under Flight Lieutenant Gordon Jones. It was to be a short-lived association, as by August the Hurricanes had gone and 80 Squadron was back to being all Gladiators again! No.33 Squadron flew its first mission on 14 June, six aircraft having deployed to Sidi Barrani. Offensive patrols and support of the Army – and the first aerial claims, with Flying Officer Dean (L9046) claiming a CR.42 and Pilot Officer Woodward and Sergeant Craig claiming a Caproni 310. The first losses came a few days later (16th) but the 'victor' was the weather … low mist claimed three aircraft; two force-landed at Kilo 73 and one, Flight Lieutenant Bolingbroke, dived into the sea and was killed. The same day Mersa Matruh was bombed by twelve SM.79s and although six Gladiators were scrambled no intercepts were made.

On 17 June, Air Commodore Collishaw, as AOC 202 Group, issued a memorandum on the 'Tactical deployment of Hurricane aircraft'; it set the scene for his views on aggressive behaviour of pilots, which was to be a theme of DAF operations:

1. Hurricane aircraft will have to be employed in the Western Desert in a different way to the tactics to be adopted where an Advanced Air Intelligence system is in existence. In the advanced Western Desert area no intelligence organization exists and therefore fighter contact with enemy bombers is largely one of chance.
2. The following is a summary of the best tactics which can be employed in the circumstances:
    a. Hurricanes to be attached to No.33 Squadron flown by special pilots.
    b. Hurricanes to operate, as far as possible, with 5-front gun Fighter Blenheims. Hurricanes and Fighter Blenheims when raid warning received in No.33 Squadron to patrol from Matruh 35 miles out to sea in a NNW direction at approx. 15,000 feet. On this patrol Hurricanes and Fighter Blenheims should be able to intercept raiders approaching Matruh or flying eastwards out to sea to attack more eastern objectives.
    c. As a special operation, Fighter Blenheims and Hurricanes (the latter after refuelling at Bug Bug) may accompany our bomber squadrons to raid El Adem and when enemy fighters appear to inflict casualties upon the Hurricanes to refuel at Bug homewards bound.
3. It is important that Hurricane fighters should adopt aggressive tactics and take the initiative for offensive action at the outset to frighten the enemy, Success in this respect will adversely affect Italian morale, as he will be fearful that Hurricane fighters may attack at any moment.

On the same day he issued 'Operational employment of 5-front gun Blenheim aircraft'; this tactical memo included:

2. The situation in the Western Desert suggests that we ought to employ the multi-gun fighter employing tasks as follows:
    b. Enemy bombers are frequently escorted by fighters. No 33 Squadron should therefore operate in close support of Fighter Blenheims so that the Gladiators may take on the enemy fighters while the multi-gun Blenheims attack the bombers.
    c. Fighter Blenheims might also with advantage be employed to fly high over El Adem and El Gubbi to report by W/T when enemy aircraft take-off (this is conspicuous as a heavy dust cloud is raised) and when the bombers proceed the shadowing aircraft could report by W/T to get No.33 Squadron into contact with them.

No.80 Squadron had its first combat on the 19th: 'Today the Squadron had its first action of the war. Flying Officer P.G. Wykeham-Barnes, who was attached to 33 Squadron for duties with No.202 Group, was patrolling the Sollum area, with four Gladiators of that squadron when they became involved in a dogfight with nine Fiat 42s of the Italian Air Force. Flying Officer Wykeham-Barnes in Hurricane 2639, immediately cut inside the turn of the leading Fiat, and shot it down into the sea. The flight continued and although the enemy were superior in numbers, they gradually retreated towards Libya. Our pilot shot down one more Fiat, which was later confirmed by the Army forces.

The main opposition – the Italian CR.42 fighter.

A somewhat weary looking Blenheim. The Blenheim was the RAF's main bomber in this theatre for the first two years.

Out of ammunition and almost out of petrol, the patrol was forced to return. They had shot down four Fiats, but lost one Gladiator, Sergeant R. Green, an old 80 Sqn pilot, being shot down. The patrol landed at Sidi Barrani.' (80 Sqn ORB)

20 June, 113 Squadron: 'Takeoff at 12.15am – one Blenheim. Bob is shepherding two Bombays. We are loaded with incendiaries and 20-pounders – don't know what the Bombays are carrying. We cross the wire at 15000ft. There's a bit of a headwind. I drop an incendiary to get a drift but it disappears. Still viz is good and we see the surf line at Sollum. We turn in to shufti Gubbi, losing altitude. Nothing! No flaming onions, no pom-pom bursts. Bob grins at me in the green glow of the flying panel. The Bombays are big ghostly figures formatting a little above us, their eyes, no doubt watching the little darting blue flames from our exhausts. Suddenly, on the ground, a big white Savoia shows up and beyond it about 30 dispersed fighters. I click down Selector 1 and press the tit to release my first stick of incendiaries and shout bombs gone. But the jettison light comes on

500lb bomb of pre-war vintage – the main (heaviest) weapon of the bombers for the first two years; Leading Aircraftman Len Wilde of 45 Squadron. (*45 Squadron*)

and Bob pulls us up suddenly in a vicious climb. As he flattens out there is a rewarding rumble - our incendiary parcels have come unstuck. I press Selector 2.

'Bob takes us round in a leisurely circuit. One Bombay is still with us. The ground below is a living sheet of flame so they must have had 'matchsticks' too. Bob goes round again and the Bombays peel off with a quick double-flash of the belly light. We steam along the dirt road to El Adem and find a lot of aircraft there too. They are well-dispersed. (The BBC news said they had 1500 so we ought not to be short of targets). We drop the other two sticks from 8000 to get the clusters to spread, and set out for home, leaving a cheerful glow behind us.

'We signal a dummy flare-path and get its number in reply. 8. Only ten miles from home. I give Bob the course, click my stopwatch. His beady eyes see the glims before Tommy does and he makes the circuit. The Chance flings a great swathe of light for two seconds as we touch down. The CO himself meets us with a gharry at the red. We hang about in the Ops tent nattering for some time while expecting news of the Bombays. Barney finally drives us up to the Mess and we pour ourselves 'nightcaps'. Rands appears just as we are breaking-up and says one Bombay came back with an undelivered load having lost touch with us. Sounds balmy, the moon was so bright. The other had a 250 hang-up and left us to give it a shake. I wonder how you shake a Bombay?" (Mike Shekleton).

Squadron Leader Shekleton's diary also adds some apt comments about desert life: 'We got into our Mess hut today – marvelous after the EPIP [European Personnel India Pattern]. Some of us built a bar with bomb boxes. The boxes duly name-labelled make excellent personal depositories for drink etc.; you just reach across to pull out your bottle of Johnny Walker. They say 55s hut has a fireplace and chimney. "Communications. Must be for sending smoke-signals," said someone. The Egyptian gaffer presented us with a pair of chameleons – instantly named Gilbert and Sullivan. Every time the door is opened a 'squadron' of blue flies surge in but Gilbert and Sullivan collect them in minutes. It's bliss.'

Getting aircraft out to the Middle East was going to prove troublesome, especially after the fall of France and positioning of German fighters in the west of France; however, even before then, the records show significant losses – one particularly tragic day was 18 June when seven Blenheims flown by the Blenheim Delivery Flight were lost *en route* from Tangmere to Malta; six crashed in France due to bad weather with only one crew surviving; the seventh overshot Malta and crashed into the sea off Tunisia, again with the loss of the crew. David Gunby and Pelham Temple have done a fine job of recording bomber losses in their *Bomber Losses in the Middle East and Mediterranean* and to some readers it may come as a shock to discover how many aircraft and crew were lost during 'non-operational' sorties. Before long, the majority of new aircraft – other than bombers – came via sea and the overland route from Takoradi, West Africa.

Despite some ground movements in June, the British seizing Fort Capuzzo and the Italians making a few border raids, nothing much happened on the ground. This was primarily because the Italian commander, Marshal Balbo, was reluctant to launch the large-scale offensive demanded

'Sand with everything'
– for people and
equipment. Two views
of one of the main
desert hazards.

Lieutenant Loftus SAAF in a Gladiator; note the ring-and-bead sight.

by Mussolini. Following his death in an accident on 28 June, his successor, General Graziani, was equally reluctant, citing lack of supplies and the fact that a defeat would quickly become a disaster. And so it was for the next few months – minor air actions but no major moves on the ground.

The pilots of 33 Squadron, including some attached from 112 Squadron, had a very successful day on 4 July when they bounced a formation of CR.42s taking-off from Menastir; in short order the squadron claimed all nine Italian aircraft, four of them falling to Flying Officer Worcester, for the loss of one aircraft, whose pilot, Flying Officer Price-Owen, parachuted to safety. Sadly, Flying Officer Worcester was killed two weeks later (18th) when he flew into a hillside while descending through cloud to Maaten Gerawla.

The same day, 80 Squadron was in action against a formation of SM.79s over Aboukir: 'A patrol of six Gladiators of B Flight was ordered at 0745 hours. The flight took off in two sub-sections of three aircraft each, although the second sub-section was late owing to engine trouble in leader's aircraft. At 12000ft, over Aboukir ten S79s were sighted heading towards Alex. One sub flight intercepted and they hurried out to sea heading North. They were engaged until they were out of range. The sub flight then turned and attacked a second sub formation of enemy aircraft which was approx. 3000ft below on the port quarter. A quarter attack was carried out all three aircraft concentrating on the right-hand enemy a/c. As our speed lessened, the Gladiators developed a No.3 attack which was continued until the leader had expended all his ammunition but the two remaining a/c continued the engagement until the EA were out of range. There was no apparent damage to the EA apart from the fact that the right hand a/c appeared to lag and lose height, but not sufficiently for either of our a/c to close to range. The other sub flight of Gladiators gave chase out to sea but were unable to catch the enemy. One fighter hit in three places and another in one. All a/c landed at Amria (sic) at 0905.' (Appendix to 80 Sqn ORB)

This account flags up a number of the key problems faced by the RAF Gladiator pilots. The reference to the attack types shows that the old pre-war 'how to engage bombers' tactics were still much in use – and they were predicated on no enemy fighters being present. The adherence to old tactics was an issue to some squadrons until 1941 and there were some hard-won lessons, although the problem was less noticeable in squadrons with more forward-looking and flexible flight commanders and COs. Secondly, the inability of the Gladiators to do serious damage – all the ammunition on lead aircraft used to no seeming effect, and then the others firing as well, was likely due to a lack of air gunnery skills. However, this is not surprising as most RAF pilots had little training or experience in air gunnery. Finally, there is the fact that the fighters could not chase down the bombers.

The Bombays of 216 Squadron had been added to the bomber strength in June but it rapidly became clear that the type was unsuited. The first Bombay had been lost on the night of 20–21 June over El Gubbi (L5850; four crew killed and one PoW). The July period though saw four lost aircraft in three days, three during the night bombing of Tobruk:

1. 14–15 July: Bombay L5815, flew into high ground south of Mersa Matruh on way back from target; three killed and two injured.
2. 14–15 July: Bombay L5819, ran out of fuel on return and force-landed near Lake Mariut, engaged by Egyptian troops and taken prisoner, but when identities confirmed, returned to squadron, aircraft written off.
3. 15–16 July: Bombay L5848, probably shot down by fighter, all five killed.

One advantage of the desert was that, with care and some skill, you could land almost anywhere … .

'We're at 15,000. There's the wire. This is Egypt. Bob begins a slow circuit staring down at the terrain. Height peels off. We'd made a 360 degree turn, we were down to 5000.

'He'd made a perfect landing and we rumbled along a patch almost free of camel thorn. We wait. We didn't wait long. A field ambulance came careering over a dune and slammed to a halt not 20ft from us. An army lieutenant jumped out of the front and two orderlies from the back. "Anyone hurt?" shouted the Lt medic striding toward us. "No, we're fine. Just out of fuel, that's all." The fueling was a bit tedious without the usual funnels which you could slap a four-gall tin on and leave it to empty itself, but it got done in the end and we got to Maaten Bagush late afternoon. They were in a bit of a tizzy because we were so late. Bob intended to go on to Helio but Group stopped him so

The Bombay started life as a 'bomber-transport' and indeed performed a number of bombing missions before, in this theatre, it adopted more of the transport role – moving people and equipment between airfields.

we had a good dinner and went early to bed. John came in an hour later. It was comforting to sleep in your own tent.' (Mike Shekleton)

On July 27, Squadron Leader Shekleton recorded: 'Group has apparently decided that as we have some fighters here temporarily – the Beaux from 30 Squadron – they might as well use them before sending them back to their base. It seems there is a certain Army unit in danger of being cut off and very low level recces are needed to size up the position and make a rescue plan. So before we turned in tonight a plan was devised. Two of our a/c would go in with a pair of Beaux on watch at 5000ft.

'At dawn the CO (with our gunner, Tommy, on loan) and Owen took off with four of the fighters. By ten a.m. a little circle of us were standing outside the Ops Tent waiting for their return. Owen came in first, followed by the two fighters. Then for 10 minutes nothing. At last we spied a speck – it was Barney. His kite sounded pretty rough. "He's flying on one," said someone. But where were the other two fighters? As the CO touched down another fighter appeared and went into the circuit. Good-o, but what's that thing. It was a supply a/c. So one fighter was missing.'

The reference to 30 Squadron is perhaps in error; the squadron had been operating Blenheims in the fighter role (Blenheim IF) since June 1940, with its main base at Ismailia and various detachments, so it likely means Blenheim fighters and not Beaux (Beaufighter?) fighters.

'In the Ops Tent we heard the whole story (I sat in on it and no one noticed me – I'd become part of the furniture now). Over the target there was a layer of stratus and Barney and Owen going down through it lost the Beaux. 32s and 42s swarmed up from Gubbi and Adem while they were making their photo runs. Barney and Owen darted in and out of the cloud to lose them but they were very persistent. Owen said both he and his nav. got disorientated for a while. They finally darted for the border in cloud.

'The CO meanwhile was hotly engaged by a trio of 42s. One got in very close and gave him heavy burst. He saw John crumple in his seat. Just as the 42s overshot, Tommy shouted triumphantly: "Got one, sir," as Barney circled, still looking hopefully for a Beau, he saw the 42 flaming to the ground. Meanwhile, a Beau had appeared and the CO's tormentors turned their attention to it. He climbed back into the cloud and to his relief saw John was recovering, so he turned toward Bardia to finish the job in hand. But here another shock awaited him. New defenses just south of Bardia, not previously seen, opened up and he found himself the center of a fierce pom-pom barrage. A terrific clonk hit the plane and the cockpit filled with fumes – a shell had gone through the well. John's tin hat parked under his seat was crunched! Weaving and twisting, the CO managed to somehow get out of the tangle and set out for home with the port engine leaking oil. He landed on one. Owen, curiously, on the same sortie, though out of touch, had a trouble free run.

'Just after the debriefing the CO's Flight-Sergeant pulled up – he said a .5 explosive had ripped through a spar, then through the observer's parked parachute pack and, finally spent, thumped John on the back. Curiously, it didn't explode. John has it as a souvenir. The a/c is badly hurt but with full revs now available, Bob, with me as passenger, flew it to Fuka for return to the Delta. Not a very comfortable trip, a bit blustery – the bomb-aimer's front Perspex panel was missing, and the undercart wouldn't retract.'

Squadron Leader Gerald Keily, 113 Squadron, was awarded an immediate DFC for his actions the following day, as the citation recorded: 'On 28th July, 1940, Squadron Leader Keily was the pilot of an aircraft detailed to carry out a special reconnaissance over Libya. The reconnaissance had to be carried out at a low altitude owing to clouds. He was attacked by five enemy aircraft but, displaying great skill, he destroyed one of them. During the engagement the air observer was hit by a bullet. Notwithstanding the handicap of having the air observer's body leaning against him, Squadron

Leader Keily continued with the reconnaissance, returning with information of great value. He has invariably displayed exceptional leadership, courage, and devotion to duty.'

Combat report of Flight Lieutenant M.T. Pattle: 'Four Gladiators took off from Sidi Barrani satellite at 1715 hours on 4th August 1940 to escort one Lysander detailed to observe enemy movements at Bir Taieb el Esem. The Lysander flew at a height of approx. 6,000ft. Two Gladiators took up position about 3,000ft above and immediately behind. The remaining two Gladiators flew at 12,000ft to one flank keeping the lower flight of Gladiators in full view.... Immediately on reaching the target the Lysander fired a Verey light signifying that it was being attacked, released its bombs on the target and flew due East at a low altitude. I was leading the top flight of Gladiators and dived down to investigate as I did not see any EA.... I heard Flying Officer Wykeham-Barnes lead his section to the attack and immediately afterwards saw 7 Breda 65s (one flight of four and one of three) flying West just behind the Lysander. Flying Officer Wykeham-Barnes attacked the formation of four so I selected the remaining three, and delivered an astern attack. ... Turning inside them I closed to about 150 yards and delivered a quarter attack on the nearest Breda. On the first burst both my port guns ceased to fire. The Breda however had been hit, for after a few more bursts from dead astern, white smoke poured out of the starboard side of the engine and it force landed satisfactorily on good ground 5 miles further on. I then broke away and attempted without luck to clear my port gun. I was then immediately attacked by 5 Fiat 42s ... a dogfight ensued in which they made repeated attacks from the quarter and beam using the speed they gained in the dive to regain altitude after each attack. My own tactics were mainly defensive, turning away from each attack and delivering a short attack on the most suitable target as it dived past. On one occasion a Fiat completing its attack turned round in front of my aircraft, presenting at excellent shot at close range. I fired a long burst and the Fiat turned slowly on its back and spun towards the ground. I last saw it spinning at 200 feet. Shortly afterward my starboards gun packed up.'

On his way back he was set on by fifteen fighters and his one remaining gun jammed. 'After a running fight lasting about 15 minutes my rudder controls were shot away. No longer able to use evasive tactics, I baled out after climbing to 400ft and landed about 4 miles inside the border.

'During the engagement I found that one of the enemy in particular stood out as an exceptional shot. He made repeated attacks using full deflection with great accuracy. Each time he attacked I was forced to use violent evasive tactics and in fact was finally brought down by turning into the shots of another when evading his fire as he came out of a loop directly above me. The remainder as a whole lacked accuracy and did not press home to a decisive range.'

After nightfall he walked towards the wire and was picked up at 1400 hours on the 5th.

Pilot Officer Linnard of 80 Squadron submitted the following combat report for the 8th: 'The patrol flew in stepped up vic formation. Just before reaching Bir-el-Gobi enemy aircraft were reported by the top flight and I sighted them at about 2 o'clock. Enemy aircraft were flying East at about 8,000ft, my height being 9,500ft. We started getting into position between enemy aircraft and their aerodrome.

'My sub flight leader put us into echelon right and turned into enemy's right flank. The lowest flight went into attack and as they were closing in the enemy formation started breaking up. We were given R/T instructions by the top flight to enter the fight. I slipped under my leader to the left and found myself in a mass of milling aircraft. I went to attack a CR42 which was on a Gladiator's tail when another CR42 passed in front of me. I gave him a deflection burst and got on to his tail – he pulled up in a loop. I followed him around giving him bursts and when he was upside down in the loop he baled out, dropping past me, his parachute opening just below me. My range would be about 50 yards or less. I got on to another CR42 and practically the same thing happened as before except that I did not get him and my engine cut as I was following him in the loop when I was in the vertical position. I saw the enemy aircraft dive past me but I was so close to him that he could not fire at me. I pushed my nose down and got my engine started and then saw a CR42 diving down on me from vertically above, but he did not hit me. I then saw a CR42 practically head on. I gave him a burst at very close range. The enemy aircraft turned over to the right on its back and went into a flat spin. I was at about 4,000ft at the time. I watched the aircraft spin for about 1,000ft and then heard gun fire which I thought was from behind but there were no enemy aircraft in range. I then looked for the spinning aircraft but all I saw was an aircraft in flames on the ground beneath me. Another CR42 dived past going very fast. I gave him a quick burst and saw some black smoke coming from him, but he kept straight on diving as fast as he could go towards Bir-el-Gobi, I did not follow him down. I then turned back towards where the fight had been but saw only one aircraft, a Gladiator (P/O Stuckey). We hung around a bit and then made for home, I caught up with F/Lt Pattle and Flg Off Graham and returned with them. I sustained no damage to self or aircraft except for one fabric panel torn out. I saw altogether 6 aircraft burning on the ground and 4 parachutes dropping.'

The account is interesting in that it gives a very vivid picture of the rapid and changing nature of such a large dogfight, a quick glance of an aircraft, a fleeting burst of fire, focusing on one wounded enemy aircraft to such an extent that another enemy could catch you unawares. And all in a very brief period of time. The majority of sorties, of course, brought no such periods of adrenalin and were fairly routine, with no enemy sighted and nothing much to report.

Relationships between the RAF and the Navy were often strained by the former's belief that the Navy fired at anything in the air and the latter's belief that the RAF was seldom around when needed! On 17 August, Gladiators of 112 Squadron were tasked to patrol over units of the Mediterranean Fleet. 'They didn't realize anything was amiss until they found themselves amongst the AA bursts from the warships (HMS *Warspite, Kent, Malaya, Ramillies* and eleven destroyers) and saw enemy aircraft and bombs falling into the sea. Twenty-five SM.79s were spotted and five were attacked. Flight Lieutenant Schwab got one, Pilot Officer Wickham got one and his own aircraft was hit by explosive bullets, and Pilot Officer Acworth was wounded in the leg but returned safely and was sent off to Fuka field hospital. In all, eight SM.79s were destroyed and there was no damage to the ships, although the Navy were a bit upset that the RAF had not seen the enemy aircraft a bit sooner.' (112 Sqn history).

Fighter squadron strength increased on 19 August with the formation – out of 33, 80 and 112 Squadrons – of 274 Squadron. Formed at Amriya, it was a mixed Gladiator and Hurricane unit, the latter types (and pilots) coming from 80 Squadron, who noted: 'Formation of 274 Squadron under Squadron Leader Dunn. The following officers and approx. 80 airmen posted from this unit to 274 Squadron [eight officers listed]. Flight Lieutenant E G Jones assumes command of 80 Squadron, The French Flight was absorbed into 274 Squadron.' (80 Sqn ORB).

On 27 August Mike Shekleton's diary recorded that 113 Squadron was now fully equipped with Blenheim IVs and 'could reach many targets in the Benghazi area. Incidentally our old friend 9319 had turned up – now with a pair of Brownings in the belly turret.'

More importantly, he recorded: 'Our grub here gets better and better. To me it is a sheer miracle. The cookhouse is a small black wooden hut that looks like a chicken coop, an effect enhanced by the fact that a few scrawny-looking fowls peck at the sand around it. At the back of this little hulk is an annex with walls built of old petrol tins (full of sand?) then oiled and sand. The cookers are Valor Perfection run on paraffin. The cooks? – one English, one Bulgarian.'

The involvement of the Australians, by land and air, was to be a significant factor in the Desert War. On 28 February 1940 it had been decided that 'for national and training reasons' the 6th Division

By late 1940 the number of Hurricane squadrons had increased and this was to be the major fighter type until the advent of the P-40 variants. A typical desert 'airfield' scene – flat nothingness and a tent. (*Michael Welchman SAAF*)

2 Squadron SAAF Gladiator. (*SAAF*)

Crashed Blenheim IV; the arrival of the Mk.IVs improved the performance of the Blenheim, but loss rates remained high. (*Peter Metelerkamp SAAF*)

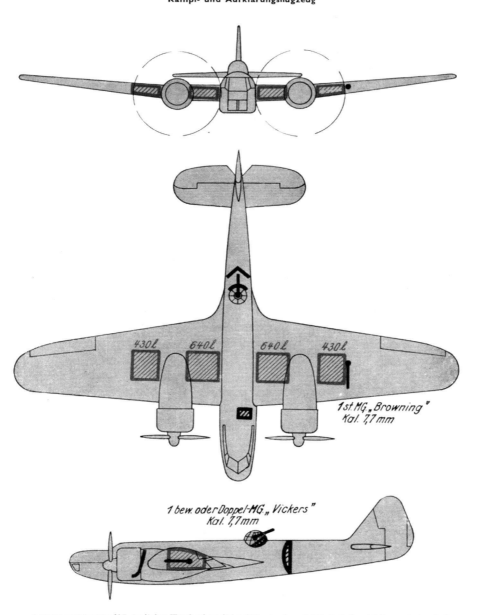

Die Kriegsflugzeuge der Feindmächte   Anlage 23 a

Großbritannien

Bristol „**Blenheim IV**" („Long-nosed")
Kampf- und Aufklärungsflugzeug

430 ℓ   640 ℓ   640 ℓ   430 ℓ

1st.MG „Browning"
Kal. 7,7 mm

1 bew. oder Doppel-MG „Vickers"
Kal. 7,7 mm

1 starres ungesteuertes MG. im linken Flügel, 1 bewegliches MG. oder Doppel-MG. in halbausfahrbarem, hydraulisch betätigtem Drehturm mit 360° Drehbereich. Neuerdings geschützte Kraftstoffbehälter.

The Luftwaffe's intelligence sheet on the Blenheim IV, showing armament and vulnerability (fuel tanks and crew).

should have an Australian squadron. Under the command of Squadron Leader I.D. McLachlan, the officers and men of 3 Squadron RAAF sailed from Sydney on 15 July, eventually arriving in the Middle East in August, and starting training as an Army co-operation squadron with Lysanders at Ismailia in early September. This was the start of what became a major contribution to the desert air war by the RAAF.

To keep combat aircraft 'in business' requires an efficient servicing and repair organization, and the fuel and munitions to 'deliver' in the direction of the enemy. While the squadron-level servicing tends to get reasonable coverage – after all they belonged to the squadron and so were part of the immediate action – the other parts, the 'second line' servicing and repair, and the supply system are frequently ignored, both by planners at the time and by historians. Sadly, the role is not 'sexy' and most readers want to read of combats and action; but in the Western Desert the role of logistics, and all that went with it, was probably more crucial – and more difficult – than in most other theatres. One such key event, was the formation of No.1 Middle East Air Explosive and Fuel Park to supply explosives and fuel to all units in the Western Desert, for which it had five main dumps:

- No.1 Main Dump at Fuka
- No.2 Reserve Dump at Burg el Arab
- No.3 Sub-dump at Qotaifiya
- No.4 Reserve Dump at Ikingi
- No.5 Reserve Dump at Amriya

The difficulties, lack of trucks, for moving material and the fluctuating front line, made the role of the supply organization difficult. It had to keep the RAF units supplied, and also keep supplies out of the hands of the enemy during any retreat.

The aggressive RAF tactics dominated the Italians and 'this moderate harassing offensive pinned the Italian air units to rear landing grounds from which they could mount only occasional raids. The air operations could, not, however, as neither could naval sweeps nor the aggressive frontier ground patrols, redress the whole strategical situation consequent on the elimination of France and the freedom of Italy to concentrate all her force against Egypt.' (RAAF history).

A number of combat accounts record that the Italian fighters often seemed reluctant to engage the RAF fighters, yet at other times they displayed a more aggressive manner and seemed happy to join a fight. Nevertheless, the overall impression is that the Italians had ceded the advantage to the RAF and that the latter had established a psychological advantage, which plays a significant role in any combat situation. On the ground the Allied position still looked tenuous, as the Italians had the edge in numbers and equipment; by early September an Italian offensive was expected: 'Cancel all order. Scram. All posts retire eastwards, repeat eastwards on Matruh.' (112 Squadron history). The Italian advance, Operation E, started on the 10th (some sources say 13th) and those orders went to the forward observation screen posts of 202 Group.

9th September, 113 Squadron: 'Today we have had fun and games over Derna, while 211 and 55 have been stirring up Tobruk West and Gubbi. It is a long time since the squadron has put up nine machines together, and it was something of a thrill to have a line abreast takeoff of two flights. The third had to come from the satellite and had a rendezvous with them on the coast. At Derna there were three targets, one for each flight – the harbour, the aerodrome and a nearby concentration of MT. We got the aerodrome and a miserable target it was. True there were about 30 a/c there but widely dispersed with 500 yards of empty desert between them.

'The journey out over the sea about 25 miles off the coast was uneventful except that Dickie, flying as usual as a wing-man to Bob, developed engine trouble and had to turn back. We carried on. The squadron split up at Derna as we turned onto our separate targets. At 16000 ft. Bob made a smooth run across a line of dispersed a/c – me squinting at the bomb sight and calling directions. And soon had the satisfaction of seeing something we'd been waiting for – a 4lb bomb falling smack in the middle of an S78. There was a violent explosion, lots of smoke and flame, so it must have been armed. The rest of the stick seemed to fall pretty close to other a/c so it looked pretty good.

'Over to our left Blomfield's bombs seemed to be hitting the sea though the other flight was knocking the MT pretty hard. I had the floorboard up to operate the blister guns and get a shufti at the bombing. Thompson said some flak had found our height, but Bob had gone into a dive anyway and we were heading out to sea. The next instant something came through my phones that sounded like "Fighters" and I heaved the guns every which way staring frantically in the mirror and seeing nothing except sea and Derna Harbour. "Where the hell are they?" I called repeatedly and got no reply. My microphone had been switched off. After a while I crawled sheepishly back into my seat and checked the coast line for a pinpoint.

'On the way back we turned toward the coast road near Sidi Barrani and searched for any sign of a forced landing – Dickie. And miraculously, we found him and his crew standing by their shiny new long nose. Bob gave him a bit of a beat-up and landed nearby. Dickie's port engine had seized up. We got them aboard and nipped back to Maaten Bagush. The CO was naturally anxious about the safety of the stranded a/c and Bob took Dickie and Samuels back to it. They made an effort to get it in the air but failed and came back after dark. It was brought back the following day.' (Mike Shekleton).

The main airfield at Sidi Barrani was attacked on the 15th by ten SM.79s, but intercepted by Gladiators, Hurricanes and even Blenheims, with seven being claimed for the loss of one 80 Squadron Gladiator. However, the airfield was then promptly abandoned and was occupied by the Italians the following day. It what was to be a regular feature of the Desert War, the base of one day became the target of the following day!

16th September, 113 Squadron: 'This evening was marred by an event so sudden and unexpected it affected us all. During the afternoon Aboukir had delivered a new long-nose and Flights had

The main Italian bomber was the SM.79, which proved to be resilient to attack, especially by the underarmed Gladiators, which also lacked the performance to chase down the bomber.

Hurricane Z5469
blowing up its own
sandstorm. (*Michael
Schoeman SAAF*)

armed it. A bit before dark young Roberts [Pilot Officer E S Roberts], lately arrived from the UK, volunteered to fly it to the satellite. For some reason known only to them, Group had cleared MB of aircraft for the night. There was, we were told, to be a squadron takeoff from there at dawn for a Benina raid.

'Roberts took off rather later than planned but the satellite is only five miles away and there was ample time for him to do it in daylight. Dickie Squires was over at Fuka waiting for one of our kites that was promised by six pm. When he didn't return it was assumed he would be staying over because our Chance Light and crew was on loan to 211 Squadron and Dickie was aware of this. In the Mess at about eight we heard the drone of a Blenheim. The CO jumped up shouting, "My God! Dickie Squires! Lights, quick!" He dashed out followed by Bob and I. The CO's car was there and two pickups ready for the morning. We all tore through the camp to the strip and made a row with headlights on. Bob's pickup had a Very pistol and a torch. We stood looking up at the sky and quickly located the errant a/c. It was making a wide circle to the north with its nav lights on. Just as Bob was loading the Very to indicate our position, to our bewilderment, Group's siren started up and a moment later the a/c which had turned beyond Group and was now headed toward us was caught in a hail of light flak. It came on towards us rapidly losing height in what seemed to be an approach. Group sounded an all-clear but by then the a/c, which may or may not have been hit, had climbed again and was headed toward the satellite where, as we heard later, a flare path had been laid out and probably picked out by the pilot.

'The CO said he'd drive over there and 'pick him up', meaning Dickie, and Bob and I drove to the Ops tent where Jock was standing anxiously at the entrance. Seconds later engines sounded again and a Blenheim dived into the airstrip with an almighty crash followed at once by the heavy thud of 250s exploding. Bob jumped straight back into the pickup and I piled in after him. He drove toward the fiery mess. Bob had done a bit of thinking and at once eliminated Dickie because *that* machine would not have been bombed up. But I had forgotten Roberts. We stood and watched as the machine burned itself out. No one could get near it though the fire truck hurled gallons of water at it.

'Roberts had already done some months of operations from the UK and had flown the Blenheim out from there to Egypt. His log book revealed he had made lots of night landings though none out here. Bob had flown with him and judged him to be an excellent pilot – indeed he had already asked Barney if he could have him for A Flight to replace poor Victor. He was only nineteen.' (Mike Shekleton). The CO, Squadron Leader Keily, himself failed to return from a mission on the 18th.

The Italians did not advance very far or very fast, and the British commander, General Wavell, was already pressing for his field commander, Lieutenant General Sir Henry Maitland Wilson, to get ready for a counter-offensive. On 20 October, 202 Group issued Op Order No.39 to 33, 55, 80, 112, 211 and 216 squadrons:

Information:
1. A battalion of the Camerons will move to an assembly point during the afternoon of 22nd October 1940 and leave it at approx. 1700 hours that day to launch an attack on an enemy position at 722373 between 0001 and 0100 hours on 23rd October. After the attack the Camerons will withdraw to the assembly point.
2. During this operation there will be covering forces at 615370 and 625357.

Intention:
3. To provide fighter protection for our forces during daylight, prior to, and after the attack.
4. To occupy and harass enemy forces in the Sidi Barrani area during the attack by our ground forces.
5. To neutralize enemy air forces which might be employed in attacking our ground forces during the withdrawal on the morning after the attack.

Method of Execution:
6. Forces to be employed: 9 Gladiators of 80 Sqn, 2 Hurricanes of 33 Sqn, 1 Bombay of 216 Sqn, 9 Blenheims of 55 Sqn, 9 Blenheims of 211 Sqn.
7. Bases: Bombers of 55 and 211 squadrons are to operate from their permanent bases. The Bombay of 216 Squadron is to operate from Fuka satellite. The fighters are to operate from Bir Kenayis.
8. Bomb Loads: Bombers of 55 and 211 squadrons are to be armed as ordered later by this HQ. The Bombay of 216 Squadron is to be armed with 150 20lb RL bombs and is to carry four reconnaissance flares.
9. Bombing Raids: By 55 and 211 squadrons are to be as ordered later by this HQ. The Bombay is to leave Fuka satellite so as to reach Sidi Barrani at 8,000ft at 0001 hours on 23rd October. The four flares are to be dropped at 0001 and bombs are then to be dropped in the Sidi Barrani area. Bombing is to cease by 0130 hours.
10. Fighter Patrols are to be maintained over Sidi Barrani area in accordance with the attached Patrol Table.
11. The roles of the fighters will be as follows. Gladiators on patrol to watch for and intervene against enemy air attacks on our ground forces. Enemy fighters which leave the vicinity of our ground forces are not to be pursued. Hurricanes on patrol to protect the Gladiators from air attack to which they are particularly vulnerable when engaged on protection of ground forces.
12. Re-arming: fighters which expend all their ammunition are to return to their operational base, re-arm and continue their patrol or stand-by to the end of the allotted period.
13. Subject to a satisfactory weather report being received, the Bombay of 216 Squadron may return direct to Heliopolis after bombing.

<u>Administrative Arrangements</u>:

14. Command at Bir Kenayis is to be exercised by OC 80 Squadron.
15. Petrol, Oil, ammunition for two sorties by each fighter are to be sent to Bir Kenayis by road under arrangements made by OCs 33 and 80 squadrons, who are to collaborate in this respect.
16. OC 33 Squadron is to be responsible for sending to Bir Kenayis such necessary personnel and equipment as will be required for the two Hurricanes. Rations for two days are to be sent to Bir Kenayis for all personnel other than those of the detachment of 80 Squadron already there.
17. The Medical Officer of 80 Squadron is to be at Bir Kenayis from 1645 on 22nd October until the termination of operations.

The interesting points from this are the detail that is provided in the op order, which is often lost when one looks just at the records of a single unit, and the detail around the support items such as supplies, including rations, and even the presence of the medical officer.

The 33 Squadron ORB records frequent patrols during this period, with reference to Blenheim, Gladiator and Hurricane sorties, which in part reflects the frequent mixing up of units and aircraft. The operational flight was at Maaten Gerawla and included 112 Squadron. The first patrols were on the 22nd, at 0540 'three B Flight aircraft left for patrol – no activity reported.' Later the same day, 'Blenheim and Hurricane aircraft took off for interception, none made, returned to base.' At 0430 the next day, 'patrols carried out by Hurricane, Blenheims and three Gladiator adjacent to Mersa Matruh.' The aircraft returned at 0630 with nothing to report. It was similar over the next few days, and on the 29th six Gladiators were detached to Sidi Barrani for offensive patrols in the Amseat–Sidi Azeiz area. The late morning patrol met with success when Pilot Officer P. Wickham forced down an RO.37, and a little later a formation of CR.42s were encountered and a fight ensued, with Pilot Officer V. Woodward forcing one down.

However, the major action came on the 31st. At 1240 all aircraft were brought to standby and at 1245 all serviceable aircraft took off and left for Matruh area: '1315, 12 aircraft were in the air and were engaging EA over Matruh, Qasaba and Bagush. EA on this occasion were escorted by 12 CR42 fighters, who caused the Hurricanes some inconvenience as they were intercepted during the climb up. Flying Officer Litt.. [not clear] a/c was considerably shot up. Flying Officer St Quintin, after shooting down 1 S79 and setting fire to the starboard engine of another, forced landed at Qasaba with holed petrol tank. He was later able to return to base under his own power. Flying Officer Holman intercepted and shot down a CR42 after a running fight. Flying Officer Leveille [not clear] after bagging 2 S79s (witnessed and confirmed by ground forces) was caught by 4 CR42 and forced to abandon his a/c. By the greatest misfortune his parachute was damaged in leaving the a/c and failed to open. No 112 Squadron also had a successful day claiming 3 CR42a and 2 S79s.' (33 Sqn ORB; this was a handwritten account and is unclear in places)

According to the 112 Squadron history: 'There was a fine fight to finish off the month. The Regia Aeronautica, attempting to retaliate against the bombing attacks against his Libyan communications and port, sent 15 SM.79s and 18 CR.42s to try to bomb our forward ground positions. Flight Lieutenant Abrahams, Fg Off Fraser, Fg Off Clarke, Pilot Officer Duff, 2/Lt Smith took off on patrol of the Mersa Matruh area at 1300 hours. Pilot Officer Duff sighted ten of the SM.79s and gave chase, bit did not see the escorting CR.42s. Six of them dived on him and shot him down, he escaped by parachute suffering from slight burns. The CR.42s were then engaged by Flt Lt Schwab, Plt Off Acworth (who had joined the patrol) and 2/Lt Smith. Flt Lt Schwab shot down two confirmed, but had to force land due to engine failure. Plt Off Acworth shot one down and then collided with 2nd

Lt Smith; both pilots escaped by parachute, but the latter dislocated his collar bone. Fg Off Fraser and Fg Off Clarke were also ordered off from readiness and engaged the bombers and Fg Off Fraser put one engine of an SM.79 out of action. Fg Off Clarke was posted missing after the engagement, in which the enemy lost at least eight aircraft.'

A few weeks later, on 20 November, the squadron had an even more successful day, claiming eight CR.42s for no loss. Flying Officer Joe Fraser was awarded a DFC around this period, the citation reading: 'This officer has led a detached flight with great success. He has destroyed at least 10 enemy aircraft, 9 of which he destroyed within a period of 14 days. He has proved a skillful and courageous fighter pilot.'

In October 1940, the CO of 55 Squadron, Squadron Leader Wing Commander Robert Stowell, was awarded the DFC, the citation read: 'Since the outbreak of war with Italy, Wing Commander Stowell has led his squadron against the enemy on 38 occasions often attacking his objectives after having forced his way past superior numbers of enemy fighters. His leadership has inspired his squadron with high morale, and he has shown exceptional valour, courage and devotion to duty.'

This squadron was one that had a long history in the Middle East, having been reformed at Suez in February 1920, spending the 1920s in Iraq (Mesopotamia) with DH.9A day bombers and helping develop – and implement – the RAF's Air Control Policy tactics. By the outbreak of war, it was at Ismailia with Blenheim Is, and from June it was based at Fuka and was heavily engaged in operations, although not suffering its first loss until the loss of L8397 on 31 August, the crew being killed when the Blenheim crashed near Mersa Matruh after an engine problem.

Another award to 55 Squadron was announced in the same bulletin; Flying Officer Grenville Green's citation read: 'In October, 1940, Flying Officer Green, although wounded and with the hydraulic gun control and instrument board out of action, successfully bombed the enemy concentration of aircraft at El Adem and, regardless of prolonged attacks by enemy fighters, brought his aircraft and crew safely home.'

And for 113 Squadron, a DFC to Squadron Leader Robert Baterson: 'Squadron Leader Bateson has displayed great devotion to duty when leading his squadron during extensive operations during September and October, 1940. His leadership has in fact played a considerable part in forcing the enemy to abandon several of his military base ports. He has led operational formations on thirty-six occasions and often, after objectives have been attacked, he has had to force his way through superior numbers of enemy fighters. Squadron Leader Bateson has also carried out a long series of hazardous reconnaissances and has obtained vital information. Throughout the period of active operations he has displayed rare courage and devotion to duty.'

The Australians of 3 Squadron RAAF moved an operational detachment of Gladiators and Gauntlets to Gerawala in early November, with the Lysander flight remaining back at Helwan. 'Tactical reconnaissances of enemy positions between Sofafi and Nibeiwa began on 13th November, and during the fourth of these on the 19th, No.3 recorded its first combat. Flight Lieutenant Pelly, escorted by Squadron Leader Heath, Flying Officers Rawlinson and Boyd, was reconnoitring seven miles east of Rabia when, about 2 p.m., eighteen CR-42 aircraft appeared. The enemy fighters broke formation, nine attacking Pelly and the others his escort, their primary object seeming to be to isolate each aircraft in turn and destroy it by sheer weight of numbers. This they almost succeeded in doing to Pelly, who had to withstand nine distinct attacks, but, although the engagement lasted twenty-five minutes, and Heath was shot down and killed, the Gladiators had much the better of the fight. Pelly reported one enemy aircraft destroyed and another damaged; Boyd claimed to have seen four of the attackers spin out of control; and Rawlinson also shot down one. Army units found three crashed enemy aircraft and as the battle began beyond the enemy lines it is possible that all six were actually destroyed. The rest of the month passed quietly, the main activity being an exercise with Western Desert Force in which mock dive-bombing attacks were made. From 28 November one Gladiator was maintained daily at standby notice and two at five-minute readiness to act as a fighter patrol when required, but they were never ordered into the air. Only one other operation came before the opening of the British offensive, when two Gladiators formed part of the escort for an aircraft from No.208 Squadron RAF which photographed Italian positions.' (RAAF history)

Meanwhile, 112 Squadron was finding November a little quiet. There were patrols over the Mersa area and some escorts for Lysanders, but other than light and inaccurate AA fire, there was usually nothing to report. On the 18th Flight Lieutenant Schwab intercepted a lone SM.79 and shot it down, but the only significant action for the month was on the 20th when six aircraft intercepted a formation of eighteen CR.42s. They claimed eight for no loss, scores going to Pilot Officer Bartley (2), Flight Lieutenant Abrahams (1.5), Pilot Officer Ackworth (1.5), Flying Officer Bennett (1), Pilot Officer Costello (1), Sergeant Donaldson (1).

One reason for the lack of action in November was the switch of attention to Greece. The Italians launched their attack on 28 October from Albania. The Greeks called on Britain to honour the guarantees made by Chamberlain in April 1939 and Churchill communicated to General Metaxas, the Premier of Greece, 'We will give you all the help in our power. We will fight a common foe and we will share a united victory.' Good Churchillian rhetoric but there was little the British could do, and even that little had to come from the stretched resources in the Middle East. Of immediate strategic concern to the British was to secure Crete from Axis occupation, as its airfields and ports, especially Suda Bay, could significantly influence the Eastern Mediterranean theatre, with implications for Malta and for the Desert War. The immediate assistance requested was for air power, and by the end of November the RAF had 'contributed' three Blenheim squadrons (30, 84, 211) and one Gladiator squadron (80) – and more were to follow.

Churchill had been unimpressed with what he thought was Middle East Command's less than enthusiastic move to secure Crete, and especially Suda Bay … 'how far short was the action taken by the Middle East Command of what was ordered and what we all desired. It remains astonishing to

Lysander and
Blenheims at Mariut
(Maryut) 1940.

me that we should have failed to make Suda Bay the amphibious citadel of which all Crete was the fortress.' (*The Second World War*, W.S. Churchill). He was far happier with the news of the offensive plan from General Wavell and General Wilson.

On the nights of 7 and 8 December, the Western Desert Force under Major General Richard O'Connor, and comprising primarily the 7th Armoured Division, 4th Indian Infantry Division, and the 16th Infantry Brigade, moved up to their start points for Operation Compass, while the RAF flew reconnaissance sorties and bombing missions against Italian airfields. The assault started on the 9th on what became known as the Battle of the Camps, or to some, the Battle of Sidi Barrani. The Italians were aware of the moves and on 9 December a formation of SM.79s was tasked to attack British troops in the Sidi Barrani-Bir Enba area, the formation being escorted by 19 CR.42s of 9 Gruppo, led by Maggiore Ernesto Botto from El Adem. The mission did not go according to plan and most of the Italian fighters ended up on a free sweep looking for enemy aircraft; one formation spotted Gladiators at low level and swooped to attack, only to be bounced by Hurricanes and a major dogfight developed, with both sides making claims.

Sergeant-Maggiore Biffani claimed a Hurricane but was himself shot down and taken prisoner: 'In the afternoon of 9 December we were flying between Mersa Matruh and Buq-Buq, when my wingman, Sottotenente Alvaro Querci, warned me that we had enemies behind us. I alerted Botto by shooting a burst [Note that the CR.42 had no radio during this period], then I realized they were near my tail, so I made a 180-degree turn and I saw them pass: they were three Hurricanes. I climbed almost vertically and saw the 73a Squadriglia in front, the three Hurricanes behind it and 96a and 97a Squadriglia behind them, all in a vertical line that went down to the ground. Then I discovered a Hurricane that was breaking off from the combat, clearly he had seen the other Italian fighters on its tail. I continued to climb, now I was the highest fighter of them all, then I dived down at full throttle [towards the escaping Hurricane]. I arrived near it and then I reduced speed and put the revolutions between 1850 and 2250 because otherwise I would have cut my propeller as happened to Gon and others, because the airscrew went out of gear and the round was fired when it passed in front of the gun … . When I closed to it, I opened fire. I aimed and saw the explosive bullets that exploded on the wing. Why didn't anything happen? Was there no fuel at all? I fired at the other wing but it was the same, the bullets exploded but nothing happened. I fired into the engine, nothing happened. I saw the tracers very well, and after all, it wasn't the first time I was shooting. At Gorizia I used to hit the target balloon with ten rounds only. In the meantime, I was losing speed and falling behind, O.K. Goodbye! It passed and turned towards me again – so I hadn't caused any damage to it, and I did the same. We found ourselves face to face at a distance of around 500–600 metres. I started firing and saw my tracers hitting it, then its wings lit up and in the same moment my plane caught fire, it was just an instant. My plane was severely damaged and while I was trying to land, I saw the Hurricane that dived into the ground and exploded. I saw no parachute. I force-landed among British MTs and was immediately taken prisoner. I went back home after 63 months of POW!'

The Italians claimed seven shot down and three probable (later reduced to four and three) for the loss of one CR.42, and a further three damaged that had to force-land. The Hurricanes were from 33 Squadron and 274 Squadron; the ORB of 33 Squadron noted for the 9th: 'The Squadron's role is to ground strafe the enemy's rear areas, concentrating on troops and MT. 12 a/c, leaving at 10 minute intervals successfully machine-gunned troops and MT causing heavy damage. 3 formations of EA were intercepted and 3 CR42s were shot down confirmed. 1 CR42 seen to go down out of control. 1 Hurricane force landed but pilot safe.'

The same day was also the first combat outing for 39 Squadron's Blenheims in the Western Desert. The Squadron had moved from Aden in early December and while re-equipping at Helwan, sent a detachment to operate with 45 Squadron. The first mission included two aircraft of 39 Squadron on a high-level raid on the airfield at Sollum. On 12 December a lone Blenheim on a decoy raid at El Gubbi was intercepted by twelve CR.42 fighters. The pilot adopted the standard evasion technique by putting the nose of the aircraft down into a steep dive and going flat out for low level. The guns on the Blenheim jammed soon after the encounter began but nevertheless the aircraft reached low level and sped off across the desert, jinking violently. The fighters soon gave up the chase, having caused no damage whatever to the Blenheim in spite of the odds.

The squadron's introduction to the desert also included the problems of airfields when one day in December a Blenheim was sent to the landing ground at Mersa Matruh in Egypt to investigate the feasibility of establishing a forward base there. The crew were a little suspicious when they arrived as the field was deserted; the many bomb craters along the runway made landing difficult and the pilot had to keep swerving the aircraft to avoid these obstacles. Unfortunately, at the end of the landing run the port wheel slid into a crater and it took thirty minutes of heaving and shoving to get it out again. Having formed an adverse opinion of the place, the crew wasted no time in getting airborne again – although finding a clear path through the craters did prove difficult. Their report on their experience caused great consternation at Headquarters, as officially, Mersa Matruh had been abandoned and mined!

73 Squadron, December 1940, ORB, Heliopolis: 'The whole of the Squadron, with the exception of the pilots, at Heliopolis where they proceeded to take over the HQ allotted and to unpack stores and equipment. The pilots were on their way to Heliopolis via Desert route from Takoradi: Squadron Leader Murray, Pilot Officer Humphries, Pilot Officer Legge, Sergeants Laing, Stenhouse and Brimble were being escorted across the desert by a Blenheim which lost its bearings due to W/T failure and all seven aircraft force landed in the desert as darkness was falling. Sergeant Brimble was killed, another Hurricane was written off, and the remaining four aircraft were damaged.

By the 9th the ORB recorded that all pilots had arrived save for four who were waiting the damaged four Hurricanes to be made fit to fly, and, 'rumours of a pending move are rife and it is understood that the Squadron will shortly be called upon to detach certain pilots in operational units in Egypt, pending the sorting out of the Squadron stores and equipment.' The latter comment related to the mix up of equipment with the crates for a number of squadrons being marked the same, which caused confusion and wasted time. Eight pilots went to the Fleet Air Arm at Dekheilia and four to Sidi Haneish attached to 274 Squadron. These latter opened the 73 Squadron score, when on the 16th, during a patrol near Bardia, Sergeant Marshall claimed two SM.79s destroyed and Flight Lieutenant Smith claimed one, as well as a probable on a CR.42.

'Three times on 11 and 12 December the Gauntlets [of 3 Squadron RAAF] bombed the Sofafi force which had been sealed off from the battle by the thrust of the 7th Armoured Division. The Gauntlets were then withdrawn as the efforts needed to service these obsolete aircraft were not justified by the results they achieved. The Gladiators on the other hand continued to operate regularly over the forward army units as they approached the frontier. Most patrols were uneventful but shortly after noon on the 12th, five Gladiators intercepted a formation of seventeen CR42s about six miles north-west of Sofafi. Six or seven of the enemy remained to fight while the others climbed, circled once and flew away. After a short engagement the Australians again had a bloodless victory, three CR42s being destroyed.' (RAAF history).

Even at the end of 1940 it was still frequently a biplane fighter battle (CR.42 vs. Gladiator!). The reference to Gauntlets is interesting, as this type had very much vanished from the RAF operational inventory by this time! 'The Gladiators, though invariably outnumbered, had performed with considerable success since the opening of the battle, but the next day was one of disaster.

Six Gladiators on an early-morning patrol discovered five SM-79 bombers attacking our troops near Salum. One Savoia was shot down, a second probably destroyed and the rest dispersed, but before the Gladiators could re-form, the enemy fighter escort of eight CR42s were upon them. A confused fight followed in which two Italians were shot down, but the Australians suffered heavy losses. Gaden crashed and was killed; Flying Officers Arthur and Wintens were obliged to bale out; Boyd and Gatward were forced down although the damage to Boyd's aircraft was quickly repaired and he returned to base with Gatward as passenger. This engagement thus cost the squadron one pilot, four aircraft destroyed and two damaged, and as one of the Gladiators transferring from Gerawla that day also crashed on landing, the position became critical. On the following day a single Australian Gladiator flew two sorties; the squadron temporarily ceased operations on 15th December.' (RAAF history)

'Its (3 Squadron RAAF) Gladiator aircraft, though old and lacking the speed and climbing ability of its normal opponent, the Italian CR42, were manoeuvrable, and in the hands of determined pilots were able to engage on approximately equal terms. During the five conclusive engagements it fought during the campaign in Cyrenaica, No.3 claimed the destruction of twelve enemy aircraft for the loss of five Gladiators and two pilots killed. Such results, valuable in themselves, exemplified how the constant offensive pressure exerted by the RAF, drove the Italians to adopt purely defensive patrols, wasted away their striking power, and finally prevented them from putting their aircraft into the air at all.' (RAAF history).

One challenge for the Italian pilots was that these fighters had no radios, and so co-ordinating with other members of the formation – for warnings or co-ordinated attacks – was difficult, to say the least.

Sidi Barrani was captured on the 10th, and by 15 December Sollum and Halfaya had been captured, along with large numbers of Italian prisoners – indeed far more than expected (around 38,000), which caused problems in how to handle them. The ground forces had also advanced so quickly that they were soon raising an issue that was to plague both sides in the desert campaign, lack of supplies. Egypt was now clear of Italians, and the British were reorganizing for the next advance against Bardia.

The 33 Squadron ORB account for the period from the 9th (covered above) to the 15th indicates typical missions, successes and losses:

10th: Further heavy damage caused in ground strafe attacks. CR42s again intercepted, two of which were shot down confirmed and one probable claimed. During an evening recco of the road west of S. Barrani, Lt Fiscles, SAAF, failed to return and during the day one a/c force landed but pilot unhurt. Ground strafing are now Buq-Buq – Bardia and westwards.

11th: Harassing the enemy's retreat continued in Sollum area and westwards. Formations of Breda 65, CR42 and S79s intercepted of which 1 S79, 2 CR42 and 1 B65 were shot down confirmed, and 1 B65 and 1 CR42 were claimed as probable. Two of out a/c were damaged and 1 failed to return (Flg F/O C Dyson DFC). Pilots scoring victories included F/Lt J M Littler and Flight Sergeant Goodchild.

12th: Ground strafing continued in Bardia area. 1 B65 and 2 CR42 seen on new LG near Sollum.

13th: Ground strafing area now Bardia – Tobruk road. During day, Squadron shot down 2 S79s, 3 CR42s confirmed and 1 S79 and 1 CR42 probably destroyed.

14th: With 274 and 112 squadrons carried out patrols over forward area. During afternoon 2 S79s intercepted over Sollum. One last seen with port engine smoking, 2nd believed damaged.

15th: Patrols of Tobruk – Bardia road. Two formations of S79s met and forced to jettison their bombs. 1 Hurricane missing.

While there were no ops on the 16th, the next day brought more strafing and another claim for a CR.42, but of more import was: 'About this time F/O Dyson returned, having been missing since 11/12. During his patrol he shot down 6 CR42s and probably destroyed one, before finally forced down near Sollum. He was picked up by our forward troops and subsequently led back a column of 800 Italian prisoners to Matruh. For this effort he receives a Bar to his DFC.'

The award of his bar to DFC was one of many instances where no specific citation was included other than the comment in AMB 3405 in March 1941 that: 'One officer destroyed five enemy aircraft on one day. Later when the enemy was employing large masses of aircraft he encountered six fighters and shot them all down.' No.33 Squadron recorded for December: thirty-six destroyed, ten probably destroyed and eleven damaged.

Among the gallantry awards for this general period: A DFC was awarded to Squadron Leader James Gordon-Finlayson of 211 Squadron in December, the citation reading: 'This officer has completed more than 40 day and night raids and reconnaissances over enemy territory in Greece and the Western Desert. Undaunted by continual severe anti-aircraft fire and attacks by fighters he has shown superb courage, determination and devotion to duty. The accuracy of his bombing has resulted in great damage to enemy positions and transport concentration, and his determined leadership of his squadron has enabled most effective results to be secured.' Another of the Blenheim day bomber units, 211 Squadron had been in Egypt since 1938.

On the 30th the main party of 73 Squadron moved to Sidi Haneish – with mixed feelings and impressions: 'Rations were taken but it was almost impossible to consume them on the road owing to a severe sandstorm. The men and officers slept the night in crowded tents because the Advance Party had not had the opportunity of erecting all the required tents. The Squadron was received by 112 Squadron which was due to leave for Amriya the following morning. The impression was gained – perhaps unjustifiably, that the officers of 112 Squadron were too anxious to see to their own move to bother much with the comfort and arrangements of this Squadron. The Adjutant of 112 expected Fg Off Hoole, officer in charge of the Squadron canteen, to take over the contents of their canteen at 1930 hours when it was dark and seemed slightly annoyed at his refusal to sign for various articles until he had assured himself that the articles were in fact in the canteen.'

It is interesting that 'minor' admin issues took up more space in the ORB than the operational success of the pilots detached to 274 Squadron! And the ORB writer was not done yet: 'Heard crackling sounds outside their tent and saw the reflection of flames. It was the Officers Mess on fire. Within half an hour it was completely burnt out, but most of the contents were saved. The cause of the fire is unknown and it is perhaps a little unfair to blame the officers of 112 Squadron. The fire started in the kitchen and presumably by accident.'

The 112 Squadron record is a 'little different': 'On 31st there was another party, a farewell one, to mark the end of the squadron's stay in the Western Desert, being relieved by 73 Squadron. That night fire razed the Officers' Mess in the small hours and the squadron left 73 with nothing but a marquee, sandstorms and cold. The Squadron was not sorry to go and was thankful to see the end of 'gruelling patrols … work was carried on under impossible conditions, machines on several occasions being brought home when visibility due to dust was practically nil.'

Blenheim L6663 with Flying Officer Cubby Thomas, December 1940. (*45 Squadron*)

SAAF armourers work on a 1 Squadron Hurricane. (*Hannes Faure SAAF*)

Sand … as referenced above … and more sand. The abiding memory of all those who served in the desert was 'sand with everything'. Getting used to the reality that any and all food included sand – all that varied was the quantity and the grittiness.

The Luftwaffe Arrives

On 19 December the Italians formally requested German military assistance for their campaigns in North Africa and Greece. The Germans had actually ordered 'Special Operation Mediterranean' on 10 December, designating one German fighter wing to be 'committed from southern Italian bases for a limited time.' According to Directive 22 for Sonnenblume (Sunflower), the initial mission for Xth Air Corps, which transferred to southern Italy, was to combat the British naval forces and to interdict British waterways between the western and eastern Mediterranean. This involved using its main bases in Sicily but also bases in Tripolitania, from which it could also give direct support to Army Group Graziani. The Germans also committed a 'blocking force' – the 5th Light Division. The transfer of Xth Air Corps, under Lieutenant General Geisler, from Norway to the Mediterranean began in mid-December and the airfields of southern Italy gradually became home to:

- Bombers: Ju.88 of 3rd Group of 30th Bomber Wing
- Dive-bombers: Ju.87 of 2nd and 3rd Groups of 1st Dive-Bomber Wing
- Fighters: Bf.109s of 1st Group of Fighter Wing 27.

The Luftwaffe operational strength by mid-January 1941 was some 240 aircraft. They scored their first success on 10 January with attacks on a Malta-bound convoy from Gibraltar. To support the key mission aim of destroying British naval power, Malta was a key target for the new formation, as it was a major naval base and strategically placed between Gibraltar and Alexandria. The success of air operations from Sicily also had a direct effect on both the Greece and Western Desert campaigns, in that the British had to re-route supply convoys, including aircraft supplies – the latter now going by sea to Takoradi where aircraft were assembled and flown on the 'Takoradi route' to Egypt. But for now, the Luftwaffe was not operational in the desert theatre.

O'Connor resumed his offensive on 3 January with his now reorganized and renamed XIII Corps. In a series of classic manoeuvre encounters, the Allies quickly cut off Italian forces, taking Bardia on the 5th – along with 45,000 prisoners and a large amount of equipment. The Allies rolled on to their next target, Tobruk, the Italians being harassed from the air and from naval bombardment and being unable to form a new defensive line. During this offensive the squadrons of 202 Group provided essential air support.

The Wellingtons of 257 Wing were based in the Canal Zone and were tasked to support ops in the Mediterranean and Western Desert. No.37 Squadron had been based in the Canal Zone (Fayid) since 1 December and in January 1941 flew fifteen night sorties, all but two of which were against airfield and port targets.

Date	Target	Aircraft
Jan 2–3	Bardia	4
3–4	Tobruk	2
4–5	Tobruk	2
5–6	Tobruk	7
7–8	Benghazi	8
8–9	Benghazi	8

Date	Target	Aircraft
10–11	Benina airfield	3
10–11	Berca airfield	4
13–14	Benghazi	7
14–15	Benghazi	1
15–16	Maritza airfield	4
17–18	Tobruk	8
20–21	Tobruk	5
21–22	Derna	3
22–23	Maritza airfield	2

The Wellingtons of 37 and 70 Squadrons were kept busy on these types of target, as well as sending a detachment to Greece and, later, Crete. The 70 Squadron diarist recorded the rationale behind the run of attacks on airfields, for all the Wellington units were attacking such targets 'for the purpose of rendering enemy aerodromes unserviceable. Delayed action bombing was used as it was believed that the enemy do not use their aerodromes for seventy-two hours after being bombed by DA bombs.'

No.70 Squadron was another Middle East veteran, having spent the 1920s and 1930s in and around Iraq, primarily in the transport role. It had arrived in Egypt in August 1939 with its Valentias; it re-equipped with Wellington Is in September 1940. Crews had returned to the UK to collect aircraft and one of these was destroyed at Malta on the outbound flight; T2830 was strafed by Italian fighters and destroyed, but two airmen – Cpl Joseph Davis and AC1 Thomas McCann – risked their lives by rescuing machine guns and ammunition from the flaming aircraft, which earned each of them a BEM.

The citation read: 'During September 1940, these airmen approached a burning aircraft and succeeded in detaching Vickers guns and magazines of ammunition and removing them to a place of safety. Both displayed conspicuous gallantry in disregarding imminent personal danger from exploding ammunition and the likelihood that the petrol tanks might explode.' (AMB 2792)

January had been a busy month for 38 Squadron, its operational summary for the month showing:

Sorties: 46 with 441.10 operational hours
Bombs dropped: 455 × 250lb GP, total 113,750lb
Incendiaries: 3,259 × 4lb, total 13,036lb
Incendiaries: 204 × 25lb, total 5,100lb
Fragmentation: 252 × 20lb, total 5,040lb
Total: 135,926lb

The assault on the Tobruk garrison was launched on the morning of the 21st and the following day the garrison surrendered, and another 20,000 PoWs needed to be processed. The advance continued and on the 26th Derna was captured. Once again the ground offensive was outrunning supplies, and vehicles were suffering from lack of maintenance. To maintain pressure on the Italians to ensure they evacuate Cyrenaica, which they had in fact already decided to do, the RAF flew harassing raids

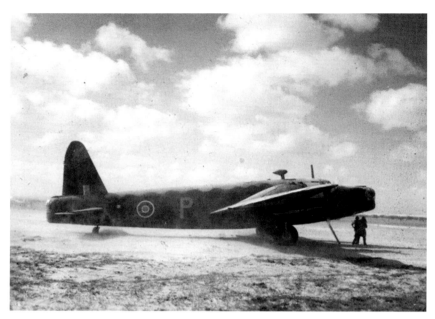

The Wellington was the only strategic bomber in theatre and the limited number of squadrons were kept busy attacking ports outside the range of types such as the Blenheim. (*George Muir SAAF*)

and the land forces made an armoured thrust in one direction and an infantry thrust, by 'Combe Force', in another direction.

The Battle of Beda Fomm ended on 7 February and when the British forces reached El Agheila on the 9th they were ordered to halt. The major reason for the termination of the offensive was a decision by Churchill to send land forces to Greece, and the forces available were those busily driving back the Italians. This has remained one of the great debatable points of the Second World War. While the British reinforcements did little to affect the military outcome of the conflict in Greece, the weakening of the forces the Western Desert certainly had an impact.

The campaign had been a massive success and netted more than 130,000 prisoners (twenty-two generals among them) and large amounts of material, including more than 400 tanks. Churchill wrote: 'The Desert Army had in six weeks advanced over 200 miles of waterless and foodless space, had taken by assault two strongly defended fortified seaports with permanent air and marine defences, and captured 113,000 prisoners and over 700 guns.'

Egypt and Cyrenaica had been cleared and the Italians were now digging in on the frontiers of Tripolitania, and receiving significant reinforcements that made up their losses. However, they had suffered a major defeat and the British forces, air and ground, had gained both a physical and psychological ascendency. Indeed, this latter may be said to have verged on over-confidence – and a severe shock was soon to come.

Nevertheless, it looked like the signs for 1941 were good; the Italians had been well and truly beaten, the RAF was ascendant and, despite still being outnumbered, dominated the skies, and land force morale was good after the recent successful advance. However, it was all about to change … not helped by the diversion (and losses) with the Greek campaign. There is not space in this book to cover the Greece and Crete campaign in detail but before moving on the developments of 1941 in the Western Desert, we will take a quick overview of the campaign.

Greece and Crete

On 28 October 1940 Italian forces invaded Greece from Albania. In response to Greek requests, British air forces moved there from Egypt, followed some time later by ground troops. The initial RAF effort comprised three squadrons of Blenheims (30, 84 and 211) plus the Gladiators of 80 Squadron, and all were soon engaged on successful operations against the Italians as the latter found their 'simple' conquest turning into defeat. Air Vice-Marshal Sir John D'Albiac was given additional squadrons, in part to make up for a reduction in the combat strength of the Hellenic Air Force. The heavy bombers were also engaged in the Greek operation, Wellington detachments moving from Egypt to Greece; the first detachment was by 70 Squadron to Eleusis, but targets such as Valona continued to take its toll of bombers that 'visited' in daylight.

The second half of December was busier from an operational point of view for 80 Squadron:

19 December: Offensive patrol Tepeleni area. Five S79s engaged and one claimed as destroyed. Plt Off Cooper shot down and baled out. Sgt Hewett was hit by AA and landed 20 miles North of Yannina, his aircraft was badly damaged. Later heard that Cooper had died of his wounds.

20 December: Offensive patrol Tepeleni-Kelcyre area. A formation of 9 S79s were engaged and one was destroyed. Later 6 S81s were sighted and of these, P/O Vales and F/Lt Pattle each brought one down. A large formation of enemy fighters patrolled overhead throughout the engagement without attacking the Gladiators.

21 December: Larissa was bombed in the morning and one fell less than 50 yards from the Officers Mess, breaking many windows of the house. An offensive patrol Argyrokastron area carried out by 10 Gladiators led by the CO engaged with 6 bombers, result indecisive, as escort of 54 CR42s engaged our aircraft. In the following dog-fight 8 CR42s were definitely destroyed and three were unconfirmed, P/O Vale accounting for three. The CO and F/O Ripley did not return from this sortie.'

Additional squadrons arrived in January and the situation appeared quite promising. One of those units was 112 Squadron; on the 9th a detachment moved to Yannina to join 80 Squadron in operations over the front line. That same day, Pilot Officer Vale of 80 Squadron was involved in a combat that again seemed to confirm the Italian reluctance to engage: 'At 1040 hours, 14 Gladiators took off on an offensive patrol over Klissoura area, led by S/Ldr Jones. Just after reaching the patrol area "tally ho" was given on sighting three enemy bombers, which turned back before an interception could be made. Two Gladiators had to leave the formation with engine trouble. The patrol was carried on until about 1155 hours "tally ho" was given for a formation of five CR42s, which apparently did not observe our formation until very late and then three broke away and went down to the North. I was slightly behind the main formation and headed the two CR42s off until they both broke away downwards, followed by two Gladiators.

'I then observed about six more formations of 5 CR42s above us and so I gave "tally ho" and I immediately climbed. A dogfight started and from my position the policy of the EA seemed to be diving attacks and gaining height straight away. One CR42 dived on me from above but I managed to evade his fire by pulling round and up towards him. I fired a short burst which seemed to scare him away. I then saw a CR42 diving down on to a Gladiator and so carried out a diving quarter attack and he pulled away which left me in an astern position close in. I carried on firing until the EA turned over on its back and the pilot left the machine. I saw his parachute open and so gained height and fired a long burst at a CR42 which dived down on me from above. I then broke away from the combat and owing to shortage of ammunition and fuel returned to base with Fg Off Cullen who came up and formated with me.'

The Hurricanes of 33 Squadron arrived in Greece in late February, the first op, an escort to Blenheims, taking place on the 25th. The target for 11 and 211 Squadron was Buzat. The first success came on the 28th when the squadron contributed four Hurricanes in a fighter force that also included six Hurricanes and seven Gladiators of 80 Squadron and eleven Gladiators of 112 Squadron. The formation intercepted fifty bombers and fighters in the Tepelene area and a major fight ensued.

The 112 Squadron history for 28 February states: 'This was a record day in the Squadron's history. Eleven pilots joined in a general offensive over Sarande-Argyrokraston-Valona-Tepelene with the result that five G.50s and five CR.42s were shot down and two CR.42s and one BR.20 damaged.'

By March, 33 Squadron was operating from Eleusis with a detachment at Paramythia, the latter with 112 Squadron. The ORB recorded for 4 March: 'With 4 Hurricanes of 80 Squadrons, 18 Gladiators of 112 Squadron, 6 Hurricanes of 33 Squadron, escorted 9 Blenheims of 211, 5 and 84 Squadrons to attack 6 warships bombarding Himara, 10 miles South of Valona. No direct hits were made. The fighters were engaged and W/O Goodchild shot down in flames North of Corfu. The main party meanwhile was en route to Larissa, its next home.'

No.112 Squadron continued intensive ops in early March against what the diary referred to as 'Mussolini's bedraggled Eagles'.

The Germans declared war on Greece and Yugoslavia on 5 April, and their offensive opened the following day, driving the Allies away from the Metaxa Line and into headlong retreat. An Me 110 was seen on the 10th and the pilots of 112 Squadron had no illusions that their Gladiators were no match for the Luftwaffe. The squadron diary commented: 'If any Gladiators are left their next appearance no doubt will be in the British Museum.'

The 33 Squadron ORB records: 'On April 6th Germany declared war against Greece. On April 7th, 12 Hurricanes led by S/Ldr Pattle carried out a fighter sweep over the Rupel Pass area of Bulgaria during the later afternoon. During this patrol S/Ldr Pattle surprised and shot down two ME109s confirmed, whilst F/O Wickham, further North was engaging three more ME109s and shot down one of them confirmed. F/Sgt Cottingham, still further North in the Rupel Valley, shot down one more ME109, the pilot bailing out. While the parachute was falling, another 109 circled round to give protection, and this aircraft was also shot down by F/Sgt Collingham.' This was an excellent start, but within a few days the tables would turn and the Allied aircraft would lose their air advantage.

Yannina was abandoned on the 16th, 112 Squadron heading for Agrinion. The operational wings were disbanded and control returned to HQ British Air Forces Greece, although the Allied retreat was rapid and somewhat confused, so control was something of a misnomer.

On 19 April Pat Pattle recorded his most successful single day, downing six, which took his score to between forty-five and fifty, some even suggest as high as sixty, as he was well known for being particularly reluctant to claim anything that was not definite. Sadly, he took off the following day against advice, as he appeared to have a fever, and was shot down and killed.

From the desert to the mountains; 80 Squadron on the move in Greece, October 1940.

Hurricane and pilots of 33 Squadron; one of the fighter squadrons moved to Greece. Pattle, the lead ace of the period, is sixth from the right.

Most of the Blenheims were destroyed on the ground by Luftwaffe attacks, against which the few RAF fighters could make no impact. The RAF was running out of airfields and by the 19th was confined to airfields in the Athens area – not that Air Commodore D'Albiac had many aircraft left. When the Germans attacked the Athens airfields on the 20th, the attack was opposed by fifteen Hurricanes, with five shot down and others damaged, at a cost to the Germans of maybe eight aircraft. With total air superiority, the Luftwaffe turned its attention to shipping, destroying a number of Greek ships over the next few days, while the Allied ground forces tried to move to the Isthmus of Corinth and the Greek equivalent of Dunkirk.

Crete

It was obvious that Crete would be next, as the Germans could not allow the Allies to keep possession of the island, not least because it had a number of good airfields (Maleme, Canea, Retimo, Heraklion) that could be used by bomber forces to threaten German strategic asserts. The RAF aircraft strength for the defence of Crete amounted to a small number of Hurricanes and Gladiators, a mixed bag from 33, 80 and 112 squadrons, and twenty-three Blenheims of 30 and 203 squadrons. The initial task was to provide air cover for ships arriving from Greece and those departing from Suda Bay for Egypt.

The Blenheims soon left and by mid-May the British garrison of around 28,000 troops had maybe twenty to twenty-five fighters as their air cover, and it is recorded that only 50 per cent were serviceable. Overall command rested with General Freyberg, with Group Captain Beamish as the air commander. As German air attacks intensified, the Army was not impressed with the RAF; the 112 Squadron diary recorded that its task was made no easier by the 'attitude of the army units around our aerodrome … the spiteful and ignorant criticisms which were hurled at us were most annoying … to the army an aircraft on the ground was an aircraft fit to fly.'

The German airborne assault on Maleme proved costly but successful and became a bridgehead for German reinforcements. On the evening of the 21st, the 33 Squadron ORB recorded: 'At nightfall the Squadron was nearly surrounded again, but the Maoris managed to clear the road to Canea, leaving the Squadron in a safer position.'

Meanwhile, Admiral Cunningham had deployed the Mediterranean fleet to guard the sea lanes, and a task force of battleships, cruisers, destroyers – plus the carrier HMS *Formidable*. It was a risk but one that had been taken. The air-sea battle began on the 21st when an Italian supply convoy was destroyed by the British fleet – but Richthofen's pilots joined the battle, sank the destroyer *Juno* and damaged the cruiser *Ajax*. It was an indication of what was to come the following day.

The German build-up continued and in essence the Battle of Crete was over by the 23rd, although action on land, air and sea continued for a few more weeks, the final surrender taking place on 1 June. For 33 Squadron, and others, the retreat continued on the 22nd and 23rd towards Canaea and then on to Traivoros, east of Suda, hiding from the frequent air attacks. On the 26th: 'Party left Traivoros packed very tightly in lorries, and travelling throughout the night over a 7,000ft mountain range to the South coast of Crete, they reached a sport about 5 miles East of Sparkia. All transports were then systematically wrecked.'

Note: A more extensive account of the campaign in Greece and Crete is included in *Malta Strikes Back: The Role of Malta in the Mediterranean Theatre 1940–1942*, Ken Delve, forthcoming.

Chapter 3

From Victory to Defeat and Stalemate

At the end of January 1941, all looked well in the desert theatre, and even in Greece and East Africa. The Allies had faced Italian advances in all those locations but, despite the superiority in air and ground strength of the much vaunted 'new Roman Empire', it had proved deficient in actual military capability. Mussolini had called on Hitler for help, and in the first half of 1941 the German intervention in Greece and North Africa proved decisive; for much of the year it was a tale of woe for the Allies as gains were lost and casualties were high.

The Luftwaffe's first 'outing' in the Western Desert was not connected to the ground battle but was part of the strategic campaign against shipping supply routes and was made in response to intelligence of a major convoy heading for the Suez Canal from Aden. The commander of this special force, Colonel Harlinghausen, reported that: 'On 17th January I landed with about 12–15 aircraft of the 2nd Group of Bomber Wing 30 in Benghazi. From there I sent 3 bomber aircraft on a reconnaissance flight to find the convoy. One of the planes observed the convoy approaching Suez, so that its arrival during the following night seemed probable. On landing at Benghazi, two of the returning aircraft collided, so that only 8 were available for the attack. We started at dusk, each plane with an auxiliary tank and two tons of bombs. None of the planes found the convoy; they dropped their bombs on secondary targets on port and canal installations. I saw a few ships in the roads of Suez, but their number did not in any way correspond to the convoy that had been reported. The attack was therefore unsuccessful. Only one of the 8 planes returned undamaged to Benghazi; three crews had to make emergency landings behind British lines because of the headwind they suddenly encountered. They were taken prisoner. I had to make a forced landing in the desert some 150 miles SE of Benghazi, where I was found three days later.' (Major General Harlinghausen, letter July 1954).

The mission was not in any way a success – but the presence of German aircraft must have come as a surprise to the Allies … and it was about to get much worse.

One of the keys to the Luftwaffe's achieving a degree of air superiority was the presence of the Bf 109E and 109F variants – flown by experienced combat pilots. Although both still suffered from short range through limited fuel capacity, they remained faster than their opponents and more manoeuvrable than the fighter types in service with the RAF in the Western Desert. By late February, RAF recce aircraft had picked up clear evidence of large-scale German reinforcement; the opportunity to clear Cyrenaica had been lost. Although Hurricanes featured in our account of the 1940 air battles, much of that account was also the RAF biplane (Gladiator) against the Italian biplane (CR.42). Both sides fielded what were, in theory, modern bombers, a situation that was a hangover from the 1930s strategic bomber theory that saw more investment in bomber types than fighters. The new year of 1941 was when that all changed.

Air Brigade Africa was initially designated to support the new German land force in Africa, with the 15th Panzer Division (initially forty-five light and ninety medium tanks plus a self-propelled anti-tank battalion) joining the 5th Light Division to form the German Africa Corps, with General Rommel arriving in Tripoli on 13 February, while at around the same time the Italian Supreme Command in theatre had also changed, with General Gariboldi replacing the discredited Graziani.

The main German enemy – Ju 87 Stuka escorted by Bf 109. The Stukas had established a psychological supremacy over ground forces and it was essential for the Allies to counter this … as they soon did with a number of 'Stuka Parties'.

Bf 109E of JG 27, the main fighter unit – and one with which a number of aces built up high scores.

A number of Stukas ended up in Allied hands and were put into flying condition, sometimes for 'fun' and sometimes for other uses – 39 Squadron flew its for Royal Navy gun-laying exercises over Alexandria harbour … bold, considering the naval predilection to shoot at anything and ask questions later!

Gariboldi was ordered to 'hold Tripolitania by mobile defence in the Syrte desert' and Rommel was given command of all mobile German and Italian units. The Germans had little confidence in the equipment or capabilities of the Italians, and some of their own units were not due to arrive until May. They also projected that the British had superior equipment, numbers (divisions) and morale and so an early offensive was expected. Rommel immediately demonstrated his aggressive style of command, sending elements of 5th Division to bolster Italian units, gauge their capability, and improve morale. Part of this involved pushing patrols forward to probe the Allied positions, something the Allies had not seen with the Italians. This, combined with local air reconnaissance by Henschel Hs 126s and long-range recce from bases in Sicily, quickly revealed weaknesses and a lack of defensive preparedness in Allied positions, a direct consequence of the removal of land and air units for the Greek campaign.

Elements of Xth Air Corps arrived at Bir Dufan (100 miles south of Tripoli) and Castel Benito in mid-February, with 1st Squadron of 1st DB Group, 2nd Squadron of 2nd DB Group, and 1st Squadron of the 27th Fighter Group. The first dive-bombing attack was made on 14 February, the targets being in the El Agheila area. Major General Froehlich was appointed Air Brigade Commander Africa on 20 February, his mission being: 'The Air Brigade Commander Africa will direct and commit the elements of the GAF employed in the African theatre of war, such as flying and anti-aircraft units, in a manner that will guarantee maximum support of the Army units employed in the area.'

Additional units were scheduled to arrive in May, but in the meantime the air brigade had a major task in creating a support structure and in positioning units, with squadrons moving to Timit and El Machina, both near Syrte, in mid-March.

The German records also express surprise at the lack of British air reconnaissance and intervention in the German military movements into the ports and forward positions. In fact, British reconnaissance and intelligence had picked up the presence of German units in the front lines, but commanders in Cairo were of the opinion that it did not involve major units and posed no immediate threat. General Wavell reported that he did not expect a major German offensive before the end of the summer because of the long distance from Tripoli to Benghazi, the scarcity of Axis shipping capacity and the approaching hot season. All good conventional military wisdom – but Rommel was not conventional and he now had enough intelligence on Allied weaknesses to plan his assault.

Enemy air attacks were soon extended to Tobruk and to British troops forward in the Agedabia area, and by 17 February 3 Squadron RAAF was being called on for some assistance. 'During the following three days, 26 sorties were flown in six patrols over the forward area and on two occasions enemy aircraft were encountered. The first engagement was on 18th February when three Hurricanes attacked a force of approximately twelve Junkers Ju 87s near Marsa Brega. The Stukas' dived quickly from 1,000 feet to fifty feet and scattered, but not before one had been shot down and eight damaged. The following morning three Hurricanes found nine Ju 87s, again bombing British troops and in an immediate attack Flight Lieutenant Perrin shot one down. Perrin and Gatward were then attacked by several Messerschmitt 110s which appeared without warning, Gatward being shot down and killed. At this point Perrin, finding himself alone, attacked and set on fire the nearest enemy machine, but while attacking a second Messerschmitt, his own aircraft was hit in the petrol tank. He continued attacking until his ammunition was expended, and then, too low to bale out, he crash-landed in flames. As he ran from the aircraft one of the enemy continued to fire at him but, escaping serious wounds, he was later picked up by a British patrol. The third pilot had lost contact after the original attack on the Stukas. Unable to find his comrades, he had landed at Agedabia.' (RAAF history)

Flight Lieutenant John Perrin's DFC citation reads: 'In February, 1941, while leading a formation of three Hurricanes on patrol, this officer observed nine Junkers 87s dive bombing and machine gunning near Mersa El Berga. He immediately called his flight by radio telephone but, failing to make himself understood, dived to the attack accompanied by only one of his section. They were immediately attacked by 15 Messerschmitt 110s and, in the ensuing combat, Flight Lieutenant Perrin shot down a Junkers and a Messerschmitt before a cannon shell burst in his petrol tank, covering him with petrol, setting his aircraft on fire, and slightly wounding his right eye. Despite this, he continued to attack another Messerschmitt at a low level until his ammunition was expended. He then crash-landed his aircraft. Throughout the engagement this officer displayed outstanding leadership and courage in the face of greatly superior numbers of enemy forces.'

Having crash-landed, Perrin quickly jumped out of the aircraft, as it was being strafed, and ran for the shelter of a tree! 'It was the fastest 100 yards I have ever run, and when I barged into that tree in my haste, I saw a thousand stars,' he recalled. He was picked up and taken to Benina for a short spell in hospital, and then back to the squadron.

No.450 Squadron had been formed at Williamtown, New South Wales, on 16 February 1941 for service in the Middle East; the ORB starts in February 1941: 'This and 451 Squadron are to be infiltration squadrons, i.e. a nucleus of RAF experienced officers and other ranks will be posted to the Unit on arrival in the Middle East. When the squadron becomes sufficiently experienced, the RAF personnel will be replaced by RAAF personnel and it will consist completely of Australians.'

This was, in part, a political move and the reality was to be that most squadrons in the Desert Air Force remained somewhat mixed, although 'dominated' in terms of numbers by their home nationality. The other major contributors to the war in this theatre were the South Africans both in terms of squadrons but also personnel, especially pilots operating with RAF squadrons and, from 1942 onwards, the Canadians.

February also saw the award of the DFC to Wing Commander Ian McLachlan, CO of 3 Squadron, RAAF, the citation stating: 'This officer has displayed fine qualities as a fighter pilot. Under his determined leadership many fine military feats have been accomplished, often against overwhelming numbers of enemy aircraft.' McLachlan had been CO since the squadron arrived in the Middle East in July 1940 and it was largely through his efforts that the squadron overcame numerous challenges, not least around equipment, training and organization that led to it becoming one of the most efficient and effective fighter squadrons in the DAF.

Nightly attacks on Axis ports and airfields, as well as advanced bases, had both a material and morale effect. No.148 Squadron had been operating from Malta, primarily attacking targets in Italy, which, along with targets in Albania, Rhodes and other Axis locations were also on the night-time sorties of the Middle East Wellington squadrons. The squadron was probably happy to leave the very dangerous Malta base; it had lost seven aircraft in an air raid on 25 February and Luqa was rapidly becoming untenable for the number of aircraft that were there.

On 22 March all RAF squadrons were warned to be ready to move at short notice and to prepare demolition plans. They would be required to operate throughout a withdrawal under the following general plan (Operational Instruction No.4 issued by AOC Cyrenaica):

- Army co-operation squadron (6 Sqn) to maintain tactical reconnaissance.
- Bomber squadron (55 Sqn) to maintain strategical reconnaissance and carry out bombing attacks in direct and close support of the army.
- Fighter squadrons (73 Sqn and 3 Sqn RAAF) to protect Tobruk port and the forward troops, especially armoured unit.

With an impressive variety of clothing, pilots of 73 Squadron pose with a Hurricane. Having gained its reputation as a fighter unit in France, the squadron moved to the Middle East at the end of 1940.

Stewart 'Bomb' Finney of 1 Squadron SAAF taxies his Hurricane across the desert. Finney served with 1 Squadron (Nov 1941–Dec 1942 and Sep 1943–Mar 1944) and a spell at 73 OTU (Mar–Sep 1943), and later with 2 Squadron (1944). (*'Bomb' Finney SAAF*)

Moving between desert strips was a frequent occurrence – and was fraught with dangers. (*Tom Meek SAAF*)

RAF strength had continued to increase, albeit slowly as resources were limited and the Middle East was still not the highest priority, and the campaign in Greece was still absorbing resources. However, significantly, the bomber strength of 257 Wing was increased to four Wellington squadrons with the arrival of 148 Squadron at Kabrit in March. This was important as it showed the increased value placed on strategic night bombing.

Rommel Attacks

On 31 March 1941 Rommel launched his attack; the advance was rapid and ably supported by the Luftwaffe. That same day the Axis forces captured Mersa el Bregha, and on 2 April they took Agadabia. Cyrenaica was now open and Benghazi was a strategic key point with its port and other facilities. His original discussions with Hitler had suggested a defensive strategy, but Rommel now had an option for a direct assault on Benghazi or a sweep through the desert to Gazala to cut off the Allied retreat. Benghazi fell on 4 April but the desert sweep hit problems when 5th Panzer Regiment lost its way and then ran out of fuel, partly because low-level air attacks had destroyed supply vehicles, while those that did get through were unable to find the regimental combat vehicles. This early 'desert sweep' thus highlighted a number of elements that would become key to the rest of the Desert War:

1. Navigation in the desert was tricky.
2. It is a big desert, so finding formations (from the air or ground) was not easy.
3. Fuel was the key … armoured vehicles consumed large amounts and without fuel there could be no advance, or indeed retreat.

'As the British fell back the RAF attempted to stem the advance by attacking supply lines and providing CAS for beleaguered ground units. Wellingtons bombed Tripoli and Sirte air bases; Blenheims bombed and machine-gunned the advancing enemy columns, while 3 Squadron RAAF, assisted after the first day by a flight of 73 Squadron, strove with some success to protect the retiring British forces from enemy aircraft, which, now that the battle was joined, accepted more risks than formerly. At 11.40 a.m. on the 31st patrolling Hurricanes sighted two Me 110s about to bomb troops south of Agedabia and Campbell destroyed one while the other fled. Only five minutes later two Italian formations each of five Fiat BR-20 bombers were dispersed before they could complete their attacks.' (RAAF history)

On the morning of 3 April, Benina was evacuated. Anything of value that could not be taken was destroyed and all aircraft, even those from other units under repair, were flown off. Operations were not disrupted as nine Hurricanes took off from Benina, patrolled between Agedabia and Antelat, and then landed at Sceiledima, whence a second similar patrol was made. This time the Australians landed at Gotes Sultan and during the afternoon operated for the third time. During the second of these patrols, seven Hurricanes of 3 Squadron, with four of 73 Squadron, dived unseen on a number of Me 110s and Ju 87s, probably eight of each, which were positioning themselves to dive-bomb a target 15 miles south of Sceiledima. In this surprise attack, five enemy aircraft were destroyed, four probably destroyed and two damaged. Any elation at this victory was soon dissipated when at 10 pm the same night, the squadron was ordered back to Martuba, well east of Barce.

Nevertheless, the Axis advance continued and on 7 April it reached Mekili, bagging more than 2,000 prisoners, seven generals and large quantities of supplies. The captured vehicles and POL (petrol, oil and lubricants) enabled the advance to continue, and it became a feature of German operations that British trucks from then on formed a significant percentage of the German supply system. Derna and its important airfield was captured on 7 April and Tmimi was captured the following day. However, despite the earlier 'bag' of Allied prisoners and equipment, the majority of the Allied forces had managed to escape the trap. Again, in what became typical of the back-and-forth war, once an airfield fell to the enemy it was immediately on the target list. Thus, Derna became a key target, especially as it was also a major fuel dump for the Axis forces.

Since early February, 70 Squadron had maintained a forward detachment at El Adem; the diarist recorded the chaos prevailing in April: 'During the period 6–15 April the detachment was on the move all the time, evacuating its personnel from each base as it moved back. On 6th April El Adem was evacuated to Sidi Aziz about 70 miles east; each aircraft flew a double trip in order to get as many men and as much equipment as possible away.' (70 Squadron ORB). By 14 April the squadron was back at its old base at El Adem – dropping bombs on its new occupants!

It was a similar story for 45 Squadron's Blenheims: 'Eight aircraft (R3733, T2049, T2174, T2249, T2339, V5573, V5592 and Z5898) and crews, mostly of 'B' Flight, headed west in two groups of four on April 4th. Landing first at Marawa, they were immediately obliged to pull back to Derna where they arrived at about 1730hrs to supplement No 55 Sqn. The following day five of the squadron's Blenheims, accompanied by two of No 55 Squadron, bombed Marble Arch. On the 6th the two squadrons began a fighting withdrawal. A six-aircraft mission was flown from Derna against Agedabia, the aircraft landing at Gazala whence a further four sorties were put up against MT concentrations at Mechili. The squadron despatched seven Blenheims from Gazala to attack Mechili again on the 7th. From this raid the aircraft recovered to Gambut and then launched four more sorties, again to Mechili. Mechili was the target for another six aircraft on the 8th. (*The Flying Camels*, 45 Squadron history, Wing Commander C.G. Jefford)

Leading Aircraftman Len Wilde was a member of this party and he has provided the following graphic account of some of his personal experiences: 'We flew from Helwan to Marawa, stayed about an hour, and were then redirected to Derna. We operated from Derna and were refuelling and rearming when a bunch of six '110s arrived. The only road passed by the boundary of Derna 'drome and was crowded with retreating army units. The first sign of trouble was a loud bang as one of the trucks was hit and exploded as the planes strafed the road. Then they swung away, towards the juicier targets presented by our aircraft, and headed for us! I jumped off the mainplane and grovelled my way back to take cover under the tailplane. Bursts of gunfire passed overhead and as the last of the fighters zoomed away I sprinted for a slit trench. The rear gunners of the '110s sprayed us as we ran and the bullets were like bees around us! I looked up from the trench and saw a '110 within a few yards of the tail of a 55 Sqn Blenheim which was trying to land. The AG in the Blenheim was firing back. They seemed to be glued together but finally the '110 broke away and the Blenheim landed safely. They were lousy shots though as only one of our planes had been shot up.

'During this period we would see the squadron off on a raid, all pile aboard the remaining planes and retreat to a 'drome further back, to which the raiders would recover. After Derna we went to Gazala. At dusk we were bedding down under the planes' wings when an Australian padre arrived in a staff car. He gave each of us a tin of peaches and a wonderful bottle of beer! To this day I still remember it as the finest beer of my life – absolute nectar! Sadly the padre was killed in one of our squadron 'planes. Shortly after taking off from inside Tobruk at dawn, with him as a passenger, it was shot down into the sea. The following day was unique. The squadron had a raid to do. All the groundcrew, with their tools and kit couldn't fit in the one remaining plane. Flight Sergeant Bates volunteered to stay behind and kindly volunteered Cpl Jack Eades and myself to be his companions! One of the planes flying the raid was detailed to drop in at Gazala on the way back to pick us up. Off they went and we sat, alone and a trifle disconcerted, on our tool boxes. The escarpment to the west was alive with the movement of trucks and other vehicles; heliographs were flashing and there were the constant thuds and thumps of explosions. A staff car and a lorry circled the 'drome salvaging oil and petrol and eventually reached us. The officer in charge of the party advised us to go with them or to walk due east 'a bit sharpish'. We put our faith in the squadron and elected to wait for our promised pick-up. The salvage party set fire to a crashed Blenheim and went on their way. By this time Chiefy was getting decidedly restless but then we heard a familiar drone in the sky – our lovely squadron. One Blenheim broke away and landed and Pilot Officer Chadwick taxied over to us. He kept the engines running while we scrambled aboard in double quick time with (most of) our gear. Then we took off, right over the burning Blenheim. No sooner were we airborne than Chiefy Bates, who had been checking over the toolboxes, announced that one of the ones we had abandoned had contained his pistol. On balance, however, he decided to accept whatever retribution might come his way rather than ask the pilot to return to Gazala! We landed at Gambut to find that most of the rest of the groundcrew had now arrived I spent the next hour shooting them the biggest line possible!' (*The Flying Camels*, 45 Squadron history, Wing Commander C.G. Jefford)

The Hurricanes of 73 Squadron had their main base at El Gubbi from 9 April but, like other squadrons, also made frequent use of a number of airfields. Moving between airfields could be hazardous for the ground party; the ORB records the move from Bu Amud to El Gubbi: 'The remainder of the Squadron arrived during the afternoon – the Adjutant, F/Lt Baker-Harber having led the convoy which consisted of approx. 96 vehicles including 16 4" guns under the protection of 12 Australian MT with anti-tank guns. The first scare they had was near Great Gambut where an AFV was seen in the distance travelling at great speed – no action took place however. Near our old aerodrome at Bu Amud the convoy was halted for half an hour because a large Italian bomb dump was being demolished. Enemy aircraft attacked the convoy later but fortunately all our vehicles arrived safely.'

The same day's account also recorded that: 'Many ground strafing attacks were carried out during the day with success – several enemy MT being destroyed as well as many troops being killed in the Derna-Gazala area. All the pilots seem "browned off" with this ground strafing – we are losing too many machines which we can ill afford to do and the ultimate result puts us very much on the debit side.'

The latter is an interesting observation; in part maybe it is the fighter pilot speaking who prefers air combat and sees losses here as of less value; the overall impact of one set of such attacks might be minimal but, as is clear in our account of the Desert War, it was the use of air power to dominate and influence the land battle that was to prove significant in the final success for the Allies.

Sandstorms prevented flying on the 11th, but the following day the ORB recorded that: 'The siege is now serious and recco's returning from early morning patrols stated enemy in various degrees of concentration surrounding Tobruk.'

It was also a bad day for the squadron with losses during strafing attacks: Sergeant Wills shot down by ground fire and believed killed, Sergeant Gudeon (Free French) shot down but seen to be unhurt and so probably a PoW, Flight Lieutenant E. Ball failed to return, and Sergeant Marshall having to land 'many miles away at Mersa Matruh'.

The following day (13th) the ORB recorded: 'Sergeant Marshall returned to base at El Gubbi and was congratulated by Group Captain Brown for saving his aircraft. Marshall has put up a magnificent performance ever since he arrived in the country and his DFM is much overdue having "knocked down" (confirmed) 12 enemy aircraft.'

The diarist got his wish, the DFM for Marshall was announced on June 1941 and the citation stated: 'This airman has displayed outstanding skill, courage and devotion to duty whilst engaged on active operations against the enemy. He has personally destroyed 15 enemy aircraft. On a recent occasion he took off to engage the enemy whilst a fierce ground attack was being made against the aerodrome.' (AMB 4040)

On the 14th: 'The day started on a high note with a most determined attack on the fortress by approx. 70 enemy aircraft. Ju87s were accompanied by ME110s and G50s acted a fighter escort. They dive bombed the harbour but with little success. F/Lt Smith, probably the most popular officer in the Squadron and one lived up to being always an 'officer and a gentleman' was killed in a single handed attack on 5 G50s – he destroyed 2 and damaged another. 'Smudge' will be sadly missed by officers and men alike for his cheerfulness and courage were an inspiration to us all. Sergeant Webster – one of the old members of the Squadron and who had excellent work was also killed – a bad day indeed it had turned out to be, because P/O Lamb ('Kiwi'), the joker and one of the grandest fellows ever, also failed to return from a patrol after a further attack by a mixed formation of about 20 Ju87s and ME110s. The total bag for the day was – 1 Henschel destroyed, 2 G50s destroyed, 6 Ju87s destroyed and 2 probably destroyed and many others damaged. We had two Hurricanes damaged together with the 3 lost. In spite of the magnificent victory – we had only 8 serviceable aircraft and 34 sorties were carried out – it is one of the saddest days in the Squadron's history.'

Meanwhile, other units were also in action: 'Near Tobruk, on 14 April, Arthur and Lieutenant Tennant (South African Air Force) after a sharp fight with three Me110s sent two enemy machines diving steeply apparently out of control. The following day Jeffrey took off at noon to attack two Italian bombers reported over Sidi Aziz, but failing to find them, turned on to the Bardia-Capuzzo road to strafe enemy vehicles. Suddenly he saw four Ju52 aircraft flying south. A search having revealed no escort, he turned quickly to attack but found the transport aircraft had meanwhile landed in considerable confusion, one alighting down-wind being rammed by a second approaching cross-wind. Only one was still airborne and this Jeffrey shot down and then strafed and set on fire the three on the ground.' (RAAF history).

This was the last combat for 3 Squadron, as on the 20th it handed its Hurricanes to 274 Squadron and headed to Aboukir for a spot of well-deserved leave – before re-equipping with Tomahawks. In this first operational foray into the desert, the Squadron had flown 1,262 sorties, claimed forty-seven destroyed, ten probables and thirteen damaged, for the loss of twelve aircraft and six pilots.

The bombers too were busy; 14 April: DFC to Flight Lieutenant Duder, 38 Squadron, for an attack on Derna in a Wellington. 'Damage by enemy AA fire to W5623 on night 13/14 April 1941 (F/Lt Duder). Whilst on operations over Derna Aerodrome this aircraft was badly shot up. The port aileron control rod was almost severed, damage was caused to the near false spar and aileron hinge bracket. Another explosive shell damaged the fuselage abaft the emergency exit leaving a 3-foot gaping hole. Splinters cut the supply pipe to the rear turret putting it out of action and numerous splinters damaged geodetics on top of the fuselage in many places. The aircraft became immediately left wing low but was righted after difficulty by the Captain by driving the right wing accordingly and was flown back to Fuka Satellite safely. The Captain on the following morning flew the aircraft back to base owing to the urgent need of aircraft and knowing it was the only means of getting her repaired quickly. The aircraft landed at 1300 hours and was taken into the hangars. A rough estimate of damage had been given to the maintenance Officer by the first plane home, and he had a maintenance gang standing by. Work was started by 1330 hours and gangs worked continuously until 1600 hours the following day at which time the aircraft took off for operations which were successfully carried out. Except for brief stops for meals the repair party worked continuously 29 hours.'

Having flown a badly damaged aircraft back from the target, the pilot pressed on the following day to take it back to base to get it fixed and operational – and thus helped the squadron maintain a 100 per cent serviceability record for the number of operational airframes; a tribute to the groundcrew!

The 38 Squadron ORB records a number of awards notified in April, with DFCs to Wing Commander Wilfred Thomson, Squadron Leader Robert Gosnell, Flying Officer M.B. Smith, and Pilot Officer Jack Cowpar, and DFMs to Sergeant Edward Rosam and Sergeant Arthur Plant. No specific citations were given for any of these. However, there was a citation for Pilot Officer Ian Stephens: 'One night in March, 1941, this officer was detailed to attack a large concentration of enemy aircraft on the aerodrome of El Machina. Owing to ground mist, the location of the aerodrome was very difficult to find and, after searching for two hours, Pilot Officer Stephens had

Hans-Joachim Marseille with a downed Hurricane; an exceptional shot, he became the leading Luftwaffe ace in the theatre.

Although the Italians continued to fly the CR.42 biplane, they also used the MC 202.

to descend to 500 feet before identifying the target. He pressed home his attacks from a height of 1,000 feet in spite of heavy anti-aircraft and machine-gun fire, and destroyed five enemy aircraft and damaged others. This officer displayed great courage and set a magnificent example of leadership and devotion to duty.'

The bombers continued to operate from various locations, including Malta, against targets in Italy, the Greek Islands, and North Africa, such was the connected nature of the overall campaign.

On 18 April the first Luftwaffe single-engine fighters arrived in North Africa, Bf 109s of I./JG 27 landing at Ain-el-Gazala under Hauptmann Eduard Neumann. These combat veterans were in action the following day in the Gazala–Tobruk area and claimed four Hurricanes, two falling to Oberleutnant Karl-Wolfgang Redlich (his 100th victory). Another fell to Unteroffizier Hans Sippel, who two days later became the first casualty of the unit, when shot down and killed over Tobruk (21 April). One of the new pilots with the unit was Oberleutnant Hans-Joachim Marseille; his first victory with the unit was 23 April, a Hurricane (probably from 73 Squadron) over Tobruk. Although he already had a small number of victories over the UK, it was in the Desert War that the Star of Africa was to make his name as one of Germany's greatest fighter pilots. His next victory was a 45 Squadron Blenheim in the morning of 28 April, followed by two Hurricanes the same day. The Blenheim was probably Z5898, which was carrying passengers from Tobruk to Egypt; the aircraft was less manoeuvrable and its destruction cost the lives of the two crew and five passengers.

No.73 Squadron was one of the units heavily engaged at this period in the defence of Tobruk, a comment on 15 April that, 'Jerry has been remarkably quiet and only one formation passed over the defences' was followed over the next few days by rather more hectic activity and the first references to the 109s. The 73 Squadron ORB takes up the Tobruk story for the end of the siege:

21st April: There were 4 scrambles during the day and in the last 5 ME109s were encountered without any conclusive result. Sergeant Castlenain (Free French) had his machine badly damaged and on landing on the aerodrome he broke his arm and his machine became a write-off. Shipping patrols were carried out with no untoward incidents from dawn until 1930 hours. There were heavy attacks on the harbour and on the aerodrome during the day and in the early hours of the morning. The Squadron is reduced to 5 Hurricanes and the position is serious. Many of the Squadron pilots are showing signs of the continued strain and the morale of the Squadron is not as high as could be desired. If only additional aircraft could be supplied, the Squadron would give a good account once again of itself. It is not to be expected that pilots can, day after day, tackle 20 to 60 enemy aircraft with five Hurricanes at their disposal. Lowering of morale and lessening of enthusiasm are bound to result.

22nd April: A hectic day with no less than 6 scrambles together with other patrols to cover our troops on the perimeter and shipping approaching Tobruk. In the morning 30 Ju87s escorted by 12 ME109s and 12 G50s made a determined attack on Tobruk and the aerodrome. F/O Goodman destroyed a Ju87 and with Sous Lt Denis destroyed a second of the same type. Sgt Marshall shot down a G50 and Sous Lt Denis destroyed a Ju87. Not satisfied with his victories in company with F/O Goodman, Sous Lt Denis later destroyed an ME109 near Gazala. A highly satisfactory day. We had no losses except one Hurricane damaged on landing at base.

23rd April: A fine day again. The first scramble over Tobruk came at 0705 but no enemy aircraft were seen. About 1000 hours four Hurricanes took off on another scramble under the command of the CO, S/Ldr Wykeham-Barnes. Shortly afterwards another 3 Hurricanes were mustered. A tremendous attack on the harbour and aerodrome soon developed and the sky was full of aircraft. It was generally agreed that about 20 Ju87s, 30 ME109s and 10 ME110s were engaged against our 7 Hurricanes and the A/A defences. The Squadron put up – and the opinion expressed in full appreciation that, as a member of it, the chronicler is open to open to criticism – a magnificent exhibition. 4 Ju87s and 2 109s were destroyed. The CO got one of each type, Sgt Marshal a Ju97, S/Lt Litolff an 87 and a 109, P/O Chatfield a Ju87. We lost P/O Haldenby who was shot down in flames by an ME109 as he was trying to land. This is a great loss to the Squadron of a very fine young lad and a promising pilot. F/O Martin occasioned us a great anxiety until news came through that he had baled out and was safe. The CO baled out in full view of the camp, having been attacked and shot up by 3 ME109s. The CO was unhurt except for a strained leg. F/O Martin returned with a damaged arm. Sgt Marshall was attacked on the ground as he was preparing to have his aircraft refueled. He had a wound in his shoulder and a nasty but superficial wound in the back of his head. He was taken to Tobruk hospital. AC Webster, one of the crew, was severely wounded in one lung and also taken to hospital. The ground strafing was severe but no damage, except the above, was done and at the end of the attack we all felt we had, on the whole, escaped lightly. P/O Halliday was buried in the afternoon on No.199 grave, Tobruk cemetery. In the evening there was another big attack on the town by about 20 109s escorting 20 Ju87s. On this occasion our losses were nil in exchange for one ME109 destroyed and one probable.'

As a historian, I always appreciate when an ORB 'chronicler' records such vivid and comprehensive detail; this is often not the case, and as the ORB is the only official document with a mandatory preservation in the records, lack of such details makes it much more difficult for us to create an accurate and personal picture.

The ORB recorded that the 24th was a quiet day but on the 25th 'about 0700 hours 258 Wing asked for a nominal roll of all left on the camp and it seemed clear that some important move was afoot. The Squadron has only 5 serviceable aircraft. There was an early scramble in which 20 ME109s were seen, as there were 4 Hurricanes only, F/Lt Oliver did not engage and returned to base.'

This was the last Tobruk op for the 73 Squadron, and at 1800 hours the eight aircraft that the groundcrew had managed to get into a flyable condition departed for Sidi Haneish.

Churchill was now despondent; in his post-war history he focuses on missed opportunities and failures, often revolving around the use of ports (such as Suda Bay and Benghazi) but his overall account remains true. 'All Hurricanes in Greece had been lost, and many of those in Tobruk had been destroyed or damaged. Air Marshal Longmore considered that any further attempt to maintain a fighter squadron inside Tobruk would only result in heavy losses to no purpose. Thus the enemy would have complete air superiority over Tobruk until a fresh fighter force could be built up. ... It seemed very unsatisfactory to us at home that Benghazi, which we had failed to make a useful base, was already playing so important a part now that it passed into German hands.'

The latter was a reference to reinforcements (15th Panzer) and supplies were being unloaded at the port, which, of course, made it a primary target for the RAF's bombers. Churchill was also unimpressed with the way that 'from the outset of these new dangers General Wavell showed himself most reluctant to assume more burdens.' The new dangers were in Syria and Iraq, which created another drain on limited resources.

Iraq and Syria 1941

Iraq Revolt

The German-inspired revolt in Iraq was led by Rashid Ali and started at the beginning of April 1941. Principal targets for the rebels included the oil pipeline to Palestine, and the RAF's major (training) airfield at Habbaniya. The rebels were provided a small degree of air support by the Italian 155 Squadron and the Luftwaffe Sonderkommando Junck. By the end of April their forces were besieging the airfield at Habbaniya, home of No 4 FTS. This became a spirited little action during which the training aircraft – Audaxes, Oxfords and Gladiators – of the FTS were modified for offensive action and in which capacity they flew 1,400 sorties! The revolt was over by 31 May as British forces regained control of the rebel areas.

RAF Habbaniya, Iraq, became famous for the short but intensive campaign against a German-inspired revolt.

Syria

Vichy French control of Lebanon/Syria provided problems with supply of British areas and also provided a potential line of attack for German forces, and the Axis air support to the Iraq rebellion had gone via Syria. The decision was taken to seize these areas and an offensive (Operation Exporter) was launched on 8 June, the ground forces being supported by four and a half squadrons, these being primarily engaged on a counter-air campaign to negate the French air presence as well as providing ground support on the few occasions that the situation so demanded. A ceasefire was declared on 12 July.

Tomahawks of 3 Squadron RAAF; the squadron commenced ops in the desert theatre in November 1940, re-quipping with Tomahawks in spring 1941.

The Blenheims of 45 Squadron moved to Palestine (Ramleh and Aqir) on 19 June as part of the air support, although they were still rebuilding after the losses of April and May in the Western Desert and Greece/Crete. The first op was flown on the 23rd when three Blenheims attacked Fort Soueida, whilst a fourth aircraft flew a recce mission over Beirut. The latter was intercepted by four French fighters and damaged, which resulted in a ground loop (courtesy of a bullet through a tyre) and collapsed undercarriage but no injuries. More aircraft arrived and more missions were flown, albeit with poor bombing results: the CO was disappointed with the bombing accuracy achieved during the first few missions. He attributed the poor early results partly to the relatively unfamiliar nature of medium-level bombing and partly to the lack of experience of the mere handful of 'scratch' crews that was initially supposed to represent an eighteen–crew squadron. (45 Squadron history)

A number of other air units were involved, such as 3 Squadron RAAF with its Tomahawks. 'Bobby' (R.H.) Gibbes was a recent arrival on the squadron: 'On Sunday, the 8th of June, 1941, after a total of six hours flying on Tomahawk fighters, I was called up for briefing with the rest of the squadron pilots. The C.O. gave us "the gen." [information] on the opening blow of the squadron in the Syrian campaign. We had been half expecting to be at war with the Vichy French for some days, and the actual news of the offensive commencing was greeted with a feeling of relief, coupled with that of dismay to think that it was actually necessary to come to blows with our old allies, the French, in order to prevent German infiltration into Iraq.'

The squadron claimed a number of French fighters destroyed in the air and on the ground. It was all over by 14 July, when an Armistice was signed.

However, the successful conclusion to these 'new dangers' provided an improved strategic situation in the eastern Mediterranean and enabled focus to be turned back to the threat posed by Rommel. Having made the 600-mile leap from Tripoli to Benghazi, Rommel now faced a 400-mile leap on to Sollum. The importance of the distances is that it indicates the supply issues, especially as there was only one good road, the Via Balba, and other than that supplies had to arrive by sea, along the coast or be flown in by transport aircraft. Both sides spent a great deal of time and effort attempting to disrupt supply lines; ultimately, the Allies were far more successful in this, primarily due to air operations. While the Axis forces tried to capture Tobruk, the advance towards Egypt continued, and Bardia fell on 12 April – there being no resistance as the Allies were still retreating towards a more defendable position, the Halfaya Pass, near Sollum and the only way vehicles could easily get up to the plateau. Although the Germans captured the pass in the last week of April it was retaken by the British on 15 May, only for them to lose it again on the 27th.

On 1 May there was another restructuring, with a mobile Air Headquarters (AHQ) formed to control operations in the Western Desert, to be located close to the Army Western Desert Force HQ, while a Rear HQ was formed to provide administrative support. The wing structure was also changed, with the addition of 257 Wing (SR and bombing) and 253 Air Component Wing (close support and tactical reconnaissance (TacR).

No.204 Group had been formed under Air Commodore Raymond Collishaw to bring under one command structure the 'tactical' squadrons, which at this point comprised:

- Hurricane: 73 Sqn (Tobruk), 274 Sqn (Gerawla), 6 Sqn (Tobruk, also with Lysander).
- Blenheim: 14 Sqn (Burg El Arab), 45 Sqn (Fuka), 55 Sqn (Zimla).
- Maryland: 39 Sqn (Maaten Bagush), 24 Sqn SAAF (Fuka).

The new group also had a new airfield structure, with three 'Striking Force Bases' and six 'Subsidiary Aerodromes' for squadrons and units west of Burg el Arab, the idea being that squadrons could move into the bases and find a fully functioning support organization without having to depend on their own ground personnel (who had not yet caught up with them – going forwards or backwards). According to the maintenance history: 'The striking force bases were for the reception, administration and ground operation of squadrons or parts of squadrons being sent forward from rear areas without ground organizations, and for squadrons or parts of squadrons returning from forward areas without their ground organization. The administrative organization set up enabled squadrons to operate immediately from these bases. The subsidiary aerodromes were for the reception of squadrons and their ground organizations returning from forward areas or moving forward from the Delta area.'

Supplies of fuel, oil, bombs, ammunition, pyrotechnics and oxygen were kept at each base, and each base was supported by elements of 31 Air Stores Park and 51 RSU. This was in recognition of the likely highly mobile nature of any campaign and was sound thinking.

The planners may have had one, often rose-tinted, view of the 'airfields', the squadrons frequently had another: Fuka Satellite was typical of these desert bases, with no 'hard' permanent runways, no hangars or control tower – just stacks of petrol and oil cans and tents scattered all over the place amidst the barren desert landscape. 'The desert wind, the "Khamsin", made life even worse as the sand got into everything, food drink and clothing. There were also clouds of vicious flies that descended on any exposed food, making an already unpalatable diet even worse. Newcomers to the desert took quite a while to get used to conditions. Also, it was prudent to check beds and clothes for scorpions and other desert nasties.' (George Beckett, 39 Squadron, May–June 1941).

It was this group that, under the command of Air Vice-Marshal Arthur Coningham, later became AHQ Western Desert (and eventually the Desert Air Force). The frequent change of commander designation and organization and assignment of units is invariably confusing, and for the purposes of this book we have treated all Western Desert operations as 'DAF', even though the formal designation as AHQ Western Desert was not made until February 1942, having spent a few weeks as AHQ Libya, and Western Desert Air Force (WDAF) not until sometime later.

The Martin Marylands of 39 Squadron were an important asset for the ground commander, as they were tasked with the crucial strategic reconnaissance (SR) role; the squadron had given up its Blenheims back in January and had commenced work-up with the new type and new role. The first aircraft acquired by 39 Squadron was finished overall in blue and was quickly nicknamed *Blue Pencil* by squadron crews. In early February all crews flew the Hind for front and rear gunnery practice and as part of a general flying refresher. During the same period all the pilots went solo in *Blue Pencil* in preparation for collecting more aircraft from Takoradi. By the 24th, the squadron had received four Marylands. These aircraft were originally destined for the French Air Force and thus all the instruments were all calibrated and labelled in French. This caused one or two problems initially, especially among the navigators who, apart from contending with fairly basic equipment, also had the problem of converting the metric units to the familiar imperial. To this end conversion charts were provided alongside the equipment! Although the Maryland was basically a bomber it was primarily used as a long range high-level reconnaissance aircraft during the months it was flown by 39 Squadron. For this job, a 14in focal length Williamson camera was fitted in a vertical mounting. On 15 April 1941 four aircraft, crews and a ground support party moved to Maaten Bagush satellite, which was also occupied by 55 Squadron. Operations began the following day with a high level reconnaissance of the whole of Tripolitania and Cyrenaica.

During April and May, the squadron was making daily reconnaissance flights over the battle area and the Mediterranean and was earning great praise from the air officer commanding. However, the price was high: one Maryland failed to return from a reconnaissance over Derna on 5 May and two more were lost on 8 May.

Sid Sills recalled: 'On 11th May 1941 we took off from Fuka Satellite in AH298 (pilot – F/Off Sid Ault, WOP/AG – Sgt Taff Williams, A/G – Sgt Ginger Pulling, and myself as Nav) after the normal breakfast in the mobile kitchen – tinned sausages and tomatoes, thick bread and even thicker tea. We climbed steadily to our 25,000 feet operating height for the day and headed more or less due West. A different operating height was chosen each day just to confuse any possible enemy aircraft or AA. There were no nav aids in the Western Desert of over Libya so we used a mixture of known landmarks and DR navigation, checking course by a wrecked aircraft here, an unusual wadi there, and best of all the huge barbed wire fence and forts constructed by Mussolini. We aimed for the large port of Benghazi and the local airfields of Berca and Benina. It was, to quote a cliche, a normal milkrun.

'It was about 380/400 miles to Benghazi, nearly three hours flying on the chosen route, to pass Benghazi to the South and then approach from the sea and be heading for home when taking the photographs. En route, movement on the ground was being recorded, and there was plenty, mostly vehicle convoys and an occasional camel train, easily visible in the clear air. The horizon was some 140 miles ahead, making navigation easy. Everything was normal as we approached Benghazi and there was only desultory AA fire from below which appeared to have our rough direction but not our height. So I took photos of the port and recorded shipping positions. On this course we passed over the airfield of Benina and again took photos and noted that there seemed to be more aircraft on the ground than normal.

'To reach Benina we had to change course slightly but maintained height, indicated speed being 140 miles per hour. As we neared Benina it was obvious that something was happening there. We had been over the day before and there was very little activity, whereas today there must have been more than 100 aircraft on the ground, mostly Ju52s. Over the airfield we flew, taking photos the whole time and deciding this was most important, flew back again and took more. After discussion among ourselves it was decided that something must be done, and our pilot being the only Officer aboard and therefore 'in charge' decided on attack. We flew into the desert to the East of the airfield and then, descending to a height of about 2,000 feet where we felt we were hidden from the airfield defences, we circled and then with the throttle wide open we dived on Benina, choosing a line where

Marylands of 39 Squadron; the primary role of the type was strategic recce rather than bombing.

Marylands were operated by 12 Squadron SAAF from May 1941, the unit commencing ops in the desert in July 1941.

The Maryland was not a great success as a bomber – and also suffered recognition problems, with Allied fighter pilots mistaking it for the Do 17.

the Ju52s seemed to be thickest, all front guns hose-piping. For myself I could only sit and watch and I know many aircraft were hit although we saw no fires. Keeping at ground level we continued for some twenty minutes before climbing away and returned to base five hours thirty minutes after take-off. Subsequent events showed the Ju52s to be part of the Crete invasion force and we were therefore the first to see it and to bring the news back to base.' (*The Winged Bomb*, *ibid*).

The South Africans of 24 Squadron SAAF had arrived in early May and their B Flight was attached to 39 Squadron, to learn more about the Maryland and to boost the operational strength after recent losses. No.39 Squadron subsequently had close relationships with two other Maryland units, 2 Free French Flight, attached in July, and the South Africans of 16 Squadron SAAF.

Despite Churchill's increasing lack of confidence in Wavell, the latter was well aware of the threat from Rommel and any reinforcements, and so he attempted a spoiling attack before the new troops and supplies reached the front. Operation Brevity was launched on 15 May, led by three columns under Brigadier William Gott, with limited objectives in the Sollum–Capuzzo–Bardia area. Initially, it looked promising, having caught the Axis forces off guard. However, this was short-lived and local

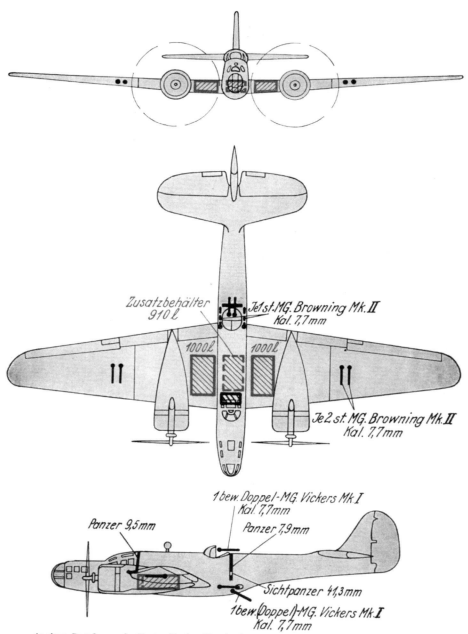

Die Kriegsflugzeuge der Feindmächte

Anlage 33 a

Großbritannien (Herkunft USA.)

Martin „Maryland"[1]
Kampf- und Aufklärungsflugzeug

Zusatzbehälter 910 ℓ

Je 1 st. MG. Browning Mk. II Kal. 7,7 mm

1000 ℓ   1000 ℓ

Je 2 st. MG. Browning Mk. II Kal. 7,7 mm

1 bew. Doppel-MG. Vickers Mk. I Kal. 7,7 mm

Panzer 9,5 mm

Panzer 7,9 mm

Sichtpanzer 41,3 mm

1 bew. Doppel-MG. Vickers Mk. I Kal. 7,7 mm

An einem Beuteflugzeug des Musters Martin „Maryland" wurde die hier angegebene, veränderte Bewaffnung und Panzerung festgestellt.

[1] USA.-Werksbezeichnung: **Martin M-167.**

The Luftwaffe's intelligence sheet on the Maryland showing armament and vulnerability (fuel tanks and crew).

counter-attacks brought the offensive to an end almost as soon as it began. After a brief occupation of the strategically important Halfaya Pass, the Allies were pushed back. Rommel continued to realign and reinforce his forces, as well as set up improved defence positions.

The ORB for May 1941 for 14 Squadron states: 'The first month of operations for this Squadron has proved rather disastrous in losses there being a very bad week when a total of 10 aircraft and crews were lost – a heavy casualty list, more particularly as experienced pilots such as Flt Lt Green, Fg Off Mackenzie, Sgt Gilmore, Sgt Taylor and Fg Off Le Cavalier, who had seen the Eritrean campaign right through were lost. The battle of Crete claimed five and Tobruk-Capuzzo the other five.'

The squadron had moved from the East African theatre to Egypt in early April, initially to Heliopolis, and on 1 May had moved sixteen aircraft to LG21, 7 miles west of El Daba to commence operations; two days later ten Blenheims flew a sector recce Sollum–Sidi Omar–Fort Maddalena–Sidi Barrani as a familiarisation to the new theatre.

Two days later, on 5 May, four pairs of aircraft attacked MT on the roads between Tobruk, Bardia and Bir Aziez. The crews reported very accurate anti-aircraft fire over Bardia. 'These 8 Blenheims were sent out to bomb moving MT on the road between Tobruk–Bardia–Bir Aziz. The leader of the second pair had to return to base with engine trouble. The other aircraft bombed various small concentrations of MT, as few direct hits were obtained. In some cases the results could not be observed because of dust. Very heavy and fairly accurate AA fire was experienced from Bardia, but all aircraft returned safety.' The sortie had been flown in pairs, starting at 0650:

0650–1013
T1994: Sqn Ldr Stapleton, Plt Off Whittard. Sgt Bartholomew
L8574: Sgt Taylor, Sgt Parker, Sgt Ritchie

0745–1009
T1856: Flt Lt Hill, Plt Off Farrell, Sgt Cooke
Z9307: Fg Off Mackenzie. Sgt Fearn, Sgt McConnel

0855–1318
Z8770: Flt Lt Buchanan. Sgt Chaplin, Sgt Ball
T8348: Lt Forrester. Sgt Fretwell, Sgt Hall

0820–1140
T8003: Fg Off Le Cavalier, Plt Off Donald. Sgt Bury
T2065: Sgt Jeudwine; Sgt Young; Sgt Luke

Blenheim of 113 Squadron; the airfield might be Maaten Bagush.

The Axis air forces were present in some strength, with a report of 150 aircraft on Derna airfield. Among the RAF squadrons to go after this tempting target on 10 May, the Blenheims of 14 Squadron flew a number of sorties. The first attempt was an early morning trip: 'Owing to extremely bad weather conditions this was the only aircraft [T1994, Pilot Officer Johnson] of four which set out to bomb Derna Satellite aerodrome to reach the target. About 100–150 aircraft of various types were seen on the landing ground. The bombs were dropped in a stick and direct hits were claimed. 60 bursts of large caliber AA fire were seen, but the aircraft sustained no damage.' (14 Squadron ORB)

The next formation left mid-afternoon: 'Three Blenheims took off to bomb Derna satellite LG. The first aircraft located and bombed the target area, but the results were not observed. The second aircraft returned to base having failed to reach the target due to bad weather. The third was attacked by a Cr.42 when over the target, and despite having had the aileron controls shot away, and being pursued for half an hour in a semi-controlled aircraft, the pilot, Sergeant Taylor, succeeded in crash landing East of Sollum, a pursuit of nearly 150 miles. Prior to crashing, the port airscrew had fallen off due to lack of lubrication, and a few minutes later the starboard engine stopped, probably through lack of petrol. The Blenheim (T2274, Sergeant Taylor, Sergeant Parker and Sergeant Hall) was severely damaged by the fire from the CR.42 but the crew were unhurt.'

The squadron had sent another formation out in the early morning on an offensive reconnaissance on the roads around Tobruk, but only one found anything to bomb: 'On the Tobruk–Bardia road the third aircraft attacked vehicles which were stationary. No results could be observed on account of the large quantity of dust.'

On 21 May five Blenheims were lost, with all fifteen aircrew, on a mission to attack MT and troop concentrations on the Capuzzo–Tobruk road; the formation was intercepted by I./JG 27 near the target. The losses were L8874 (Sergeant J. Matetich), T2173 (Pilot Officer R. Johnson), Z5979 (Sergeant N. Hoskins) V5511 (Pilot Officer R. Gilmore), and T2346 (Flight Sergeant J. Taylor); all are commemorated in the Alamein cemetery.

A few days later the squadron was again hit heavily. In the morning of 25 May, it sent six aircraft on an early morning (take-off 0415) attack on 'enemy aircraft parked on the beach and landing ground at Maleme. All the bombs fell in the target area and it is thought that at least 12 JU.52s were completely destroyed on the ground.'

A second mission later in the day (1230 take-off) to the same target resulted in the loss of all three Blenheims (T2065 – Flight Lieutenant Green, T2003 – Sergeant Jeudwins, T5510 – Lt Forrester). This is simply recorded in the ORB as 'none of these aircraft returned'. All the crew were killed in action (KIA); the Blenheims had fallen to the fighters of JG77.

Blenheim IVs of 14 Squadron. (*14 Squadron*)

With the arrival of the Luftwaffe, the Blenheims became increasingly vulnerable and it was clear that new light bomber types would be required.

Fine shot of RAF vehicles – the 'blood wagon' at Amriya; the wide range of roles performed by ground personnel are all too often glossed over, especially those not directly concerned with aircraft maintenance.

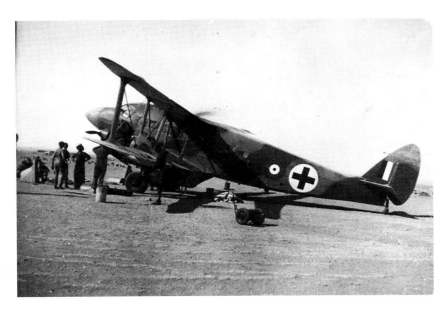

D.H.86 air ambulance – another type and role seldom given coverage. (*Ralph Harding SAAF*)

There was some good news recorded in the ORB: 'The astounding safe arrival of Fg Off Mackenzie's crew after five days in the desert without food or water needs recounting. Fg Off Mackenzie's aircraft, after having successfully attacked Maleme aerodrome did not find the coast, and force-landed some 70 miles South of Daba in the desert. All three of the aircraft crew jumped and landed quite safely. They had pre-arranged to meet at the aircraft, but Sgt Fearn and Sgt McConnell landed so far away from the aircraft they decided to head North. They were found four days later amongst some swamps, living on desert snails, berries, and what water they could find by digging. They had covered about 30 miles of desert to this area in three days without food and water. Fg Off

Squadron AX code being applied to a 1 Squadron SAAF Hurricane. (*Bomb Finney SAAF*)

In a very posed shot, Anderson and Seccombe of 1 Squadron. (*Johnny Seccombe SAAF*)

Mackenzie, although not at his aircraft, which was found two days after it crashed, laid out strips by the aircraft but has never been found since. This search was given up after an 8-day hunt, the previous three days having been spent on motor bicycles scouring the area, but no trace was found.'

The aircraft had failed to return from an attack on troop concentrations in Crete. A second Blenheim (V5593) was lost on the same sortie, the crew became lost and Flying Officer J. Le Cavalier ordered Sergeant Page and Sergeant Bury to bail out, which they did. Sergeant Page survived and walked back to Mersa Matruh. 'This line of knocks reduced the squadron to four crews and 3 serviceable aircraft. However, reinforcements are arriving, but will need a little careful training

A Lysander leaving a desert strip on a communications mission. (*Bomb Finney*)

Refuelling a Hurricane; for both sides the 'logistics war' was crucial – keeping supplies, especially fuel, out of enemy hands by moving stockpiles, and attacking supply lines. (*Peter Metelerkamp SAAF*)

before they go on their "blooding" flights.' No matter how much research and writing I do around RAF air operations, I never cease to be amazed by the way in which squadrons, or rather the people on them, were able to cope with such high loss rates.

May was also a busy month for 45 Squadron and also saw the introduction of the Blenheim IVF with its gun-pack of 4 × 0.303 in the bomb bay; the new versions were primarily used by 'A' Flight, which promptly became known as the 'Fighter Flight' although in reality the gun pack was intended, in this theatre, for ground strafing – not that this was a particularly good, or successful, idea! The squadron did have some success in the 'fighter role', sometimes working with Hurricanes, such as on 29 May when Sergeant Langrish shot down a Ju 88 that was attacking shipping, with his Hurricane partner claiming another. The squadron had been heavily engaged in May and had only received three replacement crews during that month. Although all nine of those aircrew survived the period, they had all been shot down at some point! By the end of the month the squadron could only raise six crews and, thanks to the efforts of the groundcrew, eight aircraft. The squadron was declared non-operational and left the active zone.

May brought a DFC for Squadron Leader Peter Jeffrey, CO of 3 Squadron RAAF, with the citation recording: 'This officer has commanded and led his squadron with exceptional skill. By his untiring efforts and his high standard of efficiency he has contributed materially to the success obtained by his squadron in protecting our ground forces under extremely trying conditions. On a recent occasion, he carried out a low flying attack on an enemy landing ground during which he shot down a Junkers 52 and destroyed a further 3 of these aircraft on the ground.'

Flight Lieutenant L.W. Coleman of 148 Sqn was the first New Zealander to be awarded a bar to the DFC for operations in the Middle East, his award being announced in May 1941. The citation read: 'One night in May 1941 this officer was the captain of an aircraft which carried out an attack on the aerodrome at Benine. He displayed great skill and tenacity in locating his target, and carried out his attack with great determination, bombing and machine gunning the aerodrome, from different heights, sometimes from less than 1,000ft. He destroyed at least 2 Junkers 52s on the ground and damaged others. Just after he had returned from this attack, an incoming aircraft crashed and caught fire. Though the petrol tanks and bombs on the crashed aircraft were exploding, Flight Lieutenant Coleman ran to another aircraft standing nearby, started the engines and taxied it away to safety. He had continuously displayed outstanding courage and devotion to duty.' (AMB 3959).

Flight Lieutenant Coleman's original DFC had been awarded in November 1940 when he was operating with 149 Squadron. Coleman, by then squadron leader, was KIA on 11 March 1942.

The desert squadrons continued to support operations in Crete, the escapades of 73 Squadron over 23 to 25 May are worth recounting here, but before that, on the 22nd a very important mission was flown: 'P/O Goord flew the Lysander to the dispersal ground with cigarettes etc. for our ground party down there.'

23rd: 'Apart from one scramble over base it was a quiet morning which indeed proved to be the lull before the storm. At 1100 hours we were ordered to send six Hurricanes in company with a Blenheim escort over to the Isle of Crete. The orders were to land at Heraklion, refuel and proceed to Maleme aerodrome and carry out strafing attacks on German troops reported to have landed there by parachute, Ju52s and troop-carrying gliders. It was also reported that these Ju52s were coming over in large numbers unescorted. In spite of the hazardous sea trip, the job seemed to hold promise of good results, and conjecture was rife among those left behind as to how unescorted Ju52s would cope with our Hurricanes. The Blenheim arrived and F/O Goodman, F/O Donati, P/O Moss, P/O Ward and Sgt Laing took off. Two hours later our pilots returned with the exception of Sgt

Laing. F/O Goodman reported that they had flown over a number of British Naval Vessels which had put up a tremendous barrage of anti-aircraft fire, scattering the formation in all directions, our aircraft lost the Blenheim, it was thought at the time that she must have come down in the sea. Group provided another escort, this time a Maryland. P/O Likeman took off with the others as it was uncertain what had happened to Sgt Laing. Shortly after, the escorting Blenheim returned and reported that after getting separated from five of the Hurricanes over the fleet he had carried on with one Hurricane, which landed at Heraklion.'

24th: 'Sand started to rise at about 0700 and by 0800 there was a moderate dust storm blowing, vis. About 200 yards. At 0820 one Hurricane appeared on the aerodrome out of the sand haze and to the amazement of our Australian Defence Officers two pilots clambered out of the cockpit – F/O Goodman had flown Sgt Laing back from Crete, managing to find the aerodrome in spite of the adverse weather conditions, as did P/O Ward who arrived shortly afterwards. F/O Goodman reported that they had arrived at Heraklion about 1730 hours the previous day, and found an air raid in progress by about 20 Ju88s. P/O Ward and F/O Goodman had only very little petrol left but attacked the 88s damaging two, owing to the fuel shortage they were unable to pursue the damaged machines to attain a conclusive result. The LG had been badly bombed and was full of craters including the runways, two landing wheels were broken on landing. The aerodrome was under almost continual fire from the parachutists who had positioned themselves behind rocks etc. all round the perimeter. As the pilots made their way from the aircraft to the mess they had to constantly throw themselves to the ground to avoid this fire. The ground crews managed to refuel two of the aircraft which enabled two of the pilots to carry out a patrol until dusk, no enemy aircraft were encountered. Sergeant Laing's machine was burnt out on the ground when some Ju88s strafed the aerodrome shortly after his arrival.

'The remaining pilots were to carry out ground strafing attacks on the parachutists around the drome before leaving. All the aircraft got off including those with damaged tail wheels. P/O Ward who was last to take off arrived back alone shortly after F/O Goodman. A few hours later P/O Donati rang to say he was down ay Fuka where he had been forced to land owing to shortage of fuel rendering his already damaged tail wheel completely u/s. Late in the afternoon P/O Moss rang up to say he had landed at about 0900 this morning. He landed just inside at Ras el Kanazis having run out of petrol. Unfortunately, his machine was damaged, Cat III, in doing so. It had taken him nearly all day to make his way to the nearest telephone. There is no news of P/O Goord or P/O Likeman, it is thought there is possible hope that they may have returned to Crete. We have two serviceable aircraft back from the seven we sent over, and two pilots missing.' (73 Squadron ORB).

So the promise of easy picking of Ju 52s proved elusive! The following day six non-tropicalized Hurricanes of 213 Squadron were attached for 'special duties over Crete', while on the 26th five pilots went to the Delta to collect more Hurricanes. No.213 Squadron had arrived in the Middle East aboard HMS *Furious* in late May and so this attachment to 73 Squadron was its first action in the desert, having been a UK-based fighter squadron.

26th: All serviceable aircraft were brought to standby to fly defensive patrols over the damaged aircraft carrier HMS *Formidable*, flights of three Hurricanes were rotated on standing patrols, the second patrol encountering a lone Ju 88, which Squadron Leader Wykeham-Barnes, 'attacked and damaged it, unfortunately the reflector sight went out at the crucial moment, and if the other two members of the section had chased it they would have been drawn too far away from the Formidable. The days flying played havoc with the aircraft we received yesterday, at least two will have to go back to base, and of the six non-tropicalized Hurricanes which had to be used in the emergency only one is serviceable. Generally, the troubles are minor ones, loose fittings, shorts in the electrical circuits, etc. It is hoped that our ground crews will be able to manage most of the work here.'

And on the 27th: 'Our ground crews have performed wonders on the u/s machines, rendering all the non-tropicalized machines serviceable, and three more of our own.'

In May Air Marshal Tedder took over as AOC HQ Middle East, having been Deputy AOC (to Longmore). A First World War fighter pilot, he was also an 'air strategist' and had developed his own ideas as to the way to organize and employ air assets in the fluid campaigns required in the Western Desert.

As Wing Commander H.L. Thompson recalls in *New Zealanders with the Royal Air Force*: 'Here he was presented with a unique opportunity for defining, developing and organizing the role that the air arm should play in the Mediterranean war. That opportunity he firmly grasped and he soon became pre-eminent as a strategist and in the framing of policy. He was also able to inspire the willing service of officers and airmen from the highest to the lowest and by skillful leadership weld them into a highly successful team. Apart from his undoubted military gifts, Tedder possessed a cheerful personality of which pleasant features were his addiction to a pipe of longish stem and to the "forage" or field service cap – better known to the irreverent as the "fore-and-after". He also had the happy knack of meeting his men on their own level, and many of those who served with the DAF can recall pleasant moments on desert airfields when their leader dropped in for a chat to see how things were going.

'Steps were therefore taken to create self-contained fighter and light-bomber wings each with its own vehicles, its own operational headquarters and its own servicing team, all of which could be moved rapidly from one area to another. At the same time mobile radar posts and air-support controls were established in the forward area, the latter an important innovation by which it was hoped to provide closer and more immediate help to the ground forces. In all these various ways, the RAF gradually began to create its Desert Air Force capable of highly mobile operations in the wilderness of sand and stone but firmly based on a well-organized, safely dispersed system of supply and maintenance.

The Western Desert campaigns were where the tactical doctrine of Close Air Support (CAS) were truly developed – and applied. This was in large part due to the nature of the campaign and also a particularly successful blending of commanders; on the air side, Tedder was a vital strategist but a key part of the success that was to come was down to his new AOC Desert Air Force, Air Vice-Marshal Arthur Coningham, who took over in July and, 'was to achieve outstanding success in this new role; indeed, it was not long before he outshone every other contemporary commander of tactical air forces in his ability to foresee, prepare for and meet situations and, above all, to give the ground forces the close air support they needed.' (*New Zealanders with the Royal Air Force*)

By June, 14 Squadron was dropping a new weapon – 'spikes' – along with the normal bombs … designed to drop over aerodromes and severely damage an unsuspecting landing or taking off aircraft. The initial use was on 7 June, the spikes being dropped on Great Gambut (probably Gambut Main) and an LG north of Capuzzo. June was the squadron's last operational month and it moved to Palestine in early July to re-quip. A sister unit, 45 Squadron, had first used the new weapon in early May. The spikes were triangular steel plates about 4in square and with barbed corners that meant that no matter how they landed at least one sharp point was upwards. They were packed in containers that held around 3,000 spikes and when the lids were sprung the spikes scattered over a sizeable area.

113 Squadron
Blenheims operated
in the Western Desert
from June 1940 to
the end of 1941.
(*45 Squadron*)

In theory it was a good idea and could have caused major problems for aircraft and vehicle tyres, and if it burst an aircraft tyre on take-off or landing it could have been catastrophic. However, according to one report: 'The efficacy of these was disproved by a prisoner of war captured near Capuzzo by the Army, who merely states that the whole camp was roused early in the morning to walk across the aerodrome to pick up these spikes.' (14 Squadron ORB). On the other hand, 45 Squadron could attest to their success, 'when a "spiker" inadvertently released its load at Fuka. Within hours much of the squadron's MT was immobilized with punctured tyres. The whole squadron had to turn out and sweep the airstrip line-abreast to retrieve the offending objects.' (45 Squadron history). The new weapon appears to have been confined to the scrap heap within a few months.

Operation Battleaxe

Wavell tried again in mid-June with Operation Battleaxe, the intent this time to raise the siege of Tobruk. The attack stumbled in the face of strong German defensive positions, losing some 50 per cent of tank strength, in part due to the Germans' use of the superlative 88mm anti-aircraft gun in a direct fire anti-tank role … in which it proved incredibly effective. The second day was mixed but by the third day the Germans had the upper hand and only a swift retreat prevented a major British defeat. For once the British did not have the air reconnaissance essential to battlefield air superiority. Churchill later wrote: 'The withdrawal of the whole force was carried out in good order, protected by our fighter aircraft. The enemy did not press his pursuit, partly no doubt because his armour was heavily attacked by RAF bombers.'

Also, Rommel had suffered losses, especially in tanks and he knew that he had to build up his forces before advancing on the strong defences of the Egyptian frontier. Churchill finally lost what little patience he had with Wavell and replaced him as Commander-in-Chief Middle East with General Claude Auchinleck, who had been Commander-in-Chief of the Indian Army. The German accounts of this three-day battle recorded that it took place under a 'fighter umbrella, above all at the beginning of the battle, from low-level attacks on the battlefield and in the rear areas.' The army accounts were also scathing about the lack of German (or even Italian) aircraft.

The Defence Committee approved a programme of reinforcements for Middle East Command aimed at raising strength to forty and a half squadrons by 15 July, this force structure to include five Wellington bomber squadrons each with twenty aircraft.

'The programme was increased to sixty-two and a half squadrons after the failure of the June offensive. It was further stated that: provided that delivery of Wellingtons by air via Gibraltar and Malta continued be practicable it was thought possible to achieve and keep up the proposed force

The German 88mm anti-aircraft gun was first used both to defend targets against air attack, in which it was moderately successful. However, in the desert it became a tank killer in the ground role.

of five squadrons. It was necessary, however, to introduce the Wellington II as far as possible as the Wellington I had not proved altogether satisfactory under summer conditions in the Middle East. Supplies of Wellington IIs for the Middle East would for some months be limited as Bomber Command had first claim on these aircraft.

'The increase in strength brought its own problems, not least that of crew training as most multi-engine aircrew arriving in the Middle East were straight from Service Flying Training School (SFTSs) in Iraq, Africa or Australia; an Operational Training Flight (OTF) for Wellingtons had been formed at Kabrit in early 1941 but this was unable to keep pace with the expansion. However, the Air Ministry refused to recognize the Wellington Flight at Kabrit as an OTU nucleus as replacement crews for heavy bomber and general reconnaissance aircraft were to be provided by crews flying out aircraft from the UK. In the Middle East it was found, however, that refresher courses were necessary for Wellington crews. To eliminate this need it was decided in April [1941] that 15 OTU in England was to be employed exclusively on training fresh Wellington crews for the Middle East.' (AHB Narrative, Middle East Campaigns)

Two more 39 Squadron aircraft were lost on consecutive days in mid-June. However, it was not only the enemy that were proving a threat to squadron aircraft. Due to the inability of allied fighter pilots to recognize the Maryland, a tour was made of fighter bases to give the fighter pilots an opportunity of having a close look at one – and then, hopefully, they would repeat their mistakes! This tour took place on 7 June when Flying Officer Ault took a Maryland to the Hurricane bases at Sidi Haneish, Quasaba and Gerawla. It appeared that the Maryland was being mistaken for the Ju 88, a not unnatural error when you consider the similar silhouette of the Maryland, especially from below.

'During this second attempt the RAF was required to provide the advancing land forces with an "umbrella" against air attack. For army commanders, after their experience in Greece and

Maryland on final approach with one undercarriage leg down and one up. (*Johnny Seccombe SAAF*)

Crete, had developed a strong preference for the reassuring sight of friendly aircraft overhead and the exercise of air power out of sight, though often infinitely more effective, tended to be out of mind for the troops below. The RAF complied with the requirements and its fighter force was duly concentrated on this defensive task to the detriment of more rewarding operations. Fortunately the bombers were still free to take the offensive and their attacks on the enemy's advancing columns and against his supply lines were most successful.' (*New Zealanders with the Royal Air Force, Volume III*)

For three days from 14 June, 250 Squadron flew a series of standing patrols over the battlefield, meeting very few enemy aircraft; but when, on 18 June, the land battle swung very much in the enemy's favour, Tedder intervened and ordered all fighters to concentrate on ground strafing. This was done, the Tomahawks of 250 Squadron concentrating on the main Capuzzo–El Adem roads. Although effective this was relatively costly, as four pilots including one Australian were lost on one such operation. Owing to its tank losses the Western Desert Force had already begun to withdraw to its original positions and the enemy made no attempt to exploit his success on the ground. This was one of the newly formed squadrons, forming on 1 April 1941 from 'K' Flight at Aqir in Palestine with Tomahawks IIBs. The same month it was operating detachments at Amriya and Nicosia (Cyprus), but it was the move to Maryut in May that brought it into the Desert War.

On 14 June one of the experienced pilots, Ken Driver, was shot down over Gazala; he was one of four Hurricanes, accompanied by a single Maryland of 24 Squadron SAAF on a raid against the Gazala South airfield. The formation became split up in poor visibility and only the Maryland and Ken Driver made it to the target area – and were promptly engaged by anti-aircraft fire and attacked by fighters, with Oberleutnant Franzisket of I./JG 27 claiming both allied aircraft. His account, given in *Fighters over the Desert*, reads: 'The 14 June 1941 started a few minutes before dawn with bombs dropping and ground attacks being made on the south-east corner of the landing ground at Ain el Gazala, where 3 Staffel of JG 27 was stationed. At that time 1 Staffel were on alert. One alert rotte scrambled from the western edge of the airfield and pursued the low-flying Hurricanes in a westerly direction towards Tobruk where they caught them up.'

Running up a Tomahawk engine – manpower to hold down the tail! (*Eric Johnson SAAF*)

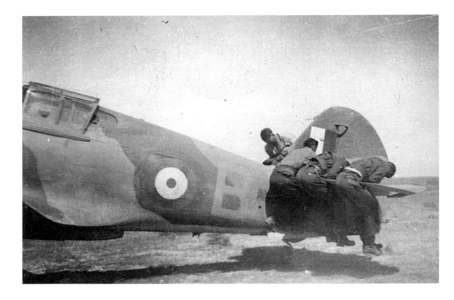

It could be that the Hurricanes referred to were those of 73 Squadron RAF that had taken off nearly an hour before Ken Driver and had run into very heavy flak. Franzisket goes on: 'In the few minutes between the first and second waves of the attack, I jumped out of my bed and took off from the southern edge of the airfield. While closing the roof of my cockpit the mechanic showed me a twin-engine aircraft approaching from an easterly direction. I took off and closed in in a right-hand turn, at which I was fired on very violently by our own flak. While still climbing at 1500 metres a single Hurricane closed in on me from in front, and somewhat higher. As my aircraft was climbing very slowly I had no other choice than to point my Bf 109 at the Hurricane, approaching "Schnauze-auf-Schnauze" (head-on), and to fire. The Hurricane fired likewise, but his bursts were too high, as I could see very clearly by the tracer. We both fired until the last second, and the aircraft touched each other. Just before this I had seen hits on the engine of the Hurricane, and Captain Driver told me afterwards that a cannon hit had set on fire the gravity tank of his Hurricane. This tank was in front of the seat and the darting flame burned his neck. When both aircraft collided, my airscrew touched the right wingtip of the Hurricane and Driver's airscrew touched the right wingtip of my Bf 109. I saw the Hurricane going down in a steep dive, and watched the pilot bale out. The Hurricane crashed some hundred metres south of the airfield, and Driver landed nearby. I turned and flew back to the airfield in a northern direction when suddenly I observed a Martin Maryland some hundred metres north-east of Gazala airfield at 1,500 metres. Although my aircraft was flying with one wing slightly low because of the damaged wingtip, I closed in and fired. The Maryland made a slight right-hand turn, I fired again, my burst going from the right engine along the whole fuselage to the tail. The right engine caught fire, the Maryland went into a flat spin and one man baled out, the bomber diving steeply and crashing some hundreds of metres north of the Via Balbia.' Ken Driver remained a PoW for the rest of the war.

While 'B Flight' of 112 Squadron had been having adventures in Crete in May and June, 'A Flight' was at Lydda refitting and gaining experience on Hurricanes, flying 80 Squadron's aircraft. It moved to Fayid in early June to complete re-equipment but not as expected with Hurricanes, instead with P-40 Tomahawk Mk.Is. The first aircraft was delivered from 102 MU on 14 June – and promptly crashed on landing! The next one was available on the 25th and the CO, Squadron Leader

Schwab, decided to collect it himself. It was his last act as CO, as the following day he was posted out and Squadron Leader D.W. Balden arrived to take command. It was also learnt that the old CO had been awarded the DFC, along with a Greek DFC. His citation read: 'This officer has led his squadron in combat against the enemy with considerable skill and has personally destroyed eleven of their aircraft. He has displayed great courage and determination.'

The same month brought a DFC for the CO of 113 Squadron, Squadron Leader Roderick Spencer: 'In June, 1941, this officer led his squadron in successive low flying attacks against a force of 100 enemy tanks which threatened our lines of communication. His determined leadership when attacking proved of great value to the ultimate success of the operations. Throughout the numerous missions in which he has participated both in the Western Desert and in Greece, Squadron Leader Spencer has displayed outstanding skill and determination.'

There was also a DFC for Flying Officer Clive Davis of 38 Squadron: 'One night in June, 1941, this officer carried out a successful attack on a target at Benghazi, afterwards flying on to Benina where, in spite of heavy anti-aircraft fire, he machine gunned aircraft on the ground from a low altitude. This officer has carried out 34 operational flights, and has at all times displayed exceptional keenness, skill and determination.'

June also saw the first success for Clive Caldwell, when 250 Squadron moved to Sidi Haneish as part of the air reinforcement for the offensive. The squadron had arrived at Mariut with Tomahawk IIBs in April and spent the rest of its war with the Desert Air Force, establishing a reputation for aggressiveness and effectiveness, as well as having a number of characters that helped ensure both its success and its fame. Caldwell had joined the squadron in early May and after a ground strafe mission on the 14th, was involved in his first air combat the following day, as he recalled: 'The next day the push up for Tobruk's relief started and the air became pretty busy. We lost a plane that day on a patrol, and had a bit of skirmishing but though we damaged a couple couldn't get a confirmation of one even. This confirmation is pretty tough – you have to give your word that you saw it actually hit the ground and two other independent reports saying the same are required before it's OK, so that, if you are over enemy country, as we mostly are, it is not easy to get the two independents even if you do see it all yourself, unless the army blokes see it and report duly …'

Battleaxe had stalled almost before it started, as Rommel launched his own thrust on 17 June, but the RAF was able to help stem this armoured drive, with General Wavell commenting: 'The enemy tanks which were heavily attacked by bombers of the R.A.F. made only half-hearted attempts to close with our forces.' He would have been accurate if he had stated that the RAF low-level attacks destroyed supplies, as once again it was the POL situation that was critical, as well as general disruption of an advancing column, as direct destruction of tanks was still difficult – they were small targets and the aircraft carried inadequate weapons.

The bald statements that RAF attacks helped is a typical matter of fact statement; looked at from the cockpit it was somewhat more exciting that that; Clive Caldwell had this to say about ground strafing in his early missions during this period: 'You can't make too many mistakes in this business for at the bottom of your dive, you are travelling like a comet with plenty to do. It's chancy work, too, for the most ill-directed shot from some gunner on the ground may sink you. Everyone is firing at you, and although most of them are wide of the mark, it is easy to run into a stray bullet.'

18th June: 'We took off at dawn and I had to land again with electrical trouble. The other seven pushed on and when I got off again 15 minutes later, they were some 60 miles on their way. Anyhow, I knew where we were to go and what needed doing, so I pushed along on my pat malone to give a bit of a personal performance. Being a bit scared of the Jerries getting me, I kept pretty low down in the seat skirting the Gulf of Sollum and cutting across the wire just below Bardia and hitting the road, Bardia to Tobruk, about 5 miles west of Bardia. Flying at about 15 feet at 250 mph, I suddenly came on two lorries. As I closed toward 'em, the crews jumped out and dived into the ditch at the roadside. I opened fire on the first truck at about 500 yards and then suddenly another chap popped out of the second truck. I gave the rudder a touch and knocked him off like a ninepin. He fairly leapt into the air and came down flat on his back in the road! Well I turned and gave the lorries another splash just to fix 'em for sure, then put a burst across the 3 Jerries lying in plain view in the ditch and so did them in.'

'About 10 miles further along, I found five lorries all dispersed in a circle and had a go at them, putting 3 out of action. In the meantime, they opened up with machine guns and a bit of tracer was flying about. I had a stab at one gun post and silenced that, fixing the two gunners and pushed off toward Tobruk. On the way I found an odd one about and gave 'em a short I sec' burst with few results. When I covered the 90 odd miles of coast I turned round and came back down it for luck, getting in another attack at the still parked 5 tracks and catching one chap mucking about with an engine, so of course he went unserviceable too. As I passed the original two lorries the four blokes were still there and hadn't wriggled so no doubt they were good and cold. Well as I got near Bardia the road goes to the right towards Sollum and I thought it might be a bit of a shock to the Jerries if I buzzed thru the middle of their big do at Bardia, so keeping right down on the deck, I ducked over the rise and was right in the middle of them before I hardly knew it myself. Well they fired all sorts of things at me but beyond a few in the tail, I came to no grief: their shooting was lousy.'

The embattled garrison at Tobruk, cut off after Rommel's advance, continued to hold out through the sheer determination of its defenders, and also the air support provided by the RAF, which included protecting shipping that took essential supplies to the garrison, as well as bombing of enemy positons, and fighter cover, albeit never enough to prevent attacks on the garrison.

On 26 June, Caldwell had his first combat success, downing a Bf 109 during a bomber escort mission to Gazala: 'All of a sudden as we sort of stooged around, down they came on us like bombs. In the first rush no one was hurt and they carried on away down in their dive. As we got near Tobruk the AA opened up and we shifted away a bit, then they arrived in force and about 40 machines got going on us. I was sort of flopping about all over the sky trying to get fixed and having a shot now and then as one flashed by. I got on one chap's tail and was just going along well when I heard a couple of sharp taps and saw some holes appear in my wing and tracer slipping by just beside the cockpit so I deduced that one must be on my tail and took plenty of violent action to spook him off. When I recovered from the shock I was at about 9000 feet and more or less unattached.'

'Then just below me, out of the general ruck … an ME109 quickly flew straight and level, so I winged over and dived on it. He saw me and dived too, but I managed to close to about 150 feet and let him have the lot. We raced on down, me firing like hell and as we got truly low, I began to pull out and he just kept right on, hit the ground and exploded with a hell of a flash. I bobbed back up to about 6000 feet and got in a go at a G–50 who got away, firing off a bit of white stuff, either smoke or glycol. I don't know which as I was again in bother from behind and had to leave. Well I got back to our advance landing ground, found a couple of my mates there and reviewed the damage. In all, I saw about 6 planes hit and explode and one or two others a bit off true. I had 16 holes in the old crate and the wireless shot away just over my head, so I was a bit lucky.'

The account of the incident in the 250 Squadron diary records Caldwell's excitement during the action and states that: 'P/O Caldwell shot down an ME 109, having shouted over the R/T for five minutes 109, 109, 109 … he has at last seen an E/A in the air and also shot it down.'

Shadow Shooting

One of the major problems for fighter pilots in the rapid turning and twisting of air combat is to get in the shot that destroys the enemy, while of course keeping a wary eye out for those others trying to shoot you down. A number of pilots, especially the Poles and Czechs in the Battle of Britain when attacking bombers, believed in getting in as close as possible in order for the bullets to have maximum effect and not to miss. Others, especially, when the target was a manoeuvring fighter, became masters of the deflection shot – in other words shooting where the enemy and bullets would be and not aiming at the aircraft directly.

We do not have the space to look at this interesting debate at length in this book, but suffice it to say that the vast majority of pilots hit nothing on the occasions they fired in air combat! Various pilots, and various leaders, came up with techniques for trying to improve air shooting, and some training was done in specialist schools. However, Clive Caldwell is thought to have been the first to introduce the idea of 'shadow shooting'. One of the noticeable things about flying low over the desert is how clear the aircraft shadows and Caldwell stated that: 'When we flew low over the desert the early morning sun cast racing shadows on the sand. When I tried to hit a colleague's shadow I missed; I fired over the shadow and well behind, but with more practice and self-correcting I soon mastered the art of deflection shooting with fixed guns.'

30th June: Captain Malcolm 'Bennie' Osler of 1 Squadron SAAF was one of two pilots to claim a Ju 87 (the other being Lieutenant Ronnie Simpson) when the squadron intercepted a formation of eight Ju 87s and eight Bf 109s. As Captain Vivian Voss recounted in *The Story of No.1 Squadron SAAF*: 'Uneventful operations had been carried out for several days, but on the last day of June our pilots ran into a formidable force of enemy aircraft. The job was a protective patrol of a convoy of ships taking stores to the garrison in Tobruk. The three pilots who took off at 1240 hours, to take over from the previous section, were Captain Bennie Osler, Lt. Ronnie Simpson and Lt. A. S. Russell. They were patrolling from south to north at respectively 8,000ft, 11,000ft and 15,000ft feet when Lt. Russell sighted eight Ju87s approaching from the south in a wide vic, with eight Me 109s as escort above them. He warned the other two over the R/T (radio telephone) and at the same time the Stukas went into line astern and dived on the ships. Both Capt. Osler and Lt. Simpson attacked

Bennie Ossler climbs out of the Squadron's 'pet' 109 – which was soon nabbed by HQ. (*Tom Meek, SAAF*)

the Stukas, each of them putting a rear-gunner out of action, and shortly afterwards the two Ju87s crashed into the sea. Two Me109s came down on Captain Osler, who broke away from the bombers to engage them, and he succeeded in out manoeuvring them and getting a long burst from quarter astern into one of them. This left the formation and headed west, with Capt. Osler on its tail. It was evidently damaged as it was losing height steadily and although normally the faster machine, was gradually being overhauled by the Hurricane. But the latter had been shot through the oil tank, and the oil temperature was rising rapidly. Capt. Osler had no option but to make for Sidi Barrani. When he left the 109, it was down to 200 feet above the sea, with small chance of reaching its base.

'When Ronnie Simpson attacked the first Ju87 he was so close to it that he nearly rammed it. As he was firing at a second Ju87 he was attacked by a Me109 and had to break away. After some quick manoeuvring he was about to deliver a frontal attack, from below, on the 109, when his guns jammed, and he had to run for Sidi Barrani. As he left the ships he found two 109s above his tail, and two more below on the starboard side. To increase his speed he pulled the plug, and although the e/a (enemy aircraft) were still gaining on him they turned back to rejoin the Stukas. Lt. Russell did not return. After his initial warning nothing more was heard or seen of him, and it was not known what part he took in the combat. His death had later to be presumed.'

Harry Gaynor in 1 Squadron SAAF Hurricane AX-X. The squadron arrived in Egypt in April 1941. (*Bomb Finney SAAF*)

Hurricane squadrons increasingly took part in strafing of ground targets, which was a hazardous operation but one that caused consternation amongst the Italian troops. (*Hannes Faure SAAF*)

Tobruk's continued survival in Allied hands also denied the Axis forces an important port. The logistics aspect of the Desert War was without doubt a key element in strategy, and success or failure of an offensive was largely dependent on supplies. The Axis forces in summer 1941 had their main base back to Tripoli, some 1,000 miles away, and even the closest port, Benghazi, was some 375 miles from the front line. That length of supply consumed significant quantities of petrol and the ports and roads were vulnerable to attack. Even more significant was the 400-mile sea journey from Italy to those ports, and Axis convoys were a prime target for Allied attack by naval and air forces. Tankers were a particularly sought-after target, and every tanker that was lost was a major blow to Rommel's capabilities.

The anti-shipping war was one of the most critical aspects of success for the Allies, with aircraft operating from desert bases and from Malta. The bombing of shipping was by now considered to be not as effective as the use of torpedo attacks. By summer 1941 the decision had been taken to increase the air torpedo attack capability by introducing the Bristol Beaufort to the Mediterranean theatre. The unit chosen to convert to the new type was 39 Squadron and although it maintained an operational Maryland detachment into early 1942, the bulk of the squadron moved in early September to Wadi Natrun for the conversion process. Many of the aircrew were from the UK-based 22 and 86 Squadrons

Beaufort of 39 Squadron at Wadi Natrun; the squadron acquired Beauforts in August 1941.

The Beaufort was primarily used for anti-shipping, initially with bombs but later, and effectively, with torpedoes.

and had flown ops over Europe – the clear blue skies in the Med provided no cover and in the endless black humour of aircrew became known as 'Beaufort Weather'.

Minelaying was considered to be a vital part of any campaign of attack on enemy ports and a number of Allied aircraft types undertook this work, including the Wellingtons from July onwards; the first such sortie was flown by 38 Squadron on 16 July when aircraft dropped mines in Benghazi harbour. The maritime war, or more precisely in later 1941 and 1942 – the supplies and fuel war – was to be prosecuted with vigour by the Allies from Africa and from Malta, an effective tactic. The details of this campaign, while of direct relevance to the Desert War, are only covered in brief in this book, and details can be found in *Malta Strikes Back,*, Ken Delve, forthcoming.

However, it was not just the Axis forces that had to worry about protecting shipping. A significant percentage of RAF sorties were being flown to protect coastal shipping and, in the case of Tobruk, the port area. Typical of this was 15 July when the RAF fighters were on shipping patrol; many of these ops were mixed units, with aircraft and pilots attached to other squadrons.

The long-range Hurricanes were in demand. 'The long-range aircraft did a patrol over ships which entailed 4 hours constant flying,' recorded the 73 Squadron ORB. 'At 2130 in the evening Wing informed us that our pilots had been in action and accounted for a few Huns. The details emerged the following day: 'Our pilots were just going out on their second patrol when they saw bombs falling near the lighters. An Me110 was sighted and the whole formation immediately gave chase. The Me 110 realized that he could not reach the coast and changed his course. He led our aircraft to a formation of 15 JU87s which had hitherto remained unseen, flying at about 500ft above the water. P/O Jones remained as guard whilst the others dived down onto the 87s. F/Lt smith destroyed one 87 and damaged one, P/O Wareham destroyed an 87 and a 110, P/O McDougal two 87s and a probable Me110, and P/O Edgehill bagged one 87 and damaged one. P/O Johns sighted an Me110 about to attack our machines. He dived on it and chased it a point west of Tobruk. As he was not gaining on the Hun he then turned back. On the return journey he saw 8 Ju87s crossing the coast North of Gambut. He attacked them, sending a long burst into a section of three, sending one of them down in flames. Our casualties were P/O Moss (73) and P/O Lauder (229) missing, and S/Ldr Rosier's machine badly damaged.'

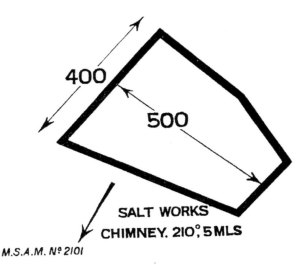

It doesn't get much more basic than this – the official plan of Wadi Natrun! A simple marked out area of desert.

The period June to November was one in which both sides looked to build up strength and supplies, and, in the case of the eighth Army, undergo extensive training that would turn it into a formidable force. With Tobruk still under siege and the Allies continuing to improve the defences of the Egyptian frontier it was in many respects a stalemate on the ground. In the air, as can be seen from our account, there was plenty of action. It was all a matter now of who would be ready first – and who would be enabled by the commanders out of theatre to be ready. Rommel was restricted in his options by the German focus on Russia, the invasion of June 1941 taking a massive amount of resources from all theatres. The British were also under pressure in the Far East and other theatres.

The long-rehearsed 'debate' as to control of air assets and their employment rose to new heights: 'The main controversy centred round the extent and control of air support for the Army. And after various conferences had failed to settle the matter, Churchill gave his ruling in a strongly worded directive. The RAF had its own dominant strategic role to play and must not, he said, "be frittered away in providing small umbrellas for the Army as it seemed to have been in the recent battle." It was unsound to distribute aircraft in this way and no air force could stand the application of such 'a mischievous practice'. On the other hand the RAF had its obligations to the Army and, Churchill declared, "When a land battle is in prospect the Army Commander-in-Chief is to specify to the Air Officer Commander-in-Chief the targets and tasks he requires to be performed both in the preparatory attack and during the battle. It would be for the Air Officer Commanding to use his maximum force for these objectives in the manner most effective." These decisions were of the utmost importance for they recognized and defined the role of the RAF and prevented any attempt to follow the German pattern of complete subordination to the Army. It was now up to all parties to realize each other's problems and to work out a satisfactory system of team work. How well they achieved this, the following years were to demonstrate.' (*New Zealanders with the Royal Air Force*)

The reorganization owed much to Tedder and as well as structural changes there were also command changes; one of the key figures to arrive in July was Air Vice-Marshal Arthur Coningham, who was to establish himself as an energetic and innovative commander of the Desert Air Force. One of his key achievements was to establish an effective relationship with the Army, not least by having Air HQ move with Army HQ, close contact led to mutual confidence. Another key player, but one often overlooked, was another New Zealander, Group Captain H.B. Russell, who served as senior air staff officer, a key role held by an experienced – but not dogmatic – fighter pilot.

The lack of a similar air-land understanding, co-operation and structure was a major failure of the German organization, the lessons of battles such as Sollum having seemingly had no effect. In fairness to the Luftwaffe in North Africa, it was also given priorities that prevented or restricted such collaboration. For example, the losses of shipping, especially supply shipping, led to an Armed Force High Command directive that: 'The X Air Corps will immediately concentrate on protecting the convoys moving along the west coast to Benghazi and Derna as well as coastal traffic between these two ports. For particularly important convoys moving from Italy to Tripoli the X Air Corps will provide air protection that will overlap by temporary transfer of fighter units to Sicily and/or North Africa.' (Oberkommando der Wehrmacht (OKW), 20 Sep 1941).

At a time when the British had woken up to the threat to Egypt, the Suez Canal and the whole Middle East, Hitler's strategic focus turned 100 per cent to Russia with the launch of the great offensive in the East … the real battle as far as he was concerned. Across the Mediterranean, from Malta to Greece and Crete, and into North Africa and, even in the Levant, the Germans were in a position from which to make major advances, and the supporting air forces had been built to a position of at least local air superiority. Additional resources would be more limited, and there was always the threat of forces being withdrawn. The win or lose scenario remained finely balanced.

Desert Life

Most RAF personnel arrived in the Middle East from more 'civilized' facilities and ordered locations, either from training bases or operational units. In the desert, away from the permanent airfields near Cairo and the Canal Zone they now led a nomadic life – a patch of desert, with or without scrub and stones, no hangars and buildings, no tarmac runways, but a collection of tents of various types and sizes, and a motley collection of trucks and other vehicles.

The men, like the 'facilities', were not dressed as one would find in 'normal' locations but instead to suit these conditions and the blue uniform of the RAF was rarely seen. In summer everyone wore khaki shorts, shirt and an RAF cap; in winter the uniform was khaki battle dress, augmented by every sweater and jersey on which the wearer could lay his hands, so cold were the nights.

The weather was also a challenge: in summer it was extremely hot and flies plagued everyone by day, but the cool of the evening was perfect, the nights silent and splendid under the brightest dome of stars and a big, round, almost 'day-bright' moon, which, however, lost a little of its fascination for it was usually as it waxed full that the landing grounds were bombed by the enemy. In winter the days were usually bright but the nights bitter, and sometimes there were torrential rains that bogged down aircraft and turned every rutted track into a morass through which truck drivers floundered and cursed.

The chief torment of the desert was, of course, the dust storms. They came more frequently with the *khamsin* of the spring, a hot wind from the south with the strength to rip down a tent. It was like a London fog, but a fog laden with grit! Under a desert dust storm the whole area darkened into half-night; a man driving a car could not see its bonnet and two men sitting in a creaking straining tent could barely discern each other across its width. While the dust storm lasted unabated, bringing gritty misery, all flying was impossible.

Desert life had its compensations; for one thing, it was extremely healthy and with the exception of desert sores – small cuts festered for months when sand filtered into them – there was almost no sickness. Life was simple and the hours of sleep were long. The food might be only bully beef for weeks on end, though usually there was something else as well, but it sufficed. There was nearly always enough water for a cup of tea and even for a bath when one had learned to bathe with a tin drinking mug.

George Beckett, of 39 Squadron, comments: 'Living conditions were reasonable with comfortable messes at the main airfields, and the bonus of relaxation on the beach of the lagoon at Maaten Bagush – each aircrew member was, in theory, meant to "relax" there at least every third day. It goes almost without saying that this admirable arrangement very rarely worked in practice! Life was not always this comfortable, however, since the Squadron frequently found itself living in tents. This is particularly true of the period late 1941 to 1943 when the Squadron moved from place to place at frequent intervals, often operating from semi-prepared stretches of desert – and most LGs were just that, there being a great profusion of these Landing Grounds throughout the desert. The basic tent could be improved by digging out the internal area of the tent for both extra space and temperature comfort and with up to six people in a ridge tent it was important to make the living area as comfortable as possible. It was quite amazing what some people were able to achieve with the meagre resources available. Alternately scorching hot by day and cold by night, the desert was an undeniably hostile environment.

'Life in camp centred on boredom, lack of palatable drinking water (it was invariably highly chlorinated, very salty and dispensed from a bowser), monotonous rations and very basic hygiene and sanitation – especially when assailed by a bout of dysentery. Plumbing was non-existent; holes in the ground sheltered by sacking being the norm – although on occasions a rough wooden seat was provided. Such facilities were not to the liking of 39 Squadron and so six Yorkshire lads were provided with a 3-tonner lorry and verbal instructions to scour the desert and "obtain" any items of furniture and such like that could be of use to the Squadron. They had been away for a week with no word and were just about given up for lost when, on the eighth day, they returned – with a lorry laden with "obtained" items including sides of beef, live chickens, tables, chairs, crockery and cutlery; and furthermore, towed behind the lorry was the piece de resistance – a six-seater wooden lavatory (bearing the insignia of a famous Guards regiment). These items of desert flotsam and jetsam were quickly divided up in democratic fashion (and no questions asked) – two seats to the officers, two to the NCOs and two to the airmen. Shortly afterwards, a number of signals flashed around the Western Desert concerning a series of "nocturnal raids by persons not thought to be German or Italian". Sadly, the magnificent throne later became the victim of a German bombing raid; fortunately, it was not occupied at the time!'

Allied airfields were under regular surveillance and key airfields were subject to night bombing, such as that of 9–10 July, with the Allies losing twenty-six aircraft destroyed and forty-nine damaged. No.2 SAAF Squadron appeared to be having more luck with the Tomahawk and departed Fayid on the 11th to start ops in the Western Desert. Seven pilots left for Takoradi on the 14th to pick up aircraft; in the meantime, three more Tomahawks were collected from the MU and the last of the Gladiators were flown away. At the end of the month news was received that approval had been given to 112 Squadron for its badge of an 'Egyptian cat Sejant' and the motto 'Swift in Destruction'. The cat had been chosen because of the squadron's association with Egypt. A number of squadrons that

Pilots of 2 Squadron SAAF; Angus Farrell is fourth from the left. (*Angus Farrell SAAF*)

made their name in the desert campaign adopted symbols for their badges that related to the region; for more on this, and the RAF Heraldry Trust project, see Appendix I, p.223.

Combat Report by Flight Lieutenant Smith, 73 Squadron, 15 July: 'At 1930 hours on 15.7.41 I was leading 8 Hurricanes of 73/229 Squadron when I sighted bomb bursts around the ships. Then I saw directly ahead two twin-engine aircraft at 10,000ft and climbed to intercept. The A/C sighted the formation and dived to get away. I followed him down but owing to a rough running engine I was overtaken by another Hurricane which proceeded to attack the Me.110. By this time we were about 1,000ft and I sighted the formation of Ju87s on the port bow. Only Blue Leader remained at 10,000ft as above guard the remaining 2 pilots in his flight following my flight down.

'My first attack on the 87 formation produced no visible result but in my second attack I closed to within 50 yards and the 87 burst into flames and nose-dived into the sea. I then looked around and saw two more 87s in formation and went after them. Just as I was about to open fire the leading 87 who was trailing white smoke suddenly burst into flames and dived into the sea. He was not being attacked by anyone at the time so was probably not claimed. I attacked the second 87 and knocked pieces of metal off him but when I closed right in to the give the final burst I ran out of ammunition and returned to base. Formation used is flexible and with practice should prove very effective.'

Flight Lieutenant Smith was on a shipping protection sortie 50 miles north-west of Sidi Barrani and the enemy formation comprised fifteen Ju 87s and five Me 110s. The formation claimed six Ju 87s and one Me 110 for the loss of two aircraft missing. The cover sheet to his report also had the comment: 'Formation was straggling owing to slowness of the LR Hurricanes compared with the SR; only leader of Blue Flt remained up as above guard owing to insufficient practice in squadron formation.'

July saw another change of commander, with General Sir Claude Auchinleck replacing Wavell as C-in-C Middle East, at the instigation of Churchill. Auchinleck was moved from command in India to take over the Middle East. Another new arrival was Air Vice-Marshal G.G. Dawson, who had previously worked with Lord Beaverbrook in the Ministry of Aircraft Production (MAP). This might seem a strange choice but in fact Dawson played a significant role in the success of Allied air operations – by ensuring that aircraft and other vital equipment was available. He was largely responsible for putting in place or improving the lines of communication from Takoradi, the crashed aircraft recovery organization, maintenance and repair facilities, and supply dumps. This 'behind the scenes' organization was to be critical in keeping the operational units equipped with aircraft, weapons, fuel and the other necessities of operating combat aircraft. Some people are particularly good at this, and Dawson was one of that breed. He subsequently (17 February 1943) was appointed *Senior Air Staff Officer* (SASO), Mediterranean Air Command.

The Axis forces were not the only ones with supply problems; the Allies had to move supplies around the Cape – the bottom of Africa – then up through the Suez Canal and then on to the front line or to storage depots. The RAF created a number of stores to hold the increasing scale of resupply; to protect the vital supplies from air attack a depot was created in the Mokattam Hills on the east bank of the Nile, clearing out caves that had been created by the Ancient Egyptians. The depots also became part of an extensive salvage and repair organization, whose tentacles spread out to recover crashed aircraft and salvage equipment. 'A special unit was established for transporting crashed aircraft from the front for reconstruction at these depots; and up in the forward area there appeared new salvage sections which, equipped with mobile cranes and special trucks, ranged the desert to bring back damaged aircraft, and mobile repair units capable of making minor repairs on the spot or else of patching up aircraft sufficiently to enable them to be flown back for more extensive treatment.' (*New Zealanders with the Royal Air Force*)

August brought mixed fortunes to 112 Squadron; conversion to the Tomahawk was the focus of the month, but with two fatal accidents the aircraft's reputation suffered, although one accident (Sergeant Johnstone) was the result of low level aerobatics over Mariut, and the second (Sergeant Mills) was down to loss of control.

On 29 August, Caldwell was one of ten Tomahawks on shipping patrol near Sidi Barrani, when they tangled with I./JG 27. Caldwell, acting as weaver, was attacked by two 109s and was hit, his aircraft being badly damaged. His combat report states: 'At approximately 1905 hours whilst acting as weaver 4 … I was attacked by two Me-109s, one coming from astern and the other from port side, neither of which I saw personally. Bullets from astern damaged tail, tail trimming gear, fuselage and starboard main plane, while the aileron on that side was destroyed and a sizeable hole made in the trailing edge and flap, evidently by cannon shells, a quantity of splinters from which pierced the cowling and side of the cockpit, some entering my right side and legs. Fire from the port side … damaged the fuselage, a number of bullets entering my left shoulder and hip, small pieces of glass embedding in my face, my helmet and goggles being pulled askew across my nose and eyes – no doubt by a near miss. As a result of the hits on the mainplane and probable excessive avoiding action the aircraft spun out of control. Checking the spin, I blacked out when pulling out of the ensuing dive, recovering to find flames in the cockpit. Pulling the pin from the safety harness I started to climb out to abandon the aircraft, when the fire, evidently caused by burning oil and not petrol as I thought, died out, so I decided to remain and attempt a landing. Looking behind me as I crossed the coast at about 500 feet some six miles east of Sidi Barrani … I saw a number of planes manoeuvring … in a manner suggesting an engagement. As my plane seemed to answer controls fairly well, apart from turns … I made a gradual turn and climbed back towards said aircraft finally carrying out an attack on what I believed to be an Me-109. Having previously lost the pin to my harness I was holding the straps in my left hand for security which together with damage sustained to aircraft made it inadvisable to attempt much in the way of quick change of altitude so I carried straight on to very low level and continued to base arriving at 2010 hours. Using half flap only I landed to find the starboard tyre flat as the result of a bullet hole.'

Nursing his damaged aircraft back to base he was still able to shoot down a 109. Despite his injuries he made a good landing. The 250 Squadron diary noted Caldwell's only comment was: 'I didn't think it could ever happen to me.' He was subsequently awarded a DFC, the citation reading: 'This officer has performed splendid work in the Middle East operations. He has at all times shown dogged determination and high devotion to duty which have proved an inspiration to his fellow pilots. On one occasion, during a patrol, he was attacked by 2 Messerschmitt 109's. His aircraft was badly damaged, while he himself received wounds on his face, arms and legs. Nevertheless, be courageously returned to the attack and shot down one of the hostile aircraft. Flight Lieutenant Caldwell has destroyed at least 4 enemy aircraft.' (Later in the war he was awarded the DSO – Wing Commander Caldwell, 19 Oct 1943, no specific citation: 'The King has been graciously pleased on the advice of Australian Ministers to approve the following appointments and awards in recognition of conspicuous service in operations against the Japanese.')

In August there was a DFC awarded to Flying Officer William Anstey of 70 Squadron, with the citation noting: 'This officer, as captain of aircraft, carried out 7 long distance night bombing attacks during the first 14 days in August, 1941. 4 attacks were made on shipping at Benghazi, 2 attacks on the Corinth canal and 1 on the aerodrome at Berca. Good results were obtained on each occasion. Throughout, Flying Officer Anstey displayed great efficiency and physical endurance. He has completed 43 operational missions, involving nearly 300 hours flying.'

On 8 September the main party of 112 Squadron moved to LG.102 (Sidi Barrani), the aircraft arriving on the 12th and the squadron flying its first combat patrol two days later when eleven aircraft patrolled the local area. 'The formation was alerted of a bandit over Mersa Matruh at 19,000ft; the formation climbed to 16,000ft and spotted an SM.79 below them. All aircraft dived to attack. Pilot Officer Bowker (AN218) fired his wing guns only as his cannon had jammed, but in a turn he reset his cannons and returned to the attack. At 150 yards he observed petrol streaming from both tanks of the enemy aircraft, and with both cannons now working, he pumped shots into the starboard engine and the fuselage. The enemy aircraft then blew up, slightly damaging the Tomahawk.' (112 Squadron ORB)

This was the first Tomahawk victory – but on the 16th there was another fatal accident, which meant three aircraft and pilots had been lost, and so the tarnished reputation of the Tomahawk continued.

Bert Houle was part of a Hurricane reinforcement that had been ferried by into the Med on HMS *Ark Royal* and had then flown off to Malta; this was only a brief stop and the fighters were destined for Egypt (Mersa Matruh) as soon as the weather was favourable. 'Sure enough, the weather was OK the next morning [14th Sep] and we were up and fed before four o'clock. A Wellington was to lead us across this stretch of water and we all lined up behind it for take-off. The hop was quite uneventful except for being tiresome and hard on the behind. We lost one aircraft, which developed engine trouble and force-landed in the sea, the pilot was never heard from again. We all landed without mishap. The sand stirred up and drifted in great clouds behind the taxiing aircraft as they made for a petrol bowser standing near a small building. This turned out to be a canteen, which could only provide us with a bottle of warm beer to slake our thirst and a hot dog to stave off hunger. After that, we sat around until all our aircraft had been refueled, all the while speculating on our future in this barren-looking land. With perspiration already streaming down our backs, we climbed into cockpits which, by this time, had become too hot to touch with bare skin. The sun was a steady, unwinking ball of fire beating down on us so that we could almost feel the weight of its rays. Hot air lifted up from the sand, baking and parching anything it touched.

'Soon, long V-shaped columns of dust spread out behind each aircraft as we took-off. These dust clouds were a certain give-away to an enemy aircraft flying high overhead; this had been, and would still be, the cause of many aircraft being shot down without any chance to fight back.' (*All the Fine Young Eagles*; pp95–96).

Hurricanes of 94 Squadron were also undertaking night defence patrols, often referred to in the UK as 'Cats Eye' patrols. Lieutenant D. Gibson (SAAF) submitted a combat report for the night of 9/10th September: 'At approx. 0430 hours an E/A (a Ju88) was picked up by two searchlights South West of Ismailia aerodrome. The E/A was then travelling from East to West. He then put his navigation lights on and I saw a Hurricane open fire. The E/A turned right and dived past me towards the North. I chased him down from 10,000ft to about 3,000ft firing bursts at close range all the while, and he returned fire. At the bottom of his dive he flattened out and turned left. I then lost him completely. The searchlights NW of Abu Sueir picked him up again, travelling NW. I again opened up with a short burst but on his evasive action (a turn to the right) I lost him. I fired 1,870 rounds in all, and on landing I found that my aircraft had been hit three times.'

The squadron had a number of pilots airborne the same night: Lieutenant R.B. Palm (SAAF) was on layer patrol at 7,500ft over Ismailia when he saw an aircraft with navigation lights on. 'At first I thought it was a Hurricane until I saw a stream of tracer coming from its rear. I dived down after it gaining rapidly. When I caught up with it, it was very close to the ground doing violent steep turns, and the rear gunner was continuous firing at a downwards angle and also slightly upwards which made me realize that there was a fighter chasing it.

'Also I saw tracer bullets bounce off the fighter. I then opened fire at the spot where the enemy tracer was coming from and after a long burst the enemy fire ceased. Then I saw the fire from the fighter enter the E/A and I opened fire again and saw where the fighter was. I had to be careful so that I did not hit the fighter as I was slightly behind and to his right. After another burst from my comrade, I saw flames coming from the E/A. I then got in another long burst, exhausting my ammunition. I shouted over the R/T that we had got the E/A just as it crashed. I then put on my navigation lights to avoid colliding with him, and circled the E/A to see if there was anyone coming out of it. I called up our control and told them I was coming in to rearm.'

The other Hurricane was that of Lieutenant A.D. Lawrenson (SAAF) and he commented: 'I carried out an attack from astern and slightly above, firing three more long bursts until my guns stopped. I saw the port engine of the E/A catch fire and followed it until the E/A crash landed in a marsh 10 miles W of Kantara. On landing I discovered that my engine was hit in two places, also my tail unit, and one hole through the fuselage. Oil was leaking badly.'

Or maybe Lieutenant Lawrenson was involved with Lieutenant A.H. Moolman (SAAF), whose combat report is similar, although he believed his comrade in the attack was Lieutenant Garner. He too expended all his ammunition (2,400 rounds) in his attacks. Lieutenant Garner reported: 'I eventually closed to within 40 yards and fired a long burst from astern and slightly quarter and its immediate result was that his port engine burst into flames. The E/A force landed shortly afterwards on shallow water.' His aircraft was also damaged.

These combats illustrate a number of points: the initial pick up was usually through searchlight activity, it was easy to lose the target during evasion, plenty of ammunition was used, close range gave best results, and enemy gunners were pretty accurate despite the evasion!

The Luftwaffe was outnumbered but it still had a number of advantages in fighter aircraft performance and tactics. The autumn of 1941 saw the rise of a number of Luftwaffe aces in the Desert Air War, the most famous of which was Hans-Joachim Marseille of JG 27. It was also a period in which the Bf 109s proved themselves superior to the Hurricanes and Tomahawks. In one combat in the afternoon of 24 September, Marseille claimed four victories in fifteen minutes when I./JG 27 tangled with fifteen to twenty Allied fighters. Three other Allied fighters were destroyed in the same fight.

The following day, 112 Squadron recorded its first tangle with 109s: 'The patrol … was attacked out of the sun by two Bf109s. The formation, which was flying in a vic of three pairs stepped up, with two weaving aircraft above and one below, was at that time making figures of eight in a N-S direction keeping the sun on its flanks, above the fleet. Plt Off Westenra must have been one of the top cover as about 1650 he suddenly found himself being attacked. He saw them coming in time to take evasive action and call on the R/T. No one, however, heard him. Flt Lt Harrison leading No.3 Section suspected that he saw an Me 109 and then realized that an attack was developing and gave the alarm – again no one heard him! Nothing happened for about 10 minutes until, for the second time, Plt Off Westenra was also attacked and he lost the tip of his starboard wing and aileron. By keeping his stick hard over and keeping above 200kts, he was able to keep his aircraft on an even keel, but near Sidi Barrani smoke started coming from his aircraft and his .5 ammunition started to explode. At this point he baled-out successfully.' Tomahawk AK495 was the first of many 112 Squadron aircraft to be lost to German fighters.

The aircraft of 112 Squadron became well known for the 'shark teeth' painted on the aircraft noses. The squadron history records: 'The Tomahawk lends itself to a design of this sort, with the large gaping intake beneath the propeller boss, and it doesn't seem to have been long before someone on the squadron thought of the idea. There is a squadron legend that one of the groundcrew tried painting the 'Helwan Cat' on one of the Tomahawks but the result looked so like a fish that it was decided to have a shark instead. Either some anonymous fitter, or, as one authority states, Plt Off Westenra, decided that what the radiator needed was a mouth, and so to distinguish his own aircraft from a distance, he painted on the first sharks teeth. Unfortunately for him, everyone liked the idea, and soon every aircraft carried the design. No other squadron used the design and it was not long before 112 became well known for it. The squadron went by a variety of names as a result – 'The Killer Sharks', 'The Tiger Sharks' or 'The Shark Squadron'. The colouring of the teeth and eyes were as follows: lips black, teeth white, interior of mouth bottom-half red and top-half aircraft

GL-coded Hurricanes
of 5 Squadron SAAF.
(*Fritz Johl SAAF*)

Hurricanes of 1
Squadron; the
squadron operated
IIBs during 1941.
(*Hannes Faure SAAF*)

background colour, usually desert brown. The eyes were also black, white and red. When there was time, the teeth were painted on very carefully, but in times of operational haste, when aircraft came and went on the squadron with alarming rapidity, the artistic efforts were not quite of the same standard.'

In the same month, the Eighth Army was formed and the RAF underwent reorganization as Air Headquarters Western Desert with six operational wings:

3 (SAAF) Wing:	11, 12, 21 Squadrons SAAF
253 Wing:	208, 237, 451 Squadrons
258 Wing:	1, 2, 3 SAAF Squadrons + 94, 238, 274 Squadrons
262 Wing:	4 SAAF + 112, 80, 229, 250, 260 Squadrons
270 Wing:	8, 14, 45, 55 Squadrons + Lorraine Squadron
269 Wing:	30 Squadron FAA

Worthy of note here is the number of SAAF squadrons – the SAAF made a major contribution to the campaign from 1941 onwards. From small beginnings of a single squadron, to entire wings of SAAF units.

No.237 (Rhodesian) Squadron had arrived in Egypt in June, after an adventurous time spent with the East African Campaign with a mixed bag of antiquated types. On arrival at the RAF Pool at Kasfareet it at last was given new aircraft, Hurricane Is, and a period of intensive training at LG Y, near Ismailia, on both the type (for pilots and groundcrew) and the operational theatre, in preparation for the planned autumn offensive.

The summer period had been relatively quiet from a strategic point of view as both sides tried to build up reinforcements, a race that the Allies were winning in that they averaged 150,000 tons a month as against just over 50,000 tons for the Axis, which was barely enough to sustain existing operations never mind from strategic reserves. Now operating Beauforts, 39 Squadron was engaged with Operation Plug from late September. This was the codename given to sea reconnaissance sorties carried out in search of enemy supply ships and was carried out twice a day by two aircraft flying on parallel courses. Such sorties were needed because Axis shipping was suspected of trying

Kittyhawk of 112 Squadron; the distinctive shark's mouths were unique for an RAF squadron. For most of 1941 the squadron was operating Tomahawks.

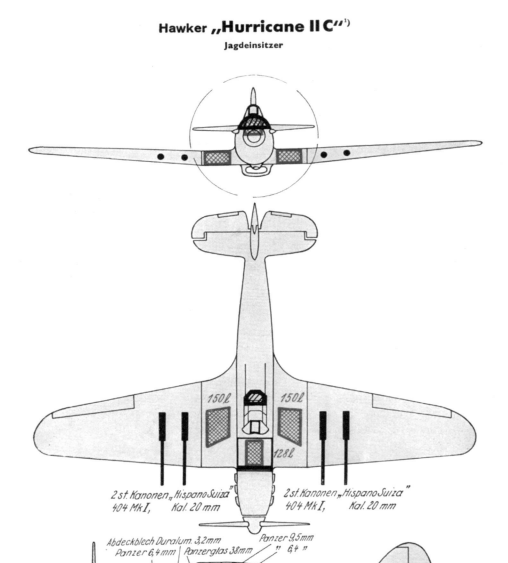

Die Kriegsflugzeuge der Feindmächte

Anlage 8 a

Großbritannien

Hawker „**Hurricane II C**"[1)]
Jagdeinsitzer

150 ℓ   150 ℓ

128 ℓ

2 st. Kanonen „Hispano Suiza"   2 st. Kanonen „Hispano Suiza"
404 MkI,   Kal. 20 mm   404 MkI,   Kal. 20 mm

Abdeckblech Duralum. 3,2mm   Panzer 9,5mm
Panzer 6,4mm   Panzerglas 38mm   " 6,4 "

[1)] Ausführung mit Kanonen, Kal. 20 mm.

The Luftwaffe's intelligence sheet on the Hurricane IIC showing armament and vulnerability (fuel tanks and crew).

to avoid the aircraft based in Malta by sailing towards south-west Greece and then turning south for a dash for Benghazi. Although tasked with compiling and passing sighting reports for use in planning larger attacks, squadron aircraft also carried out bomb and machine gun attacks on enemy merchant vessels (MVs). To reduce the effort involved in long transits to the reconnaissance areas a policy was implemented at the end of September of sending detachments of aircraft to operate from advanced landing grounds (ALGs) in the Western Desert. Mariut thus became the base landing ground (BLG) for the squadron and from there aircraft moved to the ALGs in preparation for specific operations.

Luftwaffe strength was also increased with the arrival of II./JG 27 from Russia, having re-equipped with Bf 109Fs for their new theatre of operations … but this still only gave sixty or so Bf 109s between the two units of JG 27. However, the German fighters, with experienced pilots and effective tactics, were making an impact on the air war; on 12 October 112 Squadron lost two aircraft in a dogfight, but claimed two 109s and a G.50; even better was that both pilots (Pilot Officer Parker and Sergeant Leu) were picked up, injured, by the Coldstream Guards the following day; control of the area in which combat took place was crucial in the recovery of aircrew, as well as the recovery of aircraft (and more so for the Army with tanks and vehicles). As far as salvage of aircraft was concerned, the sterling work of the recovery and salvage units (RSUs) has largely been unnoticed and unremarked, and yet that role was both dangerous and important.

Back to the issue of the 109s; 112 Squadron's history records: 'To combat the new Bf109Fs that were starting to appear over the battlefield new aerial tactics were devised. Instead of flying straight during offensive sweeps, with one or two aircraft 'weaving' at the rear, whole squadrons now 'weaved'. 'I should hate to tackle one of those formations,' wrote Tedder, 'which looks like a swarm of angry bees.' The arrival of the 109F was indeed a shock. Late September saw the arrival of II./JG 27, under Hauptmann Wolfgang Lippert, and the rotation back to Germany of I./JG 27, each Staffel taking turns to pick up new 109Fs.

Flying Officer Roberts of 3 Squadron RAAF recorded in his diary entry on 12 October: 'Took off at 7.30 to do cover over Fort Sheferzen [in the front line]. At 0900 six 109Fs attacked us from astern and high. I steep-turned and my elevators were shot away and a shell burst in my port wing. I pulled her out of the dive somehow and landed her on the wheels, taxied four miles to H.Q. of a South African unit and journeyed over the country, had prisoners, made one carry my chute. Eventually

Beaufort N1170 crash-landed at Sidi Barrani.

got back to my crate with my [ground] crew. Took tail-unit off Frank Parker's 112 Squadron kite, fixed it on mine and flew it back. Spent two nights in desert and got back to base on 14th.'

He also recorded on the 27th that the squadron was trying out new tactics: 'All the boys are practising tactical formation latterly. The C.O. has invented it. Too sixes and sevens [disorganized] to be successful. Squadrons are continually arriving round here; No.30 night fighters are here on the drome now and others coming up. I think Jerry is going to get a kick in the pants this time. Changes in Squadron routine have been made lately. One thing is the introduction of the "Pilots' Mess" instead

John Perrin of 3 Squadron RAAF.

A warning to pilots that gremlins were ever ready to cause problems to unwary pilots! (*Tom Meek SAAF*)

of Sergeants and Officers separately. Operations are dealt out equally to the squadrons now and we haven't had a great deal of work to do. Christmas is coming and the boys are all sending home cards. We have had a special card for the Squadron made, which is quite good. The last couple of days we have been hard at it censoring, etc. I'm gradually picking up my mail some time when energetic. I'll write a story about the Squadron, but that's when I'm energetic. Boys practised formation in a Wing. It was a horrible show, more a dogfight than aught else.'

And on the 29th: 'Put on our new formation, which came out successfully when several 109s tried to attack us but they couldn't. One Jerry flew along with us for a while and when he saw us turn for him he went like a bat out of hell for earth, all three squadrons after him. We gave up the chase after a while. One Tac-R lost and two of 250 Squadron. 250 got two 109s. Landed back at base and a dust storm came up which lasted all afternoon and last night. Everything covered in fine filthy dust.'

Strategic bombers were increasingly important, and to control the five Wellington squadrons in the Middle East, 205 (Heavy Bomber) Group was formed with effect from 23 October at RAF Shallufa in place of 257 (HB) Wing; it remained under the command of Group Captain L.L. Maclean. The group was not placed under the jurisdiction AHQ Egypt but remained directly under the AOC-in-C. Operational control could be granted to the AOC Western Desert when the situation demanded it. The non-fighter types are often ignored in accounts of the Desert War, but the role of the bombers, and especially types such as the Wellington, was important in the battle over supplies (anti-shipping and anti-port) as well as against direct targets such as airfields and ground formations. The table below shows the Wellington order of battle (ORBAT) just before Operation Crusader.

Kittyhawk formation; by late 1941 the number of P-40 squadrons (Tomahawk and Kittyhawk) was increasing, for example, 250 Squadron formed in April 1941 and 450 Squadron re-equipped from Hurricanes at the end of the year.

Command	Unit	Base	Aircraft
250 Wing	1 GRU	Ismailia	7 Wellington I
205 Gp	37 Sqn	Shallufa	18 Wellington IC
	38 Sqn	Shallufa	21 Wellington IC
	70 Sqn	Kabrit	18 Wellington IC
	148 Sqn	Kabrit	8 Wellington IC, 23 Wellington II
	108 Sqn	Fayid	19 Wellington IC
201 Gp	Sea Rescue Fit	LG152	4 Wellington IC
HQ Malta	40 Sqn det	Luqa	Wellington IC

The bombers of 205 Group were kept busy on strategic targets, with ports remaining the top priority in an effort to stem the flow of supplies, which meant Benghazi was 'visited' on a regular basis, so regular in fact that some squadrons referred to it as the 'Mail Run'. In the period mid-June to mid-October, the Germans recorded 72 heavy air raids on Tripoli and 102 on Benghazi.

Flying Officer J.R. Anderson was operating with 108 Squadron based at airfields in the Daba–Fuka area.

'Taxying out for take-off in the dark and swirling sand raised by other machines could be quite harrowing when the flarepath became obscured and other aircraft and obstructions not clearly definable. With take-off safely accomplished the flight to the target was usually uneventful, consisting of one long climb trying to get as much height as possible. Over Benghazi the flak was concentrated and pretty accurate – gunners and searchlight operators there had plenty of practice for there was rarely a night when no aircraft visited them. Bombing raids were seldom made above 12,000 feet as this was the best a Wellington IC could manage in the thin air even when stripped of all possible equipment. A typical mail run trip took about seven hours from the advanced base and on return there crews would

A significant number of RAF aircrew 'walked out' having crashed or baled out; this pair are probably Sergeant K. Wood and Flight Sergeant R. Spencer of 40 Squadron, who were part of the crew of Wellington DV504 lost over Tobruk.

The Wellingtons of 205 Group were an essential part of denying supplies to Rommel.

be interrogated and then after a short rest until dawn their aircraft would be refuelled for the return to base.

'We had a rather eventful trip one night towards the end of October while making our bombing run over Benghazi. We were caught in a searchlight cone and then hit several times by anti-aircraft fire. The fuselage was badly holed, hydraulic pipeline severed and the undercarriage fell down and bomb doors jammed open. The extra drag reduced our speed on the flight back and when we were about ten miles short of our advanced base one of the engines cut out owing to lack of petrol so I gave the order to bale out. Just after they had gone the other engine stopped and the aircraft began to go down in a glide. There was no time for me to leave the controls and clip on my parachute so I switched on the landing lamps, did up my straps and hoped for the best. Fortunately the ground was reasonably level and the Wellington ploughed along and made a fairly good landing.

'This was an anti-climax but a very pleasant one after my thoughts during the last few minutes. A moment later, to my surprise, the wireless operator and rear gunner popped their heads through the door from the rear cabin to join me in wiping away the perspiration. They had missed the order to bale out.

'We rested until dawn and then leaving the two of my crew to guard the aircraft I walked north and found the road four miles away where a passing lorry gave me a lift to our advanced landing ground where two of the others had already arrived. We commandeered a truck and soon found both the aircraft and the other "caterpillars".'

The anti-shipping war was going well, with Axis losses of forty major ships, a total of 178,577 metric tons, in the period June to October, of which twenty-four were confirmed lost to direct air attack. A further ninety smaller vessels were lost. The combined loss was 270,000 tons.

Although air losses are difficult to pin down, especially in fluid combat situation and in the absence of accurate records, it appears that in the period June to October they were: Allied 198 shot down and 48 destroyed on the ground and Axis 170: 89 Italian and 81 German (air and ground). The exact numbers may not be correct, but it is interesting to note that the Allies lost significantly more aircraft than the Axis. However, a number of those Allied aircraft were recovered and returned to service, or stripped to help others return to service, whereas the Axis never established an effective recover, salvage and repair organization. Air losses on both sides were to be significant in the remainder of 1941, as the British launched a major offensive.

A Hurricane during strafing practice on the range; the sturdy nature of the type, and the fact it was a stable gun platform, made it a good ground attack machine.

Chapter 4

Operation Crusader

The Crusader offensive was launched in November and the newly constituted Desert Air Force soon gained a measure of air superiority, although it was a hard fight. It was also a period when many lessons were learned, not least in the tactical air support role. In mid-October Wing Commander Andrew Geddes was assigned from HQ Army Co-operation Command to act as an RAF liaison officer with HQ 13 Corps; he produced a report on his period in this role, and this 'Libya Oct–Dec 1941' document makes fascinating reading in that it provides a detailed account and analysis. Extracts of the report are included in the text below.

The Allies entered the offensive with 910 operational aircraft in the Middle East area, with a further 458 under repair, of which it was expected that 273 would be serviceable within fourteen days. The intense campaign put strains on the supply of aircraft, but there was never a major crisis and the squadrons were kept supplied – a bigger challenge was the drain on experienced pilots, with some squadrons suffering significant losses. The Allies estimated Axis air strength at 400–450 German and 160 Italian aircraft, although different sources give widely varying numbers, especially by type and availability!

Geddes arrived at Maaten Bagush, HQ of the Eighth Army and the DAF – 'located in holes in the sand', in the third week of October and met Air Vice-Marshal Coningham to be briefed on his role and the role of the DAF in the forthcoming offensive. While in Cairo he had been given a copy of the new training pamphlet *Direct Air Support*, which was the tactical 'bible' for air support to be used by the RAF and Army. At Maaten Bagush he was kitted out for his new role: 'It had been decided that 5 RAF Liaison Officers should be sent to Corps and Divisional HQs for the coming offensive. I was to go to 13 Infantry Corps (Lt Gen Godwin-Austin), W/Cdr Charles to 30 Armoured Corps (Lt Gen Willoughby Norrie), W/Cdr Ferrers to 4 Indian Division (Lt Gen Masservy), W/Cdr Gill to the New Zealand Division (Lt Gen Freyberg VC).

'Each RAFLO was provided with a driver and a Ford deluxe Utility-body heavy passenger car which had to carry bivouac tents, a reserve of 16 gallons of petrol, 12 gallons of water, a personal kit, arms and ammunition and navigational equipment (sun and prismatic compass) for seven days self-contained existence in an emergency.

'I attended two full-scale exercises of Direct Support involving a move of Army HQ and two Corps and their sub-formation HQs into leaguers in the desert, SW of Mersa Matruh on top of the escarpment. I visited all the squadrons detailed for Air Support at their base aerodromes and I spent a day with HQ 13 Corps and their affiliated AC Squadron, 451 Squadron RAAF (Squadron Leader Williams).

'At this time, No.253 Wing (W/Cdr Charles) was still in being and attached to HQ 13 Corps and controlling the three AC squadrons (208, 451, 237) operating on the front of the Army during the preparatory phase of the battle.'

It had been decided that the direct support tactics needed to be modified in order to make best use of the thirty-two squadrons available (sixteen fighter and sixteen bomber). 'By mutual consent of GOC Eighth Army (General Cunningham) and AOC WDAF (AVM Coningham) … it was essential that local air superiority over our advance must be maintained and that Direct Support could only be effective when the GOC and AOC were satisfied that the employment of the Air Force for Direct Support would not jeopardize the retention of local air superiority by our Air Forces.'

This led to a command and control decision that has always caused debate between 'land' and 'air' that, 'It was essential therefore that the AOC should retain complete control of the Air Forces throughout the battle and that he should have the organization under him to accept or refuse all calls for air support.'

The system put in place was for tentacles at unit level to pass requests to their corps air support control (ASC), which filtered requests and passed them on to the Air Support Section at the Battle HQ (of WDAF), which obtained approval, or not, from the AOC, in consultation with the GOC. To speed up reaction times, pilots were briefed on possible action as soon as a request was picked up for the respective ASC, but no aircraft were actually sent out until the Battle HQ approval was received.

The new system was tested during a full-scale exercise on 5 November: 'The average times for a call to reach Corps ASC from a tentacle was 10 minutes. The average time for a call to reach the Squadron briefing room from its origin at a tentacle was 18 minutes. Specimen times from the exercise:

Tentacle	'Bombs dropped'	Time lag
0700	0932	2 hr. 32 min
0745	1000	2 hr. 15 min
1025	1305	2 hr. 40 min

'These were average times and later, during the actual advance, they were not greatly improved upon.

'In my opinion, the large time lag between the initial and the bombs being dropped was due to the following causes:

a. The poor standard or training in the majority of squadrons, whose pilots were definitely lacking in flying and operational experience. The number of aircraft unnecessarily smashed up through failure to comply with the ordinary principles of airmanship was appalling. The standard of bombing-up drills and organization of the ground staff was far inferior to that seen in England.

b. The great distances to be flown from aerodrome to target, sometimes as much as 200 miles.

c. The difficulties in navigation and identification of targets in bare desert with few landmarks when the targets themselves were probably some miles for their original indicated position by the time when the bombers arrived. Visibility was often poor due to dust haze.

d. The necessity for close fighter escorts for all bombing raids entailed a rendezvous and waste of time in forming-up raids, which, due to the enemy opposition, encountered throughout the campaign by high-flying ME.109s was unavoidable. It was seldom possible to base fighter escorts and bombers on the same aerodromes.

e. Delays between briefing and the closing-up of a formation on its way to the target were caused by having to use hastily cleared strip and dust has to be allowed to blow away before the next aircraft could see to take off. The wide dispersal all over the desert round each aerodrome, made necessary by frequent enemy low-flying cannon attacks, also delayed take-off when crews were not accustomed to 'impromptu' as opposed to 'deliberate' raids, for which they could be briefed some hours in advance.

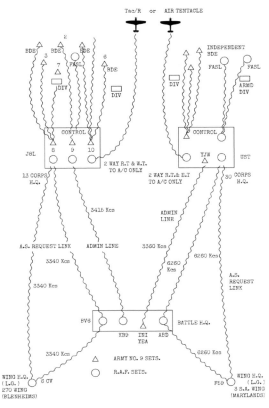

Crusader also enabled the further development of air support concepts.

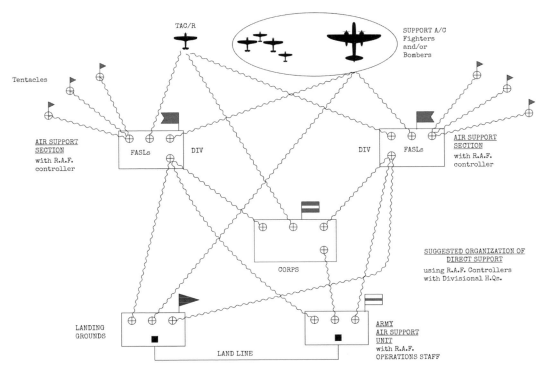

A second major exercise was conducted, but problems and results were pretty much the same. Time had run out and any improvement would have to be made as the advance progressed.

The *Crusader* Air Plan was complex. Within it, the heavy bombers of 257 Wing (205 Group by this time) were to continue their pressure on shipping and port facilities at Benghazi by night and attack such other strategic targets as might be decided on from time to time.

On the night of 1–2 November heavy losses were caused through a fog developing 'suddenly four hours before the Met expected. Of the Wellingtons operating on that occasion, seven of 148 Squadron attacked petrol dumps at Coefia, north-east of Benghazi. These aircraft were routed to alternative landing grounds as soon as the fog started to form, but all the Western Desert landing grounds were quickly obscured. Five of 148 Squadron's aircraft crash-landed, four being destroyed. Five crew members were seriously injured. Although the intensified Wellington effort resulted in further damage to port facilities and virtually stopped off-loading at night, the attempt to hit shipping at night proved the most difficult task.' (AHB Narrative, Middle East Campaigns)

It was decided that the Wellingtons should operate at maximum effort from the night of 5–6 November onwards … In their constant effort by night the Wellingtons of 257 Wing flew a total of 144 effective sorties, dropping nearly 184 short tons of bombs – including during the last week of the phase (i.e. the preparatory phase) a proportion of 4,000 pounders. The targets attacked included the moles, shipping, petrol storage, stores, and marshalling yards. There were no losses due to enemy action.

The Wellington units made use of a number of ALGs for certain of the missions, LG60, LG104 and LG106 being particularly favoured. During Phase II of the operation, and still pre-D-Day (the ground forces opening their advance on 18 November), the Wellingtons concentrated on further weakening of enemy logistics to prevent supplies reaching the battle area and also attacks on enemy airfields as part of the air superiority strategy. On many of the night missions the Fairey Albacores of 826 Squadron, Fleet Air Arm, were used as flare droppers to illuminate the target, thus ensuring that the Wellingtons could apply maximum effort to the actual bombing rather than, as previously (and subsequently), providing their own illumination aircraft.

Other reinforcements had also arrived as part of the air build-up, for example, 14 Squadron returned with its Blenheim IVs from Palestine and took over LG15 (Bagush Satellite) from 113 Squadron. Its first op took place on the night of 9–10 with six aircraft attacking dumps at Gazala North airfield.

The night raids by Wellingtons remained crucial – it was still the only type able to reach the distant ports on the North African coast. (*Michael Welchman SAAF*)

Geddes went on: 'While the majority of aircraft failed to find these targets, the alternate, the fort to the West of the aerodrome, on the edge of the bay of Mersa EL Gazala, was attacked. Bombs were dropped in the target area, one building receiving a direct hit and a fire started.' The Germans returned the favour on the afternoon of the 10th when 'two enemy aircraft dive-bombed the aerodrome; 20 bombs were dropped, of about 80kg each. One man, AC Turner, in the Photographic Section was killed. One aircraft belonging to 113 Squadron was damaged.'

The Army HQ, along with HQ WDAF, moved forward on 16 November to a patch of desert near LG75 and the railway and pipeline near Piccadilly. Geddes was ready but somewhat confused: 'As RAFLO my duties seemed rather vague, since I had no executive control of the Corps AC Squadron and the Corps Staff seemed to regard anyone who had not previously served in the desert as uneducated and unfit to give advice on air matters.'

As it turned out, the advance was to be a learning experience for everyone – with the usual highs and lows as it progressed and then petered out. The advance towards Tobruk, one of the main objectives, started well enough: 'After intensive air attacks by our bombers and fighters and heavy rainstorms along the whole of the coastal strip from Benghazi to Bug-Bug during the night of 17–18 November, a very large proportion of the enemy air force was grounded.

The ground forces rolled forward on the morning of the 18th: 'Our fighters had no engagements in the air,' reported Geddes, 'but they shot up 18 EA on aerodromes in the back areas. Our bombers attacked enemy MT and advanced aerodromes, in particular Baheira, where later 13 Corps found damaged Henschels and Me.110s.' The advance rolled on the following day, with increasing amounts of enemy armour being encountered, and the Luftwaffe making an appearance. No.1 SA Brigade was heavily attacked by Stukas. The aircraft of 451 Squadron were flying TacR and one 'gave timely warning of enemy tanks east of Sidi Omar to 4 Indian Division. HQ 13 Corps moved into LG132, on the wire at Fort Rabta, along with 451 Squadron; at 1430 hours five Me.109s followed a stray Tomahawk to the aerodrome and shot it down. They ground-strafed the aircraft of 451 Squadron at the ALG and shot-up the Corps Advanced HQ for 20 minutes; casualties – 2 Hurricanes, 3 airmen.'

Squadron serviceability dropped to five aircraft; the situation was better for 208 Squadron at Gabr Saleh and 237 Squadron at LG112. It was not all one-way traffic with ground-strafing, and 'our fighters shot-up 15 CR.42s, five Ju.87s and two Me.109s.'

The Rhodesians of 237 Squadron had been at LG112, some 30 miles east of Fort Maddalena, for a few weeks and here: 'Operations began in earnest, operations which kept everyone fully occupied. With the first dismal grey of a bitter dawn, the ground crews were out by the aircraft peering morosely at engines and checking the dials. Soon one engine would splutter reluctantly to life, then another and another, until the air was heavy with a throbbing that rose in pitch as the engines were boosted. A sharp burst of fire as the guns were tested, and the aircraft was ready for the pilot who, muffled to the ears in flying-kit, beat his chilly hands together before climbing into the cockpit. Then away the machine would taxi from the dispersal point, and, as the grey in the east brightened, the sinister, malicious-looking Hurricane, shadowy in the first light, would rise over the desert camp. Even with Hurricanes operating in pairs, army co-operation work in the Western Desert, whether it was reconnaissance or spotting for a battery, was fraught with heavy risks. Hostile aircraft were more formidable than anything the Rhodesians had met before. Lurking Macchis or Messerschmitts 109F, the new German fighters, were a frequent source of danger, and casualties were to be expected. About this time the Squadron lost Pilot Officer B.D. White, killed in action, and two pilots who crashed behind the enemy lines and were taken prisoner.' (237 Squadron history).

Time for a quick read
of *Punch* magazine
while on the move;
5 Squadron marked
its trucks with the
unit's GL code. (*Owen
McCarthy SAAF*)

Hurricane cockpit –
luxurious compared
with a 109.

No.3 Squadron RAAF was also headed to LG122 on the 20th; Harold Roberts' diary recorded:
'On the 20th some of us came into 122.LG by railway. We had 60 miles to go, rose at 0500 and arrived
here at 1600 hrs. The dammed railways are terrible. They stop every ½ hour and muck around for
hours. When we stopped for lunch a Tommy [Tomahawk] crash-landed alongside us; it was 'Slinger'
Nitschke [Pilot Officer R. Nitschke] and he had been in a scrap with Ju87s and 109s. His hydraulic
gear was shot away. He apparently shot two Ju87 and a 109. When we arrived here at LG.122, we
found we'd missed some fun. Altogether our squadron had shot down four crates. Frank Fisher had
got one 109 when he returned from a patrol with an oil throwback [engine problem]. He was coming
in to land when he tackled eight 109s strafing 451 Squadron. He got shot down, crash-landed; got
out and the Jerry shot his crate on the ground. Frank received many splinters of shrapnel in his leg

and shoulder. Buzz our pet monkey is very frisky and is jumping around our tent and crawling in with everyone; into their beds and snuggling down.' Roberts was airborne on the 22nd and was shot down, spending the next three years as a PoW.

The armoured battle was joined in earnest on the 19th and most air effort, including that of the Wellingtons, was addressed at neutralizing the enemy air force; on the three nights of 18–20 November, the 205 Group units flew 104 effective sorties against Derna, Gazala, Martuba and Tmimi, the prime targets being dispersed aircraft. The major effort was then switched to direct support of the battlefield. On 20 November there was the first use of the special Wellingtons (often referred to as 'Winston's Wellingtons' due to the Prime Minister's direct interest in such operations); a report from advanced HQ the following day stated: 'Preliminary reports from prisoners indicate tank jamming most effective causing breakdown in their communications.' Later analysis showed this to have been somewhat over-optimistic although the unit flew twenty missions during Crusader (for the loss of two of its six aircraft).

No.45 Squadron was also back in the battle, having arrived at LG75 on 14 November. On the 19th the squadron sent six individual Blenheims to attack Sidi Rezegh. One Australian crew (Z7510, Pilot Officer Magor) failed to return and a second aircraft (V5943, Squadron Leader Hughes) was shot down near Sidi Omar.

Flight Sergeant David Cliffe, in the 45 Squadron history, recalled: 'We ran out of cloud cover after leaving the target and our port engine was hit by flak. Hughes initially ordered us to prepare to bail out but changed his mind and crash landed the aircraft on its belly. In my hurry to get out of the aeroplane I did not realize that my flying helmet was still attached to the intercom plug. I found myself hanging in mid-air and had to scramble back inside to disconnect myself. We could hear the sound of heavy gunfire and saw a tank heading straight for us. We could not tell whether it was an enemy or an allied tank and could only wait anxiously to find out. The tank stopped beside our aircraft, its top hatch opened and a head emerged wearing what appeared to be a German officer's hat. The person then spoke to us and said, "I say chap are you all right?" You can imagine our relief! He was from the Dragoon Guards and he informed us that we had crash landed in the middle of a battle. We quickly scrambled into his tank which took us to the gun positions of the RHA whence we were transported to Brigade HQ. An RASC truck then took us to a forward

Formation of 84 Squadron Blenheims; Crusader was their last participation in this theatre as they moved to the Far East in January 1942.

supply depot and from there, by various means, we made our way back to the squadron which we eventually reached two days later. During our absence we had been posted missing and our next of kin had been notified. My few personal effects had been divided up by the other crews; this had included my camp bed and primus stove – two very valuable possessions in the desert. Fortunately I was able to reclaim these.'

Both sides continued to manoeuvre on the 20th, with enemy armour moving towards the Deheua ridge, being engaged by artillery, while 4th Armoured was engaging 100 or more tanks near Gabr Taieb El Essem, a duel that meant they were out of ammunition by the end of the day and had to pull back. They were resupplied that night by a Bombay aircraft, one of the unsung types of air operation in the Desert War. The division had also been the intended target of a Stuka attack, but the enemy, escorted by Me 109s, was intercepted by 250 Squadron, supported by Royal Navy fighters, and lost seven Stukas and two 109s.

'Fleets of bombers with close fighter escorts and covering sweeps passed over 13 Corps all day to bomb and drop leaflets on MT at El Adem, Gambut and in the coastal wadis north of the escarpment. Beaufighters destroyed 14 Stukas and two Me.109s on the ground at Tmimi, and two Stukas and one CR.42 in a wadi north of Capuzzo, and a further six Me.110s were destroyed in air combat. One German report states that Luftwaffe activity was low in the first few days not only because of RAF air action but also because of a torrential storm on the 16th that flooded the German–Italian airfields: 'Suddenly, high waves tore down the wadi and took everything along with them. Then tent camps in the wadis around Derna were flooded within a few minutes and several people drowned. This disaster caused by bad weather also damaged the airfields in the neighbourhood of Derna. The runway was partly flooded.' (Report by General Froehlich).

The 20th was a good day for 112 Squadron: 'The enemy made desperate efforts to support their ground troops, and the squadron got amongst them in a decisive fashion. Ten Tomahawks of

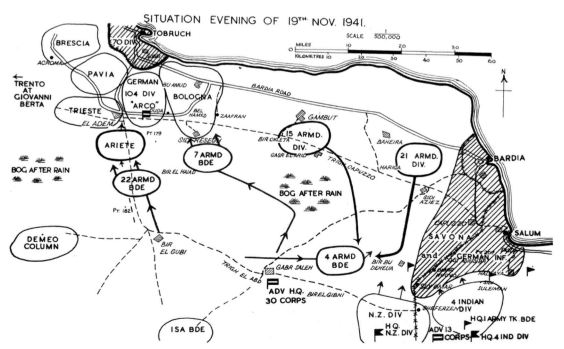

Crusader situation map, 19 November.

112 Squadron, with 12 of 3 Squadron RAAF, surprised about six Me.110 in pairs over Sidi Rezegh, our aircraft having the height advantage of about 5,000ft. Sergeant Carson made two straightforward attacks on an Me.110 that took no evasive action and was shot down with smoke pouring from it. Pilot Officer Bowker attacked another and its starboard engine blew up. As he broke away from that one he was able to attack another, which was already under fire from another Tomahawk. This aircraft eventually crashed with four Tomahawks chasing it. Pilot Officer Jeffries attacked an Me.110 which began to stream glycol or petrol from both engines, causing it to slow down and fly left-wing low. The rear gunner managed to get some hits on AN413 which resulted in Pilot Officer Jeffries having to break away. Fg Off Soden attacked two aircraft and blew the canopy off the second. The total claims for this combat were two Me.110s destroyed, one probably destroyed and two damaged. Since the RAAF squadron also claimed some destroyed it may be that most of the formation of Messerschmitts were shot down.'

Operational Summary of 80 Squadron for 21 November: '12 Hurricane escorting 16 Blenheims on bombing raid; target was MT concentrations 2 miles NW Bir Hacheim near a fort. Bombs appeared to fall well in target area, no enemy aircraft encountered. CO heard tank commanders talking on RT. 30 miles South of El Adem pilots saw puffs of smoke and sand like shell bursts in this area. A camp of semi–permanent nature 2 miles west of Half Way House on main Bardia-Tobruk road, 12 Hurricanes (bomber), bombing from 3,000 to 1,000ft at 1345 hours. All pilots claim salvoes in the camp area, wooden huts received direct hits and considerable damage caused. Ground strafing vehicles along and on either side of road going East to Dahra. Pilots claim to have damaged at least 12. Three pilots strafed persistently another camp on the North side of the escarpment NW of Gambut aerodrome. 94 × 40lb bomber dropped and 2.830 rounds of .303 fired. S/L Horgan force landed NW of Sidi Omar, his plane pancaked and he was seen to step out apparently unhurt. Much and accurate A/A fire around target area.' (80 Squadron records).

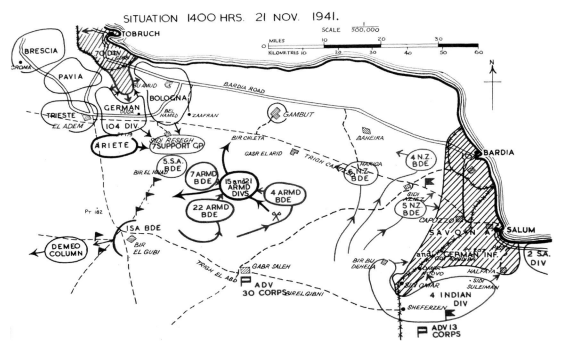

Crusader situation map, 21 November.

Tony Biden adopts the '109 stare'. (*Peter Metelerkamp SAAF*)

Posing with 112 Squadron Kittyhawk … the eyes make the overall effect more impressive. (*Ralph Harding*)

Over the next few days the ground battle continued, with gains and losses on both sides, but the loss of Sidi Rezegh aerodrome when 100 or more German tanks pushed the Allies back, meant the loss of a key feature in the drive to Tobruk. The DAF was active throughout the day, as was the Luftwaffe. On 22 November, JG 27 bounced a group of Blenheims and their Tomahawk escort, claiming four Blenheims and three Tomahawks for no loss; by the end of the day the German pilots laid claim to thirteen fighters and eight bombers, but had lost five of their own fighters – losses that were hard to replace.

The three Tomahawks were part of a twelve-aircraft escort provided by 3 Squadron RAAF to six Blenheims of 45 Squadron, the target being MT on the Acroma–El Adem road. The 109s of I./JG 27 caught them by surprise and Karl-Wolfgang Redlich and Hugo Schneider were credited with the destruction of the Tomahawks (AM378 – Eric Lane; AN416 – John Saunders; AK510 – Malcolm Watson; all the pilots were killed).

The Blenheims pressed on without escort, but were bounced by 20 Bf 109s. Only two crews made it back. Of the four aircraft shot down, seven aircrew were killed, four became PoWs, and one evaded capture and made it back. The latter was Sergeant R. Turton, who wandered the desert for two weeks heading towards Allied lines, and was eventually picked up by 2nd South African Brigade.

Ced Birkbeck was one of those who made it back and he recalls: 'In the first few moments of the attack the CO's plane was shot down as were three others. Our own plane had large shell holes in the port wing, completely wiping out the aileron. As we raced for cloud cover we noticed that some of the chaps had baled out and a few even walked back from the desert. Fortunately, there was enough cloud around to offer some protection; we were throttled back as far as possible and we stayed in cloud as long as we could. As soon as we emerged a couple of fighters would attack and we would race for the next cloud. This kept on for quite some time and resulted in our more or less flying

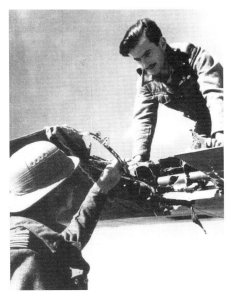

45 Squadron, Squadron Leader Austin and Sergeant Pennifer inspect damage caused by a fighter attack on 22 November. (*45 Squadron*)

in circles. Eventually the fighters must have run short of petrol; there were no more attacks and we were able to return to base. I don't think that our plane ever flew again. The other crew to return safely was that of Stuart Muller-Rowland with Phil Graebner and Ken Gardiner. Their aircraft had also been shot up.' (45 Squadron history)

113 Squadron crews use models to discuss tactics. (*113 Squadron*)

Rearming a Tomahawk.

This meant that the squadron had lost seven aircraft in the first three weeks of November and of the twenty-one aircrew involved only four had made it back, with eleven others dead, five PoWs and one wounded. The last week of the month was even busier for sorties, with eighteen flown on the 25th, the busiest single day.

The bad day for 3 Squadron was not over; an afternoon sortie had fourteen Tomahawks, with nine others from 112 Squadron, on a fighter sweep around Tobruk–El Adem. The ensuing combat with twenty or more 109s of JG 27 lasted quite some time and there were casualties on both sides:

3 Squadron, six aircraft shot down:
Pete Jeffrey (AN390) – returned to squadron
Ron Simes (AM507) – returned to squadron
Robbie Roberts (AN373) – PoW
Bill Kloster (AK390) – PoW
Lin Knowles (AN410) – KIA
Sammy Lees (AN305) – KIA

112 Squadron:
Pilot Officer Burney – returned to squadron

This had been a wing sweep led by Wing Commander Jeffreys and had been intended to find and fight the enemy. The 112 Squadron account states that 'a true picture of the combat cannot be given as it moved at great speed for the better part of an hour. For the first 15 minutes it was a free-for-all, gradually separating into individual dog-fights. Finally, 11 Tomahawks formed a defensive circle, with the Germans and Italians in a similar position slightly above. The circles flew round and round, while every now and again an aircraft, seeing some advantage, would slip out.'

Sergeant Burney was shot down but a rescue was attempted: 'Wg Cdr Rossier (who was with the formation because he was trying to get to Tobruk) landed his Hurricane beside Sergeant Burney to try to pick him up. They both tried to get off in the one aircraft but the Hurricane burst a tyre and they were forced to abandon it. There were some enemy armoured cars close by and the two pilots were obliged to make off into the gathering dusk and hike 30 miles back to our own lines where they were picked up none the worse for wear by the Indian Division.'

On a perhaps more significant note, the morning of 22nd had seen 112 Squadron undertake its first strafing sortie: 'Thirteen aircraft led by Sqn Ldr Morello carried out a very successful strafe of an enemy road column nearing El Adem on the Acroma road. It was thus that this day saw the squadron, for the very first time, turn its attention from air-to-air fighting to ground attack, which was eventually to become its only task. The formation arrived over El Adem at 1225 hours and after one circuit the motorized convoy was spotted. The CO ordered the squadron into long line astern and dived to attack. With all guns blazing the road was blitzed for about seven miles – with pieces of windscreen, fittings and wheels flying off the enemy trucks as machine after machine hedge-hopped over the line of vehicles. The whole convoy, which was mainly of tarpaulin-covered 3-ton type vehicles was brought to a standstill. The enemy opened up with small arms on the later runs, but inflicted no damage. Plt Off Sabourin was hit before the attack by flak from Sidi Omar and forced to bale out of his aircraft (AN330) which crashed in flames. He landed safely amongst the Indian Division and returned to the squadron a couple of days later.'

As part of the general focus on disrupting ground forces, the Blenheims of 14 Squadron were employed in attacking enemy MT and tanks. Typical of this activity were the sorties on 21, 22 and 23 November:

21 November: 'Seven Blenheims left LG75 for LG128, whence, escorted by fighters, and having been briefed they proceeded at 0900 hours to attack enemy MT and tanks near Bir Hacheim. In spite of some fairly accurate medium AA, excellent results were observed. One aircraft failed to release bombs due to a faulty mechanism. In all 24 x 250lb bombs were dropped. All aircraft returned safely.'

22 November: 'Sent to bomb enemy MT and tanks adjacent to El Adem–Acroma road. Flying in formation the objective was found and 4 × 250lb bombs from each aircraft fell well inside the target area. All aircraft returned to base.'

23 November: 'Concentration of enemy AFVs was found East of El Adem–Acroma road, and escorted by fighters our aircraft dropped 44 × 250lb bombs on the AFVs. Excellent results were observed and observers reported several direct hits and near misses. Bombing took place from 6,000ft. Only slight Breda type AA was experienced from El Adem itself. All our aircraft returned safely.'

The Crusader offensive was the first time that Beaufighters took part in offensive operations over the lines as opposed to long-range convoy patrols, with 272 Squadron in action. Having started life as a Coastal Command unit, 272 arrived in the Middle East in May 1941, based at Idku from mid-June with Beaufighter ICs. By the time of Crusader, it was operating from LG10. The range, firepower and rugged nature of the Beau made it suitable for freelance missions, although its large size and somewhat limited manoeuvrability also made it vulnerable. The rugged nature was tested by D.H. Hammond when they attacked Tmimi airfield: 'When their aircraft struck a telegraph pole, tearing off part of the wing, and it was only by desperately pushing the aileron control hard over that Hammond just managed to lift the damaged wing and keep on a level course. But he had not the strength to hold on for long, so he called his navigator forward and together they contrived to manage the controls and bring the aircraft safely to its base over 400 miles away, a remarkable feat of flying.' (272 Squadron ORB)

On another sortie over Tmimi, the squadron pounced on five Ju 52s that had just taken off, and promptly shot them all down, after which they strafed others on the airfield. Leaving this target, they claimed two more German aircraft, and strafed an enemy column.

Among the many stories and actions that could be told, it is worth highlighting the flying units that seldom get a mention in 'combat histories'; one such unit that arrived in the Western Desert during this period was 117 Squadron, a transport squadron that had been operating Bombays (from 216 Squadron) but on arrival with 202 Group it was equipped with the Dakota, initially in the DC-2 version, and operating from Bilbeis and Amriya.

'Transport pilots also did work during Crusader by carrying forward urgent supplies and evacuating casualties. Flying Officer Chisholm was prominent in these duties as captain of a Dakota aircraft of No.117 Squadron. At the height of the battle he helped to answer an urgent call for ammunition from British tanks near Sidi Rezegh. When the call came, ships carrying the ammunition had only reached Port Sudan in the Red Sea, so the Dakotas flew a shuttle service from that port to a landing ground near the scene of the fighting. The Dakotas continued to fly up ammunition and spares for several weeks and undoubtedly made an important contribution at a critical point in the battle. (*New Zealanders with the Royal Air Force*)

Crusader was also the first time that specialist aircraft were used for radio counter measures (RCM) in this theatre, with six special Wellingtons arriving from the UK. The aircraft were equipped to jam radio communications, the intent being to jam German communications, especially within the armour elements. The Egypt-based Wellington force also expanded with the arrival, in October, of a flight from 109 Squadron (in January the flight was renumbered becoming the Signals Squadron, until its new numberplate, 162 Squadron, was confirmed). The Signals Squadron designation indicated the unusual role of these particular Wellingtons: all were equipped for the RCM role, and in particular for electronic intelligence gathering (ELINT).

The AHB *Narrative* records this move: 'In order to hinder the enemy control of his tank forces plans were activated for the employment of Wellington ICs especially equipped for jamming inter-tank radio communications. The specialist equipment had been developed by 109 Squadron in conjunction with a number of technical experts from 80 Wing and the TRE (Telecommunications Research Establishment) ... With the use of a *Hoover* motor it was eventually found possible to convert a general purpose transmitter to emit musical jamming tones over 28–34 MCS wavebands; the power came from an ASV alternator specially fitted into the aircraft.' (AIR 26/850)

Flight trials had been conducted by 109 Squadron and in due course six of these aircraft had been flown out from England in October; experiments were subsequently carried out in Palestine with captured German tank radio sets. The Chief of Air Staff reported to the Prime Minister that: 'We should be able to jam out completely, from about 20–30 miles range, all German inter-tank signals between units 2 miles apart and perhaps less. The Wellingtons will have to fly by day and near the battle area and may, therefore, require some fighter escort, but they will not be flying all the time as the intention is to put them up only when the situation is considered opportune.'

Unfortunately, this first attempt does not appear to have met with any notable success. For one thing the Wellington aircraft themselves, flying low over the battle area, proved highly vulnerable. One night towards the end of November 1941, when Williams was on patrol over the enemy lines, his aircraft was attacked by several fighters and badly hit; the front turret was put out of action, the wireless transmitter damaged and the hydraulic tank holed. The leaking tank was plugged with rags and the wireless operator stood by holding them in place, thus enabling Williams to complete his patrol and return to base. After two of the six Wellingtons had been shot down and all the others damaged, the jamming patrols over the battle area were temporarily withdrawn.

To have effective air support over the fighting meant, as I have already highlighted, taking and using landing grounds; one of the main features of the Desert War was the constant back-and-forth over airfields, or more accurately for most locations, a patch of cleared scrub as a landing ground. It was a dangerous game in the fluid armoured conflict area and on the 23rd the recce party of 451 Squadron was sent forward to Gasr El Arid aerodrome 'but was intercepted by the enemy,' reported Geddes. 'The senior ALO, the GSO and the RE Officer in charge of the construction party were missing after their car was found burnt out 3 miles from Gasr El Arid. It was found that the area between Chleta and Gambut was not entirely free of the enemy and the ALG party must have driven straight into an enemy column. Luckily one of the heavy vehicles had a puncture and the main body of the ALG party got slightly off their course, joined by a NZ party on the Trigh Capuzzo.

'The ALG party settled down at Sidi Aziez, a good permanent German aerodrome which I inspected as soon as the Corps HQ arrived at Bir El Hariga. It has a stone-laid surface and the HQ 5 NZ Brigade with Bofors and some 25-pdrs for protection were sited alongside the aerodrome.'

The advanced HQ of 30 Corps had established itself at Gabr Saleh aerodrome and the Army commander arrived to confer with 30 Corps' commander; when he took off at 1300 the airfield was under attack by a German column. '208 Squadron ground party at the aerodrome left hurriedly and the Army Commander's Blenheim took-off through a stampede of vehicles across the aerodrome. The Bofors on the aerodrome were ordered to remain on action when they showed signs of packing up, apparently unaware of the potentialities of their weapons against tanks even when only loaded with HE.'

The German Flak 88 (an anti-aircraft weapon) was establishing a reputation as a real tank killer in the desert but the Allies tended not to follow suit with weapons like the Bofors, albeit they were not as effective as the 88 in the role.

Having been brought back up to almost full strength with new aircraft and some borrowed pilots, 451 Squadron continued its daily TacR, providing invaluable intelligence to the brigades of the corps. On the 23rd a morning sortie told the NZ Brigade that they were facing '100 tanks and MT SW of Sidi Rezegh, 160 tanks and MT to the N of Sidi Rezegh and 200 tanks and MT near Bu Amud.' Air action during the day was focused on MT between El Adem and Acroma, and pilots claimed more than 100 vehicles destroyed, as well as the destruction of a number of ammunition dumps. Claims were also made for nine enemy aircraft. At night the medium and heavy bombers attacked targets at Gazala and Benina.

Hurricane Z4795 of 451 Squadron, Sidi Aziez, December 1941.

Trying to pitch 'home'
in windy conditions;
112 Squadron.

The 22nd and 23rd had been good days for the Luftwaffe's JG 27, with claims for fourteen victories, half of which were by Wolfgang Redlich, who was the lead scorer in the gruppe at this time, for the loss of two pilots shot down and captured. The other stars of the gruppe were in 3./ JG 27 – Leutnant Hans-Joachim Marseille and Oberleutnant Gerhard Homuth; by the end of the first week of December, Marseilles, having claimed four Hurricanes in three days, was on twenty-nine confirmed victories. Total German claims over the two days were for thirty-six RAF aircraft shot down.

By this time Rommel had adopted a counter-attack tactic with his remaining armour, German and Italian, down the Trigh El Abd from El Adem and El Gubi. The central thrust crossed the wire at Sheferzen and caused havoc among the Allied supply and reinforcements, and disrupted the air control system by stranding some of the units.

Geddes reported: 'At nightfall the situation in rear of 13 Corps appeared confused with no news of 30 Corps except the report brought by General Cunningham on his visit at midday before his return to Battle HQ at Maddalena. Our bombers and fighters were turned on to attack the enemy as he approached the wire. Owing to lack of identification flags … a certain amount of indiscriminate strafing from the air took place. Since Rommel was using a large proportion of captured British vehicles, mistakes in identification were excusable. Nearly all columns both enemy and friendly in the so-called Matruh Stakes were moving in an easterly direction and it was singularly difficult for

Hannes Faure taxying
Hurricane BN173 with
1 Squadron SAAF;
the aircraft went on
to serve with an OTU
and survived to May
1945. (*Hannes Faure
SAAF*)

Engine change by the Repair and Salvage Unit (RSU); the work of recovery, salvage, and repair units enabled serviceability and aircraft availability to br kept fairly high. (*George Muir SAAF*)

Red Connor, the engineering officer for 1 Squadron ... and yet more dogs. The work of the Eng. Os and their groundcrew were greatly appreciated by the pilots. (*Bruce Rose-Christie SAAF*)

Hurricanes remained the main fighter and fighter-bomber type during Crusader, but they were increasingly outclassed by the 109s.

anyone either on the ground or in the air to pick out whether any particular cloud of dust was friend or foe.'

On 25 November, Geddes and Wing Commander Charles inspected Baheria Satellite landing ground, with the former commenting: 'Apart from a British caterpillar diesel grader and many picks and shovels left in haste by the enemy, there was nothing of interest there. We did not have time to inspect Bahia Main aerodrome north of the escarpement before darkness fell. There were some German AC aircraft there (Henschel 126s and Me.110s) damaged in our earlier ground strafes lying there. The enemy used Me.110s chiefly for AC reconnaissance. When he found that the single Me.110s were shot down, he employed pairs of Me.109s for 'dart-in' sorties, diving from a great height for a brief circuit of the target area.'

In the fluid desert, possession of the battlefield meant that you could recover damaged equipment (tanks or aircraft) and put them back into service or use them for spares, but if you did not possess the battlefield then that equipment was totally lost.

The Allied air forces were heavily engaged in the ground battle, strafing and bombing. On an early morning sortie the Tomahawks of 3 Squadron were tasked to strafe a column of tanks that were heading to the Allied lines near Sidi Omar. The Tomahawks made low-level runs and on one attack Flying Officer Roy Botwell's aircraft (AM398) was hit by ground fire and crashed; one pilot reported that he thought Bothwell had flown straight into a tank. Flying Officer Bruce Evans of the same unit was lost later in the day when his formation tangled with enemy fighters and he was last seen chasing an enemy fighter out to sea near Tobruk. A third aircraft was lost the following day when Sergeant Geoffrey Hiller was shot down by Hauptmann Karl-Wolfgang Redlich. Although he bailed out and was taken prisoner, he died of his wounds a few days later.

In the afternoon the Australians sent ten Tomahawks along with 13 from 112 Squadron on a sweep over Sidi Rezegh, led by Wing Commander Jeffreys. 'They arrived over the New Zealand troops just as they were being dive-bombed by a large force of enemy aircraft. This formation consisted of top cover of 20–25 fighters, mainly G.50s with some 109s, while in the middle were 20 medium bombers, mostly Me.110s with some Ju.88s, while at a lower level were some 15 Ju.87 dive bombers with an escort of CR.42s. No.3 Squadron attacked the Me.110s and chased them out towards the sea, the Ju.87s made for home and the top cover came down to attack 112 Squadron. The G.50s went into

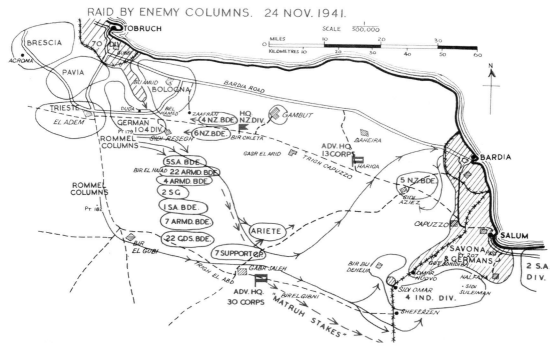

Crusader situation map, 24 November.

Rommel, November 1941; Allied air superiority was to plague Rommel in all his advances and retreats, while the disruption and destruction of his fuel supplies became a strategic decider.

a defensive circle and 112 were left to pick-off what they could. Fg Off Humphreys attacked a CR.42 which he shot down, and an Me-109F probably destroyed. Plt Off Bowker shot down an Me.110 into the sea, and Flt Lt Westenra left a CR.42 spiralling down, but he did not see what became of it. This day's fight brought the squadron's score to 88. The total for the day, including 3 Squadron, was ten destroyed, three probable and eight damaged. One aircraft of 112 Squadron, Sgt Pilot Glasgow (AK461) failed to return.' (112 Squadron ORB)

Every unit had scares as to where the enemy was; on the 25th, LG132, home of 451 Squadron, came close when 'enemy tanks passed about 5 miles to the NW. Apart from putting all their equipment on wheels and ensuring that their Bofors guns were ready to take horizontal shots, the Squadron stood firm and carried on with its job. S/Ldr Williams, OC 451 Sqn, reported that the ground party of 208 Squadron from Gabr Saleh nearly started a panic at LG132 by streaming in from Gabr Saleh reporting that the enemy tanks were just behind them. To avoid upsetting 451 Sqn they were detoured to a rendezvous near Double Cairn. 451 Sqn continued to operate from ALGs at Sidi Azeiz, LG132 and Base LG at LG75 near Piccadilly, where the Blenheims were based.' (451 Squadron ORB)

The 25th was significant in that the encirclement of Tobruk was broken when the 2nd New Zealand Division made contact with the garrison. However, in the next few days of fighting, as Rommel gradually developed a better tactical feel for the battle, this division virtually ceased to exist, with more than 2,500 men taken prisoner.

A few days later, on the 27th, part of 451 Squadron was unlucky: 'In the early morning the HQ of 5 NZ Brigade together with 451 Squadron ALG party were overrun by a force of about 35 enemy tanks supported by artillery and lorry borne infantry. F/Lt Carmichael, OC Detachment was taken prisoner. The four Hurricanes at Sidi Azeiz took off in the dark without a flare path of any kind and flew around trying to see the battle to bring back some report of what occurred. They had not enough petrol to stay up until dawn, so they flew south towards LG132 and landed in the desert, subsequently returning to their unit safely. A corporal from the ALG party later escaped by shooting a German officer with his revolver and driving a lorry full of water back to the unit. The remainder of the party except for F/Lt Carmichael [he had been moved by submarine] were recaptured in a starving condition after the fall of Bardia.'

No.84 Squadron suffered its first loss on 27 November, with Flight Sergeant Ingham-Brown being shot down by AA fire. This had been the squadron's third mission since arriving in the desert with its Blenheims, having made the move from Iraq in late September. Ken Lister writes: 'When the move took place, the aircraft were flown to Amriya just outside Alexandria with an overnight stop at Lydda which enabled the crews to see Tel Aviv and enjoy an evening out on the town.

'After their arrival at Amriya, the air party had to await the arrival of the ground crews, who were travelling in a large convoy of trucks across the desert through Jordan and Palestine. Amriya was a horrible place with the most primitive of conditions, infested with flies and subject to frequent dust storms. As we were living in tents there was little protection from either; so every opportunity was taken to get into Alexandria which catered for all kinds of entertainment, legal and otherwise.

'A reconnaissance flight was made by the two flight commanders on 31 October to inspect the proposed landing strip allocated to No.84 Squadron. They were to move there on 19 November. Notes in the PRO state that the main party arrived at Haifa on the 9th and then travelled by train. On the same day, motor transport arrived from Helwan preparatory to moving to LG. 116. An advance party led by Fg Off Bongard, the Equipment Officer, left on the 19th, followed on the 23rd by the main party led by Flt Lt B Ashmole and Flt Lt Ryan. They arrived at 1730, minus four vehicles. Two had broken down, two others had lost their way reaching Mersa Matruh and had to return via Sidi Haneish.

'The aircraft arrived the next day and, operating from nearby LG.75, flew their first operation on the 25th, bombing motor transport in the Bir Schefferzen–Gazr–el–Abid triangle. The following day, eight Blenheims escorted by 20 Hurricanes bombed troops at Magen Bel Hared. Sqn Ldr James led nine aircraft on a bombing raid on the El Cuscia area. Log books report it was very successful.' (*Scorpions Story, the Story of 84 Squadron History*, Don Neate, Air Britain).

The battle around Tobruk and towards Sollum was poised to disrupt or destroy the British 30 Corps and, according to a German account, they were saved by 'a well-planned flying mission by RAF units. The British flying units inflicted heavy losses on the Africa Corps. Strong British flying units intervened during daylight hours almost without interval in the ground fighting. They controlled the Via Balbia all day, so that vehicles could use it only during darkness.' Even more critical was the Allied domination of the Mediterranean supply routes.

The loss of landing areas started to have an impact, as Geddes highlighted: 'No ALG could now be used, since Sidi Rezegh and Gasr El Arid were not suitable and it was not possible to construct an ALG near Advanced HQ 13 Corps in the time available due to the number of slit trenches and damaged vehicles along the Trigh.' This did not stop the intensity of air action and bombers and fighters of both sides were constantly in action. Sometimes the effect of the bombing was discovered in a personal note, such as in the diary recovered from a soldier of the 361st Afrika Regiment and recorded by Geddes: 'During the bombing attack of last night the Afrika Corps stores went up in

The Maryland served with three SAAF bomber squadrons in the Middle East: 12, 21 and 60 Squadrons. (*Michael Welchman SAAF*)

The long-serving Blenheims started to give way to American types, although it was 1942 before this change really had much impact with the arrival of Bostons (pictured) and Baltimores.

flames, with 9 million cigars and cigarettes, 7½ litres of beer per man and the Schnapps and wine that go with it. This was our Christmas present.'

Geddes continued: 'During 28 November, 451 Sqn Tac/R produced splendid results. Flying under low cloud at about 1,200 feet, they repeatedly faced heavy AA to obtain detailed reports of the enemy forces surrounding 6 and 4 NZ Bdes and Adv. HQ 13 Corps, on whom they dropped special reprints of the 1/500,000 map, which showed the whole picture which was accurate and up to date. Strat/R, which was carried out by Marylands or Bostons, flying singly at about 20,000ft, reported 70–80 aircraft at Derna, 26 aircraft at Benina, 25 aircraft at Barce and 25 aircraft at Berca Satellite.'

29 November: 'Advanced HQ 13 Corps was located 400 yards SW of Gubbi Satellite aerodrome, Tobruch … immediately ordered 451 Sqn to Tobruch. Since the land route was closed, this was impossible. A night service of Bombay aircraft was requested to fly up army liaison officers and essential technical personnel. This service was very erratic and they made use of a flare path with paraffin flares (the only method available) a difficult undertaking. About four Tac/R Hurricanes were kept nightly at Tobruch in blast-proof camouflaged pens to fulfill immediate demands and normal servicing apart from refuelling was generally carried out at LG132.

'The question of endurance of the Hurricane I made sorties impossible from LG132 direct and the fighter sweeps of Hurricane IIs and Tomahawks also were forced to land at Tobruch to refuel. This required another sweep as top cover during refuelling in case of enemy fighter or bomber attacks from close range enemy aerodromes at Gazala and Tmimi and the Martubas which were all occupied. W/Cdr Black, the RAF detachment commander at Tobruch fortress, had no proper staff for this purpose and only one converted Italian water trailer as a petrol tanker. I arranged for army lorries and drivers to assist him together with a fatigue party for refueling which had to be carried out from 4 gallon tins. All the tins were old and the atmosphere was full of dust. We used to have about 4 days each week with heavy dust storms blowing. The dust and water condensation in the tins necessitated all refuelling for aircraft or MT to be carried out through a filter.

'Refuelling 24 fighters from each sweep, followed almost immediately by the 24 aircraft supplying top cover, was a tiring business for all the RAF personnel on the ground. Whenever aircraft circled to land, the enemy started shelling the aerodromes with their long-range 150mm guns which prevented any feeling of boredom during the refueling operations which were also carried out in what must have been record time.'

On the 30th a large air battle broke out when RAF fighters engaged a Ju 87 force, escorted by Maachi 200s and Me 109s as top cover, over El Gubbi, claiming ten shot down and eleven more damaged. A second battle took place over Gabr Saleh when a force of Fiat G.50s, Me 110s and Me 109s were engaged, the RAF claiming sixteen victories and eleven probable. Part of the battle involved a wing of twenty-four Tomahawks from 3 Squadron and 112 Squadron. The latter recorded: 'Intercepted a force of 35–40 enemy machines on their way to bomb our troops at Tobruk. The enemy were in several layers, 15 Ju.87s at 6,000ft, 20 G.50s and Macchi 200s from 7,000ft to 8,000ft, and five Me.109Fs as top cover. The Wing Commander detailed one section of 112 Squadron to watch the 109s, and the remainder of the squadron, with No.3, went for the lower formations. The attack forced the enemy to jettison his bombs and one Macchi 200 and two G.50s were destroyed and one Me.109F and one G.50 damaged. Our own losses were two Tomahawks, both pilots safe. Pilot Officer Bowker claimed one M.200 destroyed, but he was shot down himself by a G.50 and was forced to crash-land on the outskirts of LG122, his aircraft (AN338) being badly damaged. Pilot Officer Duke chased a G.50 for a long way and eventually shot it down. He was then attacked from astern by two or three Me.109s. He turned and gave one Me.109 a short burst and did some damage.

Being pursued home by another Me.109 he was finally hit in the port wing and main petrol tank. His machine went over onto its back at about 500ft and hit the ground just as it pulled out on its belly. The aircraft took to the air again, with a burst of power and crash landed. Pilot Officer Duke leapt out and had hardly cleared the aircraft when it was strafed by the Messerschmitts and set on fire. He was later picked up by a Lysander and returned to base.'

'Your fellows have been simply magnificent,' declared Freyberg. 'My men are full of admiration and gratitude' – his New Zealand Division had been a primary target for the Germans; Auchinleck expressed his appreciation for 'the magnificent co-operation of the R.A.F.' which had supplied 'a constant stream of valuable information', while their fighters provided 'almost complete protection' and the bombers disorganized the enemy 'often in answer to calls from my troops'.

Whitforce

An interesting feature of Crusader air operations was the attack on Rommel's supply lines south of Benghazi by a small force of thirty-two Hurricanes and Blenheims sent to operate from bases in the heart of the Cyrenaican desert. Although almost completely isolated and with its landing grounds under frequent attack by enemy bombers, this small force accounted for several hundred enemy vehicles, including some petrol tankers; and it destroyed more than thirty enemy aircraft in the air and on the ground. Wing Commander Eric Whitley was in charge of the two squadrons and the few RAF armoured cars that guarded their landing grounds. For two months he led this force with great determination in the face of all manner of difficulties and as well as planning its operations he led many of the Hurricane fighter sorties himself. Towards the end of November 1941, 'Whitforce', as it came to be known, was joined by Hurricanes of 73 Squadron.

The commander was awarded a DSO for this operation: 'Group Captain Whitley commanded a diversionary force comprising one Hurricane and one Blenheim squadron, an armoured car unit, and other army units. From November 1941 to January 1942, he led his force with great determination. Although heavily attacked on occasions, and isolated as they were in the desert region between Jarabub and Jalo, his force did great execution on the Axis forces using the main road round the Gulf of Sinta, and in attacking airfields. Group Captain Whitley planned all and led many of the operations. The number of enemy aircraft destroyed exceeded thirty. The excellent results achieved were, in a large measure, attributable to the leadership, steadiness and great courage of this officer. He has since commanded a wing with success.'

On 1 December 'Bennie' Osler took over as CO of 1 Squadron SAAF (and was promoted to major a few days later). To celebrate his new role he shot down three enemy aircraft on the 2nd: 'Scrambled from Tobruk, after enemy aircraft near El Adem. Ten Ju87s were sighted flying in vic, at 4000 feet, with a close escort of MC 200s and G-50s. Above them, at 7000 feet, was a medium cover of 10 MC 202s and above that at 10 000 feet, a high cover of 10 Bf 109s. The resultant scrap cost two Hurricanes destroyed, two damaged, and a pilot killed, for two Bf 109s and a MC 202 destroyed (the latter falling to Bennie) and a G-50 damaged.' (1 Squadron SAAF records)

He was awarded the DFC, which was announced the following month: 'This officer has displayed exceptional skill and leadership as squadron commander during the present campaign in Cyrenaica. In December, 1941, whilst on an operational flight, Major Osler and the pilot of another aircraft became involved in combat with a large force of enemy fighters and bombers. Despite the odds, Major Osier at once attacked and the section shot down 3 of the enemy's aircraft. Major Osler has destroyed 7 enemy aircraft. ('Bennie' Osler was subsequently awarded a bar to the DFC in April 1944, when serving with 601 Sqn)

The Allies were taking a toll of German aircraft every day, claiming nine definite and seven probable on the 2nd, but also on the ground when 'our armoured cars carried out a raid on Gazala and destroyed 3 Stuka and 10 MT vehicles. They were heavily engaged by enemy aircraft when withdrawing and suffered casualties. At one time, according to reports, they were attacked by 74 Me.110s.' (Geddes) A definite case of poking a stick into a hornet's nest!

By 1 December, 80 Squadron noted: 'No.1 Servicing Party received notification that it was to proceed next morning to LG.123 (some 3 miles NW of Maddelena) as the squadron was to form a temporary wing with the Royal Naval Fighter Squadron.' The RNFS was the short-term designation for the operational deployment to the Western Desert of 803, 805 and 805 squadrons, equipped with a mix of Hurricanes (sixteen) and Martlets (eight). The three units regained (but never really lost) their individual identities in March 1942.

Two days later the 80 Squadron ORB recorded: 'In the afternoon a bombing and strafing attack was carried out against large concentrations of motor transport along the Capuzzo track and wadis alongside it some 30kms East of El Adem. This was a highly successful operation led and pressed home with the greatest determination by S/Ldr Stephens, against strong A/A defence. The bombing was accurate and three pilots strafed a nearby encampment and more MT with effect. Much damage was caused by the attack. Three aircraft were badly damaged by A/A fire but luckily the pilots were unhurt.'

One of the main aims of the land battles in the first week of December was to open and then secure the corridor to Tobruk, and of course then push the enemy even further to the west. The air forces' role in this included keeping the air clear of Axis aircraft, and air combats were taking place daily, bombing of strategic targets, not least supply areas and aerodromes, as well as the vital Tac/R, and support of Allied artillery by spotting. Albacores performed the latter task for naval gunfire at night, dropping flares and calling fall of shot corrections. The land-based artillery received a similar service by day and on 3 December 451 Squadron 'carried out the first of their successful arty/r shoots against guns shelling the harbour. A direct hit on one gun was seen,' reported Geddes.

'In the air 4th December was a very successful day. During the previous night Wellingtons bombed concentrations in the El Adem road. During the previous night and throughout 4th December a series of raids by Albacores and Blenheims did much damage to MT concentrations on the Trigh Capuzzo. At 0835 hours Tomahawks engaged 30 Stukas which had bombed 11 Indian Infantry Bde 5 miles NW of El Gubbi. In the resulting battle, four Stukas were destroyed, one Stuka and one G.50 probably destroyed and five others damaged. At 1020 hours, Hurricanes met Stukas with fighter escort 15 miles NW of Bir El Gubi. Three Maachi 202s were destroyed and three probably destroyed; three Mc 202s and one 109F were damaged. We lost two Tomahawks and one Hurricane. The Stukas made off at ground level without attacking.'

Talking of Stukas, 39 Squadron had to move from Mariut when the base became flooded, the ORB recorded that its Ju 87 managed to get airborne off the somewhat wet airfield. The Ju 87 had been allocated to the squadron at the end of 1941 (November or December), being one of eleven aircraft that ran out of fuel behind Allied lines. It was allocated the serial HK827, repainted in RAF colours, serial and roundels, and flown by 39 Squadron pilots on exercises to give gun laying practice to the naval units in Alexandria harbour. Those crews who flew the aircraft prior to it being taken off squadron strength sometime in mid-1942, recall it as a 'basic, uncomfortable, utilitarian aircraft'.

A tragic accident occurred on 4 December. The squadrons of 270 Wing based at LG75 (14, 45 and 84 squadrons plus the Free French 'Lorraine' Squadron were briefed for a thirty-aircraft raid on MT at Sidi Rezegh. There was little wind to disperse the heavy haze of dust, which interfered with visibility, or to dictate the direction of take-off and there appears to have been some confusion over which 'runway' was in use. Squadron Leader Hughes was leading 45 Squadron that day and as he became airborne with the first vic of three aircraft from the end of the dirt strip nearest their dispersal area. He was horrified to see that the French were taking off in the opposite direction. The leading formations had missed colliding by seconds but the squadron's second vic was less fortunate.

This is Second Lieutenant Doug Allen's perception of what happened next: 'I was flying Z6446, with Ned Hammat in the nose and Geoff Gowing in the turret, in the Number 2 position on Tolman's right. Muller-Rowland and his crew were in the Number 3 position when we began our take off run. The Free French flight, whom we met about half way down the runway, came at us head-on. I was trying, with a somewhat ropey engine, to keep station on the leader when Ned, his eyes wide with horror, yelled something to me and pointed towards the nose of the aircraft. A glance in that direction and I was just in time to see the two lead aircraft lift off the ground and almost immediately collide! The Free French machine came cartwheeling down the runway – wingtip, nose, wingtip and so on, until it stopped right way up. We were none of us going as fast as we should have been but Muller-Rowland managed to pull his Blenheim into the air and went into a 'split-arse' turn, right on the deck and somehow escaped. Lagging as I was with my oiled-up engine, I slammed both throttles shut and kicked on right rudder. Luckily for all six of us the FF bloke decided to fly and pulled the +9 boost override. I can still see those four yellow 250 pounders passing only a couple of feet overhead!'

As the 45 Squadron history continues: 'The flight's leading Blenheim, V5991, exploded, killing Plt Off James Tolman, Fg Off Antony Hutton and Sgt Douglas Harris outright. The crew of the Lorraine Squadron Blenheim was badly injured, with one subsequently dying. The carnage on the airfield prevented eleven aircraft from getting off but the remaining 17 Blenheims formed up and doggedly continued with the mission which resulted in a particularly successful operation.'

Flying Officers A.M. Gill and G. Milson, who witnessed the accident, realized that nothing could be done to stop it. They had no telephone or Very pistol with which they might have been able to fire a red warning flare.

As Ken Lister, who was flying overhead at the time recalls: 'In view of what followed, it should be noted that radio silence had to be maintained and that all communications between aircraft was by hand signals. In any case the radio equipment was virtually useless and successful speech

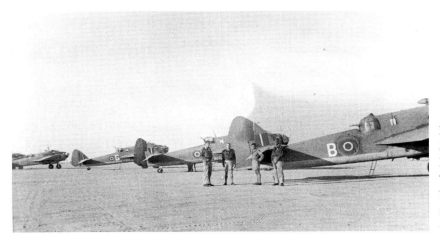

Beauforts of 39 Squadron at Gianaclis, November 1941. The squadron was by this time making a reputation for itself in the anti-shipping war.

transmission to the aircraft next to you in the formation was very rare.' (*Scorpions Story, the Story of 84 Squadron History*, Don Neate, Air Britain).

The following day, 5 December, 112 Squadron was in action with 250 Squadron: '… saw the squadron achieve as great a victory as the ones in Greece. At the end of the fight, ten enemy aircraft had been destroyed by 112 Squadron and twelve by 250 Squadron, who were led by Squadron Leader 'Killer' Caldwell. … Sighted an enemy formation of 30–40 Ju.87s in vics of three supported by 25 G.50s and M.200s as close escort. Twelve Me.109s were high flank cover in two groups of six. On sighting our aircraft a few Ju.87s jettisoned their bombs, but the majority started their bombing dive. 250 Squadron started after the Stukas and 112 engaged the fighters. The G.50s and M.200s stayed up as the Ju.87s went down, and in fact started to climb towards the Me.109s. There was a general melee, and aircraft were mixed up all around. Ju.87s got involved in the retreating G.50s and M.200s and there was a hail of fire from the ground. The final score was as follows: Plt Off Bowker destroyed three Ju.87s and damaged a G.50. Two of the Ju.87s blew up in the air, but where a formation lost an aircraft the remaining Stukas closed the gap and continued solidly towards their objective. Flt Lt Ambrose thought he had probably destroyed an M.200 and a G.50. Fg Off Soden attacked a Ju.87 and shot off its tail, which fell off by degrees in the aircraft's dive. An Me-109F that he shot at lost its engine cowling and hood but was not seen to crash. Sgt Leu attacked a M.200 from out of the sun – it did not see him coming and spun in. He also attacked a Me.109F which 'seemed to falter in the air' and then dive, but he did not see the result. Plt Off Sabourin shot down one Me.109E which fell in an uncontrolled spin with smoke coming from it, and also a G.50 which fell burning. He destroyed a Ju.87 which crashed near El Adem and in addition he damaged a G.50 and an Me.109. Plt Off Bartle shot down one Ju.87 and chased a G.50 over El Adem so that it was shot down by its own flak. Plt Off Bartle claimed this as his victory as the enemy aircraft was destroyed as

84 Squadron Blenheim; Wing Commander Boyce (CO from August 1941) and Sergeant Cherry, December 1941. (*AVM Boyce via 84 Sqn*)

a result of his action! Our own casualties were Plt Off Duke who belly-landed at Tobruk having been hit in the leg by an explosive shell.'

Squadron Leader Caldwell was leading 250 Squadron; at the end of the battle, the pilots of 112 claimed ten victories (for the loss of Pilot Officer Duke) and 250 Squadron claimed twelve.

Caldwell claimed five Stukas, and his combat report recorded: 'At 300 yards I opened fire with all my guns at the leader of one of the rear sections of three, allowing too little deflection, and hit No 2 and No 3, one of which burst into flames immediately, the other going down smoking and went into flames after losing about 1000 feet. I then attacked the leader of the rear section … from below and behind, opening fire with guns at very close range. Enemy aircraft turned over and dived steeply with the root of the starboard wing in flames … another Stuka opened fire again at close range. The enemy aircraft caught fire … and crashed in flames near some dispersed MT. … was able to pull up under the belly of the one at the rear holding the burst until very close range. The enemy aircraft dived gently straight ahead streaming smoke, caught fire and then dived into the ground … .'

Caldwell was awarded a Bar to his DFC. 'This officer continues to take his toll of enemy aircraft. One day in December 1941, Flight Lieutenant Caldwell led his flight against a number of Junkers 87s and, during the combat, he personally shot down five of the enemy's aircraft bringing his total victories to 12.'

He ended the war as the top-scoring Australian fighter pilot. In January 1942 he was promoted and moved across to 112 Squadron to become its CO.

The pilots of 80 Squadron also had a good day on the 5th: 'Two most successful operations were carried out against a large convoy of MT North of Sidi Rezegh. In the morning the convoy was moving West. Bombing except for one salvo was accurate and 7 pilots strafed lorries filled with troops causing heavy casualties. In the afternoon the same target, now stationary, was again attacked with greater effect than before. After the bombing had caused preliminary confusion, strafing was carried out by a chain of aircraft along the track leading from the Trigh Capuzzo to the main coast road. The pilots milled about the area in no uncertain fashion and with great determination against much light A/A opposition. The results of this second attack were 2 staff cars and their occupants liquidated, 2 ammunition lorries blown up, 2 fuel lorries and one light tank set on fire and many other lorries immobilized by M/G bullets. Three aircraft were damaged from both operations. S/Ldr Stephens again planned and led the attack with great skill and was followed by the squadron with enthusiasm. 80 Squadron had by now improved their tactics and its sudden and devastating sorties must have caused many a headache to the enemy.' (80 Squadron ORB).

The Axis forces around Tobruk continued to retreat and the Allied air forces continued to make life difficult for the enemy ground forces. Another convoy was set upon on the 6th by 80 Squadron: 'The target was a convoy of about 40 vehicles moving SW of El Adem. The vehicles were first scattered by accurate dive bombing after which the pilots went down and strafed at leisure. There was no opposition and the convoy, which had 2 staff cars with it, was wiped out, 11 lorries being left on fire and many casualties being caused. It was learnt later that the convoy contained an Italian Division HQ. There was no doubt that this type of target was eminently suitable for the Squadron to attack, the bigger convoys being left to Blenheims and Marylands.' (80 Squadron ORB).

On the 6th: 'Blenheims bombed MT in the El Adem area. Marylands did considerable damage to tanks and tank carriers west of El Adem. Five Stukas were destroyed by Beaufighters ground-strafing Tmimi and sweeps shot down one Me.109 and one Mc.202. During a Maryland raid on El Adem, three of the principal hangars were garnished with Red Cross flags and they had large red crosses painted on the roof. They were defended by light flak and aircraft were observed with them. One of our pilots dropped a bomb on the most suspicious of these hangars, which blew up with a heavy explosion. It was full of bombs. This so-called abuse of the Geneva Convention was seized by the Germans for propaganda and they declared on their wireless that they would retaliate. During the following three days they systematically shot up and bombed our hospitals and ambulances whenever they met them. Since none of these installations retaliated, the casualties to our sick and wounded and hospital staffs were heavy.' (Geddes). One Blenheim of GB Lorraine was lost to a fighter on this mission.

For the second night running, Tobruk was subjected to heavy air attack … 'a record bombardment which was heavy and continuous throughout the night. Little damage and no casualties resulted although there were some near misses on ships in the harbour.' (AHB Narrative, Middle East Campaign) The AA fire was mainly from Bofors, supported by various machine guns, none of which appeared to be effective, although it was impressive.

Like their counterparts in the RAF, the Luftwaffe went hunting at the airfields, as the 237 Squadron history records: 'Shortly after noon on 8th December, when many of the ground-staff and Headquarters personnel were congregated near the cookhouse, a sudden raid was made on the camp by a force of nearly a score of hostile aircraft, most of which were Messerschmitts 109 and 110. There was hardly time to reach the shelter of slit-trenches before the storm broke. The attack was short but severe. Thirty seconds of savage bombing and strafing from low level left the area a shambles of smoking debris. Four Rhodesians were killed – Corporal J. Smith, L/A/C.s A. G. Ednie and A. R. Meldrum, and AC.1 E. G. Lenthall, and ten wounded, of whom five had severe injuries. It was one of the blackest days the Squadron had known. A few days later Squadron Headquarters was shifted from Landing Ground 128 to Gambut. In this area enemy raids on camps, landing-grounds, and supply convoys were frequent, and the detached flights were lucky on several occasions to escape casualties. Sandstorms raged frequently, bringing a sinister, all-enveloping gloom, and an unpalatable grittiness to the cold bully and potatoes. At six p.m. all lights had to be out except for a hurricane-lamp in the office tent, which was hastily extinguished when the wind brought the low menacing hum of approaching enemy bombers.'

A well-known view but worth repeating – Kittyhawks on a desert strip.

Having taken on a convoy on the 7th, 80 Squadron noted for the 8th: 'Only one operation but probably the most outstanding of the whole campaign.' A formation of ten aircraft bombed the convoy on the Acroma road and 'after all aircraft had bombed, 6 pilots strafed and the remainder acted as top cover. The top cover beat off an attack by a dozen ME109s and Macchi 202s. P/O Reynolds and Sgt Mason destroying a 109 and Sgt Whyte probably destroying a Macchi 202 and damaging another. Whilst the dogfight was in progress, the six pilots led by S/Ldr Stephens strafed MT unmolested with the result that 10 lorries were left on fire and many other damaged. From this extraordinary operation all pilots returned safely though two machines were badly shot up.' The diarist praised the work of the top cover against superior numbers.

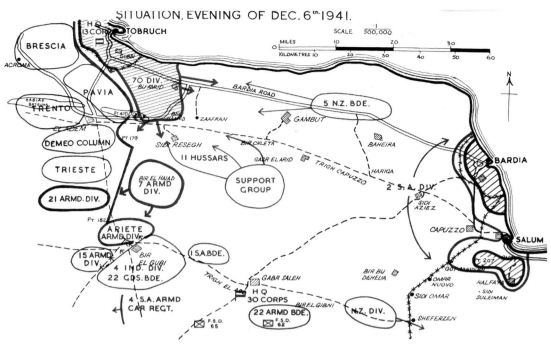

Crusader situation map, 6 December.

RAAF crew with 45 Squadron in December 1941; although there were a few specific Australian units in the desert (such as 3 Squadron RAAF), a large number of Commonwealth personnel served in RAF units. (*45 Squadron*)

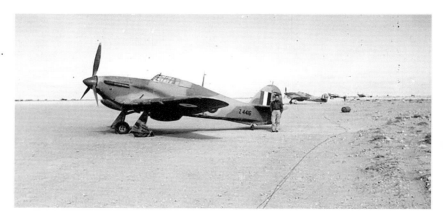

Hurricane Z4416 of 451 Squadron at Sidi Azeiz, December 1941. This Australian unit had arrived in the desert in May.

A formation of Tomahawks (nine from 3 Squadron RAAF and ten from 112 Squadron) were on a morning (9th December) sortie over the battle area when they were bounced by six 109s of I./JG 27 and three of the 3 Squadron aircraft were quickly shot down: Dave Rutter in AK378 fell to Oberleutnant Gerhard Homuth, Rex Wilson (AN457) to Unteroffizier Grimm and Tiny Cameron (AK499) to Oberleutnant Hugo Schneider (Tiny Cameron was shot down again on 11 January in combat with the same enemy, this time ending up as a prisoner); Dave Rutter and Rex Wilson were killed, while Tiny Cameron force-landed and arrived back at the squadron a few days later. Wing Commander Pete Jeffrey (AN408) force-landed at Tobruk. For 112 Squadron, Sergeant Carson's aircraft (AK533) was badly shot up and Flying Officer Sabourin (AK509) had to force-land near 20 Corps.

Squadron Leader Stephens and 80 Squadron were also busy on the 9th, and after a convoy attack were bounced by 109s: 'S/Ldr Stephens went into the dogfight and his machine was set on fire and he was wounded in both feet by a ME109F. He prepared to bail out and was actually half out of his aircraft when he saw the same enemy aircraft overshooting. He climbed back in again and shot

An attempt to camouflage a fighter in the desert – this is the only shot I have seen like this, so I assume it was not a success or frequently used. (*George Muir SAAF*)

down the ME109F, then he himself baled out. He was picked up by a Polish unit who took him into Tobruk and confirmed his victory. For courage and quick thinking S/Ldr Stephen's feat could not be bettered. Unfortunately, F/Lt Coke, Flt Sgt Rivalant and Sgt McVean were missing from this operation. Rivalant turned up again a few days later but, of the others, nothing further was heard. The loss of David Coke was a bitter blow to the squadron as his coolness, leadership and charm were a source of inspiration to all who came into contact with him. This was the first occasion on which the squadron had suffered such serious losses. No doubt it had been fortunate on other sorties but it emphasizes the need of an escort on such long trips.' (80 Squadron ORB)

It was certainly true that the Luftwaffe was more active. However, the move forwards continued and a few days later the squadron had a detachment at Gubbi Satellite, Tobruk – 'the arrival of a fighter squadron was an event for the Tobruk garrison.'

On the 10th: 'Our fighters and bombers were now getting out of range for direct support in the forward areas and equipment was brought forward from the Maddalena area to establish fighter aerodromes at Tobruch, El Adem, Bu Amud and Sidi Rezegh, with bombers at Gabr Saleh, Gabr El Arid and Sidi Azeiz. Our heavy bombers attacked the road between Cirene and Tmimi during the night, assisted by flare-dropping Albacores who kept themselves amused between dropping flares by machine-gunning the road. During the day an escorted raid of six Bostons were intercepted by 12 Me.109s which shot down 2 in flames. 3 others were missing.' (Geddes)

It was a very bad day for the Bostons of 24 Squadron SAAF; of the five aircraft lost, twelve aircrew were killed and five injured, and only three appear to have survived unhurt. The majority of the dead are commemorated on the Alamein memorial. The squadron history, in typical 'black humour' fashion refers to this as the 'Boston Tea Party'.

The following day General Ritchie and Air Vice-Marshal Coningham arrived by Blenheim to visit 13 Corps; Wing Commander Geddes escorted the AOC around a number of aerodromes. 'When we passed the derelict camp between Sidi Rezegh and Bu Amud, we came upon one of the fighter wing's advance parties with their vehicles halted in a bunch and the airmen busy looting the tents scattered in the valley which was well-sown with 'thermos' bombs and 'inkpot' grenades. When the AOC drew the attention of the OIC of the party to the danger from the men picking-up these booby-traps, which are liable to blow off limbs, the officer replied that he knew all about it as one of the men had just blown his foot off. The man had picked up a thermos bomb and, when he was told it was dangerous, he had thrown it on the ground where it had exploded and it blew his foot off.

'This incident was, in my opinion, typical of the ground discipline prevalent in the desert. It led to tremendous waste of lives and material throughout the campaign.' (Geddes). This incident highlights both the dangers of enemy locations and also the uncompromising account by Geddes.

A scare of a possible paratroop attack led to all available fighters scrambling and engaging a formation of Ju 52s and claiming four; earlier in the day a Ju 52 had been shot down by ground forces. 'The Ju.52s were not carrying paratroops but petrol which was urgently required. The enemy had about six squadrons grounded for lack of fuel. The Ju.52s had made a bad landfall east instead of west of Tobruch.' The fuel situation was made worse as 'the enemy had begun to reinforce his air forces from the Russian front and an increase in individual Ju.88 attacks was apparent.'

The Ju 88s were certainly active and, on 12 December, caught the advanced HQ of 13 Corps at Got El Talee, as Geddes reported: 'On arrival, due to exposed petrol fires cooking the food in the soldiers and officers messes, Adv. HQ was bombed from a height of about 2000ft at dusk by three Ju.88s with AP 550lb bombs intended for shipping at Tobruch. We had not had time to dig in properly and, as the ground consisted of flat slabs of rock six inches below the surface, the bombs had little crater effect and the blast and splinters travelled almost parallel with the ground. A direct hit was scored on the General's wireless truck. The casualties were two killed and seven wounded. The wireless truck was about 200 yards from me and one bomb from the stick of four fell about 40 yards from me making me slightly deaf in one ear but with otherwise little effect. An officer at G(Ops) tent saw a bomb coming and fell flat on his face. Splinters removed a piece from the back of his service cap and cut the back of his trousers behind the knees without wounding him.'

The major nuisance from the fast Ju 88s came from single aircraft making dive-bombing attacks, taking advantage of cloud cover and proving impossible to intercept.

The 12th was not a good day for 112 Squadron, with the loss of three aircraft and pilots in an early evening sortie, with claims for only one probable and one damaged. Sergeants Alves and Houston had only joined the squadron in mid-November; the former became a PoW and latter was KIA. The third pilot, Pilot Officer Jeffreys, was listed as missing. German records suggest claims of twenty-three Allied aircraft on the 12th. It was also a bad day for 80 Squadron, with four pilots failing to return when bounced by 109s and 202s, with the loss of Flying Officer Dowding, Pilot Officer Reynolds, Sergeants Whyte and Halliwell: 'More experienced pilots lost in 'Keg' Dowding and Rex Reynolds.'

In his post-war study, General der Flieger Hellmuth Felmy noted: 'On 12 December German fighters shot down 23 British planes', but of more significance, 'Since the beginning of December, German-Italian air activities had been coordinated for the first time with the ground operations of

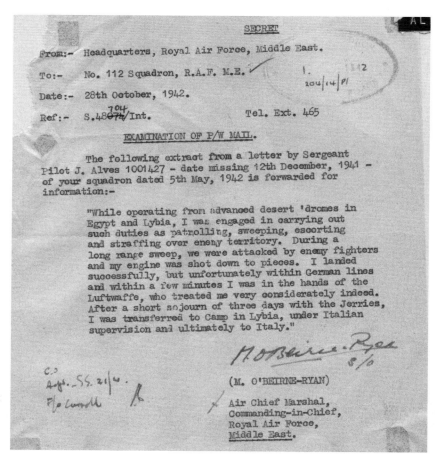

A rare and interesting survival; 'examination of P/W mail'; Sergeant Alves of 112 Squadron was shot down on 12 December.

the Panzer Group, whereupon the air operations started a noticeable influence on the course of the fighting. However, the air forces were too weak to stop the British pursuit altogether.' (*The German Air Force in the Mediterranean Theatre of War*, General der Flieger Hellmuth Felmy).

Reconnaissance showed thirty-five Ju 52s at Derna, which were promptly bombed. The transports were carrying fuel and also towing gliders full of fuel from Crete. Derna featured for 'Bobby' Gibbes on 13 December: 'We spent most of the morning on standby without being given a job, but during the afternoon we carried out a patrol in the Martuba area, led by Ed Jackson.

'We approached over Derna from the sea, below a layer of cloud at about 5,000 feet heading south. As we crossed the coast we saw six 110s escorted by 109s, and we gave chase. The enemy pilots saw us before we could close, and the 109s turned around to attack. Due to the low cloud base, they were not able to make use of the superior performance of their aircraft and could not employ their pick and zoom tactics. However, the cloud made it easier for them to take evasive action, and every aircraft which I attacked was able to pull up into the cloud. We also were not loath to make use of the cloud ourselves, and whenever I was in any danger, I would climb up into it for shelter.

'The squadron soon became split up and I found myself stooging around in company with a single Tomahawk and two 109s. One of these 109s was at this point engaged in attacking the Tomahawk, and as it took evasive action and the attacking 109 dived past and continued down, some couple of thousand feet or more below its level, I saw my chance and dived onto the second 109, carrying out a deflection shot at it from the port side, and following it around until my attack was from line astern. The 109 flicked and spun, with a wisp of smoke trailing in its wake. The Tomahawk was now on fire and going

Bobby Gibbes of 3 Squadron RAAF.

down, and its attacker started to climb up after me. If I had tried to turn into its attack, I might not have been able to get around in time, and this would leave my body exposed to its fire. If I did manage to turn in time, another head-on attack would result. (These head-on attacks always frightened the hell out of me, as I could never be sure of the enemy's method of passing. It was strange that I never was hit in these attacks, as both aircraft presented non-deflection targets to each other. When crouching low in the cockpit, watching the black smoke from the attacking aircraft guns spewing lead, and almost mesmerized by the ugly air intake of the 109 protruding from the port side of its sleek nose, I would feel the size of a house while waiting until the last second, before pushing the stick violently forward, bunting beneath it, and would breathe again, when the enemy passed close above.)

'I decided that I could climb up into the cloud before it could get into range, and I pulled up steeply at high boost. The cloud did not seem to be getting any closer; the climbing 109 was rapidly growing larger, but at last I made it just as the German pilot started to shoot. I disappeared into its friendly concealing grayness with a shower of tracer going past me and I turned hard to port in case I was still being shot at.

'I then settled onto instruments and circled within the cloud for a short period before poking my nose out below to survey the scene, fully expecting to see the fire of a burning 109 below – the aircraft I had attacked, which was still spinning when last seen – but I could only see one fire some distance away which must have been Tommy Trimble's aircraft. The second 109 had disappeared. I have since learnt that it was flown by Marseille, who had added Tommy's aircraft to his tally that day. [Marseille claimed Tomahawk AM384 of 250 Squadron, with Trimble wounded but able to crash-land, and a second victory over a 1 Squadron SAAF aircraft].

'Being now alone, I decided to make inland, hoping to find some other targets and having the cloud cover just above my level, my morale was high. I saw twelve Stukas, flying line abreast, coming towards me with their legs hanging down like eagles' reaching for their prey. These were just made for me, and I sped towards them feeling jubilant, anticipating a number of easy victories, when I suddenly saw nine 109s stalking along in line abreast at the base of the clouds, behind and above the Stukas. My plan was instantly abandoned, and I nosed up into the cloud, thinking that I hadn't been seen. I did a slow 180-degree turn and when I calculated that the enemy aircraft would have passed below me, I dived down, hoping that I would now be just behind them, and with luck, would be able to bag a 109 or two before retreating back into the cloud. I emerged amidst a milling mass of twisting and turning fighter aircraft looking for me. My guess had been wrong and I had been seen, and now, thoroughly frightened, I rapidly pulled back into the shelter of the cloud having decided to leave this little bunch well alone.

'Having regained my composure, I again dived just below the cloud and, with a wild weave, made sure that I was not in a position of any danger. Directly in front of me, heading east, were three 109s, flying away with their tails towards me. This time, I was sure that I could not have been seen and, climbing back into the cloud, I pursued them at full power. When I judged that I must be in range, I eased out of cloud and had another look. I was right behind them, but they were still out of range. I re-entered the cloud and repeated the performance. After three false attempts, and being very careful not to emerge ahead of them, I finally emerged and was in close range, but I suddenly saw that there were now only two aircraft. In a panic, I turned violently to port and was only just in time. The third aircraft was coming up at me from below and I scuttled back into cloud, almost blacking out under the high "G" force, just as he was about in range to start shooting. With my heart beating overtime, I decided that I had had enough, and would return home. Remaining in the cloud layer, I turned onto a westerly heading. After a couple of confused minutes trying to orientate myself, I calmed down sufficiently to realize my mistake and turned back, flying east.

'The cloud started to break up a little and I suddenly emerged from cloud, into a large bubble of clear air, surrounded by cloud above, below and all around, and flying sedately in this strange world, just ahead of me, was a lovely little 109. The pilot unfortunately saw me, and started climbing in a bid to escape as I closed on him and started firing, with about a 45-degree deflection, following around into a close line astern, giving him quite a hammering as he made the cloud above, and disappeared from view. I continued to spray the cloud area where he had disappeared, then I circled below waiting for him to come spinning down, but to no avail. I was sure that he must have been destroyed, so I dived below the cloud looking for his funeral pyre of black smoke, but there was no smoke. Terribly disappointed, I again turned for home remaining in cloud.

'Suddenly, I remembered the twelve Stukas, and wondered where they had been bound. It had to be near Gazala, as that was the area of our front line. I knew that I could not return home knowing about this attack, so I made towards the area. The cloud was thinning and breaking up as I approached, and on arrival, I was flying under a clear sky.

'Four Stukas were circling above the Indian troops, and about 3000 feet above were three 109s circling. I weighed up my chances of not being seen by the three fighters, and when the Stukas started into their dive, surrounded by a dense array of black puffs from exploding shells from the Bofors guns, I dived down to attack, looking up to make sure that I had not been seen by their escort. When I started to close on the Stukas, the Indians must have preferred my aircraft as their target and it seemed that every gun focused their fire on me. Perhaps this put me off as my first attack was too steep and my speed too high for accurate shooting, and my attack was abortive. I turned away, and as the three top cover aircraft were not taking any notice, I carried out a further attack on two Stukas, which had by now formed up after dropping their bombs, and I attempted to take them from abeam. As I drew into range, both aircraft turned away and their rear gunners started shooting.

'I carried out two or three attacks, but on each occasion the pilots turned their tails to me and I knew that I wouldn't be able to get the pilots who were well protected by heavy armour plate behind their seats. I saw the rear gun of one aircraft, suddenly swing up during an attack and I knew that I

'Sannie' the squadron dog of 1 Squadron SAAF, bought by Johnny Seccombe in Alexandria for 30 Piastres in November and a firm favourite with the pilots – see appendix on 'pets'. (*Johnny Seccombe SAAF*)

must have wounded or killed the gunner, but when I attacked again, the gunner in the other Stuka managed to hit my armour plate glass. There suddenly appeared a vicious looking little inner circle with spider web cracks radiating out from it, and small particles of glass came into the cockpit half blinding me. I pulled away shaking, and relieved that the glass had stopped the bullet which had been coming straight for my face. If it had been two inches to the left, there was no protective glass, and it would have been curtains for me.

'After I calmed down a little, I dived down again in search of my Stukas, but they had disappeared. I looked above and saw that the three 109s were now only little dots, heading west, out towards the Martuba aerodromes. I dived low across the front lines of our troops knowing that they must have appreciated my intervention, and I then returned to El Aden with my petrol tanks nearly empty and my ammunition almost expended. I hadn't achieved much, and all I could claim were three aircraft damaged. Others in the squadron, without having spent the hectic period that I had, had achieved better results. Tiny Cameron got one 109F confirmed and shared a second with Tommy Briggs and Nicky Barr got two, a 109 and a JU88.

There was also a DFC to Pilot Officer Geoffrey Ranger of 250 Squadron, with the citation noting: 'This officer has displayed courageous leadership and a fine fighting spirit. One day in December, 1941, during an engagement against a superior number of enemy aircraft, Pilot Officer Ranger destroyed a Junkers 88 and a Messerschmitt 109. The following day, his squadron formed part of a bomber escort in an attack on Derna. When the formation was attacked by enemy fighters, Pilot Officer Ranger shot down one of them. Two days later, over Tobruk, his section encountered a formation of enemy fighters and bombers and, in the ensuing combat Pilot Officer Ranger shot down a Messerschmitt 109F.'

Retreating air units also faced a harder task, with changes of base, lack of support infrastructure and the knowledge that you are being forced back. The pilots were tired, fuel was in short supply – and yet the Allies appeared to have an endless number of aircraft. The arrival of III./JG 27 helped and the now complete JG 27 was referred to as the 'Afrika-Geschwader'. The battles continued and by late December the unit had only six serviceable aircraft left and had lost many of its experienced pilots.

Ray Connell's Hurricane complete with damage. (*Bomb Finney SAAF*)

The Allies had their own problems, one of which was deciding on targets in the often confused and mixed up battlefield, and to avoid hitting their own side it was often the case that the bombers were ready to go but then cancelled; it was easier for the free-roaming fighter types, who had more chance to visually identify the targets.

By mid-December the advance had reached a point 1,000 miles from Cairo. This offensive, like so many in the vast Western Desert theatre, was defeated by lack of supplies and support facilities, German forces were able to disengage from their pursuers and establish a defensive line.

The RAF squadrons continued to move with the ground advance in an attempt to maintain intensive operations. On the 18th, the Blenheims of 84 Squadron moved to Gambut. Sergeant Ken Lister's comments about Gambut are well worth recording: 'At Gambut most of us found ready-made accommodation in large packing cases sunk to just below ground level which had recently been occupied by the enemy and which were still occupied, as they found later, by another adversary – FLEAS. An intensive campaign with Flit and flea powder was waged and won in a very short time. I shared quite a large and superior packing case with my observer, Alan Sharrott, my gunner Ron Pile, Ken Dicks, Alan Blackburn and two others. The case measured about twenty feet long, nine feet wide and seven feet high. On entering through the end door, one had a small ante-room about eight feet long with a table and benches along the walls and through the door at the end was sleeping accommodation with tiered bunks.

'One of the great trials of life was the shortage of water as most, if not all, of the wells were contaminated or put out of action. What water we did get was brackish and heavily chlorinated and limited to two pints per man per day. Every wash was nothing more than 'a lick and a promise' with emphasis on the promise. Tea tasted foul with salt and chlorine. Despite this water shortage, No.84 lived up to its reputation in providing a regular supply of thirst-quenching liquids at all times. This

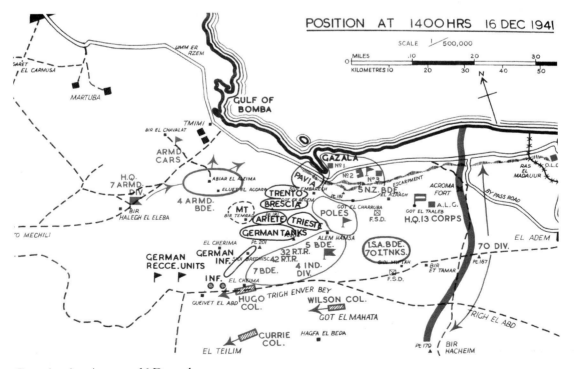

Crusader situation map, 16 December.

Another rare survival – report from the 112 Squadron intelligence officer about op on 20 December.

From:- No. 112 Squadron, Gazala.

To:-   Senior Intelligence Officer, H.Q.R.A.F.M.E.
        "   "   Advanced HQWD.
        "   "   -   No. 258 Wing.

Date:- 20th December, 1941.

Ref:-   39/Int.

Attempted Bombing of Enemy Columns on
Tocra/Benghazi Road - 20/12/41.

Seven Tomahawks of 112 Squadron, led by Squadron Leader F.V. Morello, left Gazala No. 3 Aerodrome as close escort to 12 Blenheims at 6,000 feet with 12 of 250 Squadron as top cover at 9,000 feet.

2.   On the way to the objective, when approximately 5 miles West of Maraua the whole formation was attacked by about 15 ME.109's from 10,000 feet at 1010 hours. The formation was then approaching a solid wall of cloud just ahead, i.e. a light cloud bank at 10,000' joining a heavier one rising from solid cloud base at 3,000 feet.

3.   It would seem that about 5 ME.109's dived to attack the Blenheims and were engaged by our fighters, while the remainder started a dogfight with 250 Squadron at top cover. The enemy did not appear to be in any formation, just milling around, which would suggest they had just assembled, or that some at least were on standing patrol.

4.   Our machines stayed with the Blenheims making attacks as far as possible without allowing themselves to be drawn away from the bombers.

5.   One Blenheim appeared to blow up and another was losing height with port engine on fire. A Tomahawk was also seen going down in flames.

6.   Sgt. Leu and McQueen each claim to have hit a 109F, but with no visual result, although a 109F was seen going down in flames.

7.   Squadron Leader Morello had his plane hit in several places, aileron control being shot away. His machine became temporarily uncontrollable but he managed to pull out

(continued) a few hundred feet above the ground. Coming away at this height he saw five independant fires which may have been aircraft burning on the ground.

8.   Several of the Blenheims jettisoned their bombs and split up badly, making close escort impossible, but our fighters did their best to reform the stragglers and shepherd them home. The bulk of the bomber formation disappeared in cloud and were not seen on the way back.

9.   Pilot Officer K.R. Sands and Sergeant A.H. Ferguson are missing.

10.   Sgt. McQueen reached the coast before returning home and reports heavy rain from Derna to Benghazi.

Flying Officer,
Squadron Intelligence Officer,
No. 112 Squadron, RAF.

was achieved by having two three-ton trucks regularly running between the main forward supply depot and wherever we were based. Also, whilst at Gambut, we found we were close to an abandoned enemy stores depot which I believe provided a source of wines by the carboy for those with a taste for the better things of life.

'Christmas Day was spent at Gambut and, as it was supposed to be a war between civilized nations, all fighting stopped for the day and we enjoyed something approaching a traditional Christmas dinner with lots to drink and a celebratory photograph behind a swastika flag.' (*Scorpions Sting*, *ibid*)

The squadron flew operations in the Bardia area, until the town fell on 31 December. However, a few days later the squadron received warning orders for a move to the Far East; it stopped ops on 2nd January, having flown twenty-seven sorties in its few weeks of desert ops. The significance here is that the needs of the Far East, where the war was continuing to go badly, meant that the Middle East theatre had to give up squadrons – and stop 'acquiring' aircraft that were on route to the Far East via the Middle East but that were purloined by the Middle East units!

On 19 December, the Tomahawks of 112 Squadron moved to El Adem and spent a few days escorting Blenheims on bombing raids. One such escort on the 20th highlighted the problems of such missions: 'While 250 Squadron, who were acting as top cover, engaged the majority (of the enemy fighters), five enemy aircraft got through and dived to attack the Blenheims. As our pilots were acting as close cover they could not go out to meet the enemy. One Blenheim blew up, and one started losing height with the port engine on fire. The bombers split up badly and thus invited more trouble, and gave their escort a lot of hard work. Squadron Leader Morello was hit in several places and his aileron control was shot away. He managed to pull out of the consequent dive at 500ft and make his own way home. Several of the Blenheims jettisoned their bombs and the Tomahawks had a job to shepherd them home. The bulk of the formation scattered into cloud and were not seen again. Pilot Officer Sands had developed engine trouble. He did not return to base that day and was listed as missing. Also missing was Sergeant Ferguson.'

A few days later the squadron noted that 'Sands of the Desert returns' and summarized his return: 'He force-landed about 20 miles NNW of Charuba. He ran for cover because of Me.109s flying low. Later he joined a friendly camel party of Senoussi tribesmen. They disguised him as a camel driver and took him to their tented encampment in a wadi near Si Saad by the ruins of an old fort. He spent the night on a piece of rush mat with a threadbare blanket, Arabs, goats and fleas. While they were friendly the Senoussi were not particularly anti-German, but they hated the Italians. The following day Sands looked around for friendly forces but had no success until late in the afternoon when Arabs spotted two armoured cars. Sands watched them for a long time before he made his presence known to them and they turned out to be Kings Dragoon Guards. The next day he was taken back to the Armoured Division axis and transport was provided to take him back to base.'

In addition to those quoted above, the Crusader operation brought a number of gallantry awards; the citations below are a selection.

21 Squadron SAAF, DFC to the CO, Major Johannes Britz: 'This officer, who displayed brilliant leadership in the East African campaign, continues to show outstanding qualities both as a pilot and flight commander and has led several attacks on targets in the Bardia area with distinction. On one occasion when in formation with another aircraft, during a bombing attack on Bardia both were attacked by 2 Messerschmitt 109s. The attackers shot down one of our aircraft but Major Britz fearlessly closed with the enemy and shot one of them down and, skillfully manoeuvring his aircraft, enabled his rear gunner to shoot down the other one. Throughout, this officer has displayed great courage and initiative and set an inspiring example.'

12 Squadron SAAF, DFC to Lieutenant Douglas Hillhouse: 'This officer has participated in active operations in East Africa and the Western Desert since June, 1940. He has taken part in 77 sorties, on 56 of which he has acted as air gunner and the remainder as bomb aimer. His ability to bomb his target accurately has been exceptional, and has contributed materially to the successes achieved by his unit. Lieutenant Hillhouse has shown great courage.'

107 Squadron, DFC to Wing Commander Eustace Barnes: 'This officer has performed splendid work whilst commanding the squadron. Attacks on enemy shipping in the Benghazi and Tripoli area have been attended with magnificent results and much of the successes obtained can be attributed to this officer's skill and courage. Wing Commander Barnes has also led attacks on road transports and various targets in Sicily and Italy whereby considerable damage has been inflicted on the enemy. His leadership and personal example, especially during a difficult phase of operations, have had a most beneficial effect on the morale of his flying crews. Wing Commander Barnes has carried out 35 operational missions.'

107 Sqn, DFC and DFM joint citation: Flight Lieutenant Everest Edmunds and Sergeant Sigurd Hedin: 'In November, 1941, Flight Lieutenant Edmunds and Sergeant Hedin were the pilot and navigator respectively of an aircraft which carried out an attack on shipping east of Tripoli. In spite of extremely unfavourable flying conditions Flight Lieutenant Edmunds persisted in his mission and, ably assisted by Sergeant Hedin who skillfully navigated the aircraft over 200 miles of the sea to the target area, finally attacked and scored hits on a large vessel and an escorting destroyer. Two days later, Flight Lieutenant Edmunds, with Sergeant Hedin as navigator, led a low flying attack on shipping in Navarini Bay. In spite of intense fire from the shore, several hits were scored on a 6,000 ton tanker which was set on fire. The skill and determination shown by Flight Lieutenant Edmunds, combined with the skillful and accurate navigation displayed by Sergeant Hedin, were largely responsible for the success achieved.'

80 Squadron, DFC to Flight Lieutenant David Coke: 'This officer participated in an attack on enemy transport on the El–Adem–Acroma road one day in November, 1941, in which a large number of vehicles, tanks and mechanized transport were bombed and machine-gunned. The damage inflicted played a very large part in the blocking of the road. By his skill and leadership, Flight Lieutenant Coke contributed materially to the success achieved. In addition to the low flying machine-gunning operations which have been carried out, Flight Lieutenant Coke has led the squadron with great success in air combat. During an engagement 2 days later, the squadron shared in the destruction of 5 Messerschmitt 109's.'

274 Squadron, DFC to Squadron Leader Sidney Linnard: 'This officer has shown himself to be an exceptionally resolute leader. In December, 1941, he led the squadron against a force of 15 Junkers 87's escorted by 16 fighter aircraft. The engagement resulted in the loss of 5 enemy aircraft while the remainder were dispersed. Two days later, Squadron Leader Linnard led his squadron as part of a wing escort to a formation of bombers detailed to attack enemy columns between El Adem and Sidi Rezegh. During the flight, some 30 enemy fighters were encountered but, under the skillful leadership of Squadron Leader Linnard, his squadron provided protection for the bombers for some time and, when the enemy finally attacked, 3 of their aircraft were shot down and many others damaged. Squadron Leader Linnard has participated in operational flying over a long period, including the campaigns in Greece and Syria, and has always shown courage and skill.'

Linnard had been posted to command 274 Squadron in November. On the morning of 7 December, ten Ju 87s took off with the escort of sixteen Bf 109s and twelve MC.200s to attack concentrations of motor vehicles south-east of Bir El Gobi. The MC.200s were ten fighters from the 153o Gruppo that had taken off at 10:50, together with two photo–reconnaissance MC.200s. Immediately after the dive they were attacked by about thirty enemy fighters and Maresciallo Vittorino Daffara reported: 'On 7 December, I took off from Derna airport with aircraft Macchi 200 No 5841 leader of the last section within the Gruppo led by Maggiore Favini (Ace of Clubs Group) to carry out an escort and the following photo-and-film shooting of the Stuka bombardment of the Bir El Gobi zone. Once I was over the target at an altitude of 4000 metres at 11:30, I distanced myself from the Gruppo (followed as always by my wingman) so as to be better able to make the photo-and-film shooting. I began to go down immediately after the Stukas and shot the bombardment carried out by them reaching an altitude of 500 metres.

'Once I had taken the shot, I made an about turn and got onto the return route trying to catch up with the Group of Macchis that had in the meantime made off, involved as they were in escorting the Stukas. At the same time, I observed a formation of about 30 aircraft of the Hurricane and P-40 type higher up, they were already diving down towards the Stukas to attack them. On being unable to warn the Commander of the Macchi formation of the presence of the enemy aircraft, I tried to stop them from carrying out their manoeuvre by rapidly gaining height and so swooping down from behind them.

'I managed to carry out the manoeuvre and got on their tail. I machine gunned a Hurricane that was attacking a Stuka. Instantly the British pilot broke off the attack and made off, still followed by me towards his territory. A little later I abandoned him to regain contact again with the Stukas. In this very instant, however, I noticed that another Hurricane was trying to attack a Stuka that had broken away from the formation. The greater height I was at enabled me to carry out my manoeuvre before him and get onto his tail so that I machine-gunned his aircraft successfully. The enemy, seeing that he was being pursued and the object of my rounds, started a rapid dive so as to come within a few metres of the ground followed as always by me, until with an abrupt manoeuvre similar to a spin his plane crashed into the ground at about 20 km north west of Bir El Gobi. Therefore, I reached the Stukas in time to machine-gun another Hurricane whose pilot had to change his plans and make off. I regained the altitude of 800 metres to feel more secure which was still above the Stukas that were flying a few metres from the ground. All of a sudden my attention was seized by the combat in which a Hurricane and a Macchi 200 were engaged. It just so happened that the Macchi had dragged the enemy into my immediate vicinity, so I considered that I was opportune to take him on, especially as I was a few metres higher and very fast. I fired some concentrated bursts at his tail while he tried to get out of harm's way by diving and going from side to side until some light whitish smoke came from the aircraft, he slowed down the speed of his plane so much that I had to close down almost all my plane's engine so as not to pass him.

'Therefore he landed somewhat abruptly without the undercarriage in the Giof el Baar area (south-west of El Adem). I got back with the Stukas in time to see that one of them was trying to make an emergency landing in the desert in the enemy zone. I again machine gunned another Hurricane that was attacking other Stukas but without seeing the effect. Finally, the remaining enemy aircraft made off in the vicinity of El Gazala. There was nothing else happening so I landed at Derna airfield at 12:50 after a two-hour flight.'

During a 'Jumbo' signal warning of an enemy formation in the El Adem zone, 1 Squadron SAAF and 274 Squadrons were ordered to intercept. The twelve South African Hurricanes, led by Major 'Bennie' Osler, took off from Tobruk at about 11 am. As 274 Squadron was still being refuelled it took off about ten minutes later, although a number soon returned with engine trouble.

At 11.45 am, 1 Sqn SAAF made out about nine Ju 87s at an altitude of 4,000 feet, 10 miles south-west of El Adem. They were in a V patrol with a close cover of an indefinite number of MC.200s and G.50s. The medium cover that was believed to consist of fifteen MC.202s was seen at 7000 feet (none of this type were present). Finally, there was the top cover consisting of ten Bf 109s at 10000 feet. The enemy formation must have been on its way back as it was heading west. The 1 SAAF Squadron Hurricanes were flying in pairs side by side, grouped in three sections, one of which was at a higher altitude (Blue) to cover the other two that were attacking the bombers.

The higher up section was the main concern of the Bf 109s, which were top cover. Major Osler reported: 'I was leading the Squadron on a bearing which the R/T station had given me and when at 9000 feet my attention was attracted by spurts of dust on the ground produced by fire on the formation. I saw a formation of enemy fighters and bombers some 5000 feet below. At this moment I discovered a top cover of Me 109s. They were moving into a position able to deliver an attack upon our formation. I warned the rest by means of the R.T.

'The port section of four covered my section and the starboard section while we were going down to attack the lower fighters and bombers. One of these fighters was engaged by myself and after three short bursts delivered by me, the fighter, a Mc.202, which commenced to smoke after the second attack, nosed over after the third attack to a practically vertical dive earthwards until it impacted and exploded. In conclusion 6 Me 109s made an attempt to assist the fellow I was attacking by coming in a screaming dive through us on their way home.'

The South Africans thought that the enemy formation had abandoned the battle in difficulty. In its turn 274 Squadron sighted thirty-three enemy planes (fifteen Ju 87s, six Bf 109s and twelve Macchis) west of El Adem and immediately attacked them. Its pilots observed that the German planes dived as usual and immediately regained height, while the tactics of the Italian fighters were very shoddy.

No.274 Squadron made the following claims:

- Squadron Leader Linnard (Z5064): MC.200 shot down, one probably destroyed and a third damaged
- Pilot Officer G.C. Keefer (BD880) MC.200 and a second damaged
- Pilot Officer Patrick Moriarty (Z4015) G.50 and a Ju 87
- Pilot Officer R.N. Weeks (Z4000) MC.202 as probably destroyed
- Sergeant C.R. Parbury (Z5117) claimed a damaged Ju 87, a second destroyed on the ground while it was landing to rescue the crew of another plane that had been shot down.

Three pilots were lost: Flight Lieutenant Joseph Hobbs (BD783), Pilot Officer Frank Sutton (Z5260) and Pilot Officer John Gain (Z2395).

Escort missions were never popular with fighter squadrons; however, on the 22nd a formation of six Tomahawks had a more enjoyable and successful day: 'Six aircraft attacked Magrun and took it by surprise. They waited until there were no enemy aircraft airborne in the vicinity and then attacked out of the sun. It was a case of complete surprise as there was hardly any opposition. A number of Ju.87s and a single Me.109F were just arriving or leaving and Pilot Officer Duke, after initially attacking a Ju.87, attacked the Me.109 which was not climbing to attack. South of Benghazi Pilot Officer Duke saw 15 Ju.52s coming in from the sea and attacked the tail ender. Just as this machine seemed about to catch fire, he himself was attacked by six Me.109s, which were the escort. Pilot Officer Bartle and Pilot Officer Westenra both engaged one of the Ju.87s circling Magrun and between them shot it down. Sergeant Carson attacked the attacked the Me.109 and left it side slipping uncontrollably towards the ground. He also attacked a Ju.52 on the ground.'

At Christmas it was an RAF tradition on squadrons and airfields to make the best of it at Christmas and to have a traditional, or as much as possible, Christmas dinner. As part of this many

A somewhat worn-looking Hurricane Z5348 of 1 Squadron SAAF; Jerks Maclean had a cartoon painted below the cockpit – reclining in an armchair. (*Tom Meek SAAF*)

Pilots of 4 Squadron SAAF, 1941; the squadron (the Vampires) arrived in mid-September, equipped with Tomahawks and became operational in November.

No tail wheel (it was shot off) but a safe landing and a tow back; Hurricane Z3357. (*Michael Welchman SAAF*)

units produced Christmas menus, and the author has been collecting copies of these, as they provide an interesting snapshot of unit life.

No.112 Squadron recorded that 25 December 1941 was 'a normal working day, without any trimmings. There was a sweep over El Agheila but without incident. On the return journey Lieutenant Colonel Wilmot led the singing of carols over the R/T. On 26th beer and Christmas cake arrived. Because of the terrific storm the cake was not eaten, but there seems to have been no difficulty about the beer.'

No.250 Squadron had been hoping for a special delivery of pork, but it had been waylaid and by the time it was found, it had turned green. John Waddy and some others buried the pork with due ceremony and erected a cross on the spot to the effect: 'Here lies 250 RAF Squadron's Christmas Dinner 1941'. So Christmas lunch, on a cold and windy day, was cold bully and biscuits, well salted with sand. There was no alcohol because they had drunk it all the night before. Caldwell and the others in the squadron had settled down for an afternoon of doing nothing, but after a while he and the other flight commander were lucky enough to be taken by their CO to accept an invitation from the CO of the AA defences. There they shared some very good Scotch and returned at dusk, to the news that they had orders for a show at first light on the next morning.

On 27 December, one of the 112 Squadron's established – and successful – pilots – was shot down during a strafing mission. Pilot Officer Bowker was seen running from his crashed aircraft and it was later reported that he had been taken prisoner. Neville Bowker had joined 112 Squadron in mid-February 1941, in time to take part in the operations in Greece, claiming his first victory (a G.50) on 11 March. During the remaining campaign in Greece and Crete he claimed a Bf 110 destroyed, along with two probable (G.50 and CR.42) and one damaged (SM.79). He was wounded

45 Squadron bombing positions at Agedabia (near Benghazi) on 30 December 1941. (*45 Squadron*)

The Blenheims suffered losses to the fighters, but from time to time took revenge; Flight Sergeant Cliffe or 45 Squadron poses in his turret to mark his victory over a 109 in December. (*45 Squadron*)

The desert floods! Stan Gooch 'admires' what is left of his tent and possessions at Mariut in December 1941.

The aircraft were
also bogged down.
A Beaufort caught in
the flood.

Attacking Italian MT; note tail wheel at top of photo. (*Lawrie Shuttleworth, SAAF*)

and captured on Crete but escaped the field hospital and made it back to the squadron in Egypt. By the time he was shot down he had built his total to ten confirmed destroyed (plus a share), three probable and two damaged. His Tomahawk (AK283) had been hit by small-arms fire. Taken prisoner, there was no escape this time and he remained captive to the end of the war. He was gazetted for a DFC in October 1943, with the citation reading: 'Flight Lieutenant Bowker has taken part in a large number of operational sorties. In December 1941 whilst on patrol with his squadron, he engaged and destroyed three Ju87s in air combat, bringing his total victories to at least eleven enemy aircraft destroyed. Throughout his operational career this officer has displayed an exceptional keenness to engage the enemy and outstanding courage and devotion to duty.' (AMB11627)

Chapter 5

1942 – Backwards Again

Summary: Once again the race was on to see who would be ready first for the next move: Rommel, ever ready to take a gamble, struck first, even though he had received little in the way of reinforcement. By the early summer, Tobruk had fallen and he was back in Egypt, where the Allied defence line at EI Alamein managed to halt the offensive. But for the work of the Desert Air Force squadrons the retreat would quite likely have become a disastrous rout. Rommel was brought to a halt at a pre-planned defence line, but it is equally true to say that lack of supplies was a major factor in the termination of his offensive. A great deal of the credit for this must go to the anti-shipping squadrons operating from Malta and the Western Desert. These aircraft, especially Beauforts, Blenheims and Wellingtons, hunted down Axis shipping throughout the Mediterranean, paying particular attention to the routes from Italy and Greece across to North Africa. It was this element that now played the dominant role in ensuring success for the Allied forces. So, as with other theatres of the war, 1942 was to prove a turning point.

The January ORBAT for North Africa Luftwaffe units showed a strength of 529 aircraft, with 297 being 'ready for action':

Role	Types	Available	Ready for action
Close–in Recce	Bf 110, Hs 126	16	4
Long-range Recce	Ju 88, Do 215	13	11
Fighter	Bf 109	156	86
Night–fighters	Ju 88, Bf 110	50	28
TE fighters	Bf 110	18	6
Bombers	Ju 88, He 111	146	69
Dive-bombers	Ju 87, Bf 110	72	55
Naval aircraft	Ar 196, He 60	38	27
German Total		529	297
Italian aircraft		190	?
Total		719	?

The balance of air power was fairly even, although if the nearly 200 Italian machines are excluded, the RAF had an overall superiority and, after its successes of late 1941, had built something of an ascendancy. Meanwhile, the RAF was moving its assets around and re-equipping a number of squadrons ready for what was to be a critical phase of the air campaign and the Desert War in general.

In early January the ground initiative remained with the British and the advance was continuing. However, 'the prospects for 1942 were favourable for the Luftwaffe. The assault on Malta had gained in power and volume so that another major Axis convoy reached Tripoli on 5 January 1942. The arrival of equipment for four tank companies had raised the combat effectiveness of the German armoured division quite considerably.' (*The German Air Force in the Mediterranean Theatre of War*, General der Flieger Hellmuth Felmy).

No.270 Wing Operation Order No.68 tasked 14 Squadron and 1 GB Lorraine Squadron. The format of the op order is worth showing, as this type of document frequently does not survive:

<u>Information</u>: The enemy is still holding out in fortified positions in and around Halfaya Pass. Our forces are attempting to capture Halfaya Pass in the near future. No air opposition is anticipated.

<u>Intention</u>: To assist our ground forces by preliminary bombardment of fortified positions and gun emplacements within the area held by the enemy prior to the attack, and later by direct bombing support on selected targets during the attack, if required.

<u>Execution</u>:

1. The target areas for the preliminary bombardment selected by the 30th Corps are divided into two separate targets, lettered X and Y.
2. Priority of targets is X and Y with suspected enemy HQ at 52733686 in X area as first priority.
3. Bomb line is shown.
4. Squadrons will operate independently.
5. Number of aircraft in each sortie will be laid down in a daily programme to be drawn up by this HQ.
6. Maximum number of sorties to be made in daylight hours.
7. All available aircraft in both squadrons to be at full readiness by 0730 hours daily.
8. Bombing is to be carried out between 4,000ft and 6,000ft. If AA opposition is slight bomb height should be decreased to ensure maximum accuracy.
9. Bomb load 4 × 250lb bombs GP fused NI (43) without rod adaptors.
10. Aircraft to be bombed up, but not refueled, immediately on return from each sortie. Aircraft to be refueled only on completion of days operations, unless essential to complete a sortie.
11. Photographs to be taken on each sortie.
12. Aircraft taking off for a sortie are to be given priority over aircraft returning to land from a sortie.

On 1 January, 3 Squadron RAAF took on a 109-escorted Stuka attack; three pilots claimed a Stuka each, with Sergeant Cameron reporting: 'As most of the formation appeared to be about to attack the bombers, I endeavoured to lead Blue section into the Messerschmitts and followed these with several Kittyhawks after me. When I emerged from the cloud, they were circling above and as I appeared to be alone, I decided to break off and jump them from above. I came back through the clouds, warned the Kittyhawks … then went away and climbed to 12,000 feet. When I came back I could see nothing above or below cloud so went to Agedabia to intercept them on their way home. Here the cloud base was irregular at about 3,000 feet, and after I had done a couple of circuits, three Me-109s turned up and prepared to land on Agedabia West. I let them get settled down and then dived on one, but had to alter my attack and dive on another one head-on. I had a long burst at it and saw it flick upside down as it went under me. This was at 1,000 feet. The others by this time had their wheels down so I stalked the rear one who was only about 500 feet. After only a short burst he dropped his nose and crashed. I then attacked the other from astern, saw him waver as I fired,

Bennie Osler takes to the air in the 109 that 1 Squadron restored and flew in January 1942, before handing it over to the 'authorities'. He was not greatly impressed. (*Hannes Faure SAAF*)

The Allies acquired and flew a number of German types – but it worked both ways; Hurricane V7670 at Gambut in January 1942 in German markings.

but immediately had to climb to avoid some Stukas that were now coming in. Icing conditions were severe in the cloud, my ring sight being thickly crusted and the motor showing signs of ice in the carburettor. I attacked a line of 5 or 6 Stukas just about to land and saw the rear one slide away as I shot at it then went for the leader. He kept ahead on a straight glide into the desert while the main group turned left and landed. I flew in and out of cloud for some time, but as two of my guns were stopped and the reflector sight useless, I thought it unwise to remain longer.'

The holdout garrison at Bardia surrendered on 2 January, perhaps helped in its decision by some precision bombing by 45 Squadron on New Year's Day. Doug Allen took part in one of these final missions: 'We were at that time aiming our bombs from horizontal flight and we very seldom, I think, ever hit anything we were aiming at except by sheer good luck now and again. This lack of success bugged my Nav/Bomb Aimer, Ned Hammat, more than somewhat and he talked to me quite often

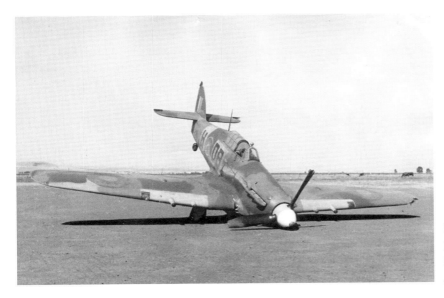

Broken prop in landing accident, 229 Squadron. (*Angus Allen-White SAAF*)

about trying a little dive-bombing with the old Blenheim. My crew, with Ken Edwards as WOp/AG in place of Geoff Gowing who was sick that day, was one of about six selected for this raid. Ned came to see me, all excitement – this he maintained was the perfect dive-bombing target and I agreed to give it a try. Ned planned to lie forward on the cockpit floor. Having located the target, I was to put the aircraft into a 45° dive, using the ring and bead sight to aim just short of the target. When Ned signalled to me by kicking one of his legs up I was to begin a nice steady pull out while he released the bombs in quick succession. On the way in I could see about three of our aircraft ahead of us and watched their bombs exploding all around the target but there were no actual hits. Throttling right back, I put the Blenheim into a fairly steep dive and at about 1,000' Ned signalled to me to pull out. We must have been back at about 1,000' in a steep climb when I got the shock of my life! The aircraft was hit by an enormous explosion, followed just seconds later by another. My first thought was that we had been hit by an 88mm 'Flak' shell and I looked over my shoulder back down the fuselage to see whether we still had a tail unit left! Ken Edwards was grinning at me delightedly from his turret and signalling a 'thumbs up' with both hands. In level flight once more I was amazed to see an enormous cloud of black smoke already above us and going on up to about 3,000 feet. A second one, at an angle to the first, probably went up to 5,000 feet. Ned had placed his first bomb just short of the blockhouse wall and the second had gone straight through the roof. The remaining two just hit the ground but, I would think, only yards beyond the building. The remaining two aircraft brought their bombs home!' (45 Squadron history). It was a fine end to what was to be 45 Squadron's last rotation in the Western Desert; the Flying Camels were headed to the Far East and a very different war.

Later in January 1942, 14 squadron was operating under 3 (South African) Wing. The squadron was based at Bu Amud (operational party), while the servicing party remained at Gambut, and had bomb racks for 500lb bombs under the wings, as part of the increasing Allied air campaign against the Axis ground forces. The Hurricanes of 33 Squadron had moved to Msus in early January and commenced standing patrols over Benghazi Harbour, adding to their score on 5 January when Sergeant Kelsall shot down a Ju 88 and damaged an Me 109, while Pilot Officer Woods damaged an He 111.

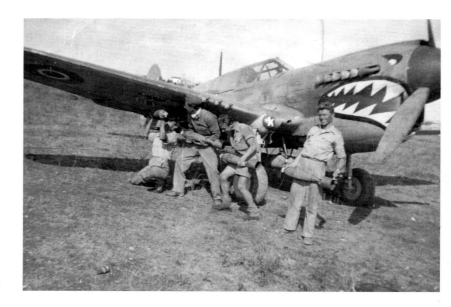

112 Squadron groundcrew manoeuvre bombs to the underwing racks.

40 Squadron Tomahawk. (*Michael Welchman SAAF*)

On 29 December the first Kittyhawk IAs had been delivered to 112 Squadron, the Tomahawks being 'donated' to 250 Squadron. By the start of the year the Squadron had fourteen Kittyhawks: 'Although there were quite a few alterations from the Tomahawk, the two aircraft were basically the same. Nevertheless, the pilots were immediately impressed with them and considered them an improvement. There was immediately the usual crop of accidents. On the 4th, Sergeant Crocker killed himself on his first flight, and on the following day news came through that Sergeant Johnson had been killed on the 1st while flying through a dust storm near Halfaya Pass.' (112 Squadron ORB)

The first mission was flown on the 9th when Flight Lieutenant Westenra led eight aircraft, plus eight Tomahawks of 250 Squadron, to escort a Blenheim raid near El Agheila. On the return leg, Sergeant Carson was attacked by an Me 109 and forced down. He returned to the squadron – as did his aircraft (AK672) 'Warrant Officer Luscombe went out with a party into the desert and towed the aircraft the 25 miles to Msus.' (112 Squadron ORB)

No.80 Squadron received Hurricane IICs at El Adem in January and from dawn on the 7th they started standing patrols over the Tobruk–El Adem area. On the same day news was received of a DSO for Squadron Leader M.M. Stephens: 'In December, 1941, this officer led a bombing and machine-gun attack on enemy mechanical transport in the Acroma area. Following the attack, Squadron Leader Stephens observed the fighter escort in combat with a force of enemy fighters, but, whilst attempting to participate in the engagement, his aircraft was severely damaged by an enemy fighter pilot whose cannon fire exploded the starboard petrol tank which, with the oil tank, burst into flames. The same burst of fire wounded Squadron Leader Stephens in both feet and blew out the starboard side of the aircraft's cockpit. Squadron Leader Stephens then prepared to abandon aircraft but, when half-way out of the cockpit, he observed an enemy aircraft fly past him. He immediately regained his seat and shot down the enemy aircraft. Squadron Leader Stephens finally left his crippled aircraft by parachute and landed safely on the ground where be beat out the flames from his burning clothing. Although 'he had landed within 300 yards of the enemy's lines Squadron Leader Stephens succeeded in regaining our own territory within three-quarters of an hour. Throughout, this officer displayed great courage and devotion to duty. Previously, Squadron Leader Stephens led his squadron on operations which were of the greatest value during the battle for Tobruk. His leadership and example proved an inspiration.'

Painting a name on
the aircraft – 'Lady
Shirley'.

A few days later the news was not so pleasant, with a letter from the 22nd New Zealand battalion stating that they had found the body of Flight Lieutenant D. Coke alongside his Hurricane about 4 miles west of Acroma on 11 December and was buried there by the unit. The squadron ORB recorded: 'The whole Squadron was sorry to hear of the definite loss of such a promising Flight Commander.'

The arrival of the cannon-armed aircraft had been greeted with delight; however, the new aircraft were proving troublesome, as these entries in the squadron ORB indicate:

17 January: 'Gun firing tests were carried out on the new Hurricane IICs which was an excellent test to demonstrate that the cannons would not fire.'

18: 'Four Hurricane IICs were flown to Gazala and back on gun tests. Again the result was disappointing. In fact, for the next few weeks all the energies of the squadron were devoted to trying to make the cannons fire.'

25: 'S/Ldr Urwin-Mann intercepted a Ju88 and got within 100 yards of it, pressed the button cannon control and nothing happened. A great disappointment and another proof that something was very wrong with the Hurricane's cannon.'

January was generally fairly quiet operationally for the fighter squadrons, with most records showing practice flying, some scrambles, most with no result, and, later in the month, some limited ground attack work, but usually by small numbers of aircraft. Typical of these was 33 Squadron, by now operating from Antelat:

17 January: 'Three a/c carried out a ground strafe of MT on the road East of El Wofilia (Tripolitania). Two heavy lorries were set on fire and considerable damage was inflicted on single lorries and troops. All our a/c returned to base, but owing to the bogged conditions of the runways, two of the aircraft were damaged on landing.' (33 Squadron ORB)

Indeed, the poor weather and the poor condition of landing grounds accounted for some of the lack of activity.

Flight Sergeant Haslam with a 213 Squadron Hurricane. The squadron continued to operate Hurricanes through to May 1944.

Hurricane IIC on approach – note only one cannon each side. (*Bomb Finney SAAF*)

Hurricane V7779 of
451 Squadron, Flight
Sergeant Wally Gale.

During a combat with JG 27 on 11 January, 3 Squadron RAAF had already lost two aircraft (Bobby Jones and 'Tiny' Cameron) and the battle was still raging. Andrew 'Nicky' Barr was focused on a 109: 'In a few seconds the Me-109 seemed to turn into a flame thrower. Brilliant fire streamed into the wind from the wing and along the fuselage. The plane twisted wildly, then dived towards the desert, crashing in a trail of smoke. There was no chance for Schneider to escape.'

The victim was Hugo Schneider, a nine-victory ace. 'Earlier, Nicky had noticed two Me-109s hovering nearby, but now the air appeared clear, so he flew back to the beach at Brega where the Kittyhawk had gone down. By now, the pilot had climbed out of his crashed plane and was standing by it. Nicky recognized him as Bobby Jones by his white gloves. (Some pilots wore lightweight gloves under the heavy leather gloves to keep their hands cool, but most were dark-coloured.) Because they were many kilometres behind enemy lines, and Jones would surely be taken prisoner, Nicky decided to attempt a rescue landing. The terrain nearby seemed suitable.

'Nicky lined up his intended landing strip, reduced power, then lowered his undercarriage. He was in the process of lowering his wing flaps to begin his landing glide when he noticed Jones, next to his plane, pointing to about ten o'clock above. Nicky turned in his seat and cursed his vulnerability. There was a 109 coming in on him very fast, all guns blazing, possibly one of the two he had noticed earlier. Luckily for Nicky, the pilot must have been inexperienced as he couldn't press his advantage. With a resounding roar, he overshot Nicky and desperately attempted to climb away,

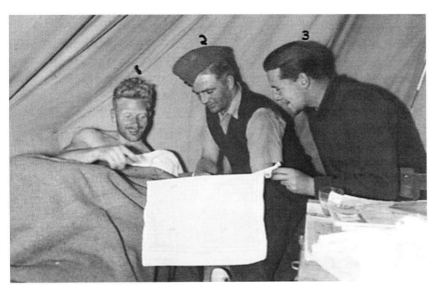

Flying Officer Nicky Barr on bed rest after walking back from being shot down, January 1942.

now realising his own precariousness. In the same instant, Nicky reacted. He pulled the flaps and wheels up, pushed on absolutely full throttle, wrenched back on the stick and braced himself. The powerful motor discharged a trail of blue smoke, lifted the Kittyhawk upwards and thrust it forward.

'The violent surge quickly closed the gap on the 109, now losing its speed in a climb. Within seconds, the German plane filled his sights. Without hesitating, Nicky fired the six .50 guns, shattering the Messerschmitt's tail and damaging the fuselage. Immediately, smoke poured out through the wing mounting. Within seconds, flames, fanned by the slipstream, seared backwards, emitting a bright red glow inside the now curling black smoke.

'The crippled plane fought to stay aloft for some time, but crashed some distance away, unseen by Nicky. In fact, Nicky's attention had been diverted as he caught sight of a second Me-109 which was now directly overhead and climbing into the sun.

'As Nicky found out later, this plane was flown by Oberfeldwebel Otto Schulz, an ace from II./ JG 27. Schulz already had nine victories from the Battle of Britain and had fought in Russia. Even though Nicky had picked up considerable speed since his abortive landing attempt, he was still flying relatively slowly, compared to Schulz. Nicky raised the nose and gained some distance, then fired a brief burst at the Messerschmitt's underbelly. His gaze followed the tracers – then bullet holes – as they penetrated the metal skin, but there was no obvious immediate reaction. Schulz then wheeled his plane around hard. He possessed a speed and height advantage, and positioned himself perfectly for a quarter attack on Nicky's plane [other reports say two aircraft attacked him]. He fired and Nicky felt the bullets rattle along the Kittyhawk's fuselage – *kathump, kathump!* Nicky didn't think he had been hit in the engine, but the plane suddenly lost power. Maybe the engine wasn't responding after the effort of coping with the prolonged intense demands for full power. He lost altitude. Then nothing responded. He was still under 1,000 feet and there was no time to lower his wheels or turn the flaps down. (Fighter planes have trimming flaps which help to adjust the plane to a horizontal position if it goes into a dive.) They were activated by a switch and controlled both ailerons as well as elevators, but nothing worked. Nicky was going to have to belly-land. In preparation, he flicked the master switch off, turned the ignition off, checked the tightness of the harness, then braced himself.

'The fighter landed with the sound of crumpling metal. A parching cloud of dust swirled around the plane as it continued to career for some distance, grinding the metal underbelly into the sandy shale. Nicky was concerned that the plane might cartwheel or even burst into flames. He desperately wanted to get out. For what seemed an eternity, the plane skidded and rocked out of control, screeching incessantly as the metal ripped a large gash in the earth. Finally, it slithered and grated against an incline to a dead halt.

'Mercifully, it didn't burst into flames. Nicky worried that the hatch might have jammed on impact, a common occurrence, but it slid back cleanly. He crawled out, trying numbly to assess his situation, when he noticed the Me-109 circling, as if it might land. It didn't, then Nicky realized it was going to blow up his Kittyhawk. As the 109 came round in a circuit and lined up for a strafing run, Nicky reasoned he wasn't far enough away to be safe if it did blow up. He decided to make it tough for the pilot and unsettle his aim by running directly at the Messerschmitt as it zoomed in low towards him and the Kittyhawk.

'Nicky sprinted towards the attacking Me-109. He was back on the athletic field again, but this time he was sprinting for his life. He lifted his knees and hands high, trying to gain purchase in the sand, his legs working like pistons, willing himself forward. The plane started firing. Nicky sidestepped as he watched the 20 mm shells spitting at him, firing beautifully through the nose of the 109. The bullets smashed into the ground just ahead and to the left of him, crashing and shattering nearby rocks. The explosion caused splinters of rock to ricochet into his legs. He collapsed and dropped to the ground as a searing pain surged through his lower limbs.

'The cannon fire continued to zip through the sand, spurting dust skyward and pock-marking the earth, tracing a lethal path to the wrecked Kittyhawk. An instant later, the plane was enveloped in flames and then exploded with a convulsive detonation that rocked the air. The pilot completed a quick circuit to supervise his handiwork, while Nicky waited to see what he would do. The blast had thrown him into a dense clump of camel-thorn and he lay there motionless, forgetting to breathe, wondering whether the pilot would try for a second run at him. To his relief, Schulz flew off, albeit rather unsteadily, as his left wing was drooping. Nicky hoped this had been caused by his own fire. In any case, Nicky assumed the German only intended on making sure the Kittyhawk wouldn't fly again.

For long moments, Nicky lay still and contemplated his situation. It had all happened so fast and he was disoriented. In the space of a few moments, he had shot down three enemy planes and had been downed himself; he had crash-landed, been strafed, then skittled, and he was still alive. Wonder of wonders. He began to feel some elation even, over the severe pain of his wounded legs.

'As he was bleeding profusely, his first task was to arrest the haemorrhaging, then to excise the rock splinters from where they had pierced his shins. Then he began to consider his next step. He was behind enemy lines, wounded and without food and water.

'After some moments, Nicky suddenly realized he was not alone. About six Arabs had materialized out of the arid surrounds and were observing him from a distance. They seemed friendly, and two came forward. They noticed his damaged legs and by now Nicky realized he also had some shrapnel in his left elbow. Communicating with them through a rudimentary sign language, some of the Arabs left and came back with some dressings. They looked to be stolen German dressings.

'*Justice*,' Nicky thought. (extract from *Nicky Barr, an Australian Ace*, Peter Dorman).

Nicky Barr walked back to Allied lines and was soon back in action, increasing his score to eight before being shot down and taken prisoner.

Brian Thompson recorded in his diary: 'Tiny' Cameron went in flames. Agheila, Bobby Jones crash landed near the beach. Curtis lost and force landed near Benghazi. Nicky Barr shot down

Ground strafing had become one of the main roles for the Hurricane squadrons. (*Hannes Faure SAAF*)

three and one probable, then tried to pick up Jones, but was jumped and managed to crash-land east of Brega. Returned to squadron later after Arabs helped him.'

Barr's actions earned him a DFC, with the citation reading: 'This officer, who commenced operational flying in November, 1941, has displayed the greatest keenness and skill as a fighter pilot. In December, 1941, during a patrol over the Derna area, he shot down a Messerschmitt 110; the next day, in the same area, he destroyed a Messerschmitt 110 and a Junkers 88. One day in January, 1942, his squadron formed part of an escort to bomber aircraft operating over El Agheila. Enemy aircraft were encountered and, in the ensuing engagement, Flying Officer Barr attacked 2 Italian fighters, one of which he shot down. He then observed one of his fellow pilots, who had been shot down, waving to him from the ground but, when preparing to make a landing in an attempt to rescue him, Flying Officer Barr was attacked by 2 Messerschmitt 109s. Although the undercarriage of his aircraft was not fully retracted, he immediately manoeuvred to engage the attackers, only to find that his guns had jammed. Quickly rectifying the fault, he delivered an accurate burst of fire which caused one of the Messerschmitts to disintegrate in the air. A further 2 enemy aircraft joined in the combat and Flying Officer Barr was wounded and forced down. While on the ground he was further wounded by the enemy's fire but, despite this, he made his way through the enemy's lines and rejoined our own forces some 3 days later. He brought back much valuable information regarding the disposition of enemy tanks and defences. Flying Officer Barr displayed the greatest courage and tenacity throughout. He has destroyed 8 enemy aircraft.'

The Kittyhawks of 112 Squadron had also been moving around, being at Antelat satellite by the 13th and also getting a new CO, with Squadron Leader Caldwell moving across from 250 Squadron. It was a short stay; the German offensive began on the 21st and the Allied retreat started. Antelat was abandoned. 'The squadron moved hurriedly out of Antelat owing to the state of the aerodrome, back 40 miles to Msus. There was a return trip to Antelat to assist No.1 Party, and one and a half hours later the Germans shelled the airfield. Everyone arrived at Msus after negotiating some bad stretches of mud. There was not much time to be had there as No.1 Party was told to be ready to leave again at dawn.' (112 Squadron ORB)

While the squadron continued to fly sweeps, the next move was already in hand: 'The rest of the aircraft were flown directly to Mechili. There was a lot of difficulty in getting away and the aircraft had to be lifted out of the mud and taxied with men under the wings and tail to keep it from bogging down and overturning. The transport was also giving trouble and No.2 Party, which left Msus at dawn had to abandon the Mess truck and a Morris, with all the Mess equipment, some pilots' kit and the HQ tentage.' (Squadron ORB)

The constant moving between airfields is often recorded in books in respect to aircraft, and of course aircraft are the rationale of an air force, but the pilots (and aircraft) are only part of the overall story and the ground personnel, especially in the Desert War, lived and worked in harsh conditions – and usually could not fly away from an advancing enemy.

Brian Thompson (3 Squadron RAAF) at Antelat recorded both the bad weather and the panic move in his diary:

19 January: Rained again. Everything bogged about the camp. This afternoon we had to see that all planes were able to taxi out to runway without getting bogged.

20: Rained again last night. Still lots of cloud about this morning. Our flight is on 'available' though runways are very wet and heavy. May be moving back to Msus tomorrow.

21: No rain today. We were supposed to move to Gazala at one stage and now it is back to Msus.2, where we originally were.

An RAF fuel tanker passes a tank somewhere in the Western Desert.

22: Up early this morning to go on patrol, but this was scrubbed as nearly all kites were hopelessly bogged. I had bad luck and I tipped 'Q'624 on her nose bending the prop. Spent the rest of the day getting the kites out in position to take off. Gibby tipped his prop taking off. After all the serviceable kites had taken off, I went back to come up in the glass house with Col Greaves. Had to get several trucks out of bogs and as we were preparing to leave a Major General came along looking for G/Capt Cross. He told us that all fuel & kites that could be moved were to be moved immediately. As 'Y' had only a flat tyre, I volunteered to fly it back and made a seat out of covers. I had no chute or helmet and was very deaf when I eventually reached Msus. Could not keep the plane straight on take-off and although she swung badly, I managed to get her in the air and proceeded to Msus. Landed here about quarter to three and got down quite OK. Landed on one wheel. Heard tonight that Jerry was eight miles south of Antelat at four thirty, so things may be doing tomorrow.'

The great thing with diaries is that they also record the more 'normal' happenings; an example is the 29th by Brian Thompson: 'Called at 7.30 and told we were to be in the air at 8.30. I was flying No.2 to Wally Mailey in Red section. We were airborne at 8.30 and patrolled the North and South roads from Derna to Barce and Tocra. Didn't see any activity on Jerry's part. Landed back at Martuba and found that 2 and 4 SAAFs were there. We had lunch there which was very decent, consisting of real boiled potatoes, bully, rice and pickles. Had quite an interesting talk with several of the chaps there. Very good crowd, these chaps. We took off at 2.30 and patrolled the same area. Saw a Hurry, which we chased and scared the wits out of him. Taught him a lesson anyhow and noticed he was weaving a lot as we left him.'

The interesting parts here are the lunch and the 'decent chaps' of the SAAF squadrons, and the having a bit of fun to sharpen up the look-out of the Hurricane; it would be interesting to know what its pilot might have recorded in his diary!

By the end of the first week of January 1942, Rommel had consolidated his forces in the El-Agheila area and was considering his options. The supply situation had improved markedly and many of his units had been brought up to strength in major equipment, including tanks. Luftwaffe

More mud ... pilots and mud at Martuba. (*Johnny Seccombe SAAF*)

reconnaissance showed that the Allies were not ready to move and also that the German forces were not well placed to defend against a concerted attack. Westphal suggested it was better to attack while the Allies were not ready and before they could launch their own attack. After initial reluctance, Rommel agreed and moved his division into place, again planning a sweeping movement to outflank and cut off the British. The orders were issued for an attack on 21 January by the newly designated Panzer Army Africa. The planned punch initially failed because the Allied forces were weaker than expected and their immediate action when threatened was a rapid retreat.

Clearly 1942 was the critical year in the Desert War and while the ultimate Allied success was the result of a number of factors, the resounding victory in the supply and fuel campaign was certainly one of the critical ones. We have alluded to the campaign in the Mediterranean to interdict the Axis supply lines, with offensive capability from Malta and Africa, and the often costly bombing attacks on Crete because of its role in the supply chain. While the Africa-based bombers had always been part of this, it was the advent of the torpedo capability with 39 Squadron's Beauforts that truly increased the anti-shipping capability. Having completed its torpedo conversion, the squadron participated in an attack on a convoy on 23 January.

A Blenheim of 203 Squadron sighted a large convoy making a dash for Tripoli and passed the details to the force that had been assembled at Berca Satellite, Benghazi, to attack shipping when it came within range. The strike force consisted of Blenheims, in the majority, Albacores of 826 Squadron and three torpedo-carrying Beauforts of 39 Squadron. The force was scrambled and, on locating the convoy, the Beauforts of 39 Squadron (piloted by Flight Lieutenant Taylor, Pilot Officer Grant and Pilot Officer Jepson) led an attack on a large merchant vessel (MV) – the 14,000-ton liner *Victoria*, described by Count Ciano 'as the pearl of the Italian merchant fleet.' The convoy was made up of MVs strongly escorted by battleships, cruisers and destroyers making some 20–30 ships in all. Although an intensive flak barrage was thrown up on all sides, the Beauforts held their course and dropped their torpedoes from 1,500 yards. All were seen to be making good tracks and a dense column of smoke was seen to come from the liner, indicating at least one hit. Thus crippled, the liner was attacked again later on in the day by the Albacores of 826 Squadron and a number of Wellingtons. A reconnaissance of the convoy the following day showed the liner to be missing – presumed sunk, for which 39 took some of the credit.

33 Squadron, 23 January 1942: 'Owing to the fluidity of the fighting area an advance party of two lorries left Msus for LG165. The remainder of the Squadron was at one-hour notice to move backwards. Sergeant Genders and Sergeant Wilson carried out a TacR of the area between Antelat and Agedabia. They reported considerable MT interspersed with tanks. Six aircraft took off to strafe the MT on the road between Antelat and Agedabia. One petrol bowser and two lorries were set on fire and 25 lorries were damaged. Pilot Officer Edy was shot down and crash landed about one mile away from the enemy MT. He was last seen running away from his aircraft in a Northerly direction. The other aircraft returned safely to base. Four airmen of the rear party arrived at Msus having safely come through the battle area. Orders came through at 2000 hours that the Squadron was to move to Mechile at first light. Sergeants Kelly and Crichton slept in the Bombay so as to be ready for an early morning take-off to Gazala.' (32 Squadron ORB)

It was only on the 23rd that the British truly became aware of the scale and intent of the German moves, the initial assessment having been that it was a 'reconnaissance in force' and perhaps some repositioning – but not a full-scale assault. Aerial reconnaissance discovered a large convoy off Misurata, which was duly attacked, whilst three supply ships and two warships were hit, the majority of supplies got through and the plan to hold a line from the coast at Beda Fomm, Antelat and Saunu looked less promising. Indeed, despite air attacks, on the 25th 'the forces on this line were so roughly

Bombays deliver supplies during the 'Gazala Gallop' retreat. (*Tom Meek SAAF*)

handled that they were in no condition to stop the enemy's advance, and it was decided to evacuate Benghazi.' (*The Eighth Army*, HMSO).

On 25 January, Auchinleck had flown to see General Ritchie, the battlefield commander, to urge him to rescind the general retreat order and to launch a counter-offensive. He was accompanied by Tedder, who subsequently reported to London: 'As a result of last night, I hope that the Army will now launch a counterattack. The only way to stop this nonsense is to hit back. Our fighters under Gp Capt Cross are in a bad mood … it seems that they are at this time the decisive and equalizing power.'

The 112 Squadron history noted on 25 January the return to the squadron of eight airmen who had been left at Antelat in the retreat. Corporals Luton and Hibbert, and Leading Aircraftmen Robinson, Flower, Keighley, Barton, Cross and Thompson, had an 'interesting' few days: 'They stayed behind at Antelat to service the remaining aircraft and MT vehicles. They had finished by 1630 hours (on the 24th) and were just packing up when an officer of an RAF Armoured Car Unit (No.1 and No.2 Companies, RAF Armoured Cars) drove up and told them that an enemy armoured column was nearby. They joined the armoured cars, who put a guard on the aircraft. The German armoured column, which was holding an escarpment on the Msus side of the Antelat Road, had already shelled some aircraft taking off. An Indian Coy now started to destroy all the ammunition on the airfield and the aircraft, and at 1900 hours the party moved off towards the Benghazi road. They traveled until about 2300 hours when they were caught up with a mixed crowd of artillery and RAOC. At dawn they continued towards the road, and they were strafed by a Me.109. At about 1100 they reached the road, but they decided to wait for a while in a wadi. They had only been there about 10 minutes when the road was shelled. At this they decided to retrace their steps to Antelat, getting back there about 1400 hours. Two armoured cars went forward to investigate, but they, and the 3.7 gun, got bogged in some soft ground. Just as they had been dug out nine German tanks appeared, firing as they came. The armoured cars turned to engage them (ten armoured cars in all) and the soft-skinned vehicles left as fast as they could. They were chased for about 45 minutes and only four vehicles got away. After refueling, they waited to see if anyone else was going to turn up but no one did. At 1630 hours they were spotted by two Kittyhawks who indicated to them the direction of Msus, where they arrived at 1800 hours.'

On the 25th, Rommel altered the axis of his advance towards Msus, where he considered the major British formations could be engaged and defeated before they could retreat east. However, despite some success, the bulk of the British forces again made good their escape. The 15th Panzer did manage to bag 85 tanks, 45 piece of artillery, 190 trucks (very valuable) and 200 prisoners. Most valuable were the supplies of POL, ammunition, rations and even mobile workshops. The next success came with the capture of Benghazi on the 29th, a port that the Allies had almost returned to usefulness – and would now start bombing again! Shortage of fuel meant that Rommel had to limit his pursuit of the retreating Allies, enough to keep them moving but not enough to be decisive.

For the last week of January, the Kittyhawks of 112 Squadron had flown at least one sweep a day to strafe enemy concentrations, and the 28th was recorded as 'the last day before the next move backwards and the last show of the Fighter Wing's lone stand against Rommel.' Four aircraft made

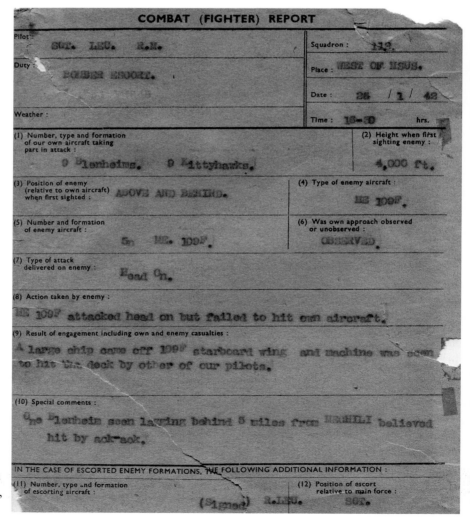

Combat Report for Sergeant Leu of 112 Squadron, 25 January.

an afternoon sweep along the Sceiledima Road and at Fort Sceiledima 'a concentration of six vehicles and a tank were selected for attention and all were raked in turn by all pilots in a run each way. There were at least twelve tanks and several hundred vehicles dispersed around the fort, and the general direction of the enemy's advance was towards Soluch.'

The Army would no doubt have been unimpressed by the 'lone stand' comment! Air attack was always viewed with dismay by ground troops, as it came unexpected and rapid, and for most ground troops there seemed little they could do to fight back – and the standard cry was 'where is the RAF' (or Luftwaffe if the Germans were on the receiving end). The psychological impact was, at this stage of the campaign, often greater than the physical damage and casualties. The firepower of the tactical aircraft was still limited and tactics were not yet developed; both of these were issues that the DAF was to rectify in 1942 and it would then become a truly effective air component of the ground campaign.

DFC to Pilot Officer John Moss, 208 Squadron: 'One day in January, 1942, this officer carried out a photographic reconnaissance of the battle area. While making his run over the area at 20,000 feet, Pilot Officer Moss observed 3 enemy fighters flying to intercept him. Nevertheless, he continued his run for some 8 minutes and, when the attackers prepared to engage him, he put his aircraft into a violent turn and spiralled down to 4,000 feet, which caused the windscreen and hood to become iced up and reduced his visibility to a minimum. When below 4,000 feet, the ice cleared and Pilot Officer Moss observed that the enemy fighters were still in pursuit but, adopting both skillful and disconcerting tactics, he cleverly evaded the enemy. He finally eluded his pursuers in a sand storm near a landing ground but he was unable to land there owing to the sand storm. Realizing, however, that his petrol was becoming exhausted, he flew clear of the tents and mechanized transports and made a safe landing with the undercarriage of his aircraft retracted and without incurring any damage to his camera. He then commandeered a vehicle and returned to his squadron with his photographs. Pilot Officer Moss displayed courage and resource in accomplishing a most valuable reconnaissance.'

No.208 was another of the long-serving desert squadrons, having formed at Qasaba in September 1939 with Lysanders in the AC role and then TacR role. It received Hurricanes in November 1940, which served to December 1943. There was a brief interlude with Tomahawks in summer 1942, and from December 1943 to the end of the war the squadron flew various marks of Spitfire.

No.80 Squadron moved to a new airfield at Sidi Aziz on 30 January and was looking forward to getting into action with its Hurricanes. 'The site of the camp was soon decided upon and the camp took shape by tiffin time.' Having just started to settle in, they moved to LG109 but within days went back to the Delta, to Sidi Haneish for more training.

At the end of 1941, 450 Squadron had given up its Hurricanes for Kittyhawks, a type that was to become synonymous with the Desert War. The squadron was at LG 'Y' when it re-equipped but moved to LG12 (Sidi Haneish) to continue its work-up, and almost immediately received an emergency signal from Advanced AHQ western Desert saying it was 'required urgently for operations under No.258 Wing'; the CO replied that the 16th was the earliest possible date. On 16 February nineteen Tomahawks duly arrived at Gambut Main and were dispersed around the airfield – the CO left for a conference with G/C Cross at 258 Wing. The squadron became known as the 'Desert Harassers', with the motto 'Harass' on their official badge, but also, according to some sources, because of a reference made by the Nazi propaganda broadcasts of Lord Haw Haw, who branded the squadron as a band of Australian mercenaries whose harassing tactics were easily beaten off by the Luftwaffe.

450 Squadron
Kittyhawk.

Kittyhawks were also the new type for 260 Squadron at LG115 in February, an original plan to re-equip from Hurricanes to Tomahawks having been cancelled. The squadron was impressed with the new aircraft, although that was in part because their Hurricane Is 'were somewhat tired'. Another piece of good news later in the month was the return of three squadron personnel who had gone missing in January – and who reappeared after having walked through the desert.

With Benghazi back in German hands the port facilities became a key target once more. If Rommel was able to get supplies unloaded at Benghazi, then much of his logistics problem would be resolved. Preventing this, by attacking convoys, ships in port and the port facilities, was therefore crucial.

LD-coded Tomahawk of 250 Squadron at El Gamil. (*Tom Meek SAAF*)

Hurricane squadron scramble. (*Bomb Finney*)

Bomb Finney with his 1 Squadron Hurricane. (*Bomb Finney SAAF*)

No.205 Group Operation Order A.282 tasked the group's squadrons with a minelaying task, one of the unsung but crucial parts of the anti-shipping campaign:

A. Form B.No.9.
B. 4th February 1942.
C. The enemy are known to be using Benghazi as a supply port for its units operating in the Benina area.
D. To lay mines in the approaches to Benghazi Harbour.
E. Night 4th/5th February 1942
F. 10 aircraft, 148 Squadron, 12 aircraft, 37 Squadron, 8 aircraft, 38 Squadron

G. i.   6 aircraft, 37 Squadron are to attacked the Central Mole defences and Guiliana point defences

ii. 2 aircraft, 148 Squadron are to attack Benghazi Town.

iii. 1 aircraft, 148 Squadron is attack Berca Main landing ground.

iv. 1 aircraft, 38 Squadron is to drop flares on the east side of Benghazi Town.

v.   7 aircraft, 148 Squadron and 2 aircraft 38 Squadron are to bomb Benghazi Town east of a line drawn through B.10 and P.10 target map B.2.

vi. 6 aircraft, 37 Squadron are to attack Berca Main landing ground.

vii. 5 aircraft, 38 Squadron are to plant Cucumbers in the areas notified to OC 38 Squadron.

K. All aircraft are to operate from, and return to, LG.09.

L. For i. time of attack is 2330 hours

For ii and iii time of attack is from 2335 to 2345 hours

For iv the time of attack is 2350 hours

For v and vi time of attack is from 2350 to 0030 hours

For vii time of attack is 0005 hours

(37 Squadron ORB)

Although the stated primary mission was laying mines, only five of the thirty aircraft were actually laying mines – the reference to Cucumbers. Minelaying was referred to as gardening and the aim was to plant (lay) vegetables (different types of mines having different vegetable names).

33 Squadron, 5 February: 'Three flights of four aircraft each strafed MT between Martuba and Gazala during the day. Ten lorries were destroyed by fire and 29 were damaged. One lorry which was destroyed was carrying a Breda gun. This lorry blew up immediately it was hit. Two of our aircraft were damaged slightly by machine gun fire. One of the pilots, Pilot Officer Tofield, was wounded by an explosive bullet. He flew his aircraft safely back to base and was taken to hospital immediately.'

The following day there was more strafing: 'Two sections of three Hurricanes each strafed MT on the road between Bomba and Tmimi. The first section destroyed one lorry and damaged five others.

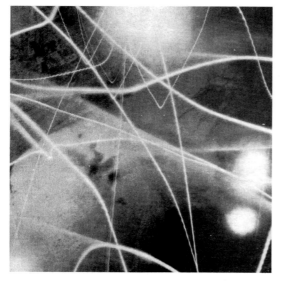

Target photo of Attacking Benghazi – searchlights, flares and flak! This important port was a regular target for the bombers of 205 Group. It was also a very well-defended target and cost many a bomber.

Two of our aircraft were hit by Breda machine gun fire. The second section only damaged three lorries as the AA opposition from Tmimi was intensive and accurate. All of our aircraft sustained damage and Fg Off Cleete had his rudder control wires shot away. All the aircraft returned to base safely.'

On the 7th, 'the Squadron was released from operations pending move to LG101 for re-equipping with long range Kittyhawks.' This was followed the next day by: 'Congratulations to you and the Squadron on the grand works and the fine spirit maintained by the Squadron. You are all to go back to base at Maaten Bagush and are to be re-equipped with Kittyhawks. In the meantime give all personnel generous leave and an easy time.' (33 Squadron ORB).

But even better: 'A Hurricane loaded with beer returned from Fuka and a farewell party was held in the Mess at Gambut. The Hurricanes were handed to 208 and 238 squadrons and 33 set out by road for Sidi Haneish.

Operating out of Gambut, 112 Squadron flew a number of sweeps and, on the 8th, a bomber escort for Blenheims to Derna. During a rearguard fight, the squadron lost three pilots (Sergeants Elwell, Donkin and Hoare) and registered three victories. Sergeant Holman was shot down a few days later, and one of the new Polish pilots, Flying Officer Matusiak, was killed in a flying accident.

The loss of five pilots in the first two weeks of the month was countered on the 14th by one of the squadron's most successful days – and for no loss. 'Ten Kittyhawks led by Pilot Officer Bartle and eight from 3 Squadron RAAF were scrambled to meet an approaching enemy formation. After flying North to Tobruk, the Kittyhawks turned West over the perimeter defences and climbed steadily until, over Acroma, No.3 Squadron were flying at 8,000ft, with 112 slightly ahead and above, just below the cloud base, and at an ideal height for the Kittyhawk. At this moment they spotted about a dozen M200s and M202 in a loose vic formation about 2,000ft below them, to the left and in front. Pilot Officer Bartle warned the Australians, who had, however, already seen a formation of enemy bombers, with a close fighter escort, flying at less than 2,000ft. 112 concentrated on the fighters, who by now were climbing to meet the attack. Their courage failed them and they hurriedly tried to form a defensive circle, in a half-hearted fashion. The Kittyhawks dived into them and in the initial attack every aircraft of 112 Squadron must have hit something. Sergeant Burney, having dived through the formation, saw the bombers below, they were BR65s, and so he carried on down and shot one down. This aircraft attempted to evade, but it hit the ground, and Burney 'strafed him to save him the walk home'. By the time he regained the formation there were no enemy fighters to be seen amongst the milling Kittyhawks. Sergeant Cordwell, in his first action, shot away about three-quarters of the wing of an Me109F, which spun out of control. Sergeant Evans attacked an M200 as it was turning and shot about two feet off its starboard wing. It dived steeply and was probably destroyed.

'Sergeant Drew, also on his first real engagement, got himself two M200s, one of which he saw hit the ground. 'It was as easy as breakfast in bed,' he is recorded as saying. Pilot Officer Duke attacked an M200 which was seen to spin in and crash by Sergeant Evans. He also attacked another Maachi at ground level from dead astern and it flew into the ground and burst into flames. This kill was shared with Sergeant Reid of 3 RAAF Squadron.

'The enemy's defence was to adopt a circle, and when evading, to dive down to ground level in rolls and vertical dives. Sergeant Leu attacked a M200 which blew up, and another one which went into the ground. Sergeant Simonsen certainly destroyed one M200, which he saw spin into the ground, and probably he damaged another. Pilot Officer Dickenson made a stern attack on another M200 which was enveloped in a sheet of flame at 1,000ft. Sergeant Christie claimed two M200s destroyed and one damaged. His account was that he dived and gave one Maachi a heavy burst so that the aircraft climbed steeply, and then spiraled and crashed, bursting into flames. He dived on the second, which stalled, pouring out black smoke and going into a dive. He had a go at a third and probably damaged it, but without any visible result. Sergeant Evans also attacked an M200 which dived away so steeply that it was doubtful whether it could have pulled out. Pilot Officer Bartle gave another M200 a good burst which sent it down out of control, and damaged a Me109F, which he chased all the way to Tmimi.

'By the end of the fight the remnants of the enemy formation had fled. Of the estimated total strength at the beginning of 32 enemy aircraft, 20 were claimed destroyed, two probably destroyed, and ten damaged. The Squadron fired 7,060 rounds of ammunition during the fight.' (112 Squadron History)

No.3 Squadron RAAF recorded 14 February as its St Valentine's Day Massacre: 'Was up at five-thirty and had breakfast at six. Left here at seven and went to El Adam where we were on standby. At nine-thirty, Pace and Reid took off to try and get Goring who was supposed to land at Martuba at 10 o'clock this morning. They returned and didn't see anything. At twelve o'clock we were scrambled with 112 Squadron and shortly after ran into a Balboa of approx. 40 enemy aircraft, mainly consisting of 109s, Maachi 200s, Maachi 202s and Ju87s. We didn't get at the 87s and Graham Pace and I shot down a Macchi 202. I thought it was a 109F. It crashed and burnt between Gazala and Acroma. Between the two squadrons we shot down 19 kites. In our Squadron Gibby got two Macchi 200s, White one 109, and damaged two 87s, Mailey two 109s and one probable. Lew Spence one 109, Reid one & half 200s and one Dornier.'

On the downside, the following day, two pilots (Frank Reid – killed and Tom Briggs – bailed out) were shot down when they scrambled to intercept raiders but were bounced by 109s.

DFC to Pilot Officer Neville Duke, 112 Squadron: 'One day in February, 1942, Pilot Officer Duke was the leader of a section of a wing when he sighted 35 enemy aircraft. He informed the wing leader and led his section to attack. In the ensuing combat 11 enemy fighters were destroyed by the squadron, 2 being destroyed by Pilot Officer Duke. This officer's leadership contributed materially to the success achieved. He has destroyed 8 enemy aircraft and probably destroyed and damaged a further 6.'

Although the victories were notable, of more significance was the fact that an enemy bombing raid had been foiled, and the DAF had taken another step towards air superiority, part of which entailed persuading the enemy that they were inferior in air combat. 'By the 14th he [Rommel] had gathered a striking force consisting of most of his Germans in this sector. But the air support on which he had counted was virtually destroyed the same day by a formation of Kittyhawks which wiped out 20 and probably 30 dive bombers and fighters in a single action.' (*The Eighth Army*, *ibid*). Seldom did an Army account give such credit to the RAF, especially for a single day's activity. It was, of course, an oversimplification but it does provide an indication of how important air cover and air support were to both sides.

Rommel now halted this advance and this also draws a close to Auchinleck's campaign that began in November with early success and promise but ended in his forces being pushed back – albeit the line had stabilized much further west than it had been before Crusader. The lull was to last some three months, to late May.

Most Allied airfields were subject to attack by fast raiders, and February seemed to be a particularly busy time for the Luftwaffe to 'visit' the major airfields such as Gambut. Brian Thompson recorded a number of attacks in the first week of the month and a general comment that: 'Jerry is making it a bit hot.' Then, on the 9th: 'Jerry visited us again this morning at about five o'clock. Put on a hell of a show too. Dropped incendiary flares right across our dispersal area and then went to work and bombed hell out of us. He hit a Tomahawk and it burnt and he also strafed five Kittyhawks, damaging them badly. The Bofors staged a good display and did a good job on the last one.'

Fred Schofield's Hurricane after engine failure at El Gamil on 18 May. (*Bomb Finney SAAF*)

And on the 12th: 'This evening at about seven o'clock Jerry came over with about six planes and started to drop flares around the aerodrome which made night like day. He dropped incendiary flares and proceeded to bomb around them, right through our camp. I was in Frank Reid's slit trench for a while and one stick went right across us. He didn't hit anything and left us at about eight o'clock, after which I managed to get some tea.'

On the 27th, Pilot Officer Bartle (112 Squadron) took eleven Kittyhawks to Gambut Main to hold readiness. 'They had hardly left their aircraft for the safety of the pilots' dug-out when the airfield was attacked by five Me.109s, who strafed the airfield leaving two burning, two badly shot-up, two Cat.2 and another damaged. The remaining four scrambled later, and Sergeant Jackson, pulling too tight a turn, spun in. The crash had not been located by the end of the day.' (112 Squadron ORB).

In the period between mid-November, the start of Crusader, and mid-February (the stablization after the retreat), the Desert Air Forces had flown more than 10,000 sorties and claimed more than 500 enemy aircraft (air and ground). The salvage and repair organization had 'rescued' 1,035 damaged aircraft and returned 810 of those back to the battle, an impressive and invaluable contribution. More importantly, the RAF operations had played a key role in preventing a fluid retreat from becoming a rout.

While the ground forces on both sides went into a period of quiet rebuilding and resupply, the air forces kept the battle going. The DAF was also continuing to reorganize: 'The fighter squadrons were now placed under separate operational control; this was organized on the 'leapfrog' principle with two identical operations rooms, one forward and one rear, which under fluid conditions could act in the same way as squadron forward and rear parties and so maintain continuity of operations in spite of frequent moves.

Simultaneously the principles of air support were defined more clearly for the benefit of air and ground forces alike, and in order to overcome the vexed problem of identification of ground targets agreement was finally reached on the marking of all British vehicles with the RAF roundel. The maintenance and repair organizations were further developed and expanded while airfield construction was pushed ahead and facilities improved.' (*New Zealanders with the Royal Air Force*)

March was to see the first classic torpedo strike by 39 Squadron in the Mediterranean. Eight Beauforts led by Flight Lieutenant A.M. Taylor took off in the afternoon of 9 March to search for a convoy reported to be heading for Tripoli. At 1640 the formation located the convoy of four MVs, three cruisers and six or seven destroyers at position 3325N 01746E (approximately 170 miles north-east of Tripoli), steering a course of 045 degrees at some 10 to 12 knots. The convoy had an air escort of three Ju 88s plus at least one Me 110. The Beauforts should have had an escort of Beaufighters but this had failed to turn up at the rendezvous and Taylor had elected to press on without it.

Approaching the convoy, he called the formation into line astern and commenced his attack run. He elected to make his main attack against the cruiser force, which was considerably in front and to port of the main body of the convoy and therefore more vulnerable. All eight aircraft made successful drops, with one torpedo aimed at the largest MV and the other seven at the cruisers. Forcing a way through the barrage of flak, the formation emerged on the far side of the convoy – to be met by the escorting Ju 88s and Me 110s. This time, however, it was to be the Beauforts' day; one Ju 88 was shot down by Flying Officer Bee's aircraft and, not to be outdone, Flying Officer Leaning's gunner damaged an Me 110. All eight Beauforts broke through the defences and flew back to North Africa, four making night landings at Bu Amud and four at Sidi Barrani. The outcome of the strike was one MV hit, one cruiser hit, one destroyer hit and possibly sunk, one Ju 88 destroyed and one Me 110 damaged – all for the cost of one Beaufort slightly damaged.

The squadron received a signal of congratulations from the C-in-C Mediterranean and Alistair Taylor was granted the immediate award of the DFC. It was a very successful strike, although unusual in the small degree of damage suffered by the Beauforts.

Sadly, it was not always so 'easy'; for example, the squadron lost five aircraft and crews on 22 April: 'Keeping low over the water, the Beauforts continued their search and sighted the convoy at 1645. The four MVs, two of 12,000 tons and two of 10,000 tons, were escorted by six destroyers on the flanks and by no less than ninety-six aircraft (Me109s, Me110s and Ju88s). The Beauforts moved into attack formation, hugging the waves, hoping that they would not be seen until the last moment. Their luck was out, for as they neared the release point they were spotted by the circling fighters and waves of fighters peeled off to attack the forlorn striking force. It was a race for time and although all eight Beauforts managed to drop their torps, almost immediately three aircraft were shot down as they were swamped by fighters. Shortly afterwards. Pilot Officer Belfield's aircraft was hit and damaged; he cleared the convoy and ditched safely, all the crew took to the dinghy and were later picked up. A fifth aircraft, that of Pilot Officer Seddon, was so badly damaged that it was forced to ditch six miles from Malta.' (*The Winged Bomb, ibid*)

Meanwhile, on 10th March there was a significant development at 112 Squadron, which was attempting to make its Kittyhawks more effective ground attack aircraft. 'Squadron Leader Caldwell made the first practice bombing dive, carrying an unfused 250lb bomb, to see whether it could be dropped without carrying away the propeller. Since this might mean a crash it was done over the sea with the ASR organization laid on. This experiment was a success and it was repeated during the afternoon with a live bomb.' The following day four pilots did some practice bombing and 'at dusk the CO went off to have a go at the enemy at Martuba, but the bomb fell wide of the target.' (112 Squadron ORB).

This development of increasingly turning the Kittyhawks into Kittybombers – with a more 'useful' bomb load – was one of the most significant of 1942. Although these early experiments were with a 250lb bomb it was not long before the Kitty was carrying 500lb and 1,000lb bombs – and not just single bombs. Billy Drake was among the fighter pilots now faced with a change of role and tactics: 'Our AOC, 'Mary' Coningham, wanted us to changeover to the ground-attack role. He had recently had it demonstrated to him that the Kittyhawk could carry a useful bomb-load, and as fighter-bombers he felt we could do more to assist the army than in the past. This was a completely new role for most of us in the RAF, and we became the forerunners of the tactical ground-attack units of the DAF. Initially we carried a 250lb bomb beneath the fuselage, usually fitted with an extension rod to the fuse in the nose, so that it would explode just above the ground surface, allowing maximum damage to be caused to soft-skinned vehicles and personnel. So began a sharp learning curve. As we were no longer just escorting bomber formations, or undertaking sweeps or patrols over the front line, we quickly learned that navigation had become much more important in allowing us to find our targets. We also had to learn to deliver our bombs in a medium-to-steep dive of 30–45 degrees, using the gun-sight.' (*Billy Drake, Fighter Leader p44*)

It was also a time of reorganization, in part because more than 300 fighters and nearly 200 bombers had been transferred to the Far East, the war situation looking even worse there. 'Nevertheless the reduced force was trained to a high pitch and remoulded in the light of practical difficulties encountered during the second Cyrenaican campaign. Fighters were gathered into a new operational group (No.211) and at the same time were organized for administrative purposes into wings of four squadrons. Each wing could be located on a single airfield and these four-squadron bases simplified arrangements for offence, defence and training. At the same time problems of direct support for ground troops and the ever-recurring difficulty of recognition of friendly units from the air were partly solved by an increase in positive liaison facilities between army and air force headquarters, and by the decision to arm as many squadrons as possible with fighter-bombers which could intervene in confused ground battles and be certain of attacking only enemy forces. The small light-bomber forces were also regrouped in wings each of two squadrons and stationed at Bir el Baheira only twenty miles from Gambut, where the fighters were concentrated. This proximity allowed joint tactics to be evolved. Additional reasons for the concentration of the fighters at Gambut, rather than the more forward airfields at El Adem and Gazala, were the prevalent dust storms and the increasing frequency of enemy attack in those areas. Communication problems were easier in the Gambut area, the existing early-warning organization was adequate, and fighters could still operate over the front lines.' (RAAF history).

Tactics are a subject that features frequently in first-hand accounts by Allied pilots: Michael Lavigne moved to 260 Squadron: 'Sometimes the Squadron was lucky and sometimes it wasn't. 260 still flew the stupid old Hurricane formation with six aircraft in a Flight. There were three Section Leaders and three weavers flying behind. Everyone looked after their own tails and no one coordinated anything when the 109s showed up. It seemed that everyone was for himself and the weavers had a hell of a time trying to keep with their leader while weaving and watching behind.

'As a defensive formation, it was a confused glob of aircraft that could be turned into a confused shambles by a small number of 109s attacking from above. With their superior speed and height, the Messerschmitts had the superior initiative to engage or disengage at will. No tactics were discussed to combat the 109s or avoid being shot down. It always seemed, particularly on bomber escort, we were easy pickings for the 109s. We were there to divert attention from the bombers, and in order not to become victim to the enemy, we were on our own. We had to turn sharply into the attacker, but to do so was to be alone, jumping from the frying pan into the fire.' (*All the Fine Young Eagles*; pp136–137).

Having moved to Gambut in early March, 80 Squadron was back on ops on the 13th and the first combats took place on the 19th when a patrol in the Tobruk area was attacked by ten Bf 109s; Pilot Officer Mason claimed a 109 and Pilot Officer Richardson damaged another (or maybe a MC.202); both Hurricanes were damaged in the combats, and additionally Flight Sergeant Rivalant was shot down … he bailed out and was picked up by a Royal Navy launch from Tobruk.

Halfaya (Hell Fire)
Pass, 15 March 1942.
A key strategic
location.

Halfaya (Hell Fire) Pass, 15 March 1942. A key strategic location.

The honour of conducting the first Spitfire operations in the Middle East and Mediterranean theatre went to the PR.IVs of No.2 PRU, with four aircraft (AB312, AB421, BP883, BP904) joining the unit in March 1942 to supplement the existing Hurricanes. Photographic reconnaissance had always been a critical role within this theatre of operations and the arrival of the Spitfires added a new capability.

Typical of the missions flown was one on 29 March when BP883 took off from Gambut for a four hour fifty-five minute sortie covering northern Greece. While the Spitfire was never to appear in significant numbers at this stage of the DAF story, it later became a key type in the Italian campaign, along with the Mustang. The first unit of the Desert Air Force to operate the type was 145 Squadron, which arrived at Heliopolis from the UK in April 1942 with Spitfire Vs.

Defending Egypt – at night: The Germans were keeping up the pressure on the Allied defensive positions but were also attacking military installations in Egypt, favourite targets being the dockyards at Alexandria and the airfields and other installations in the Suez Canal Zone. The number of night fighter squadrons was limited. No.89 Squadron had been formed in the UK in late 1941 with Beaufighter Ifs, had arrived in Egypt in December under the command of Wing Commander G.H. Stainforth and was based at Abu Sueir but with numerous detachments.

Flying Officer Robert 'Moose' Fumerton and Sergeant Pat Bing proved to be an effective team and on 3 March 1942 Fumerton flew a mission that led to his first DFC. One of four Beaus airborne to intercept raiders over the Canal Zone, they picked up a radar contact and in bright moonlight spotted an He 111, which they stalked and engaged. The pilot opened fire at 100 yards and scored hits – but the German gunners fought back and put the starboard engine out of action, destroyed the reflector sight and wounded Fumerton in the leg. A second attack set the Heinkel on fire, but the port engine of the Beau also stopped. A crash-landing looked inevitable, but one engine picked up again and the crew managed to make a wheels up landing at one of the Canal Zone airfields.

The citation to the DFC read: 'One night in March, 1942, this officer engaged a Heinkel during an enemy air raid over the Suez Canal zone. Observing the enemy aircraft in the moonlight, Flying Officer Fumerton delivered a good burst and, although he was wounded and his aircraft

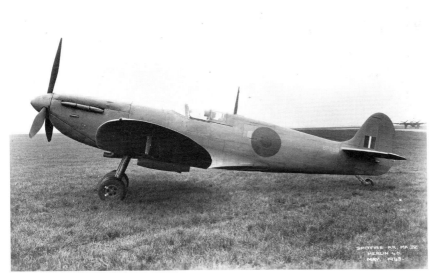

The first Spitfires in theatre were a limited number of PR.IVs; the Spitfire was not a significant type in this campaign until 1943.

With a shortage of night fighters such as Beaufighters, some of the Hurricane squadrons took on a night fighter role, a 'cat's eye' technique that had proved partially successful over the UK.

damaged by the enemy's return fire, he continued the attack and set the bomber on fire. Although the undercarriage of his aircraft had been put out of action, Flying Officer Fumerton made a safe landing. The raiding aircraft descended on to the sea, its crew being captured.'

A short spell in hospital for Fumerton and then back to action with 89 Squadron – and a double victory on the night of 7 April (two He 111s). Shortly afterwards he was awarded a bar to the DFC and he went on to become Canada's highest scoring night-fighter ace.

Daylight Luftwaffe attacks also continued, one of the aims being to inflict damage on the increasingly powerful Allied air forces. An attack on Gambut in 'the early morning moonlight' of 6 April caused damage to a number of 80 Squadron aircraft and the deaths of two airmen.

New Hurricane variants arrived in the spring, with the advent of the specialized tank-busting Hurricane IID variant with 6 (Army Co-operation) Squadron. The squadron had been in theatre since it reformed in February 1940, initially with Lysanders, but with a move from Palestine to the

Beaufighter night fighters were in short supply; 89 Squadron arrived at the end of 1941.

'real' theatre of ops in February 1941 it received its first Hurricanes, with which A Flight flew TacR sorties.

The IIDs arrived in late April: 'At Shandur the Squadron will commence intensive training on Hurricane IID aircraft and the 40mm S gun. These aircraft will be used in low flying attacks against enemy tanks.' (6 Squadron ORB, 20 April). The main armament was a pair of 40mm Vickers 'S' guns (cannon), one under each wing. The guns were designed to penetrate 20mm or so of armour – enough to kill the current range of German tanks! The Hurricanes kept two 0.303 machine guns; some pilots would have preferred to have more. Wing Commander Dru-Derby visited the squadron at Shandur to provide training on the aircraft. According to Allan Simpson: 'We didn't have long to train, and didn't have many aircraft. But we set up two rails from a railroad, painted a life-sized tank on a piece of canvas, and secured it to the two vertical rails. That was our practice target.

'We listened to lectures on our new aircraft and its weapon system: tanks and their vital spots (tracks, bogey wheels, drive wheels, engine, fuel tank, crew), the tactics tank formations used and the tactics we should use. Our skill level was high; we had an average of more than 70 per cent hits, firing six to ten shots per attack, not counting the machine guns.'

The squadron acquired the name 'the Flying Can Openers' and adopted a suitable logo, which has been painted on their aircraft ever since.

The Squadron ORB noted some key events:

12 May: 'Capt J Pearson is arranging for a captured German Mk.IV tank to be towed to an adjacent range some few miles from Shandur.'

14 May: 'AOC RAF Egypt, AVM Keith Park, visited the squadron today and informed Wg Cdr R C Porteous that one Flight must be completely trained and equipped ready to go to the Western Desert by 31st May 1942.'

15 May: 'Special demonstration of Hurricane and S gun on a captured German Mk.IV tank.' This is one of those frustrating times when no detail is provided.

The specialist tank-killing Hurricanes of 6 Squadron were armed with 40mm guns in underwing pods.

213 Squadron at yet another inhospitable desert location.

The heavy bombers of 205 Group continued to make nightly attacks, the main targets being ports (Benghazi and Tripoli) and airfields, with attacks on Crete also part of the routine as it was part of the Axis supply line. The light and medium bombers were heavily engaged on similar targets, as well as tactical targets in and around battle areas. This period of early to mid-1942 also saw the replacement of the ageing and vulnerable Blenheims and Marylands with Bostons and Baltimores, although, as we shall see, losses remained high.

No.38 Squadron ORB, 7–8 April 1942, loss of Wellington AD604: 'I have the honour to submit a report further to my signal dated 9 April 1942 on the loss of the above-mentioned aircraft.

'The aircraft took off from LG.08 at 2240 hours for a raid on Benghazi. It was carrying a bomb load of 8 × 250lb and 1 × 500lb GP and a petrol load of 750 gallons. At 0350 hours the 'operations completed' signal was acknowledged by Quotafiya; the aircraft had left the target area at 0330 hours. At 0500 hours the aircraft requested a QDM from Quotafiya, which was not able to give the QDM because the strength of the aircraft's transmissions was too weak. At 0523 hours another QDM was requested, but the strength was still too weak. Kabrit, however, took a snap bearing of the aircraft (281 degrees). At 0527 hours another request for QDM was made without success. Kabrit took another snap bearing (284 degrees). At 0540 hours a final request for QDM was made, but Quotafiya stated that strength was still too weak.

'Over certain areas of the Western Desert a fog had arisen; LG.09 was in fog – and aircraft were diverted to other Landing Grounds. It is presumed that this aircraft either tried to make a forced landing in the fog or mistook the fog for low cloud and crashed into the ground. From the above signals information the aircraft should have been in the Sidi Barrani area when the final request for a QDM at 0540 hours was made. There was a fresh westerly wind.'

This account is worth looking at for two reasons: firstly, it highlights the problems of aircrew with navigation and the usefulness of ground station assistance (although in this case no QDM was possible); secondly, it concludes with the loss of the aircraft and, in the absence of any further information, no detail as to why the aircraft was lost. However, in this case, the squadron ORB has a follow-on report compiled from accounts from the three crew members who survived:

1. Hit by flak over Benghazi which evidently did more damage than at first imagined.
2. Holdsworth flew back to near base when handed over to Sergeant Webb, still approx., 4000ft above cloud.
3. Navigator asked pilot to come through low cloud base in order to position from beacon. Cloud base 500ft.
4. Flying at 500ft the starboard engine cut and caught fire. Webb corrected the swing losing height, could not see the ground and did not realize how close they were, with the result they hit the ground unprepared.
5. Upon contact with the ground the aircraft broke in two level with the rear of the bomb beam, the front part somersaulted, tearing the front turret away, and caught fire. At this time the 2nd pilot was in the pilot's seat, front and rear gunners were in their turrets, while the Captain, Navigator and Wireless Operator were in the body of the aircraft.
6. Sergeant Webb was dazed in the crash and found himself clear of the A/C and noticed the front gunner still in his turret only a short distance from the blazing wreckage. Although in pain he pulled the front gunner clear, and then proceeded to render the same service to Sergeant Allaway in the rear turret. It was impossible to give any assistance to the three NCOs in the blazing forepart of the plane.

7. At dawn it was noticed that the telephone line ran across the desert some distance from the wreck and although Sergeant Webb was still in considerable pain – medical report has now revealed that he had suffered a spinal injury – he made his way to the line and was found by linesmen of the RE at about 1400 hours that day. An ambulance was summoned and the three airmen taken to No.14 CCS Misheifa, from where they were transferred to New Zealand Hospital, Mersa Matruh. Sergeants Allaway and Rothwell are now patients at 27th General Hospital and Sergeant Webb at 19th General Hospital.

Crew:

- Captain: Flight Sergeant T.A. Holdsworth
- 2nd Pilot: Sergeant J.C. Webb
- Navigator: Sergeant J.R.F. Mann
- Warrant officer: Sergeant E.C. Fiorini
- Front gunner: Sergeant A. Rothwell
- Rear gunner: Sergeant S.R. Allaway

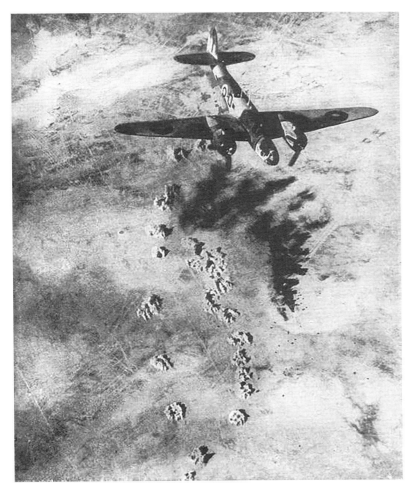

Maryland bombing troop concentrations – one of the problems of such bombing was that dispersed targets across the desert presented difficulties and it was only when they concentrated, as they had to do for an offensive, that they were profitable targets.

148 Squadron, Sergeant Spence: 'We were briefed to attack an enemy convoy steaming towards Tripoli. After flying up to advanced base in the afternoon we took off for our mission just after dark. Everything went smoothly until we crossed the coast north of Benghazi, when suddenly the port motor of our Wellington started to overheat and in a very short time it seized up; the plane started losing height very rapidly, although the starboard motor was at full throttle so the captain ordered everything possible to be jettisoned, and turned back. We crossed the coast again and let go the bombs. The plane seemed to hold its height for a time but soon the good motor started to heat and we began to lose height again.

'The night was so black we couldn't tell how far off we were from the high ground until suddenly we hit with a tremendous crash and skidded along for quite a distance. We all got out unhurt and although I had been dragged along on the floor behind the bomb bays I only received a small knock on the hip. The plane seemed to be in small pieces. We reckoned we were then about 80 miles behind the German lines, then around Gazala, so decided to try and walk back. After smashing up everything not already written off in the crash and filling our only two surviving water bottles, the six of us set off about midnight using the compass found undamaged in the wreck.

'After only a few hours walking in flying boots over the terribly rough ground in this region we were all worried with blisters. About two o'clock we almost bumped into an enemy tank and in trying to get round it came across some more. Whichever way we turned we saw tanks; we must have walked into the middle of an enemy laager in the darkness so decided the only thing to do was to try to work our way through them. In single file we crept past tank after tank and although we could hear the crews coughing and talking we were not seen and when we finally realized that we had passed through safely we were six considerably shaken men.

'Shortly after this the moon came up and we were able to see where we were placing our very sore feet. We continued walking with ten minute breaks every hour until just as it was getting light in the East, we were suddenly stopped with the cry of 'Halt', at which we all threw ourselves flat. From the voice we could tell it was not friendly so after a hurried whispered conference we crawled back the way we had come and tried to get round him to the South only to walk into another challenge. This time we decided to try the North and were able to go about 200 yards before once again the cry of 'Halt' rang out, this time accompanied by the noise of a rifle bolt being worked. We simply froze to the ground expecting a bullet every second. After a few agonizing moments we crawled back the way we had originally come.

'By this time it was getting quite light so we crept back looking for cover but could find nothing except an occasional stunted bush about a foot high, so settled down to await the coming of the search parties we were sure would be out the moment the sentries reported our presence, yet although we lay all that day in clear view of several parties of Italians, working on roads, no attempt was made to find us. However we had one or two scares, once when a motor–cyclist passed within 20 yards of us and another when about ten tanks rumbled past about 200 yards away. We had bully beef and biscuits with us but we were unable to swallow them on our ration of two mouthfuls of water each twice a day.

'As soon as it became dark enough we set off on a compass course we had worked out during the day and were able to pass the enemy parties apparently before sentries had been posted. That night we covered a considerable distance without any alarms and when morning came we reckoned we had covered about 30 miles from the crash. As there was no sign of life anywhere we decided to keep walking before we got too weak from lack of water so on we went. Our ten minute spells every hour had become by this time twenty minutes and even thirty minutes. Every step was agony. The one member of the crew who had shoes, had them fall to pieces about this time so we had to bind them up with blankets. Although we were suffering terribly from the heat at this time we still kept our blankets and Irvine jackets because the nights were so cold.

'About mid-day we saw a plane very low, flying straight for us and couldn't tell because of the haze, whether it was a Hurricane or a M.E.109. By the time we could see the markings and recognize it as a Hurricane and were able to fire our flare pistol and wave our shirts, it was right over us and we were not seen, a great disappointment. Shortly after this we came across a bird's nest among the stones with two eggs in it. They made a delightful drink when beaten up with a little of our nearly exhausted water supply. We each had two and a half spoonfuls.

'Later in the afternoon we had to climb a fairly high hill and on top we found an old observation post and in it half a bottle of red Italian wine which we shared out after a few thoughts of poison. About this time we must have started having hallucinations from lack of water because we all saw what looked like deserted British trucks and Bren carriers down the other side of the hill; but when one of the crew volunteered to climb down to search them for water he found only empty desert. After a rather longer rest than usual we set course again until after dark when we had another experience of seeing quite clearly a truck looming up out of the darkness which just disappeared as we approached.

'Soon we came to a bigger bush than usual with, of all things, green grass growing under it, so as we could go no further lay down to sleep. We must have slept for quite a time for when we woke, the grass was very wet with dew and we were able to lick off quite a bit of water before forcing ourselves to walk on. We were now down to about 15 minutes walking every hour and realized we were about at the end of our endurance, but thought we must be getting near our lines as the lack of movement convinced us we must be in "No-Mans Land".

'Just before dawn we collapsed and fell asleep where we lay. We were awakened by one of the crew shouting and we looked up to see him pointing ahead towards a group of trucks parked on the horizon facing West. We could make them out as British and guessed they were a party on the road from Tobruk to Gazala, stopped for breakfast. With new strength and very pleased with ourselves we set off, waving and trying to shout and firing off our revolvers. As we approached we could see a small group of men on a slight rise examining us through glasses and then two of them started walking in our direction. When they were about fifty yards off we realized they were German but I think we were all too far gone to take it in enough to worry.

'The officer greeted us in English and told us to follow him. Sure enough as we approached we could see that the trucks were British but were being used by the Germans. We had walked into an anti-tank group and behind the guns were the German crews watching the British tanks about two miles away. One of the officers even lent us his glasses so that we could get a good look at them. The Germans gave us what water they could spare and we were soon bundled into a staff-car and taken back by stages to Derna where we were able to get our feet attended to and as much water as we wanted.'

No.239 Wing became a reality on 26 April, comprising 112 and 250 Squadrons RAF, plus the two RAAF Kittyhawk squadrons. This 'Kittybomber' wing was under the command of Wing Commander Mayers but it was clear that unless the squadrons had extensive practice then the 'art' of fighter-bombing would not be a success.

While deliveries of Spitfires to the Middle East never kept pace with demand they did increase throughout 1942, the primary source being via the Takoradi route (shipped out to Takoradi and then flown across Africa to Egypt). The first unit of the Desert Air Force to operate the type was 145 Squadron, which arrived at Heliopolis from the UK in April 1942 with Spitfire Vs; the unit moved into the Western Desert theatre of operations in late May and flew its first mission, escort to

Spitfire Vs joined 1 Squadron in late 1942; the caption with this AX-coded Spitfire says May but the squadron did not officially re-quip until autumn. (*Bruce Rose-Christie SAAF*)

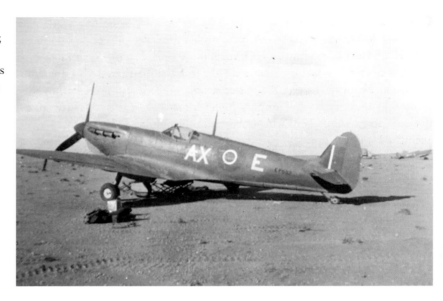

Hurricanes on a CAS mission, on 1 June. The build-up of Spitfire units was slow but at last the DAF had an aircraft to counter the threat posed by the Luftwaffe's fighters. However, it was the Mark V that really launched the Spitfire's career in the Western Desert theatre; indeed, it was in this theatre that the majority of Vcs were employed. The problems of operating in desert conditions were well known and so aircraft were fitted with the Vokes filter to preserve engine life; however, the aerodynamics of the Spitfire were affected, resulting in a significant drop in speed. The Maintenance Unit (MU) at Aboukir soon addressed the problem and produced a modified Vokes filter (often referred to as the Aboukir filter). The MU at Aboukir was also called upon to modify a number of Spitfires to counter the high-flying Ju 86P recce aircraft that frequently appeared over the Cairo area. One such modified aircraft was BR114 and this reached the amazing (for a Vb) height of 50,000ft (15,240m). Although Flying Officer Reynolds managed to damage one of the high-flying enemy on 24 August 1942, it was the 29th of the month before the first confirmed 'kill' was made.

Overall April had been a quiet month, but it gave an opportunity for reflection and training. 'The vexed allied question of a bomb line was also partially solved by the introduction of hourly signals through air support controls of the forecast military situation for two hours ahead. One of the major problems was undoubtedly the time lapse between the origin and fulfilment of requests for air support which, during Crusader, had averaged three hours due to delays in individual formations becoming airborne and for fighters to rendezvous with bombers.

Exercises during April between fighters and bombers only reduced this time by thirty-five minutes, which was a meagre improvement. Targets in desert fighting quickly grew stale, and although this time lag was palliated by a reorganization of air support control procedure to incorporate supplementary briefings and the stationing of listening posts for tactical reconnaissance aircraft with the forward tentacles, the position was still unsatisfactory. The time was doubly ripe therefore for the emergence of the fighter-bomber, which, at low level, had less difficulty in identifying its target and which did not require carefully contrived fighter escort. It was emphasized, however, that the primary role of fighters was air fighting.' (RAAF History).

Fighters were employed both on shipping protection and in low-level attack against airfields and transport behind the enemy lines. Flying Officer Makgill and Flight Lieutenant Hamm reported on

1 May: 'Three aircraft took off at dawn on strafing expedition in Agedabia area. Found and attacked five lorries near Bigrada; one towing a petrol bowser blew up in a most satisfying fashion. Later sighted twelve vehicles heading north each towing trailers carrying oil drums. Spectacular fire followed our attack. Further north came upon larger convoy and attacked with machine guns, causing fires and confusion. Soon after this "R" chased a Ju52 near the coast and it forced landed on the beach. On return his Beaufighter showed a rifle bullet hole in the fuselage directly under pilot but bullet had been deflected by elevator control. A highlight in Beaufighter operations was the low-level attack on 2 July against the group of landing grounds at Sidi Barrani, where four Ju87s and two Messerschmitts were destroyed and another thirteen other aircraft damaged.'

On 12 May four Beaufighters of 252 Squadron, with an escort of ten Kittyhawks with long-range tanks from 250 Squadron, were tasked to hunt Ju 52s on the route from Crete to Derna. After searching for two hours they found what they were looking for – sixteen Ju 52s escorted by three Bf 110s. In a head-on attack, six of the transports were shot down almost immediately; turning to engage those left, the formation claimed all but three of the enemy destroyed, with Flight Lieutenant Waddy accounting for two Ju 52s and two 110s.

At a conference between SASO and the squadron COs of 239 Wing it 'was impressed on them that the fighter bomber could only be developed and used effectively if the pilots were trained in bombing. This was the signal for conversion of 112 Squadron, who, on 16 May, became the first official F-B squadron in the DAF.' (112 Squadron ORB)

On the 16th the squadron flew its first bombing mission with six bomb carriers and four acting as top cover. 'Flight Lieutenant Bartle led the formation and chose as his target a concentration of tents in the area of Sidi Zaid. This was duly attacked and heavy flak was the answer. Everyone returned in the best of spirits.'

The following day, 'The same technique was used on a dawn sortie. This time the attack was on the Tmimi roadhouse and the surrounding area. Six bombs were dropped within a small compass and one was observed to score a direct hit on the Inn. Heavy flak, which was also accurate, was experienced and two aircraft were hit and slightly damaged. Reports of the damage say that intercepted enemy messages reported the Inn was hit and that the bombing had been very accurate.'

Flak was something new to the pilots and the dangers of ground attack were forcibly made when six Kittybombers (and four escorts) attacked enemy lines of supply on the 18th: 'Everything went well until the aircraft, having dropped their bombs, came down to deck level to strafe with cannon and machine-gun fire. The flak was very intense and two aircraft, AK763 (Pilot Officer Fisher) and AK994 (Sergeant Davey) failed to return. Pilot Officer Fisher was hit by flak and was seen to crash in flames. Sergeant Drew bent his airscrew flying too low, but managed to force-land about 12 miles south of base, out of fuel. Sergeant Davey was last seen over the target area and a report from a South African patrol stated that an aircraft had crashed near Temrad, within enemy lines. Pilot Officer Johnson returned with a shell hole in one of his wings, and two other aircraft landed at El Adem short of fuel. The results of the bombing were not known but five were seen to fall amongst tents and MT, and about 70 vehicles were shot-up in the strafe.'

The Luftwaffe's intensive campaign against Malta had certainly paid off in respect to German convoys to Africa and in the period January to March only 16,000 of 190,000 tons was lost, and in May only 10,000 from the 170,000 tons shipped. The loss of Malta's air and submarine strike capability was enabling Rommel to build up his strength and stock of supplies. The anti-shipping effort was, of course, still under way although now primarily from North Africa.

No.38 Squadron was instructed to maintain a detachment of torpedo aircraft at LG05 for the duration of the moon period. They were soon in action, a typical engagement being that of 22

May when an ASV Wellington of 221 Squadron worked with Wellingtons DV542 (Sergeant Youens) and AD597 (Sergeant Flanagan) of 38 Squadron: 'At 0130 hours Sergeant Youens received a revised position for convoy from ASV aircraft. He set course for estimated position, repeatedly checking by bearings on ASV aircraft. At 0215 hours Sergeant Youens sighted the convoy, consisting of two destroyers and two MVs, one large of about 8–10,000 tons and the other 2–3,000 tons. The convoy was in echelon 1,200yd apart with the destroyers on the flanks. He attacked the large MV, approaching to the stern of the starboard destroyer. The destroyer opened fire with 12–14 Bofors-type guns, hitting the aircraft and causing damage. As the aircraft came round to the north-east of the convoy, Sergeant Youens saw smoke screen beginning centering on the target ship. He could not see whether there was smoke coming from the stack or whether it was the result of a hit. The ASV aircraft reported that clouds of

Boston formation en route to another tactical target.

smoke were pouring from the ship and the next day a reconnaissance aircraft reported a large MV beached some 30 miles north of Benghazi with a gaping hole in the side. It is therefore claimed that Sergeant Youens hit the ship. The aircraft was damaged considerably, hits being registered on flaps, main surface and aileron of starboard wing, starboard side of fuselage, port engine cowling and port engine wheel covers. The aircraft succeeded in reaching LG05. Sergeant Flanagan did not sight the convoy until 0320 hours and it was effectively screened by smoke so that no favourable opportunity for attack was presented.' (38 Squadron ORB)

No.223 Squadron re-equipped with Baltimores from Bostons in January but acted as a training unit for a while, while its Maryland Flight remained operational to April. The first Baltimore mission was to the Tobruk area on 23 May by four unescorted aircraft, but they were intercepted by II./JG 27 and lost two aircraft (some records say three, and with the fourth having been damaged, crashing on the return trip), both falling to Marseilles (his sixty-third and sixty-fourth victories). The number of multiple victories he achieved was exceptional, for example no fewer than six Tomahawks of 5 Squadron SAAF near Bir Hacheim in early June in less than ten minutes. This ever more successful fighter pilot was later claimed to have had an incredibly low bullet to kill ratio of only fifteen rounds! It was true that he became the master of deflection shots and that once he had latched on to a target the end was almost inevitable. The 23 May mission was not an auspicious start for the Baltimore, but the type went on to have a fairly good record with the DAF, serving with a number of RAF and SAAF squadrons.

On the Defensive Again: Rommel Attacks

The next stage of the battle would be different in that Rommel was better equipped than ever, and the British had adopted a new defensive strategy for the Gazala Line based on 'boxes' that had all-round defence and, in theory, were capable of withstanding a siege as they were self-contained with infantry, artillery and tanks – and could be supported by air. They were also surrounded by, and monitored, extensive minefields, the idea being that any German advance could be slowed or held up while counter-attacks were set up by the mobile armoured reserve. The effective air strengths of the two sides were roughly equal, at around 450 aircraft, at the start of the battle, although this would change rapidly in favour of the Allies. Rommel launched his new offensive on 26 May and as the battle around 'Knightsbridge' developed, the DAF was called on to establish air superiority and to support the ground forces; for most squadrons this meant intensive operations, with, for example, the three 'sister' squadrons (3 RAAF, 112, 274) averaging 350 sorties between 27 and 31 May.

On the 27th, 112 Squadron flew thirty sorties and dropped twenty-two bombs; Flight Lieutenant Dickenson failed to return from one of these sorties but turned up the following day; he was airborne again that day and again failed to return. He had been with the squadron since November 1941, as Pilot Officer, and had reason to become 'A Flight' commander. Two other pilots were lost in the period to the end of the month.

27 May: Brian Thompson (3 Squadron): 'Push started today. Jerry made a move at twelve-thirty last night, and this morning he had a Panzer Division south west of El Adem. I went out at quarter-to-twelve with Geoff, Donald, Bray, and we bombed & strafed a supply column near Hacheim. My bomb landed near three trucks & trailers, and I strafed these after. This afternoon I led four more out – Kildey, Norman, Donald. We bombed some tanks & M/T and strafed isolated vehicles all

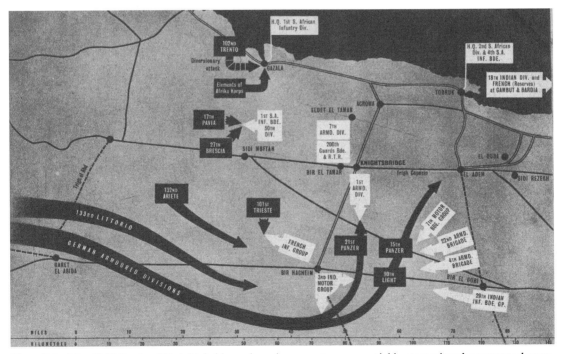

Plan of the May 1942 Battle of Knightsbridge, when air support was essential in stemming the panzer advance.

the way back. Norman strafed some tanks & I am pretty sure he went in. Thomas force-landed & is believed prisoner & Clabburn is missing from one of these shows. Lew Spence tried to pick up Thomas and burst a tyre and crash-landed my plane on the drome here. Then W/C Meyers congratulated me on my report on movements & said it was a magnificent show. Very weary tonight and although we were bombed, didn't worry much.'

Brian Thompson's diary records just how busy the next few days were:

28 May: Some of the chaps were on at dawn, but I didn't go. Went on standby at about nine o'clock and at twelve o'clock, I went off with Geoff, Vic & Mac. Geoff turned back & I took over. We found the Italian Panzer Div. after fifty minutes & bombed it. I got direct hit on truck & trailer. This evening I went out with five others & we bombed & strafed a large concentration west of El Adem – got a direct hit on truck & damaged others.

29 May: Up early at four forty-five am but didn't go out. At about twelve thirty, I led a four out to bomb the large concentration and we had 450 as close escort & 250 as top cover. We bombed first & then we all strafed. Saw three fires burning when we left. Hell of a lot of A/A. Thomas returned to squadron this morning & Clabburn walked in this evening. I went to the beach to sleep tonight with seven others, five of 450 were also down there.

30 May: Arrived back from beach at about nine o'clock and I took over from Lew Spence. We got a job about eleven. I got a direct hit on six tanks and two trailers & started a fire. Nearly went in as I dropped my bomb at 200ft. The two of 250 as top cover were shot up by 109s and earlier Burkland was killed and Chas. McWilliams walked back. 450 lost four, but believe that two are safe. Tom Birney of 112 went in today. Also McBirney and Mursey of 450. Nicky Barr and McDiarmid are missing and two Kittyhawks were seen to go in. They were jumped by 109s as they went down to bomb and strafe.

31 May: I took over from Lew at about nine o'clock, and at about ten we were given a job to bomb & strafe SE of Lumimi with 112 Sqdn. I had to return as my prop came back into full course, & Reg Pfeiffer took over. They returned O.K. & at lunch-time we received news that Nicky Barr was over at Group – safe, so poor old MacDiamid must have gone in. This afternoon Geoff took a four out with eight of 112. Kildey got hit pretty badly with A/A & one of 112 Sqn got a direct hit and went

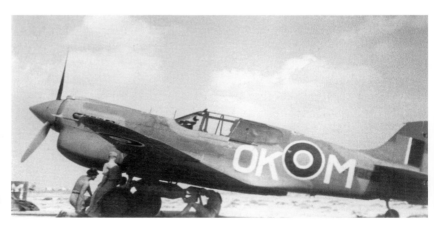

450 Squadron
Kittyhawk; the
squadron made around
twenty moves in 1942.

in. Nicky arrived back about two o'clock with Clive O'Day. 450 Sqdn lost Mick Thompson, & Dave Law & Lindsay are missing.'

On 9 June Brian Thompson was told he had been recommended for a DFM; this was gazetted in September: 'Throughout his sorties, this airman has displayed great courage and devotion to duty. He has on numerous occasions returned from fighter patrols with valuable and accurate information of the disposition and movement of ground forces. During the fighting from 26th May to 1st June, Flight Sergeant Thompson participated in numerous dive-bombing and machine gun attacks on important enemy concentrations. He always pressed home his attacks with vigour, inflicting considerable damage on equipment and troops. Each time he returned with valuable information regarding enemy movements, which proved of great importance to the Army, Flight Sergeant Thompson has destroyed at least two enemy aircraft.' (AMB 8079)

No.80 Squadron also had a particularly bad month:

3rd: Sergeant Thomas (BE360) shot down – killed
3rd: Sergeant Howard (BE494) force-landed with engine problems – OK
3rd: Pilot Officer Maynard (BE712) bailed out – OK
18th: Sergeant Nicholls (BE973) crashed on take-off – killed
23rd: Flight Sergeant Scott (BE339) shot down – killed
23rd: Sergeant Howard (BE974) shot down – killed
25th: Flight Sergeant Comfort shot down – ?
28th: Flight Sergeant Wintersdorff (BE706) shot down – OK (see below)
29th: Pilot Officer Pearson (BM991) shot down – ?
29th: Sergeant Swire (BE396) shot down – ?
29th: Sergeant Sykes (BE547) shot down – ?
29th: Flight Sergeant Campbell (BN354) force-landed – OK

23rd: 'Squadron took-off at 0815 hours to provide a cover patrol over El Adem whilst Kittyhawks were being refuelled there. We were jumped on by 109s and in the ensuing dogfight we lost Flight Sergeant Scott and Sergeant Howard, both were seen to crash in flames near Tobruk. Sergeant McCormack was also shot up but managed to land at El Adem. This has been an unfortunate week and the loss of these two popular pilots is very keenly felt.'

25th: 'Another escort of 2 Tac/R machines today. Refuelled at El Adem. When over Tmimi Flight Sergeant Comfort, who was acting as No.2 to a Tac/R aircraft dived down on the drome with the Tac/R aircraft and was not seen again. We are hoping that he made a landing and is probably a prisoner of war.' A Ju 88 was shot down over the airfield by the second shot from a Bofors gun that night.

26th: 'The day started with the sudden appearance of 4 Ju88 which appeared out of the sun. They were flying in close formation and peeled off dropping 16 bombs which destroyed the airmen's cooking trailer, two water bowsers, 3 lorries and one u/s aircraft. For their pains, one was shot down by 73 Squadron and the other three were badly damaged. The Ju88 which was shot down last night was examined. It was in a very bad state and appeared to be very old.'

The three shot down on the 29th had been part of a sweep to Bir Hacheim. Having lost eleven aircraft in the month, there was one piece of good news on 29th: 'Flight Sergeant Wintersdorff walked into ops room today. He had had great difficulty in getting out of his aircraft and was thrown out at the last minute.' (80 Squadron ORB).

On the ground it was a war of attrition; the first appearance of Grant tanks caused heavy losses to German tanks, the new type being better armed and armoured than previous types, although its shortcomings would soon become clear. The German attacks on the northern line of advance were getting nowhere, and were already running short of supplies. However, by disengaging and manoeuvring, the Axis forces were able to regain the initiative and Bir Hacheim became the focus.

The offensive by Rommel was proving very effective, although not as rapid as he had hoped, and the Allies were retreating rapidly, the DAF providing as much support as it could with attacks on enemy installations and troops, and endeavouring to provide cover for Allied troops holding out in some locations or exposed in retreating convoys. The Free French were holding a position at Bir Hacheim and a great many air sorties were flown in support.

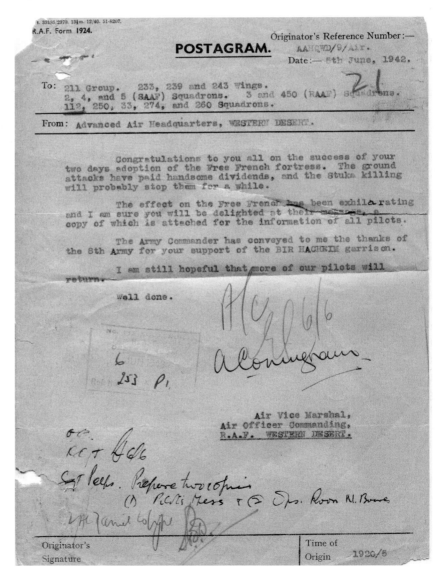

The AOC's signal of congratulations to his squadrons for support of the Free French fortress.

Billy Drake had his first air combat with 112 Squadron while leading ten Kittyhawks in a fighter-bomber sortie on 6 June: 'Near the target we spotted four Bf 109s below us. What luck, we dived on them and claimed the lot shot down – three confirmed and one probable, the latter being my personal contribution to events. We then bombed Axis vehicles claiming one in flames and six damaged. Not a bad result, we felt.' (*Billy Drake, Fighter Leader*, p45)

Drake later changed the probable to a definite with confirmation from ground forces that the 109 had crashed. Most of his total of twenty-three confirmed kills (and three shared) were scored in the Western Desert with 112 Squadron. By the end of the day, the squadron had flown thirty-eight sorties, and in addition to the aerial victories, claimed five MT destroyed and twelve severely damaged; the total could have been more but, as the squadron recorded, 'The dust and confusion of the tank battle below gave them little opportunity to intervene effectively.'

The debut mission for the Hurricane IIDs of 6 Squadron took place on the 7th with Squadron Leader F. Hayter leading five other pilots to attack tanks and MT near Bir Hacheim. One returned early with engine problems and the other five were unable to find the target. 'Pilots reported very wide dispersal of tanks amongst MT, such dispersal not being favourable to the functions of the Hurricane IID.' (6 Squadron ORB).

The following day two ops were flown, both by sections of three aircraft. Claims were made by all three pilots in the first section, but in the afternoon only Pilot Officer Bosly returned, claiming attacks on two large MTs resulting in one flamer. The other two pilots, Flight Lieutenant A.J. Simpson and Flying Officer A.E. Morrison-Bell did not return. It transpired, however, that both were safe … 9 June: 'F/O Morrison-Bell returned to the Squadron shortly after 1200 hours today. On yesterday's operation, he force landed owing to his aircraft being hit by anti-aircraft fire. He landed in our lines, near an armoured car. And after removing most of the detachable parts from his aircraft, he was taken to the HQ of the armoured car crew. The 4th Armoured Brigade has made arrangements to salvage the aircraft. F/O Morrison-Bell made two runs over the target and hit two lorries and one unidentified tank.'

And on the 11th: 'It has now been learnt that F/Lt Simpson was forced to bale out of his aircraft, which had caught fire as a result of enemy action. He was wounded by shrapnel and is, at present, in the 62nd General Hospital.' Allan Simpson recounted the sortie: 'Our mission was to relieve the pressure on them from tanks, which were lobbing shells from a few thousand yards away. As we neared the target, we dove to pick up speed and attacked level from about 1,000 yards at ten feet off the deck (later that summer, some of the boys took off their tail wheels by hitting tank turrets; one bent his propeller on a tank.' He was hit and wounded during the run-in: 'My initial reaction was to cost the enemy as much as possible, and so I continued my attack on the German Mark III tank, then lined up another at which I got a good run, and then a truck.' He then decided it was time to get out of the area as it looked likely that the aircraft would not fly much longer, and was not sure how badly wounded he was. His account, in *All the Fine Young Eagles*; pp139–140, provided more – and fascinating – detail on his action, but the end result was that he bailed out, was picked up by ambulance and a few days later was back in Egypt.

Low-level ground attack like this was fraught with dangers – not just from the amount of fire put up by the enemy (and from time-to-time one's own side), but also the risk of hitting the ground, and, of course, the prowling fighters. Losses were high. Allan Simpson was lucky that he bailed out in an area where Allied forces were able to quickly pick him up, provide treatment and get him back to his unit to fight again.

Flight Lieutenant Philip Hillier had also been awarded an immediate DFC for this mission: 'In June, 1942, this officer participated in 2 sorties against a column of enemy armoured vehicles near

Sidi Rezegh. On his first sortie, in the face of heavy fire, he made 4 low level attacks on the target, hitting several tanks. On his second sortie, he flew so low that part of the tail unit snapped off on the turret of one of the vehicles he attacked. Despite the damage sustained to his aircraft he flew it safely to base. Flight Lieutenant Hillier played a gallant part in the operations which were attended with much success.'

The French were very appreciative of the RAF support, and on the 10th they sent a signal to the AOC: 'Bravo! Merci pour le RAF!' to which the AOC replied: 'Merci pour le sport!'

On 9 June, 33 Squadron was on a sweep, with 274 Squadron, over Bir Hacheim when they were bounced by 109s and MC.202s; in the ensuing combat two 109s were shot down and one MC.202 damaged, for one Hurricane with CAT 2 damage. A few days later another dogfight resulted in no victories but one Hurricane having to force-land at El Adem. The largest dogfight for some time took place on 12 June – with 100 or more enemy aircraft. The squadron came off worst – claiming four enemy aircraft damaged but for the loss of three aircraft. The month continued badly, with Sergeant Callister being killed on the 15th when his aircraft span in, and the same day the squadron's dispersal at Gambut was bombed by two 109s in a hit-and-run attack. The shrapnel caused CAT 2 damage to three Hurricanes and killed one airman (Leading Aircraftman Wiseman) and one injured.

In the early part of June, 112 Squadron lost pilots on a regular basis:

Date: June	Pilot	Aircraft	Fate
1st	Pilot Officer Wilson		PoW
4th	Pilot Officer Atkinson		
8th	Sergeant White	AK211	Safe with forward troops
9th	Sergeant Adye		
9th	Sergeant Greaves		Safe with forward troops
12th	Sergeant Cassel		Safe with forward troops
13th	Pilot Officer Edwards	AK949	
13th	Pilot Officer Carson	AL105	PoW
16th	Sergeant Newton		

It was a similar story for 213 Squadron, with five pilots lost in the first three weeks of June and a further four in the first few days of July, three on the 3rd alone.

The Luftwaffe and Panzer Army were still finding it difficult to collaborate or agree, although on the evening of the 9th, General Waldeau reported that more than 1,000 sorties had been flown to date supporting the Bir Hacheim operation. It was agreed that a major effort would be made on the 10th, with three waves of attacks. The first attack had to be curtailed because poor visibility (haze and dust) made it hard to distinguish friend from foe. The second and third waves were more successful and by the end of the day, 140 tons of bombs had been dropped by the Ju 87s and Ju 88s, which had been covered by large numbers of fighters. A number of combats took place, during which Marseilles added four claims, to take his total to eighty-one. With other parts of the Allied line collapsing, the Bir Hacheim position had to be abandoned on 11 June, with air cover enabling most of the garrison to escape. The defence had also enabled other parts of the Allied defence line to withdraw and not be encircled and destroyed.

Macchi 202 under 'restoration' by the SAAF. (*Bomb Finney SAAF*)

Spitfire of 92 Squadron damaged by 20mm fire; the squadron became operational in the Middle East in summer 1942. (*Colin Sinclair SAAF*)

'Throughout this black fortnight, when all that our forces had so painfully won seemed to be slipping away, the Desert Air Force fought hard and continuously. During the Knightsbridge battle Bostons, Hurricanes and Kittyhawks went out hour after hour on a shuttle service of bombing and strafing, returning only to refuel, rearm and take off again. The landing grounds shimmered in the June heat under a constant cloud of dust kicked up by the take-offs. Beneath it, ground crews worked each hour of daylight and far into the darkness; they abandoned their tents and dug themselves holes in the ground beside their aircraft in the dispersal areas, flinging themselves wearily into these holes to get a few hours' sleep when exhausted. After dark they muffled their heads in blankets and worked on their aircraft by the light of pocket torches; and they continued to work

Hurricane of 1 Squadron – note four kill marks. (*Bomb Finney SAAF*)

through bombing raids in which the enemy was using peculiarly unpleasant anti-personnel missiles known as 'butterfly bombs'. And while these men toiled on the ground through the midsummer heat, the pilots and aircrews flew, fought and flew again, without time to shave their beards or change their clothes. Certainly they earned Auchinleck's acknowledgment that 'it should be made clear that R.A.F. support for the Army has been unstinted at great sacrifice throughout the present campaign.' (*New Zealanders with the Royal Air Force*)

The Knightsbridge box was abandoned on 14 June and the Allies rapidly moved back to the borders of Egypt; the RAF was leapfrogging to airfields as it retreated – and then frequently attacking the Luftwaffe, now established at airfields that the RAF had itself recently been using! The mobility of the squadrons was essential and the groundcrew had to be quick off the mark to avoid being overrun – and also to ensure that nothing useful was left behind for the enemy. Billy Drake described the way 112 Squadron leapfrogged: 'The whole of the Squadron's ground echelon

SAAF Boston; the first unit to be equipped was 12 Squadron, exchanging its Marylands in March 1942 and then operating Bostons to December 1943. (*Allan Mossop SAAF*)

was divided into two parties, A and B. As the A party moved back to a new landing ground, the B party continued to service, refuel and re-arm the aircraft as long as possible. The last to leave each airfield were the pilots and aircraft, who usually took off for an operation over the front as the B party withdrew, then landing at the new base further back, where the A party had already set up and were waiting for them.' (*Billy Drake, Fighter Leader*, p47).'

No.14 Squadron had bad luck on the night of 13 June. 'A night intruder operation was arranged for this evening, also some night flying practice for less experienced crews. The presence of enemy aircraft necessitated two of the night practice aircraft flying to a pre-arranged position until the All Clear was given. Despite efforts by all local wireless stations to recall these aircraft when the warning period had finished, it was impossible to contract them.' This highlights that losses of valuable crews and aircraft were not confined to operational flying. One of the Blenheims tasked to attack Crete on the night of the 14th also failed to return.

Searches were under way for the two missing aircraft from the 13th and, at midday on the 15th, news was received of a crashed Blenheim 8 miles south of LG10 so a road party was sent to investigate. Later the same day one of the searching Blenheims signaled that it was, 'Landing in the desert having sighted two of the crew and the wrecked aircraft missing from last night's operation. Aircraft returned to base bringing the Observer, Pilot Officer Ridley, and air gunner, Sergeant Payne, damaging undercarriage on landing. The pilot, Squadron Leader Pirie, has not yet been located having commenced to walk immediately after the aircraft crashed.' Meanwhile, the crashed Blenheim reported south of LG10 was identified as Z7517, one of the missing aircraft from the 13th, but three crew were killed in the crash. No trace was found of the other aircraft, Z6044.

On the 17th the wing bombed and strafed Gazala airfield, which the Axis air forces were using in strength; 112 Squadron was as usual in the forefront and claimed nine damaged. Billy Drake of 112 Squadron was awarded a bar to his DFC in July: 'Squadron Leader Drake is a skillful pilot and a fine leader. He has displayed great energy and has led his squadron on every sortie in the latest battle of Libya. One day in June, 1942, an attack was made against Gazala aerodrome which resulted in a number of enemy aircraft being destroyed or damaged on the ground. Squadron Leader Drake has personally scored hits on enemy transport vehicles and on a heavy tank. In addition, he has destroyed at least 5 enemy aircraft and damaged a number of others in air combats.'

On the same day, the Luftwaffe fighters flew free sweeps to counter the Allied air attacks, claiming twelve enemy aircraft shot down, with Marseilles reaching 101, which led to him being awarded the Knight's Cross with Swords and Oak Leaves, the third of his awards. JG 27 could celebrate this, but it also lost seven aircraft when RAF fighters strafed its new airfield at Gazala.

Reg Pfeiffer recalled the 'move backwards' in 1942 … and how useful it was to have beer in the aircraft: '3 Squadron was instructed to retire (retreat?) to another strip some 50-odd miles east, as enemy tanks were not far away. Then came an order to do a sweep to get some information so a few of us were told to take off, get the information and land at the new strip where the Squadron would be. Those concerned were Lou Spence, Butch Furness and I together with, I think, Lance Threlkeld and Vic Curtis, but I am not sure of the last two.

'When we landed there was not a soul within miles of the strip so we dispersed the aircraft and sat down to await the Squadron's arrival. When dusk arrived all by itself, it looked even money as to whether our next contact would be with our side or theirs. We were not equipped for night flying and doubted that there was any field within range that was so equipped, so the only choice was to sit tight and wait for first light in the morning.

'We found what had been a circular gun emplacement of sandbags about eight feet in diameter and four feet or so high so we huddled together under cockpit covers to keep out the cold wind whilst listening for tanks or other unwelcome sounds. Suddenly Lou Spence said he had a carton of canned beer in his aircraft, so he was immediately directed to go and get it. Then it was found no-one had a knife or any tool which could possibly be used as a can opener.

'Undaunted, Butch produced his .38 Smith & Wesson and proceeded to shoot a hole diagonally through the top and side of the can. To hell with lead poisoning! We cleaned up all the beer and probably would have taken on the Panzer Division had it showed up.'

Everything was being thrown into the land battle, with the heavy bombers attacking concentration areas, resupply routes and major enemy movements.

DFM to Flight Sergeant David Stewart, 70 Squadron: 'One night in June, 1942, Flight Sergeant Stewart was the captain of an aircraft detailed to attack enemy armoured vehicles and motor transport. At a very low altitude and carried out two machinegun attacks. Flight Sergeant Stewart's aircraft was then hit by machine gun and cannon fire from an enemy fighter. Displaying skilful airmanship he evaded the attacker and, despite the severe damage sustained, flew the aircraft back to base where he made a successful landing with the undercarriage retracted.'

The Wellington (DV564) had left LG104 on the evening of 25 June for its target near Sidi Barrani and, after releasing its bombs, was attacked by a Ju 88, the attack fatally wounding the rear gunner (Flight Sergeant G Wagner) and injuring two more of the crew. The fires in the aircraft were extinguished by Pilot Officer T. Howes and Stewart flew back to base and belly-landed close to the flare path. Two other Wellingtons were lost with casualties the same night; DV522 of 37 Squadron was shot down by a fighter; one crew member bailed out and was killed, the others stayed with the aircraft as it crash-landed in the desert, injuring both pilots. The crew walked towards Allied lines and were picked up by a patrol about three hours later. The other loss was Z8572 of 104 Squadron, which was hit by a bomb as it was about to take off from LG106; two of the crew were killed and the remaining four were injured.

The resistance of early June became the collapse of late June and the Allied forces tumbled back eastwards, the DAF hopping back to airfields and then mounting attacks on those airfields it had just left. The intensity of operations remained high, with 112 Squadron noting on the 26th that: 'The majority of pilots flew four sorties each, and were thoroughly tired by nightfall. The length of the sorties varied between an hour and 45 minutes. Just as the last mission returned there was a panic

B Flight of 70 Squadron at Abu Sueir, 1942; the squadron flew the entire desert campaign with Wellingtons, from September 1940 through to January 1945, when it received Liberators.

and several pilots had to forego their dinners. In the engagement that followed, Fg Off Whitmore shot down a Me.109F, and Plt Off Cudden was posted missing. The Squadron moved that night to LG106 (El Daba), the enemy approaching somewhat rapidly.'

Pilot Officer Cudden returned a few days later in an Army ambulance. Almost a month later, on 27 July, he had to force-land ET527 because of oil trouble – this time he was able to 'thumb a lift with a Lysander' and get back to the squadron the same day! Brian Thompson recorded on 22 June: 'Heard today that 25,000 [Allied] prisoners had been taken in Tobruk – bad show – things are not too good. Wonder what in hell is our army trying to do – lose the war?'

On 26 June, 450 Squadron had a busy day, flying eight bomber escorts, one with eight Kittyhawks, five with six aircraft and one with three aircraft. 'During the first two no enemy aircraft were encountered and the Bostons bombed with little or no A/A opposition. The third patrol was attacked by 3 Me 109s and one Macchi 202, but none of the aircraft were damaged. Three Me 109s attacked the fourth patrol but did not reach the Bostons. P/O T E Jones's aircraft was seen to go down in a dive, but flattened out near the ground, the final result was unobserved. Me 109s again attacked the fifth patrol and P/O M J Jones's aircraft was seen to go into a steep dive. The pilot was seen to bale out successfully. Several of our aircraft were damaged, but all the other pilots retuned safely, and one Me 109 is claimed as damaged by P/O Schaaf. The sixth patrol was as top cover to the bombers with No.233 Wing providing an umbrella of fighter aircraft at 14,000ft. Our aircraft also carried bombs on these patrols. The bombing was very effective and several hits were scored in spite of very heavy A/A fire from the target.' (450 Squadron ORB)

The drama was not yet over for the day.

'At 2030 hours an order was received from HQ 239 Wing that all serviceable aircraft are to be flown out immediately by experienced night flying pilots to Fuka aerodrome. All ground personnel are to pack immediately, leave tents standing, and move out. Orders were accordingly issued to the Squadron, the aircraft took off for Fuka, and ground staff moved off for El Daba at 2100 hours. The adjutant, some officers and ground troops, with the Staff Car, the Pick Up and one truck, remained to see that all personnel had been evacuated. Soon after this, further orders were received from HQ 239 Wing, who advised that the whole squadron was now not to move, but only B Party. Adjutant explained that this order was too late, as the entire squadron had already left and he was then instructed to remain with his small party overnight. Sergeant Simpson and P/O Schaaf both had accidents and damaged their aircraft on landing. This was due to the pilots having to make a night landing without the aid of a flare path, although 239 Wing had advised the CO that a flare path would be at Fuka aerodrome.'

J.E. 'Jack' Frost had served with the SAAF squadrons in the East Africa campaigns but had gone back to South Africa when the campaign ended. Promoted to major, he took 5 Squadron SAAF to the Western Desert and was soon in action, claiming an He 111 as probable on 11 March. His first confirmed victory was a Fiat Br.20 on 27 May, but it was in June that he, and the SAAF squadrons, really began to make their mark.

On 3 June Jack Frost got a Ju 87 near Bir Hacheim. On 5 June Jack was himself shot down in the Knightsbridge area, luckily landing in the lines of the 1st South African Division. Two days later, on 7 June, he got his revenge by getting a probable Me 109 over Knightsbridge, and damaging another on the 8th over Bir Hacheim. He got a probable (a Me 109) on the 9th over Bir Hacheim again, but it was to be his last claim.

So well had 233 Wing supported the light bombers during this period of the most intense air effort that not one bomber was lost through enemy fighter action. Those lost and damaged were due to anti-aircraft fire. On 16 June, at 1840 hours, six Tomahawks of 5 Squadron, with four of 4 Squadron, and two Kittyhawks of 2 Squadron, set off once again to escort the light bombers, Bostons of 24 Squadron, raiding enemy transport west of El Adem. No.2 Squadron provided top cover while 4 Squadron gave close cover. They were jumped by Me l09Fs and 2 Squadron lost Lieutenant De Villiers (shot down in flames, but he returned that evening) and Lieutenant Bryant, who was wounded and his aircraft badly damaged. Lieutenant McGregor of 4 Squadron was wounded in the face and his aircraft also badly damaged, but he got back safely.

No.5 Squadron was the heaviest sufferer; Lieutenant R.C, Denham and Major Jack Frost DFC were lost. Frost was heard to order 5 Squadron to reform over the landing ground, having fought a running battle to protect the bombers right back to their base, but no more was heard of him. The SAAF's top scorer of the war (credited with fourteen and a third confirmed kills at the time of

Major Jack Frost DFC and Bar, SAAF, failed to return from a mission on 16 June 1942.

his death; later figures denote at least fifteen), was gone. Oberleutnant (later Hauptmann) Hans-Joachim Marseille, the leading German scorer in the desert, credited with 151 victories there (158 in all), was in action at the time in the area and claimed four victories – one of these could have been Frost but there were several other claims and four by Feldwebel Steinhausen of the same formation as Marseille.

The loss of Frost was a heavy blow; he had doubled his score in a few days, and had led his young squadron with great vigour and elan. Repeated searches were made for him in the next few days but neither he nor his wrecked aircraft was ever found. He was awarded a bar to his DFC, although this was not announced until July 1943: 'Within a very short period of time this officer trained his squadron to a very high degree of efficiency. While operating with a wing the unit inflicted heavy casualties in the enemy in the air and in low-level attacks on objectives on the ground. Major Frost has displayed great courage and has destroyed two enemy aircraft and damaged several others.' (AMB 10937)

The bad luck of 233 Squadron with the Baltimore continued in June. Operating against Barce on 8 June, AG777 exploded over the target with the loss of all crew, causing damage (that proved unrepairable) to AG825. Another aircraft was lost on the 19th when Pilot Officer Bowley (AG772), after his attack on Tmimi, tried to belly-land in poor conditions at LG116. His wing-tip struck the ground and the aircraft crashed, causing a hung up bomb to explode, three of the crew were killed and one injured. Two aircraft were damaged by fighter attacks on the 26th and had to crash-land, and the following day three Baltimores that left LG116 to position at LG24 were shot down shortly after take-off, with all the crew killed in two of the aircraft and two injured in the other aircraft. The same month saw the experienced (Blenheim) unit, 55 Squadron, re-equip with Baltimores. What had looked like a good deal on getting rid of the vulnerable Blenheim was looking less positive. They actually lost their first aircraft on 22 June, when AG813 was written off in a landing accident, the pilot being on a solo training flight.

30 June: 'A most immediate signal from AHQ Egypt to the effect that every available aircraft is immediately to be made serviceable, to be armed and, where applicable, made ready to carry bombs. Major inspections to be ignored during present crisis.' At the end of June, the German propaganda machine was stating that Rommel would be in Cairo 'within days' – and many on both sides believed the message.

Following a conference in late June between Rommel and Kesselring, the former was all for an immediate push on Egypt. Kesselring was less convinced: 'First came a report on the situation from Rommel, who declared that there were practically no enemy forces of any significance opposing him and that his army could reach Cairo within 10 days. Even though I realized that Rommel had more insight in the situation on the ground than I, my objections would have to be raised. Any further advance, even if there was only a minimum of combat activity, would result in a maximum loss of armoured and motor vehicles. The necessary supplies would not become available for a long time. Even though there might be no sizeable British ground force reserves in Egypt, one could be sure that the first reinforcements from the Near East were already moving up. I felt confident to speak for the Luftwaffe. My flying forces would face the Nile in a completely exhausted condition with aircraft that needed overhauling and without sufficient supplies. They would be opposed by fully combat-ready units which could be further reinforced in the shortest time. As an airman I considered it madness to attack head on an airbase that was fully intact. Because of the decisive importance of the part played by aviation I had to reject from this point of view alone the continuation of the offensive that had an as objective the conquest of Egypt and the seizure of Cairo.'

The night-painted (black) Wellington provides a backdrop to the PR shot of a donkey and local with RAF personnel.

USAAF Strategic Bombers

A USAAF unit had been created, as HALPRO (The Halverson Project) in 1942 to attack Japan from China, but while transiting the Middle East the mission was changed and it was attached to 205 Group. The reason for holding the bombers in the Middle East was to provide a strike force for attacking the important oil facilities at Ploesti 'at the earliest possible time'. The mission was flown on 12 June. Thirteen bombers left Fayid between 2230 and 2300 hours on 11 June 'instructed to proceed individually to the target, attack at high level, and then continue, if possible, to an aerodrome near Ramadi, Iraq. At the objective there was broken overcast at 10,000 to 12,000 feet which practically obscured the targets. All 13 planes reached the objective. The attack, which was a surprise, was made at dawn. A majority of the aircraft bombed from below the clouds. About 10 bombed the Astra Romana Refinery at Ploesti [the biggest and most important].' (*The Ploesti Mission, USAF Historical Study #103*)

The attack seemed to do little damage, but equally no aircraft were lost to enemy action, although four ended up in neutral Turkey, where the crews were interned. It was still an amazing mission – 2,600 miles. The more successful and memorable attack on Ploesti was in August 1943, but that is outside our scope. The significance for our story is that American bombers were in theatre ... and they stayed.

The Ploesti attack was followed by participation, on the 15th, in an attack on Taranto, but at that point the unit still expected to head off to China. By mid-June the USAAF had agreed to provide strategic bombers to the theatre and US Army Air Forces in the Middle East (USAFIME) was formed under General Russell Maxwell.

'It was not the intention of the War Department that the planes of HALPRO should be employed in local tactical operations unsuited to the technical characteristics of heavy bombers. Only the extreme need of weakening the enemy close to the front, so that the effects of the attack would be felt at once on the battle area, justified the use of these bombers for this purpose.' (*The AAF in the Middle East, USAH Historical Study #108*)

HALPRO missions in June in North Africa:

21–22: Benghazi
23–24: Benghazi
26–27: Tobruk
29–30: Tobruk; first combat loss with B-24 failed to return (FTR)

By the end of June, a number of B-17s had also arrived, as well as Major General Lewis Brereton, on secondment from 10th Air Force (India). All the US bombers concentrated at Lydda in Palestine. The first B-17 mission took place on 2 July, a night mission to Tobruk with B-24s. From this point on, the weight of the US bomber effort continued to increase.

The experienced 98th BG arrived in mid-August and with 12th BG and 57th FG attached to RAF units in the desert, the American contribution to what they called the Egypt–Libya campaign became well established. With more units came another command change, with the formation of the IX Bomber Command and IX Fighter Command, and when Lieutenant General Frank Andrews took command of USAFIME in November the organization became the Ninth Air Force.

112 Squadron kept a copy of the July 1942 'well done' message sent out by the AOC-in-C.

NO. 112 SQUADRON
R.A.F.
ORDERLY ROOM
23. JUL 1942
Ref. No. 253. P3.

To: All ranks of the Allied Air Forces in the Middle East from the A.O.C.-in-C.

During the past few days I have received the messages which are printed below. I can add nothing to them except to say I am proud to be at the head of such a team as you have proved to be. In the air and on the ground, in the battle and in the no less vital work behind, you have achieved the impossible. The battle is not yet over; and there is still much to be done; I know you will do it with the same relentless determination you have already shown.

Message from the Prime Minister.

Here at home we are watching with enthusiasm the brilliant supreme exertions of the Royal Air Force in the battle now proceeding in Egypt. From every quarter the reports come in of the effect of the vital part which your officers and men are playing in this Homeric struggle for the Nile Valley. The days of the Battle of Britain are being repeated far from home. We are sure you will be to our glorious Army the friend that endureth to the end.

Message from the Secretary of State for Air.

All here have the fullest confidence in you, your Staffs and your superb Squadrons. We know that throughout this critical battle you have given and will give the last ounce of effort in support of the Army. You are writing a glorious page in the history of the Royal Air Force.

Message from the Chief of the Air Staff.

No words of mine can fully express the admiration of all the Royal Air Force for the magnificent efforts of your Air and Armoured Car Crews, your Maintenance Personnel, Commanders and Staffs during the last three weeks. At this critical time we have the utmost confidence in you all. We trust that before long you will have the chance to show the enemy that your Force is even more formidable in pursuit than it has been in retirement.

Message from Field Marshal Smuts.

Please convey to Air Chief Marshal Tedder my very warm congratulations on magnificent performance of Royal Air Force in this prolonged struggle for Egypt. Climax has been reached at El Alamein in what has been most heartening news for many weeks. May this continue until enemy is finally hurled back to whence he came. Proud to know that S.A.A.F. have had their share in this proud record of achievement. Tobruk will be more than avenged.

Message from Marshal of the Royal Air Force, Lord Trenchard.

All my heartiest congratulations to you and Coningham, your Staffs and Ground Organisation as well as the wonderful Air Crews on their magnificent work during the last fortnight. I feel all owe you and yours a debt of gratitude that cannot be expressed in words.

Message from General Freyberg, 2nd N.Z.E.F.

May I take this opportunity also of conveying to you the admiration of all ranks of N.Z. Div. for the magnificent work of Bomber and Fighter Commands in Western Desert fighting.

CAIRO.
July 1942.

The Desert Air Force and the other RAF units had scored a strategic victory over the mindset of Kesselring – but as yet the British did not know that. Furthermore, Allied air power was about to benefit, albeit in small scale initially, from the assignment of USAAF units to the Middle East.

It was a low point in British fortunes after the ups and downs of advance and retreat. The difference though was that the DAF was now able to mount hundreds of sorties – day and night – blunting Axis advances, destroying logistics and the all-important fuel supplies, and generally wearing down the Axis forces: Rommel – 'the enemy air force by its continual day and night operations has caused considerable loss among our troops, delayed and, at times, cut off our supplies … the supply situation is tense owing to continual attacks on German supplies at Tobruk and Matruh.' Also, when the Luftwaffe had concentrated on the airfields at Gazala, Tmimi and Sidi Barrani it had been subjected to heavy night attacks by 205 Group, which flew sixty or seventy sorties a night, in many cases with flare illumination provided by the Albacores of 821 and 826 Squadrons FAA.

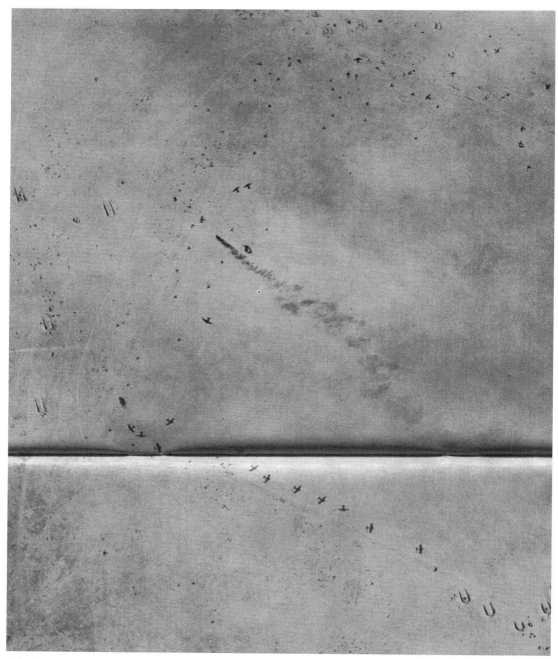

July 1942 and Axis aircraft dispersed at Sidi Barrani.

It was a defeat for sure, but it could have been a disaster: 'But the greatest achievement of Desert Air Force came during the retreat to El Alamein; for while the Eighth Army was moving back some 400 miles in a fortnight, it not only escaped destruction on the ground but it also escaped decimation from the air. This second fact was the more remarkable since, for days on end, the coastal road presented the astonishing spectacle of a congested mass of slowly moving troops and transport, a target such as pilots' dreams are made of. A little attention from Stukas and Messerschmitts and the lorries must have piled up in endless confusion. But the enemy bombers did not appear and the Eighth Army reached El Alamein virtually unmolested from the air – during one period of three days when the congestion was greatest, its casualties on the road from air attacks are recorded as being just six men and one lorry. This incredible immunity was partly due to the inability of the Luftwaffe to keep up with Rommel's advance but, when due allowance is made for this fact, the German dive-bombers could still have wrought havoc among our retreating forces had their activities not been vigorously discouraged by the Royal Air Force. Much of the work of its squadrons was done out of sight of our troops; highly effective attacks, for example, were made on the Gazala airfields as soon as they were occupied by the enemy, so crippling the German fighter effort from the start. Later, enemy squadrons were twice caught on the ground, at Tmimi and Sidi Barrani, at critical moments during the pursuit. And such fighters as the Germans did manage to bring forward were kept so busy trying to protect their own forces that they had little leisure to attack ours. But the Army realized the protection the RAF was giving it. "Thank God, you didn't let the Huns Stuka us," General Freyberg told Tedder, "because we were an appalling target."

'And even though Desert Air Force was continually forced to retire from its forward bases, the effort in the air was increased and not diminished. During the first week of the German attack Coningham's squadrons flew 2339 sorties, but in the last week, when the El Alamein line was withstanding the initial shock, they flew 5458. At the same time, the proportion of aircraft serviceable, so far from declining as the fight continued and casualties mounted, actually showed a slight improvement. All this was made possible by the strenuous and indeed heroic efforts of the air and ground crews, by the boldness of their leaders and the remarkable efficiency of the organization that had been created. Weeks before, Coningham had had plans prepared for retreat as well as for advance and the landing grounds to the rear had been stocked with petrol and bombs. His squadrons were therefore able to make a steady withdrawal, fighting all the time. And as they moved back, repair and salvage units stripped the airfields of all useful equipment and supplies. The result was that the Luftwaffe advanced on to empty desert while the Royal Air Force moved back on to well-stocked bases from which it could operate with greater intensity. (*New Zealanders with the Royal Air Force*)

Meanwhile, on the Egyptian frontier, the defence lines were strengthened and reinforcements started to arrive. The RAF was able to operate from a number of well-established bases, and with short supply lines, which enabled a high sortie rate.

Road sign – the key places and distances. (*Tom Meek SAAF*)

The debate as to if the assault on Malta, a parachute assault supported by naval landings, or the move in Egypt should receive support, had not died with the late June meetings. Hitler's view was that the Malta operation would be a costly failure as the Italian navy would not prove capable of providing the right support – and there were no German naval assets so there had to be total reliance on the Italians. He also stated that Rommel's success to date offered a unique opportunity to finish the war in this theatre. With this in mind OKW supported the drive to Egypt and the cancellation of the Malta plan; both decisions turned out to be wrong.

Kesselring's view was that, 'The Armed Forces High Command dug the grave of the German-Italian Panzer Army in the North Africa theatre of war. The responsibility for the defeat and all its consequences that made themselves felt in the overall situation rests fully with the Supreme Command of Germany's military forces.'

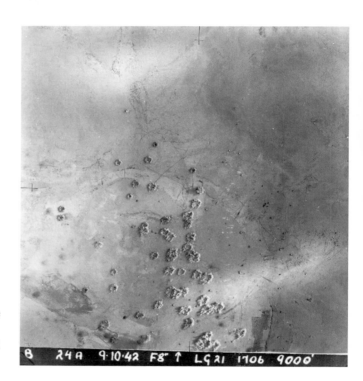

Bombing of LG21, 9 October 1942; the fighter squadrons provided cover for the bombers to attempt to hit dispersed targets. (*George Hilary, SAAF*)

Ju 52 forced down and then strafed, October 1942.

Chapter 6

Borders of Egypt: Facing Defeat

By summer 1942 the Allies were now entrenched on the El Alamein line – on the borders of Egypt and with the Axis forces close to success; one more push, one more Allied retreat and the whole of the Middle East and Levant would fall, the Suez Canal would be lost, and the whole shape of the war changed. The defence of the new position was critical and would depend on the gritty determination of the ground forces, the air support they were provided – and the war of supplies; in the back-and-forth of the desert campaigns, the latter was critical.

'Since the beginning of August the desert had been fairly quiet. The two armies faced each other on the line south from El Alamein; the two air forces flew as little as possible in order to build up their strength. The desert fighter force was indeed stronger. Not only had it increased to 21 squadrons but the standard of serviceability within the squadrons had been improved. Moreover, there were now three squadrons of Spitfires, sweeping high over the battle area and for the first time causing the Messerschmitt pilots to look apprehensively upwards instead of down. It was said a little maliciously that from that time onwards no German pilot would ever admit to having been shot down by anything but a Spitfire and no Italian pilot ever condescended to destroy anything else.' A nice piece of Spitfire mythology in *RAF Middle East* (HMSO 1943); as a wartime publication, its content is useful but also has a 'stance', and promoting the Spitfire mythology, which had started in the Battle of Britain, was part of that.

In reality, the Spitfire was never the dominant type, in numbers or achievement, in the Desert War. However, pilots were pleased; Jerry Jarrold was with 80 Squadron in the Western Desert some time later when Spitfire Vs arrived to replace the Hurricanes: 'We were overjoyed to have delivered to us Spitfire VCs – not necessarily brand new, but none the less welcome. The Spitfire was much more manoeuvrable than the Hurricane and could out-climb it and get higher, and with its reputation it was one of those aircraft that all fighter pilots wanted to fly. However, the Hurricane was a much sturdier beast, and we reckoned that in a forced-landing it would go through a house, whereas the Spitfire would simply crumple!'

By this time, 239 Wing comprised four Kittyhawk squadrons: 112 and 260 RAF, plus 3 and 450 RAAF, under the command of Wing Commander Howard Mayers, although they frequently operated with a second Kittyhawk outfit, 233 Wing, which was primarily SAAF.

For a somewhat unusual action the same month, another 112 Squadron pilot was awarded a DFC, Flight Lieutenant Geoffrey Garton: 'In June, 1942, when it became necessary to retire from a landing ground. Flight Lieutenant Garton displayed considerable skill and initiative in salvaging a bomber which had been stripped of much of its equipment. Without having flown this type of aircraft previously he successfully flew the bomber, with two passengers, to another aerodrome where he made a safe landing. Flight Lieutenant Garton has participated in many operational sorties in which he has destroyed at least 4 hostile aircraft.'

The initial assault by Rommel against the northern and central parts of the Allied position on the 1st was attacked from the air: 'The Bostons and Baltimores took off at first light and continued all day to bomb the German columns. Flying with them as part of the fighter escort went the Kittybombers.

Dust was already stirring with the early morning when they reached the target – dust that a moment later billowed up in explosive clouds, through which the Kittybombers dived to add their weight to bomb load. It went on like that all day. There was little air opposition – only one ME109 was shot down – but that was partly because other fighter squadrons were strafing the landing grounds near Sidi Barrani, where they destroyed or temporarily disabled 19 enemy aircraft.' (*RAF Middle East*, *ibid*)

Wellingtons, supported by FAA Albacores dropping flares, continued the attacks overnight, while Wellingtons and Liberators also intensified the campaign against port and support facilities, Tobruk become a frequent target. On the 3rd, 'The day-bombing pressure reached a record in the number of sorties flown and weight of bombs dropped. The day began in the usual way, with the first Boston and Baltimore raids over desert territory. But as they flew back they ran into strong formations of Messerschmitts and Macchis sweeping the battle area. There were dogfights all over the desert sky. They culminated in the evening between a formation of 15 Stukas heavily escorted by fighters, a South African Hurricane squadron [1 SAAF] and a top cover of RAF fighters. The Stukas were in three V-formations of five, the first of which was just peeling off to make its dive. As the Stukas dived, the 11 Hurricanes dived on them. The leading Hurricane pilot, Major G J Le Mesurier, hit the first Stuka, which exploded. The other Stukas panicked, put their noses down and tried to get away by skimming the ground. Only two of them may have succeeded. The remaining 13 were shot down by the South Africans. Some were chased as far as their own airfields at Fuka and shot down there. One Hurricane pilot, Flight Lieutenant R J P Collingwood himself shot down three Stukas in rapid succession.' (*RAF Middle East*, *ibid*).

80 Squadron noted: 'No.1 Squadron SAAF had a 'Stuka Party' in the evening having shot down 13 of 15, although Flt Cdr may have shot down CO by mistake, but latter radiod 'good shooting, am going to bale out.' He returned to the Squadron some days later.'

No.33 Squadron was happy to swap its Hurricane IIBs for IICs at Kilo 8 late in June, and commenced ops on 1 July. However, it did not start well … Sergeant Woollard was SD and injured (he bailed out) during the air battles of the 3rd.

The same day, Tedder was promoted to Air Chief Marshal and amongst the signals of congratulation to the AOC-in-C Middle East was one from the Secretary of State for Air: 'All here have the fullest confidence in you, your staffs and your squadrons. We know that throughout this critical battle you have given and will go on giving the last ounce of effort in support of the Army. You are writing a glorious page in the history of the RAF.'

On the 4th, General Auchinleck sent a message to all formations in the Western desert: 'Very grateful if you would convey to all ranks of the RAF the Army's deep appreciation of their magnificent efforts.' This brought an end – and a high-water mark – to the Axis advance. Although neither side knew it yet, the tide had turned and the next land battle would be the start of the Allied advance that would end with the Germans and Italians evicted from North Africa. However, there was plenty of fighting to come before that.

For 33 Squadron the initial losses with their new IICs continued, and Pilot Officer Merritt was shot down on the 4th. Another Hurricane was shot down the following day, but this time there was payback with 33 Squadron claiming two 109s destroyed and one 202 damaged. July continued badly and two more Hurricanes were shot down on the 8th.

The RAF was still learning the tactical lessons … and for 33 Squadron this meant a few days of intense training and trying a new formation with an 'attack flight' of four aircraft in line abreast of sections, supported by two flights of four aircraft line abreast port and starboard 2,000ft higher. However, the trial was not considered a success and the squadron reverted to its old tactics. The

Harry Gaynor was part of the SAAF 'Stuka Party' in July and claimed two of the thirteen Ju87s shot down by the squadron. He subsequently commanded 2 Squadron and was killed in action (strafing) in 1944. (*Fritz Johl SAAF*)

situation for the squadron did not improve in the rest of July, with seven more aircraft losses, although some of the pilots survived, including Sergeant Reading, who force-landed and walked back to Allied lines. The Hurricanes had shot down three enemy aircraft in the same period but the casualty rates were too high – which may not have impressed the five new pilots who arrived on 29 July.

LG89 and the drivers of 6 Squadron get their chance to pose for the camera … not pilots, not maintenance personnel, but drivers – a key group of men when it came to the frequent, lengthy and hazardous moving around of squadrons.

It was also important to protect against German night raids, and the NF force had been boosted in May when 46 Squadron reformed in Egypt with Beaufighters, working closely with 89 Squadron. Both units had a day and night role and, as previously mentioned, the fire power of the Beaus was very useful in attacking ground targets. Flight Lieutenant Mackenzie, with Pilot Officer Craig as his radio observer, were a most successful Beaufighter crew in No.46 Squadron; one night early in July they intercepted and shot down a Heinkel 111 bomber near Alexandria and then a few weeks later they shot another night bomber down in the sea off Aboukir; a further encounter followed in September when they caught a Heinkel approaching Alexandria and sent it down with engines on fire to explode on the ground within sight of an Allied airfield.

80 Squadron, 9 July: 'Squadron commenced ops at first light. Four aircraft ground strafed MT and tentage along the coast road, the remainder of the Squadron acting as top cover. The strafers did their stuff but it was too dark to observe results although an imposing looking tent near the beach was treated with cannon shell which had the effect of "not letting sleeping dogs lie". Were scrambled in the afternoon and saw some 109s but they were too far away for combat.'

80 Squadron, 10 July: 'Patrolled between El Alamein – Ghazal at 10,000ft. About 15 JU87s were seen flying Eastwards. Squadron was unable to intercept as they were engaged by 14 ME109s. We destroyed 2 and damaged 2 more. P/O Bradley-Smith (USA) was injured, his aircraft being Cat III. Went out again in the evening and saw many aircraft but light was too bad to engage. We were attacked by approx. 24 ME109s which were escorting a formation of Stukas. Sergeant Sykes failed to return and P/O Wales of 92 Squadron [attached to 80 Squadron] force landed and is in hospital. The bombers were forced to drop their bombs over waste ground.'

This was a typical pattern for the fighter units – patrols, scrambles, engagements and trying to prevent bombers reaching their targets. All part of protecting the lines.

On 4 July Peter Metelerkamp took over as temporary CO of 1 Squadron SAAF, a post that was confirmed as permanent in early August when he was promoted to major. He had originally joined the squadron in March and in July shot down four Ju 87s and a Bf 109. On 1 September his aircraft was badly damaged in combat with Hans-Joachim Marseille but he managed to get back to base and crash-land; he was hospitalized for a short while. Returning to combat, he added a Bf 109 to his score (to take him to five confirmed) but was then shot down by a Ju 88 gunner on 13 December. Nothing more was heard until his body was washed ashore near Benghazi (his grave is at the Benghazi War Cemetery).

There was a DFM for Sergeant Edmund Waller, 252 Squadron, July 1942: 'This airman was the observer of an aircraft which took part in an attack on the aerodrome at Derna. During the

One of the most well-known and respected SAAF pilots, Peter Metelerkamp, served with 1 Squadron from early 1942 but was shot down and killed on 13 December 1942, probably by return fire from a Ju 88 rear gunner. (*Peter Metelerkamp SAAF*)

And there was some time to visit Ancient Egypt … SAAF personnel on time out at the pyramids. (*Harold Barnett SAAF*)

operation, his pilot received wounds in both legs. Sergeant Waller immediately applied a tourniquet to his comrade's right leg and then, taking over the controls, he flew the aircraft until the pilot revived. During the return journey the pilot fainted twice, but on each occasion Sergeant Waller skillfully controlled the aircraft. Eventually a safe landing was made at base. Throughout, this airman displayed great coolness and resource.'

This Blenheim-equipped unit had arrived in the Middle East in June 1941, initially operating as part of 272 Squadron. Its primary role was anti-shipping and, from early 1942, operating mainly from Idku, it was using Beaufighter VIs in this role.

The tank-busting Hurricane IIDs of 6 Squadron recorded their first really successful day on 14 July: 'W/C Porteous [and 5 others] set out on an anti-tank sweep shared a devastating attack on a

A South African UDI entertainment visit to Wadi Natrun; shows by groups such as this, and ENSA, provided some measure of 'normality'. (*George Muir SAAF*)

column out of which one lorry escaped. Eleven lorries, one M13 and two armoured cars were hit in this column.' (6 Squadron ORB)

Flying Officer McPhee failed to return. The month remained a difficult one, with a number of sorties failing to find suitable targets, frequent damage from ground fire, more losses, but also an increasing number of targets destroyed. To emphasize how low the Hurricanes flew to attack targets: 'The attack was being carried out at 10 feet and the starboard wing root and airscrew struck one of the railway lines supporting the target' (squadron ORB); this was a training attack on the screen target and the accident was attributed to the pilot failing to pull up in time after firing. Ten feet!

As part of the Allied plan for securing the El Alamein line and disrupting German preparations, the Australian 9th Division launched an offensive on the northern flank to take the high ground at Tel El Eisa. The Australians spent the next few days fighting off heavy counter-attacks as Rommel redirected much of his forces against them. The 9th Division infantry owed much to Australian, British and South African artillery, as well as the Desert Air Force (DAF), in repelling these counter-attacks. Australians were also present in the DAF, flying with Nos. 3 and 450 Squadrons, RAAF. Allied infantrymen had varying opinions regarding armoured support, feeling that sometimes the tanks provided welcome support and protection, but also that sometimes they failed them completely.' (AWM account)

Colonel Bonner Fellers, American military attaché in Cairo, toured the campaign area to gain insights into how air–land co–operation was working. His report summarized the position well: 'We made an analysis of the RAF missions. About 70 per cent was behind the line – enemy airdromes, communications, fighter sweeps and things like that. German Air Force operation is the opposite. About 65 per cent of missions flown are over their troops in direct support to further advance units or for their protection. Now, the RAF philosophy is swinging towards that of the GAF but they may change when the emergency is over. As I came back from the front on the 19th July, the function of the RAF was to give direct support to the Eighth Army. "We had to come to it," I was told.' (*Ninth Air Force in the Western Desert Campaign, AAF Historical Studies #30*)

Tanks and motor vehicles provided the punch and mobility of the ground forces – and so petrol supplies were critical – increasingly so in the mobile nature of the back and forth conflict with Rommel. While the air forces also needed petrol it was small in comparison to the thirst of ground vehicles, especially tanks, although it was to have an impact on Luftwaffe sortie rates later in the North Africa campaign. While fuel was the key logistic element, all military supplies also had to be conveyed to the theatre – for the Axis forces this meant convoys, primarily from Italy. The Mediterranean was therefore very much part of the North African War. The effect of all this effort and endeavour is seen in the diary of the

On 4 July 1942, 1 Squadron SAAF marked a memorable day with the destruction of fifteen Ju87s. (*Peter Metelerkamp SAAF*)

Hurricane IIBs remained the main type for 1 Squadron through much of 1942, although a few IICs were used in the autumn, before Spitfire VCs arrived in November. (*Peter Metelerkamp SAAF*)

German Afrika Korps, where difficulties of supply and damage and loss caused by Allied air attacks receive repeated mention. On 21 July, Rommel himself reported that, 'The enemy air force by its continual day and night operations has caused considerable loss among our troops, delayed and, at times, cut off our supplies … the supply situation is tense owing to continual attacks on German supplies at Tobruk and Matruh.'

Air Commodore Alan Ritchie commanded the bomber force of 205 Group and in addition to the battlefield targets and airfields, his major efforts in the Western Desert were focused on the ports of Benghazi and Tobruk. His force comprised the various medium bombers and an increasing number of heavy bombers. One of his challenges was that the retreat had meant the loss of a large number of airfields and so increased the range to the main targets such as Tobruk. The medium bombers, Wellingtons, were now primarily based at the Canal Zone airfields, but making use of some refuelling locations on the Alexandria road, while the heavies, the Liberators and Halifaxes, were based in Palestine. By late summer 1942 his force comprised:

- No.231 Wing: Wellingtons of 37 and 70 Squadrons.
- No.236 Wing: Wellingtons of 108 and 148 Squadrons.
- No.238 Wing: Wellingtons of 40 and 104 Squadrons.
- No.242 Wing: Liberators of 147 and 160 Squadrons.
- No.245 Wing: Halifax detachments of 277 and 462 Squadrons, plus 14 Squadron with Marauders and Bostons.
- Special Liberator Flight.

The Wellington squadrons continued their maximum effort operations:

'Double sorties by tired aircrews, flying aircraft that were equally tired and kept serviceable only by the superhuman exertions of ground crews working without rest. Once Rommel had been checked in the first week of July, the immediate task was to prevent supplies reaching the enemy. Tobruk was the main supply port and from July onwards it became the target for all the aircraft that 205 Group could put into the air … The enemy had built up one of the most vicious concentrations of heavy and medium AA defences … one particularly dangerous and effective battery of heavy guns was christened 'Eric' by the crews. In their minds they pictured 'Eric' as a fat, bespectacled, but very cunning Hun, who waited, clock in hand, ready to give the order for his battery to fire when the night bombers arrived.

A coloured cartoon of 'Eric' hung on the wall of the briefing room and many jokes were made about this fictitious character. While over the target, however, crews treated 'Eric' with due respect. To meet the strong defences of Tobruk, the Maw Plan – initiated by the Officer Commanding No.108 Squadron – was introduced, by which the greatest possible number of bombers were brought over the target at the same moment. This plan of a Blitz time saved casualties and proved effective in attacks on other well-defended targets.' (*RAF Middle East Review No. 4*)

The Germans had put an impressive AA barrage in place to protect Tobruk. DFC to Pilot Officer J.R. Dudley, 37 Squadron: 'One night in July, 1942, this officer participated in an attack on Tobruk. In spite of heavy and accurate anti-aircraft fire, he made repeated runs over the target area and his work facilitated the attacks made by following aircraft. His aircraft was severely damaged by enemy fire but, displaying skilful airmanship, he succeeded in flying it safely back to one of our landing grounds where he made a safe landing. Throughout the operation, this officer displayed great courage and determination to

The bombing of enemy motorised transport (MT) by medium bombers, such as this Boston attack, was a key part of the land war. Such missions received strong fighter escort but were rarely intercepted as by late 1942 the Allies had achieved a high level of air superiority.

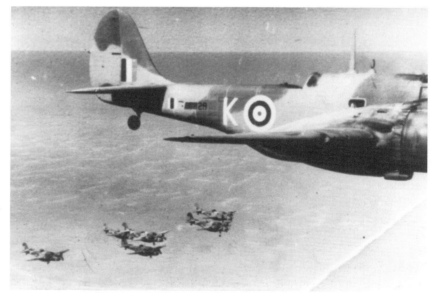

Having used Blenheims since March 1935, 55 Squadron eventually received a more modern type, the Baltimore, in May 1942.

accomplish his task. On a previous occasion, Pilot Officer Dudley displayed great courage when he vigorously attacked Tobruk from a height of 1,500 feet.' (AMB 7784). James Dudley had been tasked to drop flares over the target and rather than drop them in the usual four passes (four flares each time) he decided that his illumination would be more efficient if he picked out his placing with great care and dropped flares singly. He therefore made sixteen runs over Tobruk, remaining in the barrage for an hour and twenty minutes. His aircraft was hit on the first run and on most of the succeeding runs.

In late July it was discovered than a 7,600-ton tanker had made it to Tobruk and this became a priority target. Its destruction was claimed on the 27th by Liberators of the Halverson Detachment.

Such was the desperate nature of the supply shortage that the Axis was trying to get supplies to the El Alamein area using convoys of F-boats from Tobruk to Mersa Matruh. These 300-ton barges were not easy targets as they were armed with one 75mm and two 20mm cannon, and when in convoy could

Anti-aircraft fire was the main danger for most pilots, as increasingly the fighter units took on ground-attack roles. Damage to aileron from ground fire. (*Colin Sinclair SAAF*)

Typical log book entry for Walter Victor of 4 Squadron, July 1942. It is a great shame that not more log books are preserved and accessible as they provide excellent research material. (*SAAF*)

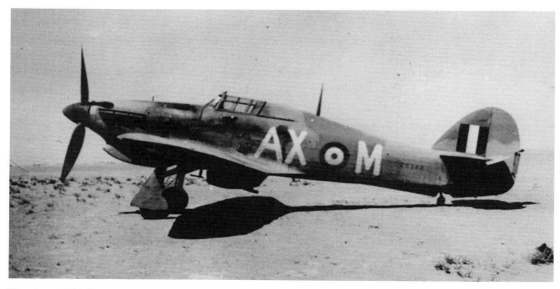

Hurricane Z5348 at LG92, July 1942. (*Michael Schoeman SAAF*)

mount a formidable defence. The Australians of 459 Squadron started their offensive operations in June, having arrived in theatre in February and being equipped with Hudsons the following month. Pilot Officer Beaton flew the first mission, but over the next few weeks the squadron flew numerous low-level dawn attacks on this type of target, claiming seventeen destroyed but losing three aircraft and crews, and with two others badly damaged. Losses continued to be high, with five aircraft lost in the period of intensive ops from 28 July to 17 August.

The most effective aircraft for hunting was the Beaufighter. 'Supplies were split up into small lots and carried forward either in trucks along the coast road or in barges, lighters and small vessels just off shore. The Beaufighters chose the shipping traffic for the first weight of their attack. Day after day they roamed in small formations up and down the coast seeking targets, always at risk of concentrated attack from the Messerschmitts and Macchis which were so readily available on the coastal airfields. During the first days of August the Beaufighters were sinking barges or setting them on fire one after the other. Some of them exploded when the cannon shells touched off their cargoes of ammunition or petrol. On 7th August they sank five barges within 12 hours. During the three weeks ending 9th August more than 20 barges and lighters were destroyed, a cargo load that was equivalent to 1,500 trucks.' (*RAF in Middle East, ibid*)

Two of the Beau units involved in this work were 227 and 272 Squadrons. DFC to the CO, Wing Commander Donald Shore, 227 Squadron, September: 'This officer has led his squadron on a number of successful attacks against enemy shipping in the Mediterranean. His squadron has also shot down numerous enemy aircraft, one of which Wing Commander Shore destroyed. Much of the success achieved can be attributed to this officer's great skill and courageous leadership.'

The medium bomber pace remained hectic. Reg Thackery joined 40 Squadron at Kabrit as a second pilot: 'In August 1942 we were all posted to No.2 Middle East Training School for conversion to night bombing on the Wellington IC. Training commenced at RAF Kabrit but was soon transferred to RAF Aqir near Tel Aviv; some sixty hours later we were back at Kabrit to join 40 Squadron. By the time I reached the squadron a regular pattern of long-range ops to Tobruk had been established under Wg Cdr Ridgway. My first trip as a second pilot was, inevitably, to Tobruk

Hurricane of 40 Squadron SAAF (WR code); the squadron moved to Egypt in December 1941, becoming operational the following month. (*Michael Welchman SAAF*)

and the skipper, a New Zealander, Flt Lt Morton, was on his second tour. He was a keen type and by Christmas 1942 had become the squadron commander. This first trip lasted eight hours and I had not previously been in the air for more than five hours and so had recourse to the caffeine tablets provided and managed to keep awake to handle the aircraft on the long flight to and from the target. The skipper, of course, did the take-off and landing and the time over the target. Our target was the dock area at Tobruk but there was a great deal of cloud and eventually Morton ordered an attack on a heavy gun position north of the harbour. During the bombing run we lost height from 13,000 to 6,000ft to avoid the Flak but saw the bursts, smelt the cordite and felt the bumps. The bomb load of 250lb and 500lb bombs were released by our observer at 9,000ft. The flight back was uneventful and we landed back at Kabrit in daylight having been airborne since 2240. I slept for about twenty-four hours after that initiation and it was a week before I was again on the order of battle – to Tobruk again.'

The Wellingtons could only reach Tobruk and so they took the major load on this target, while the heavies took on Benghazi as well as other targets outside the desert campaign. During August the bombers flew thirty-one major raids against Tobruk, some 1,600 sorties. This pounding essentially closed Tobruk as a major supply route for Rommel, 'closing the front door' as one account called it (with Benghazi as the back door). This meant that all supplies had to go to Benghazi and then make the long road journey to the front, which itself consumed fuel and wore out vehicles, as well as exposing road convoys to attack. As Benghazi was harder to hit – fewer bombers could reach it, although Malta-based aircraft now joined the attacks, it became increasingly important to sink those supplies at sea.

The Tobruk offensive took its toll on the bombers, with the following losses:

Bomber losses against Tobruk August 1942			
Date	Squadron	Aircraft	Fate
2–3	148	Wellington DV568	crash landed after engine failure, two injured
5–6	40	Wellington HF898	lost port propeller over target, all PoW
	227	Halifax W7757	one engine damaged over target; ditched and crew took to dinghy
7–8	40	Wellington DV663	mid-air with HX431 over target, all killed
	40	Wellington HX431	mid-air with DV663, bailed out but one parachute failed to open, rest PoW
	104	Wellington Z8436	Crashed after engine failure, walked for 16 days then all PoW
9–10	40	Wellington HX560	Port engine failure, starboard overheated, bailed out, all OK
10–11	108	Wellington DV667	Engine trouble over target, bailed out, all PoW
11–12	40	Wellington HX377	Engine failure, bailed out, all PoW
	108	Wellington HX484	Engine failure, crashed, all PoW
12–13	70	Wellington Z8960	Lost, ran out fuel, landed on beach, all OK
	108	Wellington T2735	Engine failure shortly after take-off, force land, 1 killed, 3 injured
	108	Wellington AD629	FTR reason not know, all killed
14–15	40	Wellington HX506	DBR on landing, 1 injured
15–16	70	Wellington HX451	Navigation error, ran out fuel, crashed, all OK
	108	Wellington DV676	Engine failed, crash landed, 1 killed, 5 injured
	148	Wellington DV606	Engine failure, bailed out, all OK
16–17	40	Wellington HX425	Engine failure on return, bailed out, all PoW
18–19	70	Wellington DV513	Ran out of fuel, force land, all OK
	104	Wellington Z8942	Engine failure, crash land, 1 killed, 3 injured
19–20	70	Wellington AD634	Engine failure, force land, all PoW
20–21	37	Wellington Z8761	FTR reason not knows, all PoW
23	81st BS	B-25	Hit by flak over target and exploded, all killed
24	159	Liberator AL537	Hit by flak, all killed (8)
30–31	76/454	Halifax W7754	Engine failure on return, all OK
31–1	108	Wellington DV887	Engine failed leaving target, crash land, all PoW
Data from Middle East Bomber Losses			

Other than the sheer number of aircraft losses – twenty-six aircraft, the majority being Wellingtons (seven with 40 Squadron) – the obvious point from this summary is that most losses were down to engine failure. While one or two of the engine problems might have been due to flak damage, the vast majority were simply technical failures. In many cases, especially with the four-engine bombers, failure of one engine led to overheating of the others. I have tried to find a report on this – and I am sure there must have been one – as it seems that servicing would have been one issue, plus perhaps engine handling, which had been a problem earlier in the war with Bomber Command.

For much of the summer the main effort against the Axis convoys had been from Malta, with 39 Squadron operating a detached Flight at Luqa – in reality this became a major strike force under the command of Wing Commander Pat Gibbs, who had, in July been given command of the combined detachments of 39, 86 and 217 squadrons. Rommel had already proved that he did not need much in the way of supplies to take the offensive, so every ship that docked with tanks or guns was critical, but more so were the tankers. The Italians had promised to deliver.

The first of Rommel's promised supply ships left Naples on 16 August. Escorted by destroyers and six aircraft, the *Rosalina Pilo*, an 8,300-ton MV carrying a mixed load of fuel, ammunition and general cargo, elected to use the shorter route round North Sicily and thence to the North African ports. The convoy was sighted by a PR Spitfire – the usual means of locating such movements – and a Beaufort strike was ordered. Six Beauforts, nine Beaufighters (235 Squadron) anti-flak and dive bombing, plus the unusual luxury of eight Spitfires, made up the attacking force. Locating the convoy some 35 miles west of Lampedusa, the strike leader led his six Beauforts into the attack, while the Spitfires engaged the convoy air escort and the Beaufighter anti-flak and dive bombers went to work distracting the enemy gunners from the six torpedo aircraft. One of the Beaufighters dropped its bomb load on the stern of the MV just as the torpedoes began their runs. As the Beauforts cleared the far side of the convoy they witnessed two devastating explosions on the MV. Post-strike reconnaissance revealed the MV abandoned and later sunk. Furthermore, one Ju 88 and one Bf 109 were shot down, all for no loss to the strike force.

The Italians, true to their word, were mounting another convoy to relieve Rommel. This was the 7,800-ton tanker *Pozarica* escorted by destroyers, a flak ship and seven aircraft. On 19 August Wing Commander Gibbs led a twelve Beaufort strike against the tanker. Unfortunately, the tanker was not as low in the water as was anticipated and so the depth setting on the torpedoes was too great, and all torpedoes ran under the ship. The attackers lost a Beaufighter and two Beauforts although both Beaufort crews were picked up by the destroyer escort.

Back at Malta thoughts were turned to a second strike, and plans were laid for a sortie the next day when up to date reconnaissance information would be available. This second strike consisted of nine Beauforts and eight anti-flak Beaufighters plus five dive-bomber Beaufighters. By this time, the convoy was nearing the Greek coast and it was here that the strike aircraft caught up with it. Gibbs scored a good hit, as did one, possibly two, other aircraft. One aircraft of the last sub flight was shot down; the crew being picked up by an escort destroyer. Post-strike PR showed the tanker stationary and leaking oil; later she was seen again, beached and abandoned.

However, the pace did not slacken as on the 24th yet another convoy was seen. This was the 1,500-ton tanker *Dielpi*. A nine-aircraft strike was mounted by 39 Squadron with the usual escort, although one Beaufort was late off and did not catch up with the rest until just before the attack. In fact, as he approached the formation, he was being chased by a Ju 88, but his problem was solved by one of the Beaufighters, which shot the pursuer down. The attack went in and, although an explosion was seen, no one claimed a hit. In fact, the tanker had been damaged and had to put in to a Greek port for repairs. A few days later, she sailed again only to be met by 39 Squadron with nine

Beauforts in a dusk attack. This time there was no escape and she received at least two direct hits and was soon ablaze and sinking. A fourth tanker, the 5,400 ton *Istria*, sailed by night to avoid the Beauforts and fell victim to a Wellington torpedo strike.

Despite persistent efforts by the Italians, Rommel had still received nothing and he was furious. The Italians tried again and sent the 5,000-ton tanker *San Andrea* at the end of August. The tanker had only one destroyer as escort and so hugged close to the Italian coast. Pat Gibbs led nine Beauforts and nine Beaufighters on the strike and elected to attack from landward and drop at close range to reduce the likelihood of the torpedoes fouling in shallow water. Gibbs' vic of three dropped at only 500 yards and as the second vic ran in, the tanker vanished in a spectacular sheet of flame and smoke. The tally for the 'campaign' was five sailed and five sunk – four of them falling to 39 Squadron – the *Rosalina Pilo* on 16 August, the *Pozarica* on the 19th, the *Dielpi* on the 24th and the *San Andrea* on the 30th – an outstanding achievement by any standards.

While the majority of ops were flown from Malta, they are included here as the lack of supplies forced Rommel's hand at El Alamein. Bar to DFC to 39 Squadron Leader Reginald (RPM) Gibbs: 'Early in June, 1942, Squadron Leader Gibbs attacked and sank a large enemy merchant vessel. Sometime afterwards this officer participated in an attack on an Italian naval force. Despite opposition from enemy fighters and in the face of defensive fire from the naval vessels, Squadron Leader Gibbs successfully launched his torpedo at the leading warship. He flew his extensively damaged aircraft safely to base where he executed a skillful landing. This officer has at all times displayed great skill and devotion to duty. He has contributed materially to the operational efficiency of his squadron.'

The CO, Wing Commander Arthur Mason, was also awarded the DFC for operations in June: 'In June 1942, this officer led an attack on an Italian naval force. Despite fighter opposition, a determined attack was made and at least 1 warship was hit by a torpedo. His leadership and courage in the face of formidable opposition were worthy of the highest praise.'

The DAF flew 'only' 5,700 sorties in August – low by recent standards (and what was to come) but nevertheless very telling on the overall campaign. In mid-August 1942 General Alexander took over command in the Middle East and General Montgomery was appointed to lead the Eighth Army. Monty had been appointed following the death of Gort, who was killed when JG 27 shot down and then strafed the Bombay in which he was travelling. Churchill's directive to Alexander being 'to take or destroy at the earliest opportunity the German Italian Army … .'

With these changes of command and the arrival of strong reinforcements, a new spirit infused Allied forces in Egypt and the way was paved for a major offensive. The Allies had strengthened a number of key positions and intended to blunt and bleed any German advance, which is precisely what happened. Montgomery was to prove an ardent supporter of air power: 'I hold that it is quite wrong for the soldier to want to exercise command over the air striking forces. The handling of an air force is a life study and therefore the air part must be kept under air force command … Eighth Army and the Desert Air Force have to be so knitted so that the two together form one entity. The resultant military effort will be so great that nothing will be able to stand up against it.' And, very tellingly: 'If you do not win the air battle first you will probably lose the land battle.'

Rommel was established inside Egypt. Cairo, Alexandria, and the Suez Canal were within striking distance. There was panic in Cairo as military personnel destroyed files, and the Egyptians became increasingly unfriendly. It remained to be seen if the Allies could maintain a defensive position while they built up men and material, and denied those things to Rommel. By late summer 1942 the situation looked dire, but within a year the Allies were to be victorious across North Africa – but the clearing of North Africa and the invasion of Italy are the subject of a forthcoming book.

Appendix I

Battle Honours and Gallantry Awards

Battle Honours

RAF squadrons were entitled to place appropriate 'battle honours' upon their standards. Before we look at these in detail it is necessary to say a few words about the standards themselves. The system was instituted on 1 April 1943 by King George VI to mark the 25th anniversary of the Royal Air Force. The basic requirement for a squadron to receive a standard is completion of twenty-five years of service; however, a standard might also be granted to a squadron that 'earned the Sovereign's appreciation for especially outstanding operations'.

The standard itself is a 4ft × 2ft 8in rectangle of RAF light blue silk, fringed and tasselled in gold and blue. It has a border of roses, thistles, shamrocks and leeks – emblems of the countries that comprise the United Kingdom – and a central motif of the approved squadron badge. The only

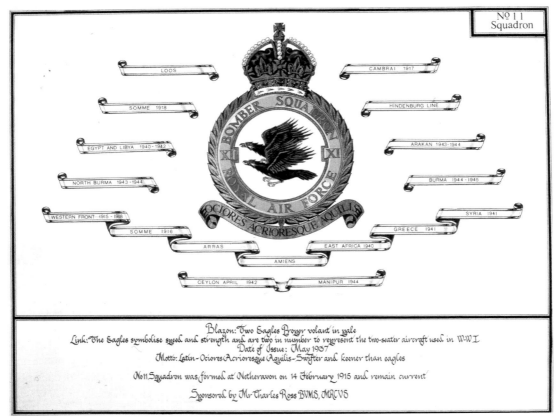

RAF Heraldry Trust project: 11 Squadron showing badge, battle honours (including four for the Middle East), and dedication. (*RAF Heraldry Trust*)

other motifs on the standard are the battle honours to which the squadron is entitled, these being depicted in scrolls. The standard is mounted on an 8ft 1in staff, surmounted by a gold eagle with outstretched (elevated) wings.

Once the squadron has completed the qualifying requirements it receives a list, from the Air Ministry/MoD, of the battle honours to which it is entitled, with a note of those that may be placed upon the standard. The squadron then selects the honours it wishes to display, to a maximum of eight, and this, along with the formal request for a standard, is forwarded to the Sovereign for approval.

A typical example is that of No 39 Squadron. Squadron Leader Coghill was CO in 1954 when the first standard was due to the squadron and he had to choose from the following list of battle honours to which the squadron was entitled: Home Defence 1916–18, North-West Frontier 1930–31, Mohmand 1933, North-West Frontier 1935–39, East Africa 1940, Egypt and Libya 1940–43, Greece 1941, Mediterranean 1941–43, Malta 1942, North Africa 1942–43 and south-east Europe 1944–45. However, with the policy decision that the operations on the North-West Frontier of India could not be displayed upon the standard, he was left with no choice and all the other honours were duly represented.

No.39 Squadron was therefore entitled to a number of – but not all – the battle honours that related to the theatre of operations and period covered in this book.

East Africa 1940–1941: Operations over Kenya, the Sudan, Abyssinia, Italian Somaliland, British Somaliland, Eritrea, and the Red Sea, during the campaigns that resulted in the conquest of Italian East Africa (10 June 1940 to 27 November 1941).

Iraq 1941: Operation in the defeat of Rashid Ali's rebellion (2 to 31 May 1941).

Habbaniya: Units engaged in the defence of Habbaniya (30 April to 6 May 1941).

Syria 1941: Operations over Syria during the campaign against the Vichy French (8 June to 12 July 1941).

Greece 1940–1941: Operations over Albania and Greece during the Italian and German invasion, whether carried out by squadrons based in Greece or operating from external bases (28 October 1940 to 30 April 1941).

Egypt and Libya 1940–1943: Operations in the defence of Egypt and the conquest of Libya, from the outbreak of war against Italy to the retreat of the Axis forces into Tunisia (10 June 1940 to 6 February 1943).

El Alamein: Operations during the retreat to El Alamein and subsequent actions (June to November 1942).

Malta 1940–1942: Squadrons participating in defensive, offensive, and reconnaissance operations from Malta during the period of enemy action against the island (10 June 1940 to 31 December 1942).

North Africa 1942–1943: Operations in connection with the campaigns in French North Africa, from the initial landings in Algeria to the expulsion of the Axis Powers from Tunisia (8 November 1942 to 13 May 1943).

Mediterranean 1940–1943: Operations over Italy, Sicily and the Mediterranean and Aegean Seas by aircraft based in the Mediterranean area (including reconnaissance, convoy protection, mining, and attacks on enemy ports and shipping) between the entry of Italy into the war and the initiation of air action preparatory to the Sicilian campaign (10 June 1940 to 30 June 1943).

You may decide to sponsor a badge for a unit with which you, a relative or a friend had a direct connection; or you may decide to join with a group of ex-RAF colleagues to sponsor a badge together.

RAF Heraldry
The centre of the squadron standard was the squadron badge, which is a study in its own right, as each device and motto has a story.

Squadron badges combined a motif (blazon) and a logo, decided between the unit and the RAF Chester Herald. They provide insights into the role of the squadron at the time of the granting of the badge.

Examples here:

112 Squadron: blazon 'a cat sejant sable' (heraldry speak for a black cat sitting down), chosen by the squadron because it formed at Helwan and at nearby ancient Memphis the cat goddess Bast was worshipped in Ancient Egypt. The logo reflects what the squadron thought it did best.

45 Squadron: blazon 'a camel azure winged gules' (a blue winged camel); the camel could have two connections – the squadron was equipped with Sopwith Camels in the First World War and had an association with Egypt in the Second World War, and the wings to reflect aviation. The logo translates as 'through difficulties I arise'. (RAF Heraldry Trust, www.rafht.co.uk)

RAF Heraldry Trust Registered Charity No: 1057097: The author is a trustee of the RAF Heraldry Trust. The RAF Heraldry Trust aims to catalogue the heraldic badges for every RAF unit (squadrons, stations, regiments, etc.) both past and present that were granted such official badges. The definitive hand-painted pages will be housed as a permanent record in RAF Cranwell's Library, where it may be consulted by interested individuals and organizations, for both educational and research purposes. The most recent set of badges was handed to the library in July 2015.

The RAFHT's aim is to preserve the heritage of the RAF, which is otherwise in danger of being lost as the members of older squadrons pass away and there is the risk that their badges are forgotten or lost. The badges are repainted by heraldic artist, Mary Denton BA (Hons), on to goatskin parchment paper using 23.75 carat gold leaf and gouache paints, which have an excellent resistance to fading. Each page includes a panel with all the badge's details, such as heraldic description and motto, date badge was issued, and unit date. It also includes a dedication specified by the badge sponsor.

MEDALS

Campaign Medals

The campaign medal for this theatre was the Africa Star. It was awarded for one or more days' service in North Africa between 10 June 1940 and 12 May 1943. The ribbon is pale buff with a central red stripe and two narrow stripes, one of dark blue and the other light blue, representing the desert, the Navy, the Army and the RAF. Qualification was to have landed in, or flown over, any of the areas that qualified for the award, or territory occupied by the enemy. Areas that qualified were North Africa, Abyssinia, the Somalilands, Eritrea, Sudan and Malta. Three bars were issued with the Africa Star: one for First Army, one for eighth Army, whilst the third was one for which RAF personnel were eligible, 'North Africa 1942–1943', for those who served under the command of AOC Western Desert, AOC NW African Air Forces, AOC Malta, or any others who operated against the Germans or Italians between 23 October 1942 and 12 May 1943.

Gallantry Awards

All the military gallantry awards were of course available to those fighting in this theatre of war. Aircrew of the Allied Squadrons received a significant number of awards; the only award not made in the theatre during this period (for an air action) was the Victoria Cross (VC) – it was awarded for an operation in Tunisia, and is covered in a future volume. The following list of gallantry awards highlights only a few typical (if one can say such a thing about a gallantry award) examples awarded in the theatre. In the very structured requirements for wearing of medal, the following shows the order for wearing. The full list is much more comprehensive, but it is limited here to those more normally awarded to RAF personnel.

Gallantry: VC, GC
Military Division of Order of the Bath: GCB, KCB, CG
Order of the British Empire: GCB, KBE, CBE, OBE, MBE
Distinguished Service Order: **DSO**
Decorations: MC, **DFC**, AFC, CGM, GM, MM, **DFM**, AFC, BEM

Distinguished Service Order (DSO)

The only Order awarded for 'distinguished services under fire', the Distinguished Service Order was established in 1886 to reward individual instances of meritorious or distinguished service in war. Within the RAF only commissioned officers are eligible for the award; any recipient who subsequently performs another suitably approved act of gallantry is awarded a bar attached to the ribbon, with a further bar for each additional qualifying act. It consists of a gold cross, enamelled white, edged gold, having on the obverse, within a wreath of laurel enamelled green, the Imperial Crown in gold and on the reverse, within a smaller wreath, the Royal Cypher. It hangs from its ribbon by a gold clasp ornamented with laurel, with another similar clasp at the top of the ribbon. The one-inch wide ribbon has narrow blue borders. Bars are worn on the ribbon or if the ribbon alone is worn, on undress uniform for example, then they are depicted by one or more small silver roses – depending on the number of bars to which the wearer is entitled. Unlike some other 'Orders' the number of members of the DSO is unlimited, although RAF awards are not common. During World War Two some 5,000 DSOs were awarded but only 870 went to the RAF – with 62 first bars, 62 second bars and two third bars.

DSO group.

Distinguished Flying Cross (DFC)

The Distinguished Flying Cross was established on 3rd June 1918 to be awarded to officers and Warrant Officers for 'an act or acts of valour, courage or devotion to duty performed whilst flying on active operations against the enemy.' The Cross is silver and consists of a cross flory terminated in the horizontal and base bars with flaming bombs and in the upper bar with a Tudor rose. This is surmounted by another cross of aeroplane propellers, with a roundel within a wreath of laurels and the letters 'RAF' on a rose–winged ensign by an Imperial Crown. On the reverse is the Royal Cypher above the date 1918. The Cross is suspended from a straight silver bar, ornamented with sprigs of laurel, and connected by a silver link. The ribbon is 1.25 inches wide and was originally of violet and white alternate horizontal stripes, although as with the AFC this was changed to a diagonal format in July 1919. Likewise, awards made during and since the Second World War carry the date of the award on the reverse lower limb. The Cross is issued un–named but recipients or family often have them engraved. Bars are awarded in the usual way and, as is common to most awards,

DFC in presentation box. (*Colin Sinclair SAAF*)

are depicted by a rosette worn on the ribbon if the medal is not worn. During the Second World War over 20,000 DFCs were awarded, with 1,550 first bars and 42 second bars, thus making it the most frequent gallantry award of the War. However, the award was never simply 'given away'; indeed, every Cross had to be earned, often in conditions of extreme danger against considerable odds. There were two general scenarios leading to the award of a DFC: firstly, an instance/incident considered worthy of an immediate award; and, secondly a non–immediate award in recognition of a period or distinguished service, sometimes highlighting one or two instances.

OBE/DFC medal group to Gordon Hampton; note the Africa Star (fourth from left). (*Gordon Hampton*)

Distinguished Flying Medal (DFM)

The Distinguished Flying Medal was instituted on June 3, 1918, and is awarded to non-commissioned officers and other ranks for "an act or acts of valour, courage, or devotion to duty performed whilst flying in active operations against the enemy". It is oval shaped and in silver. On the obverse is the Sovereign's effigy and on the reverse is Athena Nike seated on an aeroplane with a hawk rising from her right hand above the words 'FOR COURAGE'. The medal is surmounted by a bomb attached to the clasp and ribbon by two wings. The ribbon was originally thin violet and white alternate horizontal stripes. From July 1919, the stripes were similar but running at an angle of 45° from left to right. Bars are awarded for subsequent acts and since 1939 the year of award engraved on the reverse. All awards are verified in the London Gazette some of which have citations. There were 104 DFMs with two first bars awarded for World War Two. Between the wars just 79 DFMs with two first bars were awarded, of which the majority were awarded for gallantry on the North-West Frontier. During World War Two, 6,638 DFMs were awarded with 58 first bars and just one second bar.

DFM group to Sid Sills. (*Sid Sills*)

Appendix II

Pets, Parties, Christmas and Songs

Pets

There were very few squadrons that failed to acquire a dog or two during their time in the desert. Some managed to acquire more exotic pets as well.

'Sannie' (and friend) was always there to greet the returning pilots.

Prang, one of the 2 Squadron SAAF mascots. (Chrissie Kruysher, SAAF)

'Sannie' poses on the prop at LG92.

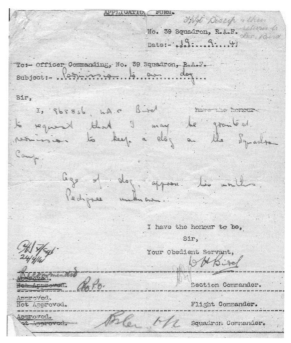

Unusual surviving document, request from Leading Aircraftman Bird of 39 Squadron to keep a dog on camp.

Dogs were frequent –
monkeys not so much!
3 Squadron RAAF
pet monkey with Cecil
Cameron.

10 Squadron SAAF
pets ... 'Ops and
Ops B'. (*Dennis Taylor
SAAF*)

Drinking and Parties

Aircrew have always been 'famed' for drinking bouts, and being in the desert was no reason not to party.

The operations log for 39 Squadron at Sheikh Othman 22 July contains a very serious note: 'Beer ran out today in the Airmen's canteen, as it has already done in the Officers and Sergeants Mess. The Command reserve of beer is now exhausted and it is reported that we shall have to wait some time for a new shipment!' In the dusty, dry conditions of Aden, beer was a vital commodity and far superior to the local water – hence the very sincere note of woe on the demise of supplies.

Flying Officer Roberts of 3 Squadron RAAF recorded in his diary:

1 Nov 1941: All the boys from the South Africans and 250 Squadron are coming over tonight for a party, so am going to bed early. At half past three this morning, Watty, Tiny and Scotty came over to the tent and got stuck into some eats and made a horrible mess in the tent. The party seems to be going very well.

2 Nov: Rose at 7.45 and Watty isn't a very happy man. Still in bed and he's not the only one there at the moment. Barney Terry is still full; he apparently was a very good host last night. If anyone

Established bars were rare – 6 Squadron Edku (Idku) 1942 – in this case ready for Christmas.

The availability of alcohol enabled many a good party ... Tobruk and the pilots' mess.

wouldn't have a drink, he told them to go home. Several of our cars were hidden by visitors and it took several hours to find them this morning. The Fleet Air Arm chaps [naval pilots] ran into a tank trap on the way over and bent the car a bit; several were injured.

Dec 1941, 80 Squadron: 'The Squadron entertained some pilots of the RNFS, 274 and 238 squadrons in the evening. Liquor refreshment was splendidly accompanied by South African delicacies provided by the thoughtful wives of F/O Trollip and P/O Reynolds. A good time was had by all.'

Jerry Jarrold of 80 Squadron: I well remember my 21st birthday. I managed to celebrate by drinking, during the day, two bottles of Seagram V.O. Canadian Whisky. The bottles had a small yellowish band of material around the neck of the bottle. After I'd finished off the two bottles, my colleagues used this to make an insignia of a medal resembling the DFC or DFM. They presented me with what they called the VO and Bar for meritorious drinking on my 21st birthday! I am afraid I was flat out (totally leg-less) and was finally carried off to my tent to sleep it off – luckily I didn't have to fly again until 9th March! I'm not sure of the date, but around this time our beloved Pilots' Mess was unfortunately burnt down. All the chairs, tables and most of the drink were lost – could this have been the time of my 21st birthday? I have photographs of the fire and also photographs of myself, and others, inside the Mess during my birthday celebrations, all looking rather the worse for wear!' (*Did You Survive the War*, Jerry Jarrold with Ken Delve)

Merry Christmas!

The RAF tradition of celebrating Christmas regardless of location and conditions has provided some interesting recollections, official, as recorded in the ORBs, and personal. In addition, many units produced menu cards, a good selection of which have been preserved by their owners. Many of these provide insights into the activities of the unit, and some have caricatures of squadron personnel (but only those who were there would be able to interpret these). The selection of food stuffs is also often enlightening, although beer and cigarettes often feature as key parts of the 'menu'. The author would be interested in hearing from readers who have such menus.

237 Sqn, December 1940, Gordons Tree, Sudan: On Christmas Eve came one of the most satisfying episodes of the month. That night Squadron Headquarters received a signal from one of the flights, which read:

Happy Christmas unto thee
We have downed a one-three-three;
If we only get our due,
We shall down a forty-two.

At first the tendency at headquarters was to regard the message as an unfortunate example of cheap facetiousness, but later signal confirmed the happy tidings. Aircraft of the flight, returning from a pamphlet-raid over Kassala, had surprised and shot down an Italian bomber.

80 Squadron, December 1940, Larissa, Greece:
24 Dec: 'Arranged for local collection of 45,000 drachmae in order to give the troops and officers an advance of pay to see them over Christmas. Ration supply ran out but the Greeks as usual helped us out.

25 Dec: 'Christmas morning was spent quietly, but at 1700 hours a Banquet was held in the local restaurant for the officers and men. The arrangements, made by Sergeant Battle, were excellent, and even the precious fluid beer, was supplied in sufficient quantities. Afterwards all ranks were invited to the Xmas tree organized by the Greek Youth movement. We all received a small souvenir and wine was liberally supplied.'

No.112 Squadron recorded that 25 December 1941 was 'a normal working day, without any trimmings. There was a sweep over El Agheila but without incident. On the return journey Lt Col Wilmot led the singing of carols over the R/T. On 26th beer and Christmas cake arrived. Because of the terrific storm the cake was not eaten, but there seems to have been no difficulty about the beer.'

33 Squadron: 'With the aid of the FAA ex Eagle Co, who were then living in the Mess, a good time was had by all and the time honoured custom of serving the troops dinner observed. The latter function being marked by the number of troops it was found possible to crowd into two EPIP tents and the number of Italian Generals and smaller fry who appeared to be present.'

250 Squadron ORB: 'There was no rest from operations on Christmas Day, and, in the company of a South African fighter squadron, he [no name in record] took off in a sweep of the Hasseat Agedabia sector. The weather was not the best: cold wind, rising dust and overcast sky. The weather got worse as they progressed and there was no sign of enemy aircraft. Someone began singing Christmas Carols over the R/T, thinking that this might bring out the enemy, but none were sighted in the air. They had been hoping for a special delivery of pork, but it had been waylaid and by the time they found it, it had turned green. John Waddy and some others buried the pork with due ceremony, and erected a cross on the spot to the effect "Here lies 250 RAF Squadron's Christmas Dinner 1941". So Christmas lunch, on a cold and windy day, was cold bully and biscuits, well salted with sand. There was no liquor because they had drunk it all the night before. Caldwell and the others in the squadron had settled down for an afternoon of doing nothing, but after a while he and the other flight commander were lucky enough to be taken by their CO to accept an invitation from the CO of the AA defences. There they shared some very good Scotch and returned at dusk, to the news that they had orders for a show at-first light on the next morning. So, that was Christmas, and the next day, business as usual.'

237 Squadron ORB: 'Christmas was spent at Tmimi with a dinner much enlivened by captured enemy rations, pea soup and Christmas pudding, though drinks were a difficulty with water scarce and beer almost unobtainable.'

Christmas 1942 was recorded by 112 Squadron as, 'the best spent by the Squadron since the start of the war.' The preparations had started on the 16th: 'The Stuka flew to Alexandria to collect Christmas supplies,' and on the 22nd, 'that evening a truck arrived with beer and cigarettes and the turkey were reported at Marble Arch.' And two days later, 'There were no operations on 24th, all efforts being channeled towards the one object of arranging the Christmas dinner. Captain Saville flew to Marble Arch to arrange transportation of the turkeys, pork and such like. The airmen's dining hall was enlarged by the addition of another tent. There was some anxiety by evening as the transport Heinkel arrived without the turkeys,' but then, on the 25th, 'food and drink were available in plenty, the airmen played the officers and NCOs and won by 3 goals to nil – due to the pilots not being very fit! The pilots also played the Americans at baseball and had slightly better success, only losing by two runs.'

213 Squadron CO and adjutant ready for Christmas … I wonder what the sign on the pig wearing glasses says, it is not quite readable.

Christmas 1942 at Benina. (*George Muir SAAF*)

December 1942: 260 Sqn, Marble Arch: 'B party spent Christmas Day at Marble Arch, there was little activity and the airmen had their Christmas Dinner in the Officers' Mess. The Dinner was a great success especially when one considers the conditions under which it was prepared. The men enjoyed this short respite from the usual activity of the desert life.'

December 1942, 6 Sqn, Edku: 'It has long been the custom of this Squadron for Flights and Sections to establish bars for the Christmas festivities and these are officially opened by the Commanding Officer and judges in the light of originality and initiative. This year the bars were extremely well constructed and some showed remarkable ingenuity and originality. First prize was awarded to M.T. Section. After the opening of the bars, final sports events were run and at 1245 hours all members of the Officers and Sergeants Messes proceeded to the Airmen's Mess to serve Christmas dinner to the airmen.'

Christmas menus provide wonderful insights into the units – both in terms of what was on offer, but also the cartoons and characters that are often part of the design. I am continuing to collect such menus … so if you have any then please let me know!

80 Squadron 1939 – no doubt each of the caricatures has meaning!

39 Squadron December 1941, with Maryland at the top and images of Egypt at the bottom … and not a bad menu.

RAF Heliopolis 1941, with a winged camel bearing Santa and Nile boats at the bottom.

81 Squadron cover sheet to menu … the characters and the dog mean something (but not recorded); the autograph page is unusual as most just had signatures placed anywhere.

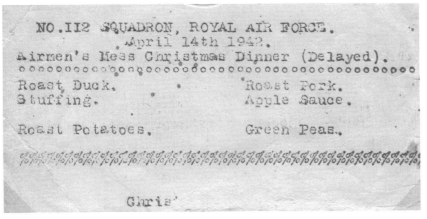

Christmas in April … 112 Squadron message for the delayed airmen's mess Christmas dinner.

Songs and Poems!

There is a long – and healthy – tradition in the Air Force of squadron songs, all part of helping bond the team together, albeit often with content that would not pass today's PC mindset. However, these songs are part of the period and display humour, including black humour, character, and various emotions. Some were 'set' to well-known tunes, while others were more like poems. Some songs were claimed or adopted by more than one unit.

'There were few who returned from the desert without some memory of a circle of men squatting outside the tent under the moon, one perhaps playing a violin or a mouth organ and the rest singing *There was a Monk of Great Renown*, *She'll be Coming Round the Mountain* or *Shaibah Blues*, all with that mixture of sentiment and ribaldry which made up the folk music of the Air Force.' (*New Zealanders with the Royal Air Force*)

One has to imagine the squadron belting out the words and feeling part of a unit … something the author was also doing during his RAF service in the 1980s and 1990s! The author is collecting such songs for an anthology on behalf of the Aviation History Centre (AHC) – so if any reader has a song to contribute then please send it in!

70 Squadron, The Mail Run Melody

To the tune of 'Clementine' (a tune that was used in more than one RAF song). Context: the squadron was frequently tasked to attack the port at Benghazi.

Down the flights each ruddy morning,
Sitting waiting for a clue,
Same old notice on the flight board,
Maximum effort – Guess where to.

Chorus:

Seventy Squadron, Seventy Squadron,
Though we say it with a sigh,
We must do the ruddy Mail Run,
Every night until we die.

Out we go on to dispersal,
To complete our Night Flying Test,
Rumour says we're going Northwards,
But we know we're going West.

Take off from the Western Desert
Fuka, 60 or 09 (Sixty or Oh-nine),
Same old Wimpy, same old aircrew,
Same old target, same old time.

'Have you lost us Navigator?'
'Come up here and have a look',
'Someone's shot our starboard wing off',
'We're alright then, that's Tobruk'.

Fifteen Wimpys on the target,
Two forced landed in the drink,
Another couple crashed on landing,
Ruddy Hell, it makes you think.

Snooping round the Western Desert,
With the gravy running low,

How I wish I could see Fuka,
Through the dust storm down below.

Trying to get your forty raids in,
Thirty-nine, now don't get hit,
If you don't, you go to Blighty,
If you do, (Well, never mind!)

Oh, to be in Piccadilly,
Selling matches by the score,
Then I shouldn't have to do that
Ruddy Mail Run any more.

112 Squadron

Context: poem composed by Flight Lieutenant D. Smith around March 1941 in Greece; the squadron had been told it was to re-equip with Hurricanes; the CO was Squadron Leader H.L.I. Brown.

In far off Egypt's desert land
There lived a little band of men
Assembled by the High Command
To fight the vile Italienne!

Their leader true, a Scottish type,
With might rump and smelly pipe,
Says 'what, what what! What are you doing'?'
And when he does – there's trouble 'Bruin.'

To Alex he led forth his crew,
Some by car and some by plane
For Middle East had promised true
To give each man a Hurricane!

All were happy, many sang,
Joe Fraser even had some leave,
And 'Stuffy' had a might 'bang'
Complete contentment to achieve!

The Adjutant was happy, too,
And went to Cabarets to woo.
No more he cursed in ranting terms
('till he, poor chap, succumbed to worms)!

But all this joy was not to last
Fate spoke out, the die was cast,
Our Hurricanes – they never flew!
… Ed again. Poor One-One-Two.

Some officer of lofty rank,
Either mad, or else he drank,
Had found on some old rubbish heap
Some Glads, Mark II, all going cheap!

'Just the very thing,' he cried,
'To send across the other side!
On whom can we these old crates shelve
Why, on the old one hundredth twelve!'

So saying, with a roguish grin
Approached with glee the horrid pile,
And from the wreckage forth he drew
Some ancient planes for One-One-Two!

They hammered nails, they tied with string,
They scrounged a tailwheel, found a wing,
Screwed in bolts and filled a piston,
Counted the cylinders that she missed on
Until the fateful day drew nigh
When all acclaimed with pride: 'They fly!'

And so one's hopes have been in vain
They've robbed us of the Hurricane.
We are the lambs without their fleece
And now we're flying Glads in Greece!

Bomber Squadron Song (Greece)

To Valona, to Valona,
Every morning just at nine,
Same old kites and same old Squadron,
Same old target, same old time.

North of Corfu dawn is breaking
And the sun begins to shine.
Macchi-hundreds and G-fifties
waiting for us dead on time.

Do four runs up says the C.O.
And make every bomb a hit.

If you do you'll go to heaven
If you don't you're in the sh*t.

On the way back, same old fighters
And the gravy's running low.
How I wish I could see Larissa
Through the snow-storm down below.

How I wish I were in Athens,
Drinking Cognacs by the score,
And I need not ever go back
To Valona any more.

113 Squadron:

Belting down the runway, throttles opened
    wide,
See the mighty Blenheim swing from side to
    side,
If you're lucky you'll leave the deck,
And if you're not you'll break your neck
We're off to Bomb Benghazi
We're off to bomb B.G.

See the mighty Blenheim loaded up for ops,
Exasperated aircrew turning both the props,

Six times around we turn the blade,
As hopes of scrubbing begin to fade,
We're off to bomb Benghazi,
We're off to bomb B.G.

Squadron Leader Lyall, leader of our band,
Couldn't find the target, too much ruddy sand
He dropped his bombs out in the blue,
And so would you, too blooming true,
If you could see Benghazi
If you could see B.G.

450 Squadron: The Ground-Strafer's Version of **Lili Marlene**

Get the right deflection;
… Check reflector-sight!
Give your skid correction,
– Make sure the range is right!

Then you can press the 'teat' old son,
And blow the Hun … to Kingdom Come,
… And poor Marlene's boy-friend,
Will NEVER see Marlene!

Belching ammunition,
Petrol trucks ahead! …
… To fill them full of lead!

A 'flamer' for you is a grave for Fritz.
He's in a Blitz, right where he sitz.
… And poor Marlene's boy-friend,
Will NEVER see Marlene!

Half-a-thousand pounds
Of Anti-Personnel.
Eighty-dozen rounds of
The stuff that gives them HELL.

Finish your bomb-dive, zoom away.
And live to fight … another day.
… And poor Marlene's boyfriend
Will NEVER see Marlene!

[Slow sentimental finale …]
… Then back to 'Harasser House' we steer,
To drink a beer; without a tear.
… And poor Marlene's boy-friend,
Will never see Marlene …

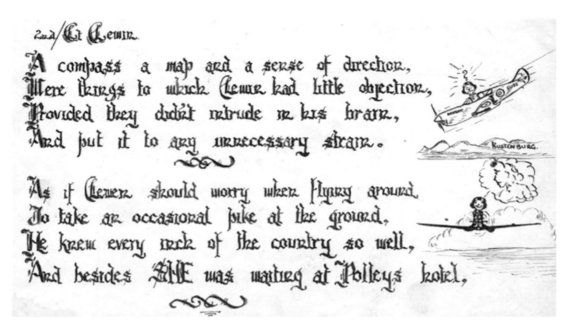

2nd/Lt Clewin.

A compass a map and a sense of direction,
Were things to which Clewin had little objection,
Provided they didn't intrude in his brain,
And put it to any unnecessary strain.

As if Clewin should worry when flying around,
To take an occasional pike at the ground,
He knew every nook of the country so well,
And besides SHE was waiting at Polleys hotel,

Songs and poems, often rude or pointed, have long been a part of military aviation. (Angus Allen-White SAAF)

Cartoons are another tradition … in this case 450 Squadron portraying Kittybombers at work.

If you happened to be at a fixed base then film shows were an option – Kasfareet cinema schedule for October 1941.

If you are in the desert and there is no entertainment, and you have Australians on the squadron, the obvious answer is a snake hunt! LG86 and 39 Squadron about to go hunting for reptiles.

3 Squadron RAAF: Brian Thompson: 'This evening I composed a song to the tune of *South of the Border* relating to the squadrons movements since Antelat.

> South of Benghazi, down Antelat way …
> That's where we met the Hun one day, when he came out to play.
> We've been to Agheila, but we did not stay …
> South of Benghazi, down Antelat way …

Walking Out ... to Walk or Not to Walk?

One of the greatest challenges to aircrew was that of bailing out or crash-landing in the 'middle of nowhere', which pretty much meant the whole of the desert theatre, as even a few miles away from a road or the coast could mean the chances of being found were very slim. The chances of being picked up by friend or foe were not great, unless you happened to come down close to the scene of fighting, and frequently the tales of 'walking out' involved contact with Arab tribesmen, who may or may not be a great deal of help! What is amazing, considering the hostile terrain and climate, is just how many airmen managed to walk out, often crossing enemy lines in the process.

The Late Arrivals Club was formed for those who had walked back 'out of the blue', its emblem being a tiny silver boot with wings. The Australians sometimes referred to the Boomerang Club (the aircrew having come back like a boomerang). Of course, a great many aircrew were simply never found; they vanished with their aircraft, they may have tried to walk out and not made it. Often a wreck was found, sometimes still with its occupants, sometimes empty meaning its occupants had either been taken as prisoners of war, started walking and not made it, or simply vanished to some other cause.

The accounts below are a small selection to give a flavour of some of the escapades, and a few others have been included in the main text.

Four members of a Wellington crew after 'walking out'; a decision crews had to make was whether to stay put and hope to be found – if in friendly territory – or walk out and, if in enemy territory, avoid capture.

DFC to Major Robert Preller, 11 Squadron SAAF, 18 October 1940:

'While carrying out a reconnaissance and attacking an enemy aircraft on the ground, Major Preller was shot down in the desert in enemy territory 70 miles from the border. He destroyed his aircraft and proceeded to walk to British territory accompanied by his crew of two who eventually became exhausted. He left them at a water hole and proceeded alone to seek aid. After 14 days, having suffered terrible hardships through lack of water and food, he made contact with British forces, and was able to give directions which led to the rescue of his crew and the recovery of a very valuable exposed film of enemy military objectives. This officer has shown marked determination in individual operations, and in leading his squadron he has imbued them with his own fighting spirit to a remarkable degree.'

On 6 February 1941, 73 Squadron's ORB recorded: 'P/O Millist has not been heard of and we are resigned to the fact that he has either been killed or captured.' His loss had been recorded on the 4th. However, on the 7th, the diarist was able to record: 'At lunch time we had a wonderful sight – P/O Millist walking in to the Mess with P/O Wareham, who had brought him from Derna. It appears that he was shot down by a CR42 and force-landed in enemy territory some 10 miles NE of Benina. He spent the rest of 4/2/41 walking and hiding. He had neither compass not revolver. He was spotted and chased by an Italian motor cycle but eluded him. He attempted to sleep in the bushes during the night but it was too cold and he continued walking on. During the night he saw what appeared to be the remnants of the Italian army marching by in retreat to Benghazi, but he was not seen. He continued walking until 1400 hours on 5/2/41 when he suddenly met an Australian Sergeant who gave him food and water. During all this time P/O Millist had been without either food or water. He had bolted as soon as he had landed his Hurricane because enemy troops were near at hand. He 'hitch hiked' to Derna and Wareham motored him here. A celebration took place in the Mess after which the CO and Millist motored to 202 Group, where they stayed for dinner.'

RAF in Middle East, ibid:

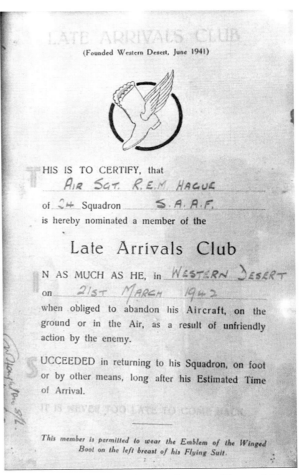

Late Arrivals Club – certificate to Sergeant Hagur of 24 Squadron SAAF.

'One day towards the end of November 1941, six Blenheims left Fuka to bomb enemy tanks and transport on the Acroma–El Adem road. In that area they were attacked by a formation of Messerschmitts and four of the Blenheims were shot down. Navigator in one of them was twenty-year-old Sergeant Turton. Bailing out of the burning aircraft, he landed safely to find that his pilot and air gunner had also survived but were both wounded and unable to walk far. While they were debating what to do some friendly natives came along and took charge of the wounded men, saying they would get them medical attention from the Germans in Acroma. Thereupon Turton, who was unharmed, decided that he would not be captured and set out to travel about one hundred miles on foot to the British lines. Fortunately, he had a small pocket compass which enabled him to go steadily south-east. Every night he passed enemy encampments at frequent intervals but he skirted them and kept on. After three days he was suffering so severely from thirst that he was forced to live on snails. Eventually he was found by a South African medical officer. His journey across enemy territory, hiding by day and walking by night, had taken him six days, and during the whole of that time he was without food and water.'

'One day while flying low as usual, I spied two men vigorously waving their shirts in a rather remote part of the desert. Thinking they might be a couple of Huns or Italians who wished to be taken prisoner, I landed on rocky ground about half a mile away. Armed with sten guns we went towards the two waifs who presented a very ragged spectacle. It transpired that one was the wireless operator and the other chap a gunner from a torpedo Wellington which had attacked a tanker in Tobruk the night before the opening of the Alamein offensive. Their aircraft had succumbed to flak and crashed outside Tobruk about dusk. The two lads had travelled one hundred and seventy miles in nineteen days without water, except dew, and only one old tin of bully beef. They were exhausted, so we lost no time in getting them back to base.'

The Boomerang Club – 450 Squadron 'scoreboard' of pilots who made their way back after baling out or force-landing in enemy territory.

Appendix IV

Takoradi Route

The RAF operated four reinforcement routes that fed aircraft to the Middle East units:

1. Takoradi (Sierra Leone, West Africa) to Cairo
2. Cape (South Africa) to Cairo
3. Port Sudan to Cairo (and Far East)
4. Basrah (Iraq) to Middle East (and Russia)

All aircraft received from the UK by sea in crates or as deck cargo had to be prepared; the role of Takoradi was to flight test them and deliver them to an Aircraft Storage Unit (ASU) prior to issue to units. The routes were operated by the Ferry Group using a number of Ferry Control Units (FCU) at Cairo, Khartoum, Aden, Habbaniya, Kisumu and Lagos. The routes and FCU areas are shown on the map. Of these by far the most important for the Middle East squadrons was that from Takoradi. Flying 3,600 miles across harsh territory, with poor facilities, very variable weather, with poor maps and virtually no navigation aids, the ferry pilots of the Aircraft Delivery Unit (ADU) played a key role in keeping the front line supplied with aircraft. By the end of the life of the West Africa Reinforcement Route they had delivered more than 5,000 aircraft (or the equivalent of more than 300 squadrons!) The Takoradi route was also used to send aircraft to the Far East theatre.

The advanced party of seven officers and fifteen other ranks (OR), under the command of Group Captain H.K. Thorold, left the UK in July 1940 to 'examine the practicality of the scheme from the point of view of the port, aerodrome and ferry route and the accommodation available at Takoradi.'

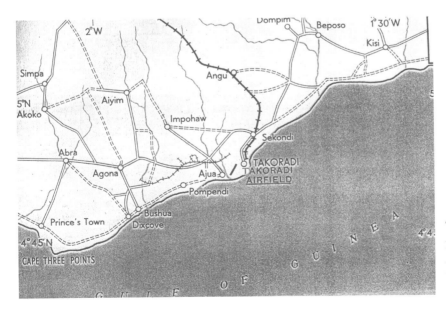

Takoradi was a key part of keeping the Allied squadrons in the Western Desert campaign supplied.

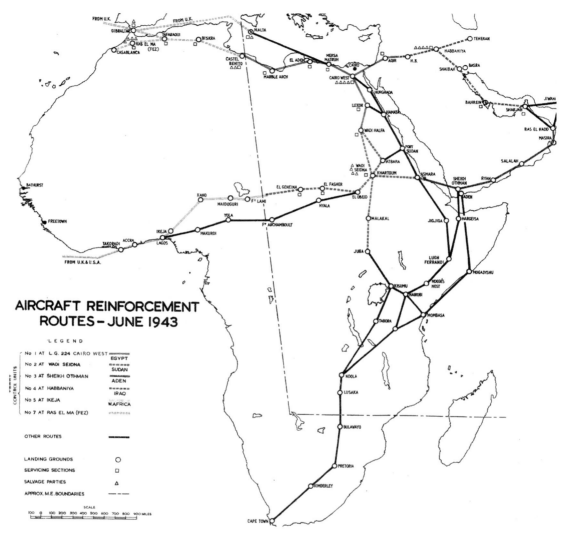

AIRCRAFT REINFORCEMENT
ROUTES – JUNE 1943

LEGEND

CONTROL UNITS

No I AT L.G. 224 CAIRO WEST — EGYPT
No 2 AT WADI SEIDNA — SUDAN
No 3 AT SHEIKH OTHMAN — ADEN
No 4 AT HABBANIYA — IRAQ
No 5 AT IKEJA — W.AFRICA
No 7 AT RAS EL MA (FEZ)

OTHER ROUTES —

LANDING GROUNDS   O
SERVICING SECTIONS   □
SALVAGE PARTIES   △
APPROX. M.E. BOUNDARIES ----

SCALE
100 0 100 200 300 400 500 600 700 800 900 MILES

The main air reinforcement routes to the Middle East.

(Air Publication AP3326 *Works*). The main party, 350 officers and men, including twenty-five ferry pilots, arrived on August 24. It is interesting to note that the air delivery route from the UK used by the bomber types in early 1940 was very hazardous, and not just with possible enemy action. The delivery flight of Blenheim IVs on 18 June, routing from Tangmere to Malta, via Marignane, led to the loss of seven aircraft and the deaths of eighteen aircrew, most having crashed in bad weather over France.

The organization was under the overall command of HQ Middle East and initially comprised the Takoradi SHQ and three independent units whose commanders were responsible to the station commander, namely port detachment, aircraft assembly unit (AAU), and communication unit.

Crated aircraft arrived by sea and were put together, tested and then flown in air convoys with a number of refuelling and night stops.

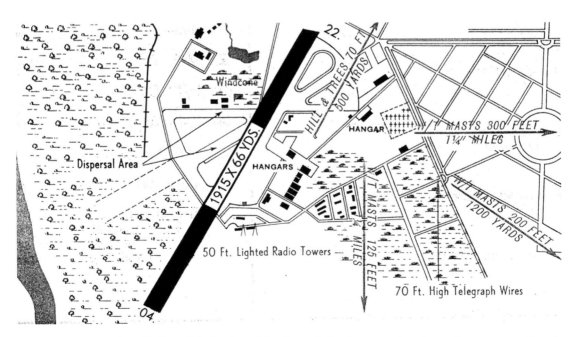

This 1946 airfield plan of Takoradi is dominated by the main hard runway, but the earlier runway pattern is still clearly visible.

Route Stages			
Stage	**Route**	**Distance**	
1st Stage	Takoradi to Lagos	370 miles	Refuel
2nd Stage	Lagos to Kano	525 miles	Night stop
3rd Stage	Kano to Maiduguri	320 miles	Refuel
	Maiduguri to Geneina	690 miles	Night stop
4th Stage	Geneina to Fasher	195 miles	Refuel
	Fasher to El Obeid	330 miles	Refuel
	El Obeid to Khartoum	230 miles	Night stop
5th Stage	Khartoum to Wadi Halfa	520 miles	Refuel
	Wadi Halfa to Cairo	506 miles	
	Total	3,686 miles	

The initial plan was for the route to provide 120–130 aircraft a month, with roughly one-third fighters and one-third bombers. The first crated aircraft, six Blenheims and six Hurricanes, arrived on 5 September, with a further thirty Hurricanes arriving aboard HMS *Argus* the following day. The first delivery flight, six Hurricanes and one Blenheim, left Takoradi on the 20th and, minus one Hurricane that was stuck on route with a technical problem, arrived safely at Khartoum on the 24th. By the end of the year more than 100 aircraft had flown the route: sixty-eight Hurricanes, twenty-seven Blenheims and twelve Fulmars. In its first year of operation the route delivered 1,454 aircraft. The monthly target had been raised to 150 a month in November, and by May 1941 it was raised to 200 a month. The main limitation, as reflected in the numbers below, was down to a lack of aircraft arriving at Takoradi.

Month	Aircraft
1940	
Sep	33
Oct	5
Nov	55
Dec	37
1941	
Jan	99
Feb	55
Mar	133

Month	Aircraft
1941	
Apr	123
May	161
Jun	203
Jul	150
Aug	123
Sep	131
Oct	146
Total	1,454

Even more impressive was the fact that around 95 per cent of these made it to their destination and into service. When this was added to the excellent work of the RSU and workshops, returning aircraft back to service, the RAF's supply of aircraft was generally able to keep pace with losses.

As a maintenance AP explained: 'From the technical point of view the major difficulties resulted from the lack of equipment and spares. Swiftly changing policy in the number and types of aircraft to be erected also caused anxiety from the equipment angle as each change needed more and in some cases different items which we not available. When the first American aircraft arrived no provisioning had been made for the necessary operational equipment, so that these aircraft were simply flying machines and nothing more. The difficulties over the lack of AGS items and tools were, however, not so great with American types as, in contrast to the British practice, each aircraft was packed with a bag of essential parts and an efficient tool kit arrived in each crate.

'The technical troubles at the staging posts were many and difficult to deal with. Numerous aircraft developed defects in the course of their progress along the route, others were damaged on landing, while some came down some distance from the landing grounds and had to be located and retrieved. The rectification and repair of these aircraft, coupled with the lack of spares and equipment, placed a very severe strain upon the limited number of personnel at the posts, and in February 1941 the number of aircraft unserviceable and awaiting spares along the route assumed alarming proportions.

'There was the occasion when the aerodrome runway at Takoradi caved in while a Hurricane was taxying, resulting in damage to the aircraft and the stoppage of flying until the runway could

Aerial photo, probably late 1943.

be rebuilt. There were several occasions when, owing to the shortage of ferry pilots, the rate of production outstripped the flying organization, resulting in the accumulation of completed aeroplanes which could not be got rid of; and the times when, because the pilots were not skilled in the types of aircraft they had been sent to collect, it was necessary for the Takoradi base to complete their training before they could be sent on their way. There was a high rate of sickness resulting from the disagreeable climate and the excessively long working periods. Finally, there were the varying and at times very bad weather conditions along the route which often resulted in aircraft being held up for days at the respective landing grounds, and called for additional efforts from the already overworked technical personnel in order that the serviceability of the accumulations could be maintained so that eventually they would be able to continue their journey.' (Air Publication *Maintenance*)

The Aircraft Delivery Unit (ADU) continued to grow in numbers of pilots, one of the early group being experienced Polish pre-war pilots who had escaped their home country but who were not considered (mainly for age reasons) suitable for the Polish fighter squadrons in the RAF. Led by Squadron Leader Rayski, a group of twenty-four Polish NCO pilots were soon regular users of the route, being joined by colleagues from the RAF and from the Rhodesian and South African Air Forces, although, as mentioned above, ferry pilots were frequently in short supply.

South African pilot Squadron Leader A.G. 'Zulu' Lewis was an experienced fighter pilot when he was posted, at his request for an overseas tour from the UK, to command 261 Squadron. His route to his new command was via Takoradi. 'On 31st flew Hurricane IIB, serial 6510, on local flying around Takoradi in Sierra Leone, West Africa. This was the port where aircraft were assembled to be flown to the Middle East.' On February 4th, 1942, still flying 6510, he led eighteen Hurricanes from Takoradi to Lagos, Nigeria; then to Kano; to Maiduguri, still in Nigeria, and on to El Genina; then solo to Khartoum and Port Sudan. He comments: 'We managed to get all our aeroplanes in convoy to destination without breaking any (sandstorms, the lot) covering 3,000 miles in three days.' While his squadron was destined for the Far East, this does illustrate the Takoradi route.

Pilots were also based at the other end of the route, with No.1 ADU in Cairo, where conditions were much better than in Takoradi. Jim Pickering was a ferry pilot on the route and recalls the 1 ADU location – Nile paddle steamers at Gezira Island on the Nile: 'On the opposite bank of the Nile there was a mooring for private river boats, some of which, according to rumour, were occupied by Axis spies with a transmitter and who were being fed with false information by British Intelligence. The paddle steamers had been operated before the war by Thomas Cook for luxury cruises up the River Nile to Luxor. One was an officers' mess, two others sergeants' messes. The Sudanese catering staff had been retained and provided excellent food, services and laundering. The cabins provided accommodation where kit and personal belongings could be safely left during absences on ferry trips, which could vary between a couple of days and a couple of weeks. While waiting for the next trip, the Gezira Sporting Club provided all desirable sporting amenities and the 'fleshpots' of Cairo were only a short taxi ride away.'

The first major test of the reinforcement programme came with the build-up (and losses) for the November 1941 Operation Crusader. The central location for aircraft from the reinforcement routes (Takoradi and Port Sudan) was Wadi Natrun, where the ADU worked with the Aircraft Reinforcement Pool, and seven days' estimated wastage (aircraft replacement requirement) was stored at Wadi Natrun.

By the end of December 1941, the route had delivered 3,822 aircraft since its inception; the increased number of aircraft using it meant an increase in the number of aircraft needing rescue, especially those that ended up force-landing. 'At the end of 1941 and beginning of 1942 there was a very considerable number of damaged aircraft scattered along the route from Takoradi to Khartoum.

It was arranged that No.203 Group should be responsible for salvaging aircraft in the Sudan sector of the Takoradi route, and to accomplish this salvage sections were established at each staging post. The salvage sections despatched parties into the bush with spare engines, etc. to endeavour to make force-landed aircraft flyable, or to deliver them to the aircraft repair depot at Khartoum for repair. They were aided by a Bombay aircraft which has been fitted up as a flying workshop and which is capable of undertaking a number of useful, if limited, engineering jobs. In this task orthodox and conventional ideas were, when necessary, disregarded.' (Maintenance)

Other Routes

The Takoradi route was the most used for the desert squadrons, but aircraft supplies came from other sources as well. By autumn 1941 the RAF base at Port Sudan was erecting Kittyhawks, Bostons and Baltimores and sending them to Summit, where the modifications and other work was completed prior to their despatch to units. Summit was chosen as it had a better climate.

The well-established airfield at Shaibah (119 MU) was also used for erecting Bostons and Baltimores; most of these were destined for Russia but some went to the Desert Air Force. No.118 MU at Basrah was also involved in erected aircraft, again primarily for Russia.

Gibraltar

As the North African campaign moved west, especially with the invasion of Tunisia in November, the lengthy reinforcement routes via Africa made less sense both in terms of effort and the number of aircraft needed. Gibraltar became the main erection site where fighter types, which arrived by ship, were erected, tested and made ready. By 7 November Gibraltar was packed with some 350 fighter types in addition to the normal operational squadrons at the airfield. It had not been easy: 'The establishment of personnel and the accommodation provided for the work were totally inadequate. The first batch of aircraft arrived before the necessary tools and spares were received. There was insufficient erection and other equipment, many aircraft had been despatched from the UK with small but essential items missing. Some components and equipment had been mishandled whilst being removed from aircraft for packing purposes before despatch. It was only by improvisation, local manufacture, the conversion of aeroplane cases into workshops and utilizing the stores and personnel of other services that the scheduled programme was met.' (Maintenance).

Airfields

Airfields are essential to any air campaign – but their significance to the Desert War was nothing short of crucial, as the fluid nature of the campaign saw frequent exchanges of territory, and the associated airfields. Airfield is often too grand a name for many of the locations, and indeed most were referred to as landing grounds (LGs). Whilst airfields are without doubt the most obvious logistics structures for RAF operations, the logistics and maintenance requirements are massive, and are inevitably glossed over in most 'operational' histories like this one. In all campaigns logistics, from infrastructure to equipment (in the case of the RAF primarily, of course, aircraft, fuel, and weapons) are essential. In this appendix and the one on Maintenance, I have attempted to partially redress that balance, and in the main text the critical importance of airfields, and the fluid nature of 'ownership' of airfields, is a fairly regular feature.

On the outbreak of war, Middle East Command (MEC) covered a vast tract of territory including Egypt, Sudan, Palestine, Malta, Iraq, Aden, Kenya and Tanganyika, with additional territories being added as the war progressed. However, as with the rest of this book, the focus will only be on those areas of direct, or supportive, relevance to the Desert campaign (in its broadest sense). On the outbreak of war there were only five permanent airfields in Egypt and three in Palestine, with the latter region playing only a minor part in the Eastern Mediterranean theatre. This meant that major expansion was essential, and the initial focus was on the Suez Canal zone to complete the five stations agreed under the 1936 Anglo–Egyptian Treaty, but without the abandonment of the stations outside the Canal Zone, as had been agreed.

These airfields were intended as 'quasi-permanent', in terms of the eventual plan for the British to leave Egypt, and were provided with extensive facilities for operational squadrons, plus aircraft

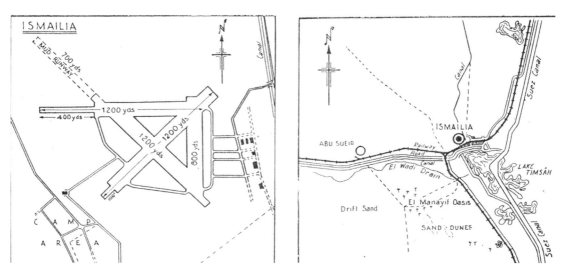

One of the pre-war airfields, Ismailia remained a key location, housing operational and training units.

Aerial view of Ismailia
aerodrome in 1938.

erection, storage and repair, as well as shore facilities for the Fleet Air Arm. The basic requirement
was facilities for two heavy bomber squadrons (or equivalent), with four Class A runways, plus
sufficient dispersals and blast pens.

The lack of suitable materials – including the right type of sand – as well as lack of equipment
and trained personnel meant that 'standard' UK construction was not possible. The runways were
laid on a sand aggregate and were essentially a 5-inch thick bituminous carpet that provided a sound
operating surface in the first part of the war but that needed reinforcing once heavier aircraft such
as the B-17 were employed; the runway surfaces were strengthened using 'an armoured coat of pre-
coated stone'.

The conditions under which extensive earthworks were carried out in Egypt appeared in terms
of home standards somewhat crude and the rate of progress slow. Every one of the wartime airfields,
together with all extensions to pre-war airfields, were constructed on desert land usually involving
earthworks in cut and fill to the extent of approximately a quarter of a million cubic yards in each
case. In one case in the Canal Zone well over a million cubic yards of excavation.

The original plan (late 1930s) had been to build six RAF Stations in the Canal Zone, but in
January 1940 the plan was changed. Secret Organizational Memorandum 61/40 stated that: 'Prior
to the outbreak of war, 6 RAF stations were to be constructed with permanent accommodation
in the Canal Zone. However, shortly after the outbreak of war it was decided to prepare Landing
Grounds only and build temporary accommodation at Kabrit for two bomber squadrons and at
Shallufa for an ATS. The six stations were Fayid, Geneifa, Kabrit, Shandur (renamed from Station
X), Shallufa (renamed from ATS), and Deversoir (renamed from Station Y).'

In addition to the new treaty stations, other pre-war stations were extended and improved, and
by 1943 some twenty major additional airfields had been provided in the canal and delta regions of
Egypt. The majority of this work was carried out by contractors, although as the war progressed
and work was needed in the Western Desert, there was an increased use of direct labour as well as
military labour.

Technical Instruction – No.3
Notes on Engineer Work of forward landing Grounds for RAF

1. INTRODUCTORY

   8th Army is developing on an increasing scale, any engineer field unit may be required to carry out work on provision of Landing Grounds. The following paragraphs are intended as a guide to Officers directing such work, subject to any specific indications that may be given any RAF in any particular case.

2. The requirements of the RAF for operational landing grounds in the Desert are as follows:

   a. Tac/R Aircraft: One runway in the direction of the prevailing wind, dimensions 1200 yds. × 200 yds.

   b. Army Co-op Sqn: Three runways each 1200 yds. × 200 yds., one in the direction of the prevailing wind, and the three forming an equilateral triangle.

   Note: For a. and b. above, in case of extreme urgency of insuperable difficulties as to ground the dimensions may be reduced, but never below minimum of 1000 yds. × 150 yds.

   c. Fighter Wings: For every four sqns, one LG 1500 yds × 1500 yds. If this is unattainable, the minimum is three runways each 1500 yds. by 150 yds. forming an equilateral triangle with one in the direction of the prevailing wind.

   Note: only as a preliminary measure may the dimensions of such runways be reduced to 1200 yds. by 300 yds. in case of special urgency or topographical difficulty.

General note a. to d.: in each case approaches should be free from obstruction (e.g. telegraph poles) for 400 yds., and the LG must be sited at least three miles from a high obstruction (e.g. a rising escarpment). It is useless to contemplate siting a LG where any portion of the area chosen requires a larger amount of work. It must always be borne in mind that LGs occupied in the first instance by Fighter Wings may be handed over to Bomber Wings as the advance progresses, therefore ground capable of development should always be selected where possible.

The ground chosen must be level and reasonably flat. It must be free from large stones and hummocks. *The tendency in the desert is to under-estimate the amount of work required to render an apparently smooth and flat piece of ground safe for aircraft to land on.* Clay pans provide the best surface, and should be selected whenever possible. In addition to requiring less engineer work, they are also free from dust. An RAF Officer will normally accompany any LG recce party, and will advise as to the suitability of the surface. The Engr. Officer must, however, himself have a good idea of the RAF requirements in order to estimate the amount of work required on the ground. Engr. Officers in forward units will also likely now be required to include in their recce reports, information about areas likely to form good LGs.

3. SETTING OUT AND CLEARING THE RUNWAYS

   a. Xxxx out by compass and car speedometer. If xx … most suitable markers for the corners, … are easily seen at a distance, and time is thereby saved.

   b. It is important to recce the whole area carefully before … the work of clearing the ground. Otherwise much labour may have already been undertaken before some small wadi or bad patch is discovered, which renders the area useless.

   c. Clearing stones and smoothing hummocks is slow work. As forward LGs are likely to be required as early as possible during any advance it is extremely important that the recce party should select ground on which the minimum of work is required. Otherwise, either aircraft will arrive before the ground is properly cleared, and a proportion of them will inevitably be damaged in landing, or else air operations will be delayed while the work is completed.

4.   MARKING OF THE COMPLETED LANDING GROUND

Experience has shown that different RAF formations have different requirements as to the marking out of LGs. Whenever practicable, user's desires should be ascertained locally in advance. In the absence of such indications, the following notes agreed by HQ, Western Desert, will serve as a guide to the likely requirements.

   a. Tac/R Landing Strips: No corner or side markings (i.e. LG is to be inconspicuous from the air). A 'T' at the leeward end of each strip.
   b. 'Runway' LGs:
      i.   'L' at each corner
      ii. Angle mark at each runway inter section
      iii. Strip marks along edge of runways at approx. 50yds intervals
      iv. Number of LG in 15-feet high letters at North-East corner of LG

Note to i. and ii.: Arms of corner and angle marks to be 40ft long × 3ft wide. See also under d. below for method of marking. In addition, each corner mark should have two tar barrels, one on top of the other, to indicate edges of the runway to pilots landing. Single barrels or flags should be placed at each inter-section and also at approx. 150yd intervals along the edges of each runway to give pilots a line down which to land.

These barrels should have broad white bands painted round them.

   c. Rectangular LGs:
      i.   'L' at each corner
      ii. Strip marks along each edge at approx. 250-yds intervals
      iii. Number of LG in 15-ft letters at North-East corner
   d. All corner, angle and strip marks should be 40-ft in length and 4-ft wide (in corners and angles each arm is 40-ft long). There are two methods of making these marks:
      i.   By laying stones 'crazy paving' style and whitewashing them (in many parts of the desert, white stone can be found locally). This takes some time but is permanent and should be done where possible.
      ii. In clay pans, by roughing the ground over the required area with a pick, pout petrol and sump oil mix over the earth, and setting light to it. This produces an effective black strip which will last for several days before requiring renewal. One Field Section can lay sufficient marks for one LG in four hours by this method.

5. REPORTS

The following information is required by the RAF as early as possible in each case:

   a. Position of LG
   b. Markings
   c. Land marks, if any
   d. Altitude
   e. Obstructions (e.g. telephone wires etc.)
   f. Special warnings
   g. Sketch plan showing dimensions and runways
   h. Nature of surface
   i. Direction of prevailing wind, if known

On 18 November, 1941, Wing Commander Geddes, RAF (Ops) with No.13 Corps RE attached this note to the document:

1. The attached has been drawn up at Army HQ, in conjunction with Air HQ, Western Desert. It will, however, be a good thing if RAF Officers will also bear these instructions in mind in recceing for airfields.
2. The dimensions given appear somewhat ambitious and will never be attained by the labour at the disposal of Corps. On the other hand, the following remarks seem to be doubtful:
    Para 2 (a) 'Tac/R Aircraft: one runway in the direction of the prevailing wind, dimensions 1200 yds. × 200 yds.' I should have thought that cross runways, with a minimum of 800 yds. × 75 yds. would have been preferable.
    Para 4 (a) 'Tac/R Landing Strips: no corner of side markings (i.e. LG is too inconspicuous from the air). A 'T' at the leeward end of the strip.' As Tac/R aircraft will often be in forward areas and unfamiliar to pilots, this seems to be rather dangerous. Presumably the 'T' would have to be put out by ground staff. An alternative is for RE Landing Ground parties to put up barrels at corners of strips on the first day of use and carry cloth strips for putting out Ts pending the arrival of Squadron ground staffs. If it is desired to keep the LG inconspicuous the barrels could then be removed when pilots are familiar with the locality and ground staffs are available to show landing ground signals.
3. If you agree with the above, I will issue instructions accordingly for units of this Corps. I would especially like to draw attention to the necessity for foreseeing possible expansion of LGs. We have been caught out over this already!
4. It is also to be noted that the use of whitewash entails a big consumption of water. If black markings can be used, even if they have to be renewed, they are preferable from this point of view. In any case, even white markings need renewal every few days owing to dust.

It would seem that his comments were well received, as on 19 November an amendment was issued to the Technical Instruction:

LG86, a typical desert strip … nothingness sprinkled with tents and a few vehicles. No.39 Squadron's 'tame' Stuka is coming in to land.

Jerks Maclean on an 'acquired' motorbike at Martuba. (*Jerks Maclean SAAF*)

Harold Kirby at LG172 … tent living! (*Harold Kirby SAAF*)

Rough surfaces took their toll on aircraft in landing or taxying accidents; types such as the Hurricane (foreground) and P-40 (right rear) were more robust in their undercarriage arrangement than the Spitfire or 109. (*Michael Welchman SAAF*)

... Reference to Para 2(a): It is rare that a strip will be found to give these dimensions with a moderate amount of work. On the other hand, a one strip LG is not safe unless it is 200 yds. wide. Moreover, it is more than likely that a Tac/R landing ground will later be developed into an Army Co-operation or even fighter or bomber LG. It is therefore short sighted to select a ground that will give one strip only. The alternatives are therefore:

    a.   One strip in the direction of prevailing wind, 1200yds x 200yds

    b.   Three strips, forming an equilateral triangle, each 1200yds by 75yds

    c.   Two strips (which could be connected by a third to form an equilateral triangle) each 120yds x 80yds

For landing grounds prepared by Corps, time and labour will always be the limiting factor, so that the selection of the above alternatives will depend on the ground. As long as the site allows for the above dimensions, the actual clearing must progress as time permits.

Impressions of Airfields

'Men newly arrived in the Western Desert found conditions rather different from those they had enjoyed in their training schools or with the operational commands in Britain. For the Desert Air Force now lived a more nomadic life, something like that of the Bedouin who inhabited these parts. There were no tarmac runways, no hangars, no neat headquarters buildings or barracks, no control tower and no concreted petrol stores. The usual desert airfield was nothing but a large space of desert scraped smooth and hard, around the edges of which were scattered a few tents and trucks, the aircraft and the protecting RAF armoured cars. Large square marquees housed the various messes, the operations control and the orderly room. Around them were dispersed ridge tents and little bivouacs as sleeping quarters, each with its V-shaped slit trench handy as an air-raid shelter. The rest of the 'outfit' stood on wheels; the office of the Commanding Officer was a caravan trailer; signals, that life-blood of the whole force, operated from a few specially fitted vehicles beneath portable aerial masts; workshops of the engineers were fitted into lorries; the cookhouse itself was often a trailer with a field kitchen dumped outside. The whole camp, tents and all, could be bundled into trucks and be on its way within an hour.' (*New Zealanders with the Royal Air Force*)

Flying Officer J.R. Anderson, 108 Sqn: 'We were based at airfields in the Daba–Fuka area and the usual procedure was for us to have a preliminary briefing there in the morning, after which crews would fly their Wellingtons to an advanced landing ground some 200 miles forward in the desert. We were bombed up at base but made this flight with a small petrol load since it made

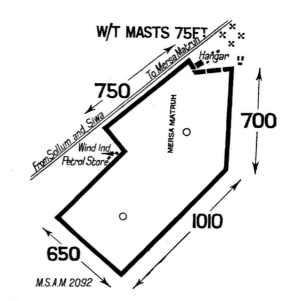

Many landing grounds were alongside roads, making them easier to find and to supply. Mersa Matruh was actually a 'major' airfield but by European standards was very ill-equipped.

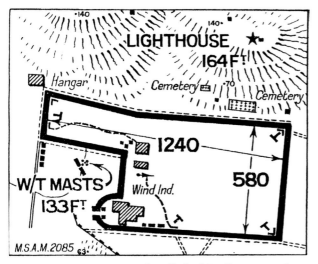

The Tobruk landing ground … limited landing area and a few buildings.

take-off easier in the heat of the day. The advanced grounds were merely patches of desert levelled off and were quite difficult to locate in dust storms – especially L.G. 60 which was some distance from the coast but much favoured because its surface, being the bed of a dried lake, was fairly smooth. On arrival at the advanced base, one member of the crew was left to guard the aircraft and make certain that the tanks were filled and minor faults rectified. After briefing and a meal there was time for a short rest if take off was late, but the only resting place available was the aircraft and it was surprising how cold a Wellington could be out in the desert.'

39 Sqn, June 1941: 'In mid-December 1941 unusually heavy rains completely waterlogged Mariut and the Squadron was forced to use Aboukir as its BLG. Fortunately, all except one of the Beauforts were away at the time at various ALGs. By the end of the month, Mariut was so waterlogged that immediate evacuation was ordered as there was a danger that the dykes holding back the waters of Lake Mariut would burst and flood the airfield. The move started on the 27th December and was completed in two days – soggy equipment and tents being packed up and the unserviceable Beaufort stripped down and sent by road. (39 Squadron)

Wadi Gazouza aerial photo, 1941.

Some of dates in the table below are outside of the period of this book; for example, they may be from mid-1943 or 1944. The majority are in the period, and the number of users gives some indication of utilization, although that may have varied from days, to weeks to a few months. The nature of the way in which squadrons came and went means that any attempt to provide a complete record is near impossible. The SD161 records (the official RAF record of unit locations) often disagrees with other sources, and even the ORBs may or may not provide accurate detail; it is very common to come across a record of a squadron at an airfield that does not feature in the location records.

Airfields: Western Desert and North Africa				
Name	LG	Country	Main Squadrons / units	Alternate Names
Aboukir	LG34	Egypt	80, 94, 112, 123, 145, 208, 237, 252, 294, 451, 603	
Aboukir Bay		Egypt	228, 230	
Abu Sueir		Egypt	6, 13, 37, 40, 46, 70, 80, 84, 89, 104, 114, 145, 203, 208, 213, 216, 223, 252, 272, 450, 458	
Abu Sueir North	LG206	Egypt		
Acroma		Libya	208	
Agedabia East		Libya	6, 145, 208	
Agedabia West		Libya		
Alem el Chel		Libya	73, 92, 250, 450, 601	
Almaza		Egypt	45, 94, 154, 216, 232, 242, 243, 318, 451	
Amiriya	LG29	Egypt	30, 33, 47, 80, 84, 94, 112, 117, 208, 216, 250, 267, 274	
Amseat No 1		Libya	55, 73	
Amseat No 2		Libya		
Antelat No 1		Libya	6, 33, 94, 112, 208, 229, 250, 260, 450	
Antelat No 2		Libya		
Apollonia		Libya	94	
Bahig South	LG40	Egypt	459	
Barce		Libya	6, 55, 113, 208, 651	
Bardia		Libya		
Bardia South		Libya		
Belandah No 1		Libya	112, 250, 260, 450	
Belandah No 2		Libya		
Benina		Libya	33, 37, 38, 55, 70, 89, 162, 208, 221, 260, 274, 294, 335, 351, 352	
Benina North		Libya		
Berka I		Libya	14, 38, 46, 47, 55, 203, 221, 227, 237, 252, 294, 454, 458, 459, 603	
Berka II		Libya		
Berka III		Libya		

Airfields: Western Desert and North Africa				
Name	LG	Country	Main Squadrons / units	Alternate Names
Bersis		Libya	33, 46, 89, 108, 134, 208, 237, 252, 335	
Bilbeis		Egypt	31, 117, 162, 267	
Bir el Beheira No 1	LG140	Libya	14, 37, 70, 148, 260, 462	
Bir el Beheira No 2	LG167	Libya		
Bir Dufan 1		Libya	73, 112, 250, 260	
Bir Dufan 2		Libya		
Bir Dufan 3		Libya		
Bir Dufan 4		Libya		
Bir Dufan 5		Libya		
Bir Dufan 6		Libya		
Bir el Gubi	LG170	Libya	208	
Bir el Regal	LG165	Libya	208, 274	
Bir Kenayis	LG43	Egypt	80, 208	
Bir Koraiyim	LG09	Egypt	11, 37, 38, 108, 148, 162, 462	
Bir Mella		Egypt	208	
Bu Amud	LG147	Libya	6, 11, 14, 39, 45, 46, 55, 73, 80, 89, 94, 108, 123, 134, 203, 229, 237, 336	
Burgh El Arab South	LG39	Egypt	39, 47, 73, 203, 450	
Burgh El Arab	LG28	Egypt		
Burrumbul		Egypt	208	
Cairo West	LG224	Egypt	6, 14, 37, 39, 46, 70, 74, 89, 104, 216, 220, 267, 450, 454	
Castel Benito		Libya	6, 73, 89, 92, 108, 112, 117, 145, 208, 250, 260, 283, 318, 417, 450, 601, 651	
Cyrene		Libya	94	
Darragh Main		Libya	92, 145, 601	
Darragh North		Libya		
Darragh South		Libya		
Dekhaila	LG32	Egypt	73, 74, 80, 89, 145, 213, 335	
Derna		Libya	6, 45, 55, 80, 148, 223, 227, 274, 294, 680	
Derna Harbour		Libya		
Deversoir		Egypt Canal Zone	6, 8, 32, 73, 213, 249, 256, 417, 680	Station Y

Airfields: Western Desert and North Africa				
Name	**LG**	**Country**	**Main Squadrons / units**	**Alternate Names**
El Adem	LG144	Libya	33, 38, 46, 47, 70, 73, 80, 94, 103, 112, 117, 178, 208, 213, 216, 221, 238, 249, 267, 274, 294, 336, 450, 459, 462, 603, 614	
El Adem South	LG157	Libya		
El Agheila		Libya		
El Assa		Libya	73, 112, 250, 260, 450	
El Ballah		Egypt	73, 94, 256	
El Daba	LG105	Egypt	30, 33, 45, 73, 74, 108, 113, 211, 238, 274	
El Dwabis		Egypt	274	
El Firdan		Egypt	14, 229, 237, 238	
El Gamil		Egypt	33, 73, 80, 89, 94, 213, 238, 250, 451	
El Gubbi East – Tobruk No 3				
El Gubbi West – Tobruk No 2				
El Khanka		Egypt	213, 216, 272, 274	
El Hassiet		Libya	92, 145, 601	
El Magrun		Libya	37, 40, 70, 73, 227, 252, 603	
El Magrun North		Libya		
El Merduma 1		Libya	73, 92, 145, 601	
El Merduma 2		Libya		
El Merduma 3		Libya		
El Merduma 4		Libya		
El Nogra		Libya	92, 601	
Fanara		Egypt	230	

El Adem airfield.
(*Hannes Faure, SAAF*)

Airfields: Western Desert and North Africa				
Name	LG	Country	Main Squadrons / units	Alternate Names
Fayid		Egypt Canal Zone	6, 13, 14, 37, 38, 70, 76, 84, 92, 108, 112, 114, 159, 178, 454, 458, 462	
Fayoum Road	LG222	Egypt	14, 40, 46, 134	
Fort Maddelena	LG124	Libya	80, 94, 208, 229, 238, 250, 260, 274	
Fort Maddelena No 2		Libya		
Fort Maddelena No 3	LG123	Libya		
Fuka East	LG19	Egypt	11, 18, 30, 33, 38, 39, 45, 55, 80, 84, 89, 203, 223, 252	
Fuka Main	LG17	Egypt		
Fuka satellite	LG16	Egypt		
Fuka South	LG18	Egypt		
Gabr Saleh	LG163	Libya	208	
Gambut No 1 Main	LG139	Libya	6, 11, 14, 33, 38, 45, 46, 47, 55, 73, 80, 84, 92, 108, 112, 113, 145, 148, 162, 203, 208, 213, 221, 227, 229, 237, 238, 250, 252, 260, 272, 274, 294, 450, 454, 458, 459, 601, 603	
Gambut No 2	LG142	Libya		
Gambut No 3	LG143	Libya		
Gambut No 4	LG156	Libya		
Gardabia East		Libya	37, 40, 70, 104, 227, 272, 462	
Gardabia Main		Libya		
Gardabia South		Libya		
Gardabia West		Libya		
Gasr el Arid	LG141	Libya	73, 94, 208, 260, 274	

Gambut area, January 1943.

Airfields: Western Desert and North Africa				
Name	LG	Country	Main Squadrons / units	Alternate Names
Gasr Garabulli		Libya	73	
Gazala No 1	LG149	Libya	33, 45, 127, 208, 318, 451	
Gazala No 2	LG150	Libya		
Gazala No 3	LG152	Libya		
Gebel Hamza	LG237	Egypt	148	
Geneifa		Egypt Canal Zone		
Gerawala	LG10	Egypt	30, 33, 112, 127, 208, 237, 238, 272, 274, 335	
Gianaclis		Egypt	38, 39, 47, 148, 221, 252, 255, 272, 459, 512	
Giarbub	LG107	Libya	6, 33, 112	
Girabub No 2	LG108	Libya		
Halfaya		Egypt	208	
Hamman South	LG37	Egypt	6, 80, 127, 274, 335	
Hamraiet East		Libya	92, 112, 145, 250, 260, 450, 601	
Hamraiet Main		Libya		
Hamraiet North		Libya		
Heliopolis		Egypt	6, 11, 14, 17, 30, 33, 39, 40, 45, 55, 58, 64, 67, 70, 73, 80, 84, 92, 113, 173, 206, 208, 211, 216, 267, 272, 417, 451, 603	
Helwan		Egypt	6, 8, 11, 18, 29, 30, 33, 39, 45, 47, 55, 70, 74, 80, 112, 113, 134, 142, 145, 206, 208, 211, 318, 601	
Hosc Raui		Libya	178, 462	
Idku	LG229	Egypt	6, 30, 33, 39, 46, 74, 80, 89, 108, 145, 162, 213, 221, 227, 237, 252, 272, 274, 294, 335, 336, 417, 451, 603	
Ikingi	LG95	Egypt	30, 55	
Ismailia		Egypt	6, 11, 14, 30, 33, 38, 45, 55, 64, 80, 94, 113, 208, 211, 213, 237, 274, 651	
Jebel Hamzi	LG237		40, 104, 108, 148, 462	
Kabrit		Egypt Canal Zone	13, 14, 32, 37, 39, 40, 55, 70, 73, 78, 80, 104, 108, 113, 114, 148, 162, 203, 204, 208, 215, 216, 219, 458,	
Kasfareet		Egypt	14, 47, 127, 237, 417, 603, 651	
Kilo 8	LG219	Egypt	73, 127, 134, 213, 336, 601, 680	
Kilo 17 – see Fayoum Road				
Kilo 26 – see Cairo West				

Airfields: Western Desert and North Africa				
Name	**LG**	**Country**	**Main Squadrons / units**	**Alternate Names**
Kilo 40 – see Gemel Hamza				
Kilo 61 – see Suez Road 2				
Lake Timsah		Egypt	230	
Lete		Libya	352	
	LG05	Egypt	18, 30, 39, 203, 213, 221, 252, 272, 459	
	LG06	Egypt	112, 237	
	LG07	Egypt	47, 112, 213, 238, 250, 272, 274, 294, 459	
	LG60	Egypt	38, 148	
	LG75	Egypt	6, 14, 33, 45, 70, 84, 112, 113, 208, 213, 237, 250, 260, 450, 451	
	LG76	Egypt	11, 14, 33, 37, 73, 112, 145, 213, 238, 250, 260, 450	
	LG79	Egypt	55, 112, 208	
	LG81	Egypt	45	
	LG85	Egypt	33, 73, 80, 213, 260, 335, 601	
	LG86	Egypt	22, 39, 55, 162, 223	

LG97, one of hundreds of desert landing grounds.
(*George Hilary SAAF*)

Airfields: Western Desert and North Africa				
Name	LG	Country	Main Squadrons / units	Alternate Names
	LG87	Egypt	47, 221	
	LG88	Egypt	14, 127, 274	
	LG89	Egypt	6, 47, 73, 127, 221, 274	
	LG90	Egypt	312, 451	
	LG91	Egypt	6, 38, 52, 112, 162, 203, 250, 252, 294, 450, 454, 458, 459, 603,	
	LG92	Egypt	80, 127, 145, 238, 274, 601	
	LG93	Egypt	229	
	LG97	Egypt	14, 260	
	LG98	Egypt	14, 55, 223	
	LG99	Egypt	55, 221, 223	
	LG101	Egypt	33, 74, 203, 213, 238, 250, 260, 450	
	LG102	Egypt	6, 30, 80, 112, 229, 250, 450	
	LG103	Egypt	80, 94, 208, 274	
	LG106	Egypt	6, 37, 70, 74, 104, 108, 112, 148, 237, 238, 250, 450, 451	
	LG109	Egypt	80, 94, 250, 260	
	LG110	Egypt	84, 112, 250, 274	
	LG111	Egypt	80, 229, 274	
	LG112	Egypt	208, 237	
	LG115	Egypt	73, 94, 112, 260	
	LG116	Egypt	11, 14, 84, 113, 223	
	LG117	Egypt	38	
	LG121	Egypt	30, 80, 134, 223, 238, 335, 336	
	LG122	Egypt	112, 250	
	LG125	Libya	33, 113, 213, 238	
	LG128	Egypt	80, 208, 237, 451	
	LG130	Egypt	274	
	LG131	Egypt	208, 451	
	LG132	Egypt	237, 451	
	LG133	Egypt	80	
	LG134	Libya	208	
	LG154		33, 145, 213, 238, 601	

Airfields: Western Desert and North Africa				
Name	LG	Country	Main Squadrons / units	Alternate Names
	LG155	Egypt	73, 145, 213, 238, 601	
	LG172	Egypt	6, 33, 127, 145, 213, 238	
	LG173		92, 145, 264, 335, 601	
	LG175		112, 417, 450	
	LG202	Egypt	208	
	LG226	Egypt	38, 203, 459	
	LG227	Egypt	47, 203, 454, 459	
Maaten Bagush	LG14	Egypt	6, 30, 31, 113, 162, 208, 213, 216	
Maaten Bagush satellite	LG15	Egypt	14, 39, 55, 127, 145, 238	
Mahsma	LG208	Egypt	459	
Marawa		Libya	6, 55, 208, 274	
Marble Arch		Libya	117, 250, 260, 267, 318, 450	

Marble Arch LG from the top of the arch.
(*George Muir SAAF*)

Airfields: Western Desert and North Africa				
Name	**LG**	**Country**	**Main Squadrons / units**	**Alternate Names**
Martuba No 1		Libya	94, 112, 208, 213, 238, 250, 260, 274, 450	
Martuba No 2		Libya		
Martuba No 3		Libya		
Martuba No 4		Libya		
Martuba No 5		Libya		
Maryut (Alexandria)		Egypt	14, 17, 39, 94, 112, 113, 202, 204, 228, 230, 250, 274, 267, 269, 270, 601	Mariut
Matariya	LG219		134, 336, 601, 680	
Matruh West	LG07	Egypt	47, 213, 238, 250, 272, 274, 294, 459	
Mechili No 1		Libya	33, 94, 112, 208, 229, 238, 250, 274	
Mechili No 2		Libya		
Mellaha		Libya	162, 274, 294, 417	
Menastir		Libya	45	
Mendalao Bay		Libya		
Mersa el Brega		Libya		
Mersah Matruh	LG08	Egypt	14, 33, 47, 74, 114, 127, 145, 162, 208, 252, 335, 336,451, 459, 621	
Misurata		Libya	33, 38, 47, 89, 162, 213, 252, 274, 603	
Msus No 1		Libya	6, 33, 92, 94, 112, 145, 208, 229, 238, 250, 260, 274, 601	
Msus No 2		Libya		
Msus No 3		Libya		
Nofilia 1		Libya		
Nofilia 2		Libya		
Qasaba	LG11	Egypt	6, 14, 30, 33, 45, 73, 208, 451	
Qassassin	LG207	Egypt	55, 203, 223, 318, 450	
Qotafiyah I	LG20	Egypt	11, 39, 40, 45, 70, 84, 104, 148, 162, 208, 211, 272, 335	
Qotafiyah II	LG104	Egypt		
Qotafiyah III	LG21	Egypt	14, 55, 73, 92, 145, 601	
Savoia		Libya	80, 94, 237	
Shalluffa		Egypt Canal Zone	6, 14, 32, 37, 38, 39, 40, 46, 70, 76, 82, 90, 104, 162, 213, 221, 252, 351, 454, 458	
Shalliufa satellite	LG251	Egypt	221	
Shandur		Egypt Canal Zone	6, 39, 42, 47, 73, 89, 108, 127, 134, 147, 160, 178, 213, 221, 223, 237	Station X

Airfields: Western Desert and North Africa				
Name	LG	Country	Main Squadrons / units	Alternate Names
Sidi Azeiz	LG148	Libya		
Sidi Azzab		Libya		
Sidi Barrani	LG02	Egypt		
Sidi Haneish North	LG12	Egypt		
Sidi Haneish South	LG13	Egypt		
Sidi Omar		Libya		
Sidi Rezegh	LG153	Libya		
Sidi Small – see Beja				
Sirtan East		Libya		
Sirte Main		Libya		
Sirte South		Libya		
Sirte West		Libya		

No runway, no problem … a good chance of putting the aircraft down in the desert. Bombay L5856 force-landed with engine problems, 7 August 1941. (*Flying Officer H.N.L. Bertam; Bertram Family Collection*)

Airfields: Western Desert and North Africa				
Name	**LG**	**Country**	**Main Squadrons / units**	**Alternate Names**
Sollum		Egypt		
Soluch		Libya		
Sorman		Libya		
Suez		Egypt		
Suez Road No 2	LG209	Egypt	223	
Sultan		Libya		
Tamet		Libya		
Terria		Libya		
Tmimi 1		Libya		
Tmimi 2		Libya		
Tobruk No 1		Libya		
Tobruk No 2	LG145	Libya		
Tobruk No 3	LG146	Libya		
Tobruk No 4		Libya		
Tocra		Libya		
Wadi Gazouza				
Wadi Surri – see Darragh North				
Wadi Natrun	LG100	Egypt	55, 208	
Waterloo – see LG68				
Zuara		Libya		

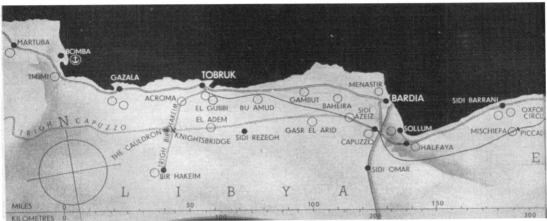

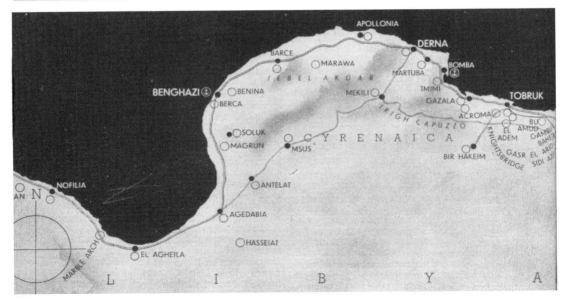

Maps showing major airfields and locations. As the full lists of 'airfields' shows, there were in fact hundreds of landing grounds across the area, most confined to the coastal strip.

Appendix VI

Chronology

1939
September
3   **KEY DATE:** Declaration of war with Germany
5   South Africa enters the war
10   Canada enters the war

October
19   Renaming of groups in the Middle East/Mediterranean
          Med GR Gp becomes 200 Gp
          ME GR Gp becomes 201 Gp
          Egyptian Gp becomes 202 Gp

1940
May
13   ACM Longmore as AOC Middle East

June
10   KEY DATE: Italy declares war
11/12 First attack on Italy (by Bomber Command; Genoa and Turin)
11   First Italian air raid on Malta
11   Start of East African campaign
11   RAF attacks targets in Libya
12   RAF bombs Tobruk harbour – first of hundreds of such sorties
14   British advance into Libya and capture of Fort Capuzzo
20   Establishment of Middle East reinforcement route via Takoradi (West Africa)
22   Italians bomb Alexandria

A slightly later shot
but including the great
desert air commanders:
Coningham, Broadhurst,
Tedder.

| 28 | First Hurricane sorties from Malta |
| 28 | Sunderland flying boat from Malta claims first aircraft sinking of an Italian U-boat |

July

| 1 | Marshal Graziani takes command of Italian forces in Libya |

August

5	Italian invasion of British Somaliland
17	No.203 (Fighter) Group formed, Khartoum
18	Evacuation of British Somaliland

September

5	First aircraft arrive at Takoradi
13	Italians cross border of Egypt
16	Italians occupy Sidi Barrani (high point of Italian offensive)

October

| 28 | Italy invades Greece |

November

| 5 | Start of RAF detachment to Greece |
| 11 | First RAF offensive mission in Greece (attack on Valona airfield) |

December

9	KEY DATE: Start of first British offensive in Western Desert (Operation Compass)
10	Capture of Sidi Barrani by Allies
16	British offensive in Italian East Africa
16	Italians driven out of Egypt, Sollum captured

1941
January

3	Luftwaffe units transferred to Mediterranean and North Africa theatre
5	Bardia captured by Allies
10	Start of first Malta 'blitz'
22	Allies capture Tobruk
30	Allies capture Derna

February

6	Allies capture Benghazi
6	Lieutenant General Rommel appointed to Africa command
9	Allied advance halted by Churchill

March

| 28–29 | Battle of Cape Matapan |
| 30 | KEY DATE: German offensive in Western Desert |

April

4	Axis captures Benghazi
6	Allies liberate Addis Ababa, Ethiopia
6	German advance into Greece and Yugoslavia
8	No.4 SFTS at Habbaniya forms 5 'operational' squadrons in preparation for Iraqi attack
10/12	Start of Siege of Tobruk
12	No.204 (Operational) Group formed, Maaten Bagush
15	British back on Egyptian border at Sollum
21	Greece requests withdrawal of Allied forces
22	Operation *Demon* (evacuation of Greece) commences
27	Germans capture Athens
27	Axis forces cross into Egypt, Halfaya Pass
30	Start of Siege of Habbaniya, Iraq (to 6 May)

May
First attacks (by Blenheims) – from Malta – on Axis convoys to North Africa
Evacuation from Greece completed

2	Siege of RAF Habbaniya (Iraq) starts (ends 6th)
15	Operation BREVITY (terminated on 16th)
17	Surrender of Italian forces in East Africa
20	German air assault on Crete
27	Axis capture Halfaya (Hell Fire) Pass
28–31	Allied evacuation from Crete
31	Armistice with Iraq

June
1	Air Marshal Tedder as AOC-in-C Middle East
8	Allied forces enter Syria
15–18	Operation Battleaxe

July
5	Auchinleck replaces Wavell as Middle East Commander
11	End of hostilities in Syria
30	Air Vice-Marshal Coningham takes post as AOC Desert Air Force

September
1	No.206 (Maintenance) Group formed

October
9	Formation of Western Desert Air Force (renaming of 204 Group)
12	No.205 (Heavy Bomber) Group formed, Shallufa (renaming of 257 Wing)

November
18	Start of Operation Crusader
26	Ritchie replaces Cunningham as Eighth Army commander

December
7/10	Siege of Tobruk ends
15	No.209 (Fighter) Group formed, Ramleh
22	German air assault on Malta
24	Allies capture Benghazi
31	Front line stabilizes at El Agheila
?	No.207 (General Purpose) Group formed, Nairobi

1942
January
1	No.214 Group formed, Habbaniya
11	Air Vice-Marshal Park takes post as AOC Egypt
21	Rommel counter-attacks, as Crusader stalls
29	Axis captures Benghazi

February
4	Front line stabilizes at Gazala-Bir Hakeim
20	Western Desert battle stabilizes at Gazala

March
7	First Spitfires to Malta
12	No.211 (Offensive Fighter) Group formed, El Adem (change of designation)

April
7/8	Peak of the first Malta blitz
16	Malta awarded the George Cross

May
1	No.215 Group formed, Basrah
11–12	First USAAF attack on Ploesti, first op in Middle East/Med theatre
26	German offensive at Gazala, the Battle for Egypt

June
11/12   First USAAF bombing op (HALPRO) from Middle East, B-24s attack Ploesti
18–26   White House Conference; decision to invade North Africa in 1942
21   Axis captures Tobruk
21   HALPRO B-24s bomb Benghazi; first attack in Desert War target by USAAF
28   Axis capture Mersa Matruh
28   General Brereton takes command of USAMEAF
30   Front line stabilizes at El Alamein

July
German offensive in Egypt halted at El Alamein

15   Air Vice-Marshal Park takes post as AOC Malta
31   57th FG arrives in Palestine

August
13–18   General Alexander as new Commander of British Forces Middle East and Montgomery as commander of Eighth Army
31   Battle of Alam El Halfa (to 6 Oct)

September
9   No.216 (Transport and Ferry) Group formed, Heliopolis
15   57th FG arrives Egypt – first USAAF FG in operational area

October
11–19   Last phase of blitz on Malta
19   KEY DATE: Allies launch El Alamein offensive pre-offensive bombing
23   El Alamein ground offensive starts

November
7   376th BG moves from Palestine to Egypt
8   KEY DATE: Start of Operation Torch, landings in North Africa
11   French (Vichy) ceasefire in North Africa
12   USAMEAF disbanded, Ninth Air Force formed under General Brereton
13   98th BG arrives in Egypt from Palestine
13   Allies capture Tobruk
14   Allies enter Tunisia
20   Allies capture Benghazi

December
1   No.212 (Fighter) Group formed, Gazala
10   No.211 (Fighter) Group formed, Maaten Bagush
13   Germans withdraw from El Agheila
15   No.213 (Operational) Group formed, Beirut (renaming Advanced HQ Levant)
17   French fleets in region (Alexandria, Dakar, North Africa) join Allies
25   Allies capture Sirte

1943
January
14–24   Allied leaders hold Casablanca Conference on war strategy
14   Allied air contingent in Algeria/Tunisia become Eastern Air Command
23   Allies capture Tripoli

February
2   Formation of Mediterranean Air Command
6   Establishment of North African Theatre of Operations

Appendix VII

Order of Battle

Nov 1939:
Middle East Command (HQ: Cairo)

Heliopolis
- 113 Sqn (Blenheim)
- 216 Sqn (Bombay)

Ismailia
- 30 Sqn (Blenheim)
- 55 Sqn (Blenheim)
- 14 Sqn (Wellesley)

Helwan
- 112 Sqn (Gladiator)
- 70 Sqn (Valentia)

Fuka
- 45 Sqn (Blenheim)

Daba
- 211 Sqn

Qasaba
- 14 Sqn – det. Flight (Wellesley)
- 208 Sqn (Lysander)

Mersa Matruh
- 33 Sqn (Gladiator)

Amriya
- 80 Sqn (Gladiator)

Sudan
- 47 Sqn (Wellesley)
- 223 Sqn (Wellesley)

Palestine
- 6 Sqn (Lysander)

Iraq (Shaibah)
- 84 Sqn (Blenheim)

May 1941:
Middle East Command (HQ Cairo)

Heliopolis
- 267 Sqn (various)
- 216 Sqn (Bombay)
- 208 Sqn (Lysander)
- 2 PRU (Maryland)

Amriya
- 247 Sqn (Hurricane)
- 89 Sqn (Hurricane)
- 450 Sqn (Hurricane)

Ismailia
- 70 OTU (various)

Alexandria
- 228 Sqn (Sunderland)
- 230 Sqn (Sunderland)

Kabrit
- 70 Sqn (Wellington)
- 148 Sqn (Wellington)

Shallufa
- 37 Sqn (Wellington)
- 38 Sqn (Wellington)

Shandur
- 39 Sqn (Blenheim)

Maaten Bagush
- 45 Sqn (Blenheim)
- 55 Sqn (Blenheim)

Sollum
- 1 GRU (Wellington)

Fuka
- 38 Sqn det. (Wellington)
- 70 Sqn det. (Wellington)
- 148 Sqn det. (Wellington)

Qasaba
- 6 Sqn (Hurricane, Lysander)

Sidi Haneish
- 73 Sqn (Hurricane)

Greece/Crete
Suda Bay
- 113 Sqn (Blenheim)

Maleme
- 33 Sqn (Hurricane)
- 30 Sqn (Blenheim)

Argos
- 11 Sqn (Blenheim

Sudan
- 117 Sqn (various)
- 251 Sqn (Gauntlet)
- 47 Sqn (Wellesley)
- 223 sqn (Wellesley)
- 14 Sqn (Blenheim)
- 237 Sqn (Lysander, Hardy)

East Africa
- SAAF squadrons

Palestine (most units at Aqir)
- 211 Sqn (Blenheim)
- 6 Sqn det. (Lysander)
- 80 Sqn (Gladiator)
- 84 Sqn (Blenheim)
- 250 Sqn (Tomahawk)

Aden
- 8 Sqn (Blenheim)
- 203 Sqn (Blenheim)

Iraq
- 70 Sqn det. (Wellington)
- 244 Sqn (Vincent)

23 October 1942
Western Desert Air Force HQ
Air Ambulance Squadron

No.3 (SAAF) (Bomber) Wing:
- 12 SAAF Sqn (Maryland)
- 21 SAAF Sqn (Baltimore)
- 24 SAAF Sqn (Boston)

No.232 (Bomber) Wing:
- 55 Sqn (Baltimore)
- 223 Sqn (Baltimore)
- 82nd BS USAAF (B–25)
- 83rd BS USAAF (B–25)
- 434th BS USAAF (B–25)

No.285 (Recce) Wing:
- 40 SAAF Sqn (TR) (Hurricane)
- 60 SAAF Survey Sqn (Photo recon) (Maryland other types)
- 1437 Flight Squadron (SR) (Baltimore)

No.211 Group
- 7 SAAF Sqn (Hurricane IID)
- 6 Sqn (Hurricane IID)
- 64th FS USAAF (P-40F Warhawk)
- 65th FS USAAF (P-40F Warhawk)

No.233 Wing:
- 2 Sqn SAAF (Kittyhawk)
- 4 Sqn SAAF (Kittyhawk)
- 5 Sqn SAAF (Tomahawk)
- 260 Sqn (Kittyhawk)

No.239 Wing:
- 112 Sqn (Kittyhawk)
- 250 Sqn (Kittyhawk)
- 260 Sqn (Tomahawk)
- 66th FS USAAF (P-40F Warhawk)

No.244 Wing:
- 145 Sqn (Spitfire Vb)
- 601 Sqn (Spitfire Vb)
- 73 Sqn (Tomahawk)
- 92 Sqn (Spitfire Vc)

No.212 Group
No.243 Wing:
- 1 SAAF Sqn (Hurricane)
- 33 Sqn (Hurricane)
- 213 Sqn (Hurricane)
- 238 Sqn (Hurricane)

No.7 (SAAF) Wing:
- 80 Sqn (Hurricane)
- 127 Sqn (Hurricane)
- 335 Sqn (Hurricane)
- 274 Sqn (Hurricane)

USAMEAF HQ
9th Bomber Command
98th Bombardment Group USAAF (all B-24)
- 343rd BS
- 344th BS
- 345th BS
- 415th BS

1st Provisional Group USAAF (31st Oct, renamed to 376th BG USAAF) (all B-24)
- 512th BS
- 513th BS
- 514th BS
- 515th BS

Desert Air Task Force
57th FG USAAF (All units Detached to RAF)
12th BG USAAF (All units but one, Detached to RAF)
81st BS (B-25)

No.205 Group ORBAT

No.231 Wing:
- 37 Sqn (Wellington)
- 70 Sqn (Wellington)

No.236 Wing:
- 108 Sqn (Wellington)
- 148 Sqn (Wellington)

No.238 Wing:
- 40 Sqn (Wellington)
- 104 Sqn (Wellington)

No.242 Wing:
- 147 Sqn (Liberator)
- 160 Sqn (Liberator)

No.245 Wing:
- 14 Sqn (Marauder)
- 227 Sqn det. (Halifax)
- 462 Sqn (Halifax)
- Special Flight (Liberator)

Squadrons

A large number of squadrons served in the Egypt–North Africa campaign, with the SAAF taking an increasing role as dedicated squadrons from 1941. Up to that point many squadrons had a very diverse mix of aircrew – less so on groundcrew – and shoulder flashes showing the nation (Canada, Australia, etc.) were common. So, even when the table below shows an RAF Squadron it gives no indication of the origins of the aircrew.

While only one RAAF squadron – 3 RAAF – is shown below, this is a false picture, as many RAAF squadrons were given numbers in the RAF's 400 series, thus 450 is actually 450 (RAAF). Furthermore, Allied nations eventually dominated some squadrons, so 335 was actually a Greek squadron.

Sqn	Aircraft	Dates
Squadrons and aircraft types used period June 1940 to May 1945, or earlier if left theatre before May 1945. Types used for only a few weeks are excluded.		
RAF	Includes Allied and Commonwealth units in the RAF squadron number sequence	
6	Lysander, Gladiator, Hurricane	Jun 1940 – May 1945
11	Blenheim	Jun 1940 – Mar 1942
13	Blenheim, Baltimore, Boston	Nov 1942 – May 1945
14	Blenheim, Baltimore, Marauder	Jun 1940 – Oct 1944
18	Blenheim, Boston	Nov 1942 – May 1945
30	Blenheim, Hurricane	Jun 1940 – Feb 1942
33	Gladiator, Hurricane, Spitfire	Jun 1940 – Apr 1944
37	Wellington, Liberator	Nov 1940 – May 1945
38	Wellington	Nov 1940 – May 1945
39	Blenheim, Beaufort, Maryland, Beaufighter, Marauder	Jun 1940 – May 1945

107 Squadron Liberator at Fayid

Sqn	Aircraft	Dates
40	Wellington, Liberator	Oct 1941– Feb 1942; May 1942 – May 1945
45	Blenheim	Jun 1940 – Feb 1942
46	Beaufighter	May 1942 – Dec 1944
47	Vincent, Wellesley, Beaufort, Beaufighter	Jun 1940 – Mar 1944
55	Blenheim, Baltimore, Boston	Jun 1940 – May 1945
70	Wellington, Liberator	Jun 1940 – May 1945
73	Hurricane, Spitfire	Nov 1940 – May 1945
74	Spitfire	Jun 1942 – Apr 1944
76	Halifax	Oct 1941 – Sep 1942
80	Gladiator, Hurricane, Spitfire	Jun1940 – Apr 1944
84	Blenheim	Jun 1940 – Jan 1942
89	Beaufighter	Dec 1941 – Oct 1943
92	Spitfire	Apr 1942 – May 1945
94	Gladiator, Hurricane, Kittyhawk, Spitfire	Jun 1940 – May 1945
104	Wellington, Liberator	Oct 1941 – May 1945
108	Wellington, Liberator, Mosquito	Aug 1941 – Dec 1942; Mar 1943 – Mar 1945
112	Gladiator, Hurricane, Tomahawk, Kittyhawk, Mustang	Jun 1940 – May 1945
113	Blenheim	Jun 1940 – Dec 1941
114	Blenheim, Boston	Nov 1942 – May 1945
117	Various transport	Apr 1941 – Nov 1943

Bombays of 117 Squadron
(*Fg Off H.N.L. Bertram RAAF,
Bertram Family Collection*)

Sqn	Aircraft	Dates
123	Spitfire	Jun 1942 – Nov 1943
134	Hurricane, Spitfire	Jun 1942 – Nov 1943
145	Spitfire	Apr 1942 – May 1945
148	Wellington, Liberator, Halifax	Dec 1940 – Dec 1942; Mar 1943 – May 1945
154	Spitfire	Nov 1942 – Aug 1944
159	Liberator	Jun 1942 – Sep 1942
162	Wellington, Blenheim, Baltimore, Mosquito	Jan 1942 – Sep 1944
178	Liberator, Halifax	Jan 1943 – May 1945
203	Blenheim, Maryland, Baltimore	Jun 1940 – Nov 1943
208	Lysander, Hurricane, Tomahawk, Spitfire	Jun 1940 – May 1945
211		
213	Hurricane, Spitfire, Mustang	May 1941 – May 1945
216	Valentia, Bombay, DH86, Hudson, Dakota	Jun 1940 – May 1945
221	Wellington	Jan 1942 – May 1945
223	Wellesley, Maryland, Blenheim, Boston, Baltimore	Jun 1940 – Aug 1944
227	Beaufighter	Aug 1942 – Aug 1944
228	Sunderland	Jun 1940 – Jun 1941
229	Hurricane, Spitfire	Sep 1941 – Apr 1944
230	Sunderland	Jun 1940 – Jan 1943
232	Spitfire	Dec 1942 – Oct 1944

213 Squadron Hurricane
on standby at Martuba

Sqn	Aircraft	Dates
237	Hardy, Lysander, Gladiator, Hurricane, Spitfire	Jun 1940 – May 1945
238	Hurricane, Spitfire	Jul 1941 – Oct 1944
242	Hurricane, Spitfire	Jan 1942 – Mar 1942; Nov 1942 – Nov 1944
243	Spitfire	Dec 1942 – Oct 1944
249	Hurricane, Spitfire	May 1941 – May 1945
250	Tomahawk, Hurricane, Kittyhawk	Apr 1941 – May 1945
252	Beaufighter	Nov 1941 – May 1945
256		
260	Hurricane, Tomahawk, Kittyhawk, Mustang	Aug 1941 – May 1945
267	Various transport	Aug 1940 – Feb 1945
272	Beaufighter	May 1941 – Apr 1945
274	Gladiator, Hurricane, Spitfire	Aug 1940 – Feb 1944
283	Walrus, Warwick	Feb 1943 – May 1945
294	Walrus, Wellington, Warwick	Sep 1943 - May 1945
318	Hurricane, Spitfire	Aug 1943 – May 1945
335	Hurricane, Spitfire	Oct 1941 – May 1945
336	Hurricane, Spitfire	Apr 1943 – May 1945
351	Hurricane	Jul 1944 – May 1945
352	Hurricane	Apr 1944 – May 1945
417	Spitfire	Jun 1942 – May 1945
450	Hurricane, Kittyhawk, Mustang	May 1941 – May 1945
451	Hurricane, Spitfire	May 1941 – Nov 1944
454	Blenheim, Baltimore	Sep 1942 – May 1945
458	Wellington	Mar 1942 – Jan 1945
459	Hudson, Baltimore	Feb 1942 – Feb 1945
462	Halifax	Sep 1942 – Feb 1944
601	Spitfire	Jun 1942 – May 1945
603	Spitfire, Beaufighter	Aug 1942 – Dec 1944
614	Blenheim	Nov 1942 – Jan 1944
651	Auster	Nov 1942 – May 1945
RAAF	The units below are only those not in the RAF sequence	
3	Gladiator, Tomahawk, Kittyhawk, Mustang	Aug 1940 – May 1945

Sqn	Aircraft	Dates
SAAF	No SAAF units were in the RAF sequence	
1	Hurricane, Spitfire	Jun 1940 – May 1945
2	Tomahawk, Kittyhawk, Spitfire	Jul 1941 – May 1945
3	Mohawk, Hurricane, Spitfire	Jan 1941 – Dec 1941; Jan 1943 – May 1945
4	Mohawk, Tomahawk, Kittyhawk, Spitfire	Apr 1941 – May 1945
5	Tomahawk, Kittyhawk, Mustang	Feb 1942 – May 1945
7	Hurricane, Spitfire	May 1942 – May 1945
9	Spitfire	May 1944 – Feb 1945
10	Spitfire	May 1944 – Oct 1944
11	Kittyhawk, Spitfire	Jun 1944 – May 1945
12	Maryland, Boston, Marauder	May 1940 – May 1945
15	Maryland, Blenheim, Baltimore	Feb 1942 – May 1945
16	Maryland, Blenheim, Beaufighter	May 1941 – May 1945
17	Blenheim, Ventura	Jan 1943 – May 1945
19	Beaufighter	Aug 1944 – May 1945
21	Maryland, Baltimore, Marauder	May 1941 – May 1945
22	Ventura	Jun 1944 – May 1945
24	Maryland, Boston, Marauder	Mar 1941 – May 1945
27	Ventura, Wellington	Jun 1944 – May 1945
28	Wellington, Anson, Dakota	Jun 1943 – May 1945
30	Marauder	Oct 1944 – May 1945
31	Liberator	Feb 1944 – May 1945
34	Liberator	Apr 1944 – May 1945
40	Hurricane, Tomahawk, Spitfire	Jun 1940 – May 1945
41	Hurricane, Spitfire	Apr 1943 – May 1945
44	Dakota	Mar 1944 – May 1945
60	Maryland, Baltimore, Mosquito	Jul 1941 – May 1945

Aircraft Strength

All squadrons were responsible for the maintenance of their own aircraft at outbreak of war, although a small air stores park, No.31 ASP, was formed at the outbreak of the war. If the repair task was beyond the squadron, it sent aircraft to the depot at Aboukir. This airfield had been in use in the First World War and by 1939 was a comprehensive facility with engine and airframe repair shops, wooden airscrew manufacture, general engineering, mechanical transport repair, and so on, along with a main stores depot. The latter undertook the erection of all aircraft that arrived crated, as well as the complete overhaul of airframes, engines, vehicles (including armoured cars), and the supply of all spares and stores for all units in Middle East Command.

On 11 September 1939 an advanced repair and salvage section was formed at Fuka to carry out repairs beyond the capabilities of the squadrons but that took fewer than seven working days; the RSU also handled crashed aircraft in the desert and the fitting of replacement engines.

The maintenance organization was slow to develop, and in June the following policy was set:

1. Squadrons on permanent stations were responsible for:
   a. All maintenance and inspections of aircraft and engines up to and including the 180-hour inspection.
   b. Repairs and replacements which were within the capacity of the units and which would not take longer to effect than the time taken for a 180-hour inspection.
   c. Modifications Class 1 and such Class 2 war modifications, the completion of which were within the capacity of the unit.

2. Squadrons at desert landing grounds in the open were made responsible for:
   a. All maintenance and inspections of aircraft and engines up to and including the 150-hour inspection.
   b. Repairs and replacements which were within the capacity of the unit and which would not take longer to effect than the time taken by a 3 Star inspection.
   c. Modifications Class 1 and such Class 2 war modifications the completion of which were within the capacity of the unit.
   d. Maintenance of parachutes and aero-engine sparking plugs.
   e. Maintenance and repairs of MT vehicles up to and including work estimated to occupy not more than 4 days.

Every aircraft recovered or moved away from advancing enemy forces was one that could potentially be returned to combat.

Sadly, this is yet another aspect that we have to gloss over; the organization for recovering and repairing aircraft continued to expand and become more experienced and effective. The ability to recover and then repair airframes and engines was critically important when any new aircraft and engines had to come such long distances, and at high risk.

The tables below provides an indication of how effective the organization was – and what an impact there would have been on combat strength if this had not been as effective. There Germans and Italians were far less effective in returning aircraft to the air.

Summary of aircraft availability Middle East			
Date	Operational Aircraft	Under Repair	Serviceable in 14 days
1941			
Nov	910	458	273
Dec	960	457	314
1942			
Jan	865	562	350
Feb	815	770	365
Mar	674	695	490
Apr	840	462	318
May	779	520	390
Jun	767	458	375
Jul	943	546	376
Aug	939	608	372
Sep	1031	680	390
Oct	1198	748	344
Nov	1235	742	372
Dec	1362	790	352
1943			
Jan	1230	750	341

Cleaning the guns; note beer cans over exhaust stubs to keep the sand out (*George Hilary SAAF*)

Summary airframe and engine repair output Middle East		
Date	Airframes	Engines
1941		
Nov	102	160
Dec	140	214
1942		
Jan	162	351
Feb	164	387
Mar	220	467
Apr	247	489
May	358	687
Jun	435	709
Jul	414	920
Aug	365	562
Sep	472	675
Oct	486	823
Nov	499	820
Dec	535	709
1943		
Jan	549	889

RSU collects more aircraft to out back into service or use for spares.